Outcomes MEASUREMENT IN THE HUMAN SERVICES

2ND EDITION

Cross-Cutting Issues and Methods in the Era *of* Health Reform

JENNIFER L. MAGNABOSCO *and* RONALD W. MANDERSCHEID
EDITORS

NASW PRESS

National Association of Social Workers
Washington, DC

Jeane W. Anastas, PhD, LMSW, *President*
Elizabeth J. Clark, PhD, ACSW, MPH, *Executive Director*

Cheryl Y. Bradley, *Publisher*
John Cassels, *Project Manager and Staff Editor*
Wayson Jones, *Copyeditor*
Lori J. Holtzinger, *Proofreader and Indexer*

Cover by Metadog Design
Interior design and composition by Rick Soldin
Printed and bound by Sheridan Books, Inc.

Library of Congress Cataloging-in-Publication Data

Outcomes measurement in the human services: cross-cutting issues and methods in the era of health reform / Jennifer L. Magnabosco, Ronald W. Manderscheid, editors. — 2nd ed.
    p. cm.
  Rev. ed. of: Outcomes measurement in the human services: cross-cutting issues and methods / Edward J. Mullen, Jennifer L. Magnabosco, editors. 1997.
  Includes bibliographic references and index.
  ISBN 978-0-87101-422-1
  1. Human services—United States—Evaluation. 2. Human services—Evaluation—Methodology. 3. Social service—United States—Evaluation. 4. Outcome assessment (Medical care). 5. Family social work—United States—Evaluation. I. Magnabosco, Jennifer L. II. Manderscheid, Ronald W.
  HV91.O97 2011
  361.00684—dc22   2011017171

Printed in the United States of America

Dedication

We dedicate this book to all consumers, clients, families, and advocates we have had the privilege of working with during the course of our careers. As we begin a new era of consumer-driven human services, we hope this book brings us one step closer to achieving the positive outcomes and strength-based approaches to care and recovery we all deserve.

Contents

PART II: Outcomes Measurement in Health

PART III: Outcomes Measurement in Mental and Behavioral Health

PART IV: Outcomes Measurement in Child and Family Services

PART V: Special Topics in Outcomes Measurement in the Human Services

Foreword

Much has transpired since the first edition of *Outcomes Measurement in the Human Services* appeared in 1997. In this second edition, Jennifer Magnabosco and Ron Manderscheid have performed a valuable service to the fields of health, human services, and social work by reconvening many of the original contributors to the 1997 edition and asking them to reflect on how outcomes measurement has changed and evolved over the past nearly 15 years.

The 1997 edition appeared at a time when health, human services, and social work were still dealing with the relatively unknown concept of *outcomes*. Consequently, the contributors to the first edition had to deal with such issues as: What is an outcome? How do you measure outcomes? Why should programs and agencies measure outcomes? At the time, there was little agreement on the relationship of outcomes and outcomes measurement to the emerging concept of government performance measurement as mandated by the federal Government Performance and Results Act of 1993. In addition, there was both concern and suspicion about outcomes and government performance measurement on the part of the scholarly evaluation community.

This second edition of *Outcomes Measurement in the Human Services* appears at a time when outcomes and outcomes measurement has become a major field of scholarly research and practice in health, human services, and social work. The chapters in this second edition make some important contributions to conceptualizing and defining outcome measures, and address a more nuanced set of issues that reflect the maturation of the field. The book helps to set the outcomes agenda for health, human services, and social work for the next decade.

For many of the issues identified by the contributing authors, there seems to be both an upside and a downside. Many funding sources, such as the United Way, foundations, most government agencies, and even whole countries now mandate the collection of outcome data, leading to the creation of large and potentially meaningful data sets. Yet there is a real concern on the part of providers, professionals, and consumers that funder-mandated quantitative outcomes infringe on their prerogatives. This practice raises a number of important subsidiary issues, including encroachment on the freedom of nonprofit human service organizations to experiment and innovate with new service delivery approaches. Likewise, evidence-based practice, focusing on greater attention to scientific considerations in decision making, is considered in some ways antithetical to the prescriptive specification of outcomes by funding sources. On another issue, qualitative research has demonstrated its effectiveness in producing valuable insights. A great deal of useful information is missed when only quantitative approaches to outcomes measurement are used, yet effective methods for incorporating qualitative findings have yet to be discovered.

One encouraging note is the recognition by several contributing authors of the many valuable outcome instruments that are now available in several fields, such as health, mental health, child and family services, substance use care, and others. The challenge now is not only to measure the accomplishment of outcomes, but also to better understand how and why they took place.

Another important topic addressed by several authors is the issue of linking outcomes, costs, and compensation. The ability of health, human services, and social work to compute their costs, specifically the costs of achieving outcomes, is increasingly important as government and private funding sources continue to move toward pay for performance by utilizing performance-based contracts and grants. With respect to the health field, outcomes and outcome measures in conjunction with evidenced-based practice hold the potential to focus not only on what works, but also at what cost. These trends have been codified, for example, in the Patient Protection and Affordable Care Act of 2010, which is intended to extend insurance coverage and improve the quality of care delivery.

The state of the art, as presented by the contributors to this volume, clearly demonstrates that significant progress in outcomes measurement has been made over the last 15 years. Yet many challenges still exist, and will continue to persist, as *human service* sectors embark upon major policy and practice reforms. It is clear that all stakeholders are not exactly on the same page. Funders, government agencies, nonprofit organizations and the general public all want to know that dollars spent for health, human services, and social work accomplish results, not just process. Those closer to consumers and direct service professionals want to be assured that treatment prerogatives are respected. This is all to say that the outcomes and performance measurement movements are perceived and judged on the basis of one's location within the system, which in effect makes it piecemeal. What these movements need to become are well-integrated systems that continually contribute to making service delivery more efficient and effective while improving productivity and maximizing the use of technology. We hope that fulfilling this need can be part of the agenda for the next decade.

All in all, this second edition does an excellent job of bringing the topics of outcomes and performance measurement up to date! Readers will understand not only where the outcomes movement is today, but also how we got where we are.

Lawrence L. Martin
Professor of Public Affairs
University of Central Florida

Peter M. Kettner
Professor Emeritus
Arizona State University

Acknowledgments

We deeply appreciate all who have contributed their inspiration, writing, and special assistance to make the second edition of *Outcomes Measurement in the Human Services* possible.

First, we thank each of the book's authors. Thank you for altruistically giving of your time, wisdom, and patience to help realize the book's vision and to meet our requests for chapter revisions. We revere your dedication and enthusiasm to participate in the second edition's effort.

We gratefully acknowledge readers who used the first edition in their own learning, curriculum, training, research, and writing. We hope that this second edition also proves to be a useful source for your current and future endeavors.

This project could not have been possible without the inspiration and support of Edward J. Mullen (coeditor of the book's first edition), our families, and other loved ones, especially Jeffrey P. Scott. Thank you for your understanding during this process and for believing in our commitment to this topic.

We thank Cynthia Gammage, Eriko A. Kennedy, Peter T. Magnabosco, and Alissa Simon for technical assistance in preparing this book. We appreciate your attention to detail and information-seeking skills.

Finally, we would like to thank Lisa M. O'Hearn, managing editor, and John Cassels, staff editor, of NASW Press for their skillful work in editing and publishing this book. Your guidance and patience during this process have been invaluable.

Jennifer L. Magnabosco
Ronald W. Manderscheid

CHAPTER 1

Introduction

Jennifer L. Magnabosco and Ronald W. Manderscheid

In 1997, the year the first edition of *Outcomes Measurement in the Human Services* was published, the United States had just begun to implement more systematic accountability of the human services through legislation (such as the Government Performance and Results Act), more contemporary approaches to human services administration that were geared toward performance measurement (such as total quality management), and more stringent approaches to fiscal accountability through evolving strategies such as managed care. At the time of this second edition's writing, our nation has once again just completed a thorough examination of how our health, mental health, and child and family services and systems are to be delivered and managed. Having just recently witnessed the passing of national health care reform, mental health parity, and new procedures to overhaul state child and welfare accountability systems, citizens in the United States are living in an unprecedented time of systemic change within our human services. Such historic change again directs much attention to human service outcomes and their measurement, and in the 21st century, new contexts for care such as prevention, consumer-, and recovery-driven (please see chapter 16 for a general definition) and strengths-based (approaches to recovery that shift from a problem-focused targeting of deficiencies perspective, to a focus on "elevating" and "magnifying strengths" perspective) care (Seligman, 2002; Seligman & Csikszentmihalyi, 2000).

This volume is intended to be in sync with information presented in the first edition. Both volumes

- Bring together prominent thinkers, researchers, practitioners, administrators,... policymakers [and consumers] to discuss issues relevant to the current impetus for accountability and measuring outcomes in health, mental and behavioral health, and child and family services

- Include chapters written by human service specialists with expertise in practice, policy and research, and advocacy

- Give students and professionals information to begin creating a comprehensive framework and to better understand the implications of outcomes measurement for the human services.

Many authors have contributed chapters to both editions, and in this edition, several authors again provide social work perspectives on outcomes measurement in the three main human service areas covered: health, mental/behavioral health, and child and family services. This volume's design and content are also grounded in a set of guiding questions similar to those of the first edition:

- *Changed context and response since 1997:* How have the contexts of outcomes measurement changed? How has outcomes measurement been usefully reconceptualized? What are the legislative and public policy contexts of outcomes measurement? Have they changed? If so, how? How have outcomes been addressed to meet legislative and public policy demands?

- *New and established approaches to outcomes measurement since 1997:* What approaches to outcomes measurement are being promulgated, and how have they changed since 1997? What can be said about the reliability, validity, and quality of existing approaches to outcomes measurement, as well as their relevance for social work and other human services?

- *Future Implications:* What are the implications of the increasing attention to outcomes measurement for social programs and for practitioners, policymakers, advocates, consumers, and researchers? What are the implications for future research, practice, policy, and advocacy?

Keeping these guiding questions in mind, authors in the second edition of *Outcomes Measurement in the Human Services* present an updated discussion of issues and methods in outcomes measurement (Mullen & Magnabosco, 1997). Where possible, and fitting, discussion regarding the effect that demands for accountability have had and will continue to have on social work practice is also included.

The Book's Organization

This introduction sets the overall context for the book, summarizing each chapter and providing a descriptor of its content in italics. Parts I through IV of the book model the first edition's overall structure. Part I addresses general overarching issues and cross-cutting themes of outcomes measurement, and parts II, III, and IV examine outcomes measurement in three select fields of human services: health, mental and behavioral health, and child and family services. Whereas one section in the first edition featured practice–research examples, in this edition we provide three such examples, one in each of the fields of practice, to illustrate the development and/or application of outcomes measurement in real-life human service scenarios. Part V is a new section that features particular areas in the human services that cut across the three main fields of practice featured and are timely and representative of important domains of interest in the 21st century. We close the book with concluding comments and recommendations for future action.

Part I: Overarching Issues and Methods

Part I "examines the overarching issues and methods that apply to all human service disciplines" (Mullen & Magnabosco, 1997, p. xxi). The themes found in these beginning chapters are echoed and particularly contextualized by chapters in parts II through V.

Orientation to Outcomes and Performance Measurement (Chapter 2)

Hatry updates the current status of outcomes and performance measurement in the public and private sectors, discussing major recent activities that have shaped the direction of such measurement in the United States and internationally. In this chapter (as in the first edition), he distinguishes among types of outcomes measurement and approaches and discusses the need for human service organizations (HSOs) to incorporate outcomes management in everyday organizational activities. He questions whether the typically collected outcomes and performance data are valid and comprehensive and raises concerns about how such data are being used. He advocates for the need to balance and integrate regular outcomes measurement and program evaluation, especially in light of the need to address disparities (inequities), and discusses various strategies being used to effectively meet accountability demands from funders, government, specific communities, and the public at large.

Qualitative and Quantitative Approaches and Outcomes Evaluation (Chapters 3 and 4)

The next two chapters provide perspectives on qualitative and quantitative approaches to outcomes measurement and outcomes evaluation. This dual perspective echoes Hatry, highlighting the necessity of both approaches and their unique contributions to the development, implementation, monitoring, and provision of outcomes and performance measurement, as well as to accountability, practice, and research purposes. In chapter 3, Patton and Gornick discuss the development, trends, and impact that qualitative data—specifically, qualitative outcomes evaluations—have had in the outcomes measurement movement and in meeting demands for accountability in the human services. They illustrate the value that qualitative methods offer in a case example evaluation of a residence for persons with long-term alcohol and drug use conditions. Patton and Gornick conclude with comments on some of the major issues in the future of outcomes evaluation, including the need to develop a common language for types of evaluation and outcome measures, as well as how increasingly important concepts, such as strengths-based care and prevention, require understanding that there may be "different meanings in different contexts."

In chapter 4, Yates provides a commentary on quantitative approaches to outcomes measurement and evaluation. On the basis of his 35 years researching and evaluating HSO programs, he reflects on issues that are common to measuring outcomes quantitatively across HSOs, such as the idea that "reliability and validity of quantitative outcomes are not just based on science anymore," and the fact that the process of selecting and quantifying outcomes for, and by, funders is not standardized. He then discusses implications for outcomes measurement in this era of change, and offers the RAPOA (Resource/Activity/Process/Outcome Analysis) model as a tool that can help HSOs measure the range of outcomes related to improving services and systems.

Controversies in Evidence-based Practice and Outcomes (Chapter 5)

Thyer discusses controversies in the measurement of outcomes and evidence-based practice (EBP). He shares views that are critically needed during this time of turbulent change in the human services: He explains why it is important to pause and reconsider the fact that EBP is really a five-step process, and that EBP "does not tell clinicians and others involved with an EBP process what to do." He thoroughly discusses the relationship between the EBP process and outcomes measurement, how to locate and assess credible evidence, and various stakeholder approaches to outcomes measurement, as well as the implications different perspectives have for human services and EBP. He concludes with thoughts on how to balance approaches to outcomes measurement and EBPs and ends on an empowering note to consumer and advocacy groups, suggesting that they become more involved with promoting EBPs in service and government organizations.

A Process for Getting to Outcomes (Chapter 6)

Acosta and Chinman describe a method for HSOs to build capacity for outcomes called Getting to Outcomes (GTO). The authors discuss how the 10-step GTO model is "more than just a process…it is also an intervention that builds the capacity of users to use outcome data for [continuous quality improvement], not just performance measurement." They illustrate the use of GTO in a current project designed to implement positive youth development programs by an adolescent coalition in Maine. They conclude with a discussion about barriers associated with measuring outcomes in HSOs and how GTO can effectively help navigate the development of capacity and outcomes.

Leadership and Outcomes Assessment (Chapter 7)

Packard and Beinecke discuss leadership development in the human services and the implications leadership can have for outcomes at multiple levels. They make it clear that human services leadership is facing a serious challenge over the next decade as many experienced human service professionals retire. They also review the main models of leadership, tenets of leadership versus management, organizational change, and pertinent studies that have shown links between leadership and outcomes in the human services. Packard and Beinecke offer a conceptual model for organizational change that can be used as a framework to develop and measure progress toward outcomes-based cultures in HSOs. They conclude with suggestions for promoting "change leaders" and outcomes measurement systems and cultures in HSOs.

Part II: Outcomes Measurement in Health

In 1997, Mullen and Magnabosco wrote, "perhaps no field of practice of human service practice has been more affected by outcomes measurement than health" (p. xxviii). This remains true today.

Integrated Service Delivery (Chapter 8)

Bartlett describes a current solution to integrated healthcare—the patient-centered medical home—and the implications it has had during health care reform and for the United States in general. Chronicling the history of primary care delivery in this country and its relation to current health care reform tenets, Bartlett describes the challenges to providing cost-effective and needed care, and to measuring integrated health care outcomes between primary care and other sectors, especially mental health and substance use. He stresses the unmistakable need to integrate health and mental health and describes several strategies that may help to bring us closer to reasonable outcomes, such as implementing the "use of brief, valid, and reliable tools" (like Zabora in chapter 12 and Corcoran and Hozak in chapter 15) and "thinking globally but acting locally" (Geddes, 1915)—that is, measuring health outcomes at all levels, with an eye toward improved population health.

Patient-reported Measures (Chapter 9)

Cherepanov and Hays provide a comprehensive discussion of measures that are critical to monitoring health and care: patient-reported outcome measures, health-related quality-of-life measures, and patient evaluations of care. The authors discuss the various types of measures in detail and their applications to practice; in particular, they discuss the Consumer Assessment of Healthcare Providers and Systems (CAHPS) Program to illustrate patient evaluation of care measures. Like other authors in the book, Cherepanov and Hays chronicle the changes made in measurement and note the available resources. In their conclusion, they predict that patient-reported outcome measures may gain greater significance during health care reform.

Assessing Services for an Aging Population (Chapter 10)

Berkman and Kaplan discuss one of the most pressing health concerns the United States will face in the next decade: our aging population. They describe the characteristics of this population and how they will affect the context of health care delivery, regardless of health care reform. Berkman and Kaplan review the state of outcomes measurement in aging and provide a range of instruments and measures that are especially relevant and useful. Like other authors in the book, they highlight the role that social workers will have as the face of health care delivery is changed by this population's needs and by health care reform.

Complementary Alternative Medicine (CAM) and Integrative Medicine (IM) (Chapter 11)

Coulter and Khorsan discuss an aspect of health care that is widespread but not routinely included in mainstream discussions: the use of CAM and integrative medicine. The authors explain the nature and modalities (for example, acupuncture, chiropractic medicine) of CAM and IM, their paradigms, the controversies and challenges associated with integrating CAM and IM, and the challenges associated with conducting research and outcomes measurement. They conclude with recommendations and comments about useful approaches (for example, observational studies) and theoretical models (for example, systems theory), the principles upon which CAM outcomes measurement should be based (for example, "elevate the notion of person-centered care and patient-centered care"), and an agenda for outcomes measurement in CAM that can be used for comparative effectiveness research and other health care reform efforts.

Research-to-Practice Example: Chronic Care and Psychological Distress (Chapter 12)

Zabora illustrates the importance of using appropriate and comprehensive screening and outcomes assessment tools to determine the range of needs chronic care patients, especially oncology patients, have during the course of care and over the longer term. Zabora focuses on screening and assessments for psychological distress—one of the most serious effects of chronic illness—in the context of hospital settings. This focus is of particular note because screening for such distress often goes unperformed, largely because of a lack of comprehensive tools and measures. He concludes with a discussion of barriers to such assessments, how particular members of the health care team—such as social workers—are better poised to take on this responsibility, and how such instruments and measures can be especially useful in health care reform efforts that seek quick and valid approaches.

Part III: Outcomes Measurement in Mental and Behavioral Health

The contributors to part III examine mental and behavioral health services outcomes measurement. As in the first edition, the terms *mental health* and *behavioral health* are sometimes used interchangeably when discussing outcomes measurement. In 1997, the term *behavioral health* typically was used to designate services that applied to people with substance abuse and mental health problems in a managed care context (Freeman & Trabin, 1994; Mullen & Magnabosco, 1997). Today, behavioral health carries a similar meaning, with two differences: First, *substance use* is used in place of *substance abuse*. Second, the overall meaning of *substance use* is not determined as much by the managed care context. Rather, it is informed by the fact that consumers, and the wide range of stakeholders in the fields of mental health and substance use, have come to accept a broader and more integrated approach to the spectrum of mental health and substance use care. Although the use of the terms "substance use" and "substance abuse" largely depend on ideology, practice, and societal context, the former represents recognition that persons with this disorder have a real illness and that the issues associated with this illness are multidimensional, taking into account the holistic individual, not just his or her drug using or drug "abusing." Hence, in the United States, we have more readily come to use the term *substance use* to "connote measurability or an emphasis on behavioral functioning" (Mullen & Magnabosco, 1997).

Transformation and Outcomes (Chapter 13)

Kelly examines mental health policy in the United States, factors leading to the recent emphasis on mental health transformation or reform, and recommendations for what is needed to transform the country's mental health system into an outcomes-oriented culture of care. Based on his recent book, this chapter, like Thyer's, provides the author's views on the use of EBPs and how various instruments can support the measurement of service effectiveness, as well as different stakeholder views on the use of EBPs and outcomes measurement. He concludes with a "blueprint for change" that can help the United States transform to a national outcomes-based mental health system, including the caution that we need to correctly implement "outcome data for all parties" that help guarantee community-based recovery for persons with mental illness.

Integrated Measures for Mental Health and Substance Use Care (Chapter 14)

Siemianowski and Kirk provide an overview of identity and integration issues for the field of mental health and substance use generally, the implications of these issues for integrated outcomes measurement for the two fields, and the specific implications for persons with co-occurring disorders (persons with mental health and substance use conditions). They use an example of multi-level integration that has occurred in the state of Connecticut to illustrate how transformation in organizational culture, strong leadership, and working with a variety of stakeholders—especially consumers—have resulted in a system that is driven by recovery, outcomes, and performance measurement. They conclude with recommendations for outcomes that can reflect an integrated system of mental health and substance use care under health care reform, and that can support integration with primary care, so that those in need can receive the comprehensive services required for their recovery.

Emergence of Rapid Assessment Instruments (RAIs) (Chapter 15)

This chapter updates Corcoran's 1997 chapter on RAIs with expanded commentary with his colleague Hozack. Just as Corcoran discussed the importance of RAIs as an important extension of outcomes measurement during managed care and in social work clinical practice, Corcoran and Hozack describe how RAIs can be useful in health care reform today. Although these tools have been in use for a long time, in routine practice they have not superseded reliance on wisdom, clinical judgments, and intuition in decision making. Corcoran and Hozack believe this will continue. However, they think that RAIs can provide evidence about medical necessity and be used as quick and valid measures of treatment outcomes, or as estimations of the clinical or real-life significance of usual treatment and/or interventions. They conclude with cautions about properly linking different populations to standardized and normed instruments and measures, as well as endorse appropriate uses of RAIs to meet various clinical and reform goals.

Consumer-operated Service Programs (COSPs) (Chapter 16)

Campbell describes the evolution of the consumer movement since the late 1990s, with specific emphasis on contributions of consumers, consumer researchers, and other stakeholders in the study and integration of COSPs within the continuum of behavioral health care in the United States. She describes the range of COSP service models and highlights salient research that has investigated their effectiveness, including results from the only national survey on COSP services, completed in 2002. Much of this chapter also focuses on rating the evidence of COSP studies—in the form of a mini-research synthesis—to question the appropriateness and types of evidence-based lenses through which to assess COSPs, and to set directions for future research and outcomes measurement in this area.

Research-to-Practice Example: Assertive Community Treatment Measures (Chapter 17)

Teague and Monroe-DeVita describe the evolution of measurement for one EBP—Assertive Community Treatment (ACT)—and provide an example of a live project that is testing refined aspects of ACT to improve service quality and outcomes for persons with severe mental illness. This example illustrates the relationship between fidelity, quality, outcomes, and effectiveness of ACT services, concluding with empowering comments—partially inspired by Kelly's arguments about mental health system transformation—regarding the need to promote outcomes measurement, quality improvement, and outcomes-based culture.

Part IV: Outcomes Measurement in Child and Family Services

Part IV examines the common and unique aspects of outcomes measurement in child and family services. Although the move toward outcomes measurement has been most evident in health and mental and behavioral health since 1997, the field of child and family services has been making great strides. Child and family services share many of the same contexts that have shaped outcomes measurement in other human service fields. The chapters in this section speak to these commonalities and, at the same time, highlight some of the unique measurement issues faced by child and family services.

Multilevel Measurement Approaches in Children's Programs (Chapter 18)

Ethridge and colleagues describe how history, current policy changes, and systemwide reforms in the field of child and family services have shaped existing and emerging approaches to measuring outcomes and performance measures in this field of practice. They discuss outcomes and performance measurement domains (which are also discussed in chapter 20) and the challenges associated with using certain methodologies, measures, and research in daily management, practice, policy, and advocacy. They illustrate how these challenges are being addressed in an outcomes measurement process that was developed and implemented across child and family services in Kent County, Michigan, in the United States. The authors conclude with recommendations for improving the delivery and outcomes of child and family services, including the need for cross-system collaboration and the development of infrastructures and working practices that enhance the sharing of information across human service sectors.

Linking Costs and Outcomes for Children (Chapter 19)

Kilburn describes the challenges and solutions to measuring cost and outcomes of childhood services and programs and family well-being. She discusses why it is important to incorporate cost and outcomes analysis into human services research and decision making, describing the different methods by which this is possible: cost analysis, cost-effectiveness analysis, and cost–benefit analysis. Kilburn illustrates the use of these methods with examples from the child services literature, but she makes it clear in her discussion that these methods are usable in any human services domain. She concludes with implications for how cost and outcomes analysis can enhance policy, research, and practice in the child and family services field.

Research-to-Practice Example: Standardization of Process and Outcomes in Child Service and Welfare Evaluations (Chapter 20)

McGowan and Walsh discuss lessons learned from child services and welfare evaluations and the push for standardization of process and outcomes (for safety, permanency, and child and family well-being) at the state level. They describe how the new results-oriented approach in accountability first came into play in 2000, its subsequent statewide assessment review process, and how this movement is helping to address some of the "methodological shortcomings" (Wulcyzn, 1997) in outcomes measurement and promoting new approaches to child welfare practice.

Part V: Special Topics in the Human Services

Part V brings together four topical areas not typically represented in general discussions of outcomes measurement in the human services that can be helpful as we begin to think more holistically about outcomes measurement, performance measurement, and outcomes evaluation across the human services.

Transformation of the Veterans Health Administration (VHA) (Chapter 21)

Francis discusses lessons learned from the VHA during its transformation into a Cabinet-level government agency determined to incorporate innovative and evidence-based clinical, administrative, and management practices to provide better health care to U.S. veterans. He describes how the VHA evolved its outcomes and performance measurement system and its integrated electronic health record, as well as how instituting a systemwide Quality Enhancement Research Initiative has improved the implementation of EBPs and performance measurement in everyday practice. He concludes by noting the importance of accountable leadership in forging change in measurement and quality-improvement systems and why this process, which includes the determination of measures, needs to be more patient centered.

Outcomes in Criminal Justice (Chapter 22)

Turner provides an overview of outcomes measurement in the U.S. criminal justice system and the challenges associated with measuring outcomes at multiple levels: individual, agency, and state. She bases her discussion in two main outcomes measurement domains: crime rates and recidivism. She discusses how new measurement systems, such as CompStat, have helped to improve correctional institutions' internal processes and outcomes, and in turn, community outcomes in both of these domains. Turner concludes with some lessons learned from the field of criminal justice that other human services may find useful in their quest to become more automated and collaborative with the various sectors involved in providing comprehensive care.

Outcomes in Faith-based Organizations (FBOs) (Chapter 23)

Flory and colleagues discuss the role that FBOs and services play in the United States and how more formalized programming and funding of such services have evolved over the past 15 years. They discuss the research upon which effectiveness evaluations have been based and directions for research that can help to better measure important components of such services, such as how the "faith factor" may influence clients and play a special role in measurement. They conclude by suggesting the development of a typology and language for FBOs and of forums that can help to better share lessons learned.

Social, Health, and Mental Health Outcomes: Global Linkages (Chapter 24)

Ganju provides an international perspective on health, mental health, and social outcomes. Like several other authors, he highlights the importance of linking several life domains and their associated outcomes together to better understand how we can improve the quality of life globally. In particular, he discusses a conundrum: Although a "natural imperative" exists that links mental health and substance use to broader societal and community goals (such as reduction in poverty, increased employment), we have yet to comfortably and effectively recognize, prioritize, and equalize mental health and substance use outcomes when evaluating global welfare. Ganju discusses the tensions underlying this and offers recommendations to help promote an international outcomes agenda for health, mental health, and substance use.

Concluding Comments

Since 1997, human services has grown in its "wealth" (Mullen & Magnabosco, 1997) of approaches, instruments, and types of outcomes and performance measures, as well as its capacity to integrate research and measurement processes into everyday clinical and administrative practice, policymaking, and advocacy. Regardless, much still needs to be done to critically assess the field of outcomes measurement and how effective its evidence bases are in meeting the myriad demands that clients, collaborators, communities, funders, and other stakeholders place on HSOs. This volume brings together an array of information that can be used as a starting point toward that end. We will return to this theme in our conclusion. We hope your reading of this volume will provide a contemporary understanding of some of the most salient cross-cutting and field-specific, issues, methods, and tools in outcomes measurement in the human services today.

References

Freeman, M.A., & Trabin, T. (1994). *Managed behavioral healthcare: History, models, key issues and future course.* Rockville, MD: U.S. Center for Mental Health Services.

Geddes, P. (1915). *Cities in evolution.* London: Williams.

Mullen, E.J., & Magnabosco, J. L. (Eds.). (1997). *Outcomes measurement in the human services: Cross-cutting issues and methods.* Washington, DC: NASW Press.

Seligman, M. (2002). Positive psychology, positive prevention, and positive therapy. In C. R. Snyder & S. J. Lopez (Eds.), *The handbook of positive psychology* (pp. 3–12). New York: Oxford University Press.

Seligman, M., & Csikszentmihalyi, M. (2000). Positive psychology: An introduction. *American Psychologist, 55,* 5–14.

Wulczyn, F. H. (1997). Methodological considerations in outcomes measurement in family and child welfare. In E. J. Mullen. & J. L. Magnabosco (Eds.), *Outcomes measurement in the human services: Cross-cutting issues and methods* (pp. 181–183). Washington, DC: NASW Press.

PART I

Overarching Issues and Methods

CHAPTER 2

Outcomes Measurement in the Human Services:

Lessons Learned from Public and Private Sectors

Harry P. Hatry

Since the first edition of *Outcomes Measurement in the Human Services* was published in 1997, a deluge of outcomes and performance measurement activity has taken place in the human services. This trend is occurring not only in the United States, but in many other developed and developing countries. The chapters in this book's second edition are testimony to the advances in activity and thinking that have occurred in outcomes measurement. To date, the bulk of this activity has been aimed at responding to the increasing demands for accountability put forth by funders of human services. However, the quality of this measurement work and its use by human service organizations (HSOs) for improving services are questionable. This chapter will shed light on this issue and discuss major outcomes measurement activity that has occurred in the public and private sectors over the past dozen years, as well as emerging issues in outcomes measurement.

(In this chapter, *outcome measurement* generally refers to the regular tracking, at least annually but almost always more frequently, by an organization of the outcomes of its individual services and programs. *Outcomes management* refers to the use of outcome information by organization managers to help them manage better, such as better allocated resources and better formulated and justified budgets. The term *performance measurement* is frequently used to cover outcome measurement. Performance measurement covers not only the measurement of service outcomes, but also the measurement of the amount of physical output produced by an organization, such as the number of sessions held with clients. The word *outcomes* refers to what results occurred from the outputs. Performance measurement also covers the measurement of a service's efficiency, usually expressed as the cost per unit of output or, where possible, the cost per unit of outcome.)

Major Recent Activities in Outcomes and Performance Measurement

During the past dozen years, many factors and activities have shaped the approaches to outcome measurement in HSOs.

Government Performance and Results Act

The U.S. federal government fully implemented the 1993 Government Performance and Results Act (GPRA) in fiscal year 1999. The years since then have seen an increase in the quality of the reported performance indicators. Each federal department and major independent agency annually develops a performance plan as part of the budget process and, within six months after each fiscal year, provides a Performance and Accountability Report. These reports contain numerous outcome indicators covering each of the agency's major programs. This clearly has had a major effect on performance measurement in the federal government. For example, the Department of Health and Human Services (DHHS) Administration for Children and Families, through its Adoption and Foster Care Analysis and Reporting System, has pressed the states (not always without controversy) for more valid data on the outcomes of child welfare clients (such as placement frequencies and outcomes of children who entered foster care).

The George W. Bush administration added another component to GPRA, the Performance Assessment Rating Tool (PART), which was in use from 2002 to 2008. The intention was both to encourage improved performance measurement and to use the information in the Office of Management and Budget (OMB) budget review process. By the end of 2008, the OMB had examined approximately 1,000 federal programs, including more than 100 in the DHHS. A major element of this effort was an examination of a small number of key outcome indicators for each of the programs (an average of approximately five performance indicators per program). These run the gamut from response times, to client satisfaction ratings (for example, Administration on Aging's "percent of home-delivered meals, transportation, and family caregiver services clients rating quality of services either good or excellent"), to improved condition levels (for example, Substance Abuse Prevention program's "percentage of participants who used illicit drugs at pretest who report a decrease in use at post-test," and Child Welfare Services' percentage children in care less than 12 months who had no more than two placement settings).

The PART process focused considerable attention on the performance management process in federal programs, rating elements of the program's purpose and design, strategic planning, and program management. OMB's ratings on these process elements indicated considerable improvement over the period. However, PART was considerably less successful in assessing the overall effectiveness of the programs. Although much has been written about this controversial PART process (Accenture Institute for Public Service Value, Georgetown Public Policy Institute & OMB Watch, 2009), much less has been written about the parallel Performance and Accountability Report process that provided considerably more detailed data on program outcomes (see, for example, work reported by George Mason University's Mercatus Center).

OMB Performance Data on State and Local HSOs

The pressure on U.S. federal departments to provide national performance data to the OMB and Congress has had a substantial effect on state and local HSOs in a myriad ways. Much of the human service outcome data originate at those lower levels of government. When accepting federal funds, HSOs often are required to provide performance data on selected outcome indicators, often ones selected by the DHHS program. This has required states and local governments to implement many outcomes measurement procedures that would unlikely have been implemented without such pressure.

Foundation Reporting Requirements

A number of major foundations in the United States (such as Kellogg, Hewlett, Gates, and Robert Wood Johnson) now often require reports and other information that document the results associated with the funding they provide. Sometimes they themselves sponsor in-depth evaluations of at least some of their programs. As with the federal government, this has put considerable pressure on HSOs that receive or want to receive funding from these foundations to undertake outcomes measurement or to cooperate with evaluations done by other organizations.

Focus on Community-Level Indicators

U.S. HSOs in the private, nonprofit sector were also encouraged to begin outcomes measurement in the mid-1990s by United Way of America with the 1996 release of its bestseller (more than 100,000 copies sold) report *Measuring Program Outcomes: A Practical Approach*. Other major national associations such as the Boys and Girls Clubs of America and the American Red Cross have shown leadership to their affiliates by providing support for local outcomes and performance measurement efforts.

The United Way movement has shifted to a focus on communitywide needs and community indicators. To do this effectively, partnering is required among many community groups and organizations. Other national groups, such as the Community Indicators Consortium, have emerged to help identify the communitywide outcome indicators needed to help communities tackle their problems in a more coordinated way.

Evidence-based Practice

Around the beginning of the 21st century, considerable attention began to be focused on implementing evidence-based practices in various domains (for example, health, mental health, child welfare) in an attempt is to identify which polices and procedures work well. This focus will likely continue into the future. However, what is meant by *evidence-based practice* has not been well defined. Which evaluation and measurement methods are sufficient to meet this criterion? Initially, the U.S. federal government pressed for the evidence to come from randomized controlled trials. However, it became apparent that this would greatly limit the applicability of such evaluations for many—probably most—public services, including human services. The pressure for rigorous studies has continued, but use of a larger range of evaluation methods is now acceptable. This pressure will likely considerably increase the use and volume of program evaluation in human services (Orszag, 2009).

Technology

Tremendous technological developments have made the collection and processing of substantial amounts of outcome data considerably more practical and affordable for many HSOs. This trend has added substantially to HSOs' ability to process, analyze, and report data in more sophisticated, attractive, and useful ways. For example, it is now technologically feasible to link case management records that identify an individual client's demographic characteristics and the types and amounts of services received to outcome information on that client. This can be done across services if confidentiality and privacy considerations are resolved. Such information made available to service managers can provide them a wealth of information on what is working well (or poorly) for which groups of clients and under which conditions. However, as of this writing, such opportunities have not been widely, if at all, realized.

International Focus on Outcomes Measurement and Evaluation

Several countries in addition to the United States have introduced outcomes measurement (and evaluation) systems covering human services with a national focus, including Australia, Canada, New Zealand, and the United Kingdom. This has had ripple effects, affecting these countries' state/provincial governments as well, requiring their human service agencies to provide outcome data and encouraging implementation of outcomes measurement and evaluation.

Internationally, major organizations such as The World Bank, Inter-American Development Bank, and other multilateral funders (nongovernmental organizations that use funds obtained from many countries to help developing countries), as well as bilateral funders (countries that use their own funds to directly aid developing counties) such as the United States (through its Agency for International Development), Canada, Germany, Japan, and the United Kingdom, have pressed for outcome and evaluation information,

Numerous international HSOs that provide services to citizens in needy countries, using funds that have been obtained at least in part from the above organizations and countries, have also been encouraged to introduce outcomes measurement and evaluation practices. (These HSOs include, for example, such organizations as Heifer International, Women for Women International, Partners in Health, and the International Rescue Committee.)

Emerging Issues and Developments

Considering the expansion in interest, requirements, and need for outcome measurement, and evaluation in the United States and abroad, several questions arise:

- Are the outcome data that are being collected sufficiently valid and comprehensive? Do the data cover enough of the outcome dimensions important to HSOs and others, and especially the clients they serve? Are the data being collected and reported in a reasonably sound, valid way?

- How is outcomes and performance measurement information being used? Is it being collected mainly for accountability purposes? To what extent are the data being used to improve services and programs, and thus improve outcomes for the clients of HSOs?

The remainder of this section discusses a number of the key issues related to answering these questions and other emerging issues and developments in outcome measurement for human services in the United States.

Need to Intertwine and Balance Outcomes Measurement and Program Evaluation

To be of most use by human service program managers, outcomes data are likely to be needed frequently, such as quarterly, if not monthly, at least for some indicators. This greater frequency lets managers obtain feedback in a more timely way, providing opportunities to undertake midcourse corrections. Outcomes measurement is analogous to information commonly available to the manager of any sports team: the running score. Managers keep track of the score to tell whether their teams are winning or losing. However, the scores do not provide information about why the teams are winning or losing.

A major misunderstanding among public officials, and probably the media and public, is that the government agencies and nongovernmental organizations that measure and report the outcomes information have complete control over these results. But these outcomes only tell what the score is. They do not indicate who or what is responsible for why the outcome occurred as it did. Many factors inevitably affect all outcome measures—the weather, the international economy, other levels of government, the parents, and so on.

Outcomes measurement, not in-depth program evaluation, has been the major focus of both public and private HSOs, both because it provides considerably more timely information and because it does not require the more sophisticated methods and statistical tools usually needed for program evaluations. Outcomes measurement, however, provides little if any evidence as to why the outcomes occurred.

In-depth, ad hoc program evaluations attempt to identify not only the outcomes for a program, but also the causes of the outcomes. HSO program evaluations are essentially intended to focus on the question, "Are the program's clients better off than they would have been without the program?" These evaluations require a substantial amount of time, both of people to do the evaluations and calendar time. Program evaluation also generally requires evaluators who have had special training, training seldom taken by HSO staffs. Program evaluations can provide HSOs with information that adds to information that is solely focused on outcomes.

Both these approaches—outcomes measurement and program evaluation—have advantages and disadvantages. However, because outcomes measurement is an ongoing process, it is likely to be considerably more useful to HSOs and their managers. Outcomes measurement is less expensive than in-depth program evaluations, requires less specialized and sophisticated technical skills, and can be applied on a continuing basis to many programs. In-depth evaluations typically require special technical skills, often require many months if not years to complete, and are costly. Generally, program evaluations need to be contracted out, or a university may be coaxed into doing them for free.

Overall, the feasibility of undertaking full in-depth program evaluations in more than a very small percentage of HSOs is unlikely. Few private, nonprofit HSOs are able to afford in-depth evaluation of their own programs, at least not without major funding from a foundation or government agency. Even in government, only a few human service programs are given a full evaluation in any given year. This is also mainly due to cost and the limited amount of time government staff have to conduct or oversee such activities. The great growth in computer technology has made outcomes measurement much more feasible for HSOs. Today's technology is also making the design and implementation of outcomes measurement systems more useful, with capabilities that can integrate multiple human service sectors and client bases and move us toward workable electronic medical and human service records.

Need to Address Disparities (Inequities)

A major issue in human services is addressing the significant disparities in service access, delivery, and quality between advantaged and disadvantaged populations. In past decades, closing the gap in funding allocation disparities has been the focus. With the heightened emphasis on outcomes measurement, a second major dimension can be added to this strategy: The outcomes for populations of disadvantaged populations can be compared more definitively with those of more advantaged populations, as well as within and across their own groups. The latter comparison is of special concern because outcomes for disadvantaged populations that are served by many public programs vary according to client characteristics, including gender, age, and geographical location (such as rural versus urban).

With the considerably more powerful computers and software technology now available, comparisons between (and among) disadvantaged and advantaged populations have started to become a relatively easy and innovative process. For example, geographic information systems and other technology make mapping readily feasible and inexpensive, helping HSOs not only to identify geographical differences, but also to report the information considerably more effectively, and more dramatically, to HSO officials and the public.

Emergence of the "How Are We Doing"/STAT Movement

Recent years have seen the emergence of a potentially terrific management tool designed to take advantage of newly available outcome information. It is based on the simple idea that periodically, an upper-level manager meets with his or her key employees to discuss the latest performance report that addresses such questions as, "Where are we doing well? Can it be transferred elsewhere? Where are we doing poorly? Why is that? What can we do to improve this?" Then, in later meetings, the group would be asked to address the question, "Did our changes made previously have the results that we hoped for?"

This process is similar to that of regular meetings agency managers traditionally hold with their key staff. However, in this new approach, a major focus of the meeting is on examining outcomes. This approach is based on the STAT ("statistics") movement that was started in the 1990s by the New York Police Department (called CompStat; see also chapter 22 in this volume). A number of other New York City agencies adapted the CompStat approach to their own human service focus. Likewise, a number of local and state (for example, Washington and Maryland) governments have adopted the approach, and some federal agencies (for example, the Veterans Health Administration) are also experimenting with it. For example, the city of Baltimore's CitiStat process has included staff from each city agency in its biweekly mayor's meeting to discuss the agency's performance.

Most of these STAT programs have used a formal process for obtaining the outcome and related data in advance from the organization unit being reviewed, assigning dedicated staff to review the agencies' data, and establishing formal meeting rooms where the data are displayed on large screens for use by high-level officials. This type of approach to the development and use of outcome and performance measures—whether or not full STAT process has been employed—has considerable potential for the improvement of public or private HSOs. Yet, it is not likely to be necessary for a HSO to have the extensive infrastructure that has been characteristic of most STAT programs. In other words, modeling as many aspects of STAT as possible can still likely help an HSO improve its outcomes or performance measurement process, and in turn, its outcomes.

Improving Strategies that Integrate Outcomes across Programs and Agencies

A related concern is how HSOs can more effectively and efficiently track the outcomes of clients who receive multiple services and receive services in more than one agency. The concern about how to handle information flow among public services and public and private nongovernmental organization programs is certainly not new to the human services community.

In addition, we have had in the last decade experiments in "performance partnerships." These partnerships recognize that key outcomes are produced jointly. Each partner has a role in producing those outcomes and in how the desired outcomes are to be achieved. For example, in 2009, the New York State Department of Education introduced its Literacy Zone Program, which focused on partnerships in a number of communities throughout the state. These partnerships were created to improve a number of key outcomes that involved not only multiple state and local government agencies but also many public and private educational, health, and social services organizations in the community. The program used literacy improvement as a starting point for outcomes, and later added outcomes related to employment and health.

An earlier example of such partnerships in HSOs is the Harlem Children's Zone in New York City. Beginning in the 1990s, that program undertook a major effort to provide a wide variety of child development programs for disadvantaged children. "The Harlem Children's Zone is a program designed to address the entire range of community needs with a focus on changing the outcomes for children growing up in poverty" (Page & Stone, 2010). The very special element of this partnership, and the most ambitious, is a linked set of services that continues to support the enrolled children until they become of age. A major thrust has been a focus on results and the continual measurement of progress. This highly publicized program has led to the federal government's "Promise Neighborhoods" program.

Such a comprehensive program is likely to be very difficult to successfully accomplish. It requires sustained resources being available over a long period of time for a wide range of services. This set of substantial resources has not typically been available to HSOs.

Increasing the Use of Outcome Information to Motivate Service Providers

The push for performance contracting began under the Nixon administration in the 1980s, when the federal government began encouraging more private sector organizations to help deliver public services. Over the years, a substantial number of attempts have been made to introduce performance contracting incentives for public services. For example, financial payments to service providers from public agencies have been made for such outcomes as placing the unemployed in jobs (for example, in the 1990s, the Oklahoma Department of Rehabilitation's innovative employment incentive program paid a portion of the contractors' payment based on placing clients in jobs, both for initial placements and, more unusually, for clients who were still employed several months later). Another example is the North Carolina Department of Health and Human Services' program. It paid adoption agencies on the basis of the number of placements and intact placements as of one year after the decree of adoption (Liner et al., 2001).

The federal government has used outcome program incentives with states for particular services. For example, for state efforts to seek child support payments, financial incentives are provided on the basis of each state's success in payment collections. Payment to states are based on factors such as establishment of paternity, support orders, current child support payments, and amount of payments overdue, with annual actual values compared with targeted values such as those outlined in the 1998 Child Support Performance and Incentive Act. Another example of federal program incentives involves the No Child Left Behind Act program. This incentive program has primarily used negative incentives, including takeover of schools for not meeting progress in test scores. In another example, for child care, states have used intermediate, proxy outcomes that sanction individual child care programs for not including specific service characteristics that evidence indicates are related to more successful child development.

Such outcome-based incentives can be a powerful tool for use in the human services when appropriate outcome measurements are available. They require careful planning and oversight to ensure that they are not easy to defraud. It is likely that the country will continue to increase the uses of such incentives as outcome measurement continues to grow.

Improving the Quality and Comparability of Outcome Measurement Data

The quality of outcome indicators has improved considerably since the early days of GPRA, at all levels of government and to a more limited extent in private, nonprofit organizations. Initial efforts in many organizations focused on using such indicators as response times to calls for services. Many federal agencies have also attempted to introduce more standardization of outcome indicators across states, to be able to both better compare outcomes across states and to validly aggregate data to provide national figures. However, differences among states make complete standardization very difficult for outcomes for which a federal agency depends on data from states. For example, the Department of Agriculture's Food Stamp program seeks data on the amount of incorrect under- and overpayments and depends on the auditing procedures of individual states.

With regard to improving the quality of the outcome indicators, an example is DHHS's Adoption and Foster Care Analysis and Reporting System. Although it is now yielding improved state comparison data, a debate continues about how to best calculate some outcome indicators, such as the percentage of children placed in a permanent home via adoption or foster care (Wulczyn, 1997). In recent years, considerably more use of outcome information obtained from clients (most often by surveys) has occurred, in an attempt to better understand their conditions and their perceptions regarding the helpfulness of the services they have received. Probably one of the biggest gaps today in human services outcome measurement is the lack of follow-up data on clients after they have completed services. For regular outcome measurement, the follow-up period should probably not exceed 12 months. Assessment of longer term impacts on clients is likely to require considerable added resources and would likely be better done by in-depth program evaluation approaches. Although service providers may not believe that such follow-ups are feasible or possible because of cost, such information can be valuable to the planning, monitoring, continuous quality improvement, and sustainability of HSO services and programs. Client follow-up seems highly desirable for those programs for which the major intended benefits to the client cannot be expected at the time he or she completes the service, such as drug, alcohol, smoking cessation, family support, employment, and child placement programs. Such client follow-ups have been done for employment programs. There is a history of federal government requirements for such follow-ups to identify the number of persons who have remained employed for at least several months after initially placement.

More effective marketing of the usefulness of such follow-up information for improving human services and the identification of more practical data collection procedures is needed. A major way to incorporate such postservice follow-ups is to treat them as part of an aftercare activity, with some funding provided for the activity (Nayyar-Stone & Hatry, 2003). Overall, the pressure from funders for outcome information that enables them to compare outcomes of similar services across service delivery organizations appears likely to continue. Considerable improvement in outcome measurement has occurred, but major gaps remain.

Increasing Outcome Management: Use of Outcome Information to Improve Services

Little evidence is currently available that outcome information has or is being used by HSOs to help improve services and make them more effective for their clients. Nor does the outcome information seem to have been used for formulating and justifying budgets. A primary reason for this may be that most outcome measurement systems have been introduced from the top down and with the primary purpose of accountability. Even for budgeting, the perception appears to exist that most agencies have produced outcome information primarily for reporting as part of the budget process, as required by Congress or state legislatures, the OMB, or by foundations. The use of outcome information to formulate the budget and then justify the budget appears to have occurred to a much lesser extent.

Even the more extensively researched federal PART process used by OMB in the eight years of the George W. Bush administration has been controversial as to how the information has been used. Critics have noted that outcome information, when used at all, has been used primarily to cut or delete programs that the administration did not like. However the outcome information available in the PART process, and how it is used to develop effectiveness ratings on individual federal programs, is quite limited. Making major program decisions based to any significant extent on the PART effectiveness ratings would be highly questionable. In addition, it has been widely documented that Congress has paid little attention to the PART data, only a small proportion of which is actually devoted to outcome information (Accenture Institute for Public Service Value, Georgetown Public Policy Institute, & OMB Watch, 2009).

Although human services are only a small portion of the federal budget, the lack of real use of outcomes and performance measurement in budget formulation and service improvement is a problem common to other levels of government and to nonprofit organizations. This problem remains a significant issue for outcome measurement.

Summary

It should be clear by examining the chapters in this book that the use of outcomes measurement information has increased greatly in human services in the past dozen years. The outcome information available, however, while substantially improved in quality as well as quantity, nevertheless still has substantial limitations. Advances in technology and comprehensive approaches to integrating outcomes and performance measurement into clinical and administrative practice, such as STAT, are making it possible to see the emerging potential for considerably more enriched data that can link client and service characteristics to outcomes. It will likely take at least the next dozen years for the human services to realize this potential.

References

Accenture Institute for Public Service Value, Georgetown Public Policy Institute, & OMB Watch. (2009). *Building a better government performance system: Recommendations to the Obama administration.* Retrieved from http://www.ombwatch.org/files/performance/buildingabettergovernmentperformancesystem.pdf

Child Support Performance and Incentive Act of 1998, 42 U.S.C. § 1305 (1998).

Liner, B., Hatry, H. P., Vinson, E., Allen, R., Dusenbury, P., Bryant, S., & Snell, R. (2001). *Making results-based state government work.* Washington, DC: Urban Institute Press. Retrieved from http://www.urban.org/uploaded-pdf/310069_results-based-stategovt.pdf

Nayyar-Stone, R., & Hatry, H. (2003). *Finding out what happens to former clients.* Washington DC: Urban Institute Press.

Orszag, P. R. (2009, October 7). *Memorandum for the heads of executive departments and agencies: Increased emphasis on program evaluation* (M-10-01). Washington, DC: U.S. Office of Management and Budget.

Page, E. E., & Stone, A. M. (2010). *From Harlem children's zone to promise neighborhoods: Creating the tipping point for success.* Washington, DC: Georgetown Public Policy Institute.

Wulczyn, F. W. (1997). Methodological considerations in outcomes measurement in family and child welfare. In E. J. Mullen & J. L. Magnabosco (Eds.), *Outcomes measurement in the human services: Cross-cutting issues and methods* (pp. 181–183). Washington DC: NASW Press.

CHAPTER 3

Qualitative Approaches to Outcomes Evaluation

Michael Quinn Patton and Jean K. Gornick

Outcomes Evaluation: Values and Approaches

The increasing valuing and use of qualitative outcomes evaluation has developed within a larger public policy context that includes increased calls for accountability, greater emphasis on evidence-based policy and best practices, and reduced resources for human services of all kinds as a result of the national and global financial crisis. In such an environment, qualitative evaluation of outcomes makes an important contribution by identifying and validating especially effective, evidence-based practices.

It is important in this regard to distinguish outcomes evaluation from outcomes measurement. *Outcomes evaluation* refers generally to determining the results and impacts of an intervention. Did the youth development program lead to increased youth strengths and assets? Did the HIV/AIDS prevention program lead to safer sex practices and reduce the incidence and prevalence of HIV/AIDS? Outcomes evaluation includes any data brought to bear on these questions, both qualitative and quantitative. *Outcomes measurement*, in contrast, refers only to quantitative indicators of outcomes and is, therefore, a narrower frame of reference.

It is also important and helpful to distinguish program evaluation from routine monitoring and management information system data. Routine monitoring data are used to manage programs, for example, to track the flow of inputs (resources), participation rates, and participant completion of program activities. Management information systems data are descriptive. Such routine data report on the basic functioning of a program, often in comparison with targets. For example, an immunization program may aim to reach 100 percent of preschool children. The monitoring data report what percentage were actually vaccinated (for example, 90 percent). Program evaluation asks not only what was occurred and what was accomplished, but why. What was the model being implemented? To what extent was the model implemented as designed (the fidelity question)? What are variations in participation, and what explains those variations? What are variations in outcomes, and what explains those variations? To what extent can documented outcomes be attributed to the intervention (the attribution question)? What, if any, unanticipated outcomes and impacts occurred? These are evaluation questions. Thus, it is important to distinguish routine monitoring data from program evaluation (for more on these distinctions, including different kinds of program evaluation, see Mathison, 2005; Patton, 2008). Qualitative outcomes evaluation contributes to answering these general evaluation questions.

Although funders value outcomes measurement and want to know outcome statistics, they also need case studies, stories, and the personal perspectives of program participants to make sense of the numbers and to place the results in a larger community context. Program staff members use case studies to reflect on their practices and improve programs. Policymakers and politicians understand that they need to know both the level of outcomes (quantitative data) and the meaning of those outcomes to the people whose lives have been affected. Qualitative data illuminate those meanings.

What Are Qualitative Data?

Qualitative data come from open-ended interviews, focus groups, observations, and documents like client case files and organization reports. The results can be presented as case studies; patterns and themes that appear in the data; comparisons of different kinds of outcomes presented in the context of people's lives; and stories of people, programs, and communities that illuminate the nature and significance of outcomes. Qualitative outcomes can be and increasingly are presented with quantitative data (*mixed methods*) to present a fuller picture of both the level and meaning of outcomes attained (or not attained). The following three examples illustrate the kinds of qualitative outcomes evaluations that have become more valued, and therefore more common, over the last decade:

1. A study of child protection services documents the number and types of cases, adding qualitative case studies to illuminate the family situations that gave rise to the abuse; capture details about the services provided; and gather evidence from those affected about the effects on their lives over time, including how services did (or did not) support child safety and a more functional and healthy family situation. These findings are used to improve the program.

2. An evaluation of a residential center to get chronic alcoholics off the streets uses in-depth case studies to follow the effects on the health and well-being of residents and how they interact with each other, staff, and people in the community to help funders and policymakers decide whether to continue and/or expand the program.

3. An in-depth, longitudinal case study of a neighborhood documents its community development efforts, including examining collaboration among human service and health organizations and capturing the perspectives and experiences of community leaders and residents to help government and philanthropic funders assess both the extent to which targeted community outcomes have been attained and the meaning of those outcomes to people in the community.

The Development of Qualitative Outcomes Evaluation over the Past Decade

Large-scale, multisite, comparative case study projects are increasingly being conducted. This is driven by the increased importance of comparative analysis in qualitative approaches to outcomes measurement. For example, a national community development organization is supporting case studies in neighborhoods throughout the United States. These neighborhood case studies include interviews of persons with key influence and knowledge about changes occurring over time, focus groups with residents, documentation of implementation and outcomes for specific health and human services initiatives, and tracking of community indicators. The evaluation researchers for the separate neighborhoods come together nationally to compare findings, identify significant contrasts, and generate insights about patterns and themes in effective community development. At the same time, each specific neighborhood case study provides feedback to local community development staff and residents about how their plans are unfolding and the outcomes being attained for children, families, and participants in human services programs within those communities.

These kinds of large-scale comparative studies have been made more manageable as a result of developments in software to organize qualitative data and support analysis. Qualitative software does not analyze data, but it does help significantly in managing the voluminous data that emerge from fieldwork and open-ended interviews. Researchers and evaluators still have to assign codes to quotations and categorize observations into those that are similar and different. Those analyzing qualitative data have to decide how to label emergent patterns and themes. But software makes it easier to deal with large data sets, which makes it possible to increase the number of cases studied and facilitates team analysis as researchers work independently to code the same data set, thereby increasing the reliability of findings when the same codes are arrived at separately and compared across cases. For example, in analyzing case studies of female sexual offenders, several analysts independently determined that almost all cases resulted from the women being involved in abuse perpetrated by male sex offenders rather than initiating or participating in abuse on their own. These findings had increased credibility because independent analysts arrived at the same conclusion. Qualitative software development has thus enhanced the capacity to conduct large-scale outcomes evaluations involving many case studies of diverse people, programs, and communities.

Indeed, capturing diversity is one of the major contributions of qualitative outcome studies. Statistics tend to focus on central tendencies and standardized outcome dimensions. Qualitative data capture and portray individual, family, and community differences. This facilitates attention to the significance and implications of diverse outcomes while also identifying common patterns of outcomes. The potential to capture and document diversity leads to yet another important way in which qualitative outcomes evaluation has developed and been reconceptualized over the past decade. Outcomes evaluation has traditionally focused on individual outcomes resulting from program participation. Although individual outcomes remain important, other units of analysis have arisen as important for outcomes evaluation:

- Family outcomes, for example, documenting changes in family systems and among families members as the unit of inquiry and analysis

- Community case studies of community changes and outcomes, the qualitative equivalent of community indicators

- Neighborhood outcomes that focus, for example, on neighborhood change and quality of life

- Organizational outcomes, for example, increased capacity and enhanced organizational effectiveness.

The attention to diverse units of analysis to document outcomes at different levels includes capturing the ways in which unanticipated outcomes intersect with targeted outcomes. This potential of qualitative fieldwork to uncover unanticipated outcomes deserves emphasis and is another reason qualitative studies have become more valued. Statistical studies of outcomes can measure only what has been thought of, conceptualized, and operationalized in advance. The open-ended nature of qualitative inquiry, in contrast, is especially useful in capturing unanticipated outcomes. Indeed, one can reveal side effects, ripple effects, and unanticipated outcomes only through open-ended fieldwork.

Recognition of the importance of attending to unanticipated outcomes has increased dramatically over the past decade with greater attention to systems thinking and complexity theory in program evaluation (Patton, 2010; Williams & Imaj, 2006). Outcomes evaluation has been dominated by linear logic models of program interventions. Reconceptualizing programs as complex, nonlinear, and dynamic systems in which unpredictable interactions affect targeted outcomes and give rise to unanticipated and emergent outcomes has increased the value of in-depth qualitative case studies that can document and portray such dynamic systems. For example, in the residential program for chronic alcoholics mentioned previously, the original targeted outcomes focused on individual well-being and functioning patterns, but the in-depth individual interviews, case studies, and focus groups revealed that the interactions among participants was critical, that their relationships with staff went beyond the narrow mandates of the residence program, and that how residents interacted in the community was an important outcome.

Over the past decade, several additional and noteworthy trends have emerged that affect qualitative outcomes evaluation. Participatory, capacity-building, empowering, assets-based, and learning-oriented approaches have emerged as particularly appropriate for qualitative inquiry into human services outcomes. For example, participants in a welfare-to-work program kept empowerment journals in which they documented empowering and disempowering experiences. These journals offered a rich source of qualitative data about the journey from the stigma of welfare to the empowerment of increased self-sufficiency. The qualitative evaluator worked with the program participants to analyze patterns in their stories and factors that affected the extent to which they attained their desired employment outcomes.

Outcomes measurement tied to theories of change is being encouraged by funders. A theory of change formalizes a program model and depicts the mechanisms that are hypothesized to lead to attainment of targeted outcomes. For example, a program aimed at supporting incarcerated African American men in the transition from prison to functioning effectively in the community employed as trainers African American men who had successfully made the transition. Creators of the program hypothesized that this would provide positive role models and that teaching the participants empowerment skills would support their transition to employment. An empowerment curriculum was developed specifically aimed at the needs and backgrounds of this population. The qualitative evaluation based on interviews with and case studies of participants found that the program could not effectively proceed directly to empowerment training without first attending more specifically to basic human needs like housing and safety.

In another human services example, a philanthropic funder wanted to create a pilot program based on a theory of change which posited that young people in poverty would respond positively to small financial incentives for attaining specific measureable outcomes, such as completing a Graduate Equivalency Diploma. Longitudinal interviews captured the participants' perceptions of the incentives and found that the relationships they formed with staff were at least as important as, and often more important than, the incentives they received. A relationship-focused theory of change is different in important ways from a financial incentive–centered theory of change. The qualitative data helped illuminate this difference.

Mixed methods are becoming understood as providing a more balanced picture of outcomes than either quantitative or qualitative data alone. In a weight loss intervention aimed at reducing obesity, the number of people who attained the desired targets indicates achievement of quantitative outcomes. What it meant to people to succeed in losing weight (or failing to meet targets in other cases) and how weight loss affected other aspects of their health and lives involve qualitative data. Integrating these data sources provides a more complete picture of outcomes and their meanings.

Credibility and Quality of Qualitative Outcomes Evaluation

The preceding discussion has described some of the major approaches to qualitative evaluation and important emergent trends. One of the things that has not changed, however, is concern about the credibility and quality of qualitative outcomes evaluation. This section discusses credibility and quality.

Credibility in evaluation begins with asking to whom the evaluation is relevant. No evaluation can answer all possible questions that might be asked. Programs have multiple and diverse stakeholder constituencies including funders, policymakers, administrators, program staff, participants, community members, and the media. Determining which outcomes to evaluate involves deciding who the primary intended users of the evaluation will be and working with them to determine their priority questions. There is a substantial body of evidence from utilization studies which indicates that actively involving primary intended users in focusing the evaluation and selecting evaluation methods increases credibility, which increases use (Patton, 2008). Thus, evaluators should not determine what outcomes to evaluate, document (qualitatively), and measure (quantitatively) on their own.

Now we turn to methodological issues related to credibility and quality. Research credibility and quality have traditionally centered on validity, reliability, and generalizability, but because these terms derive from quantitative and experimental traditions, the past decade has given rise to credibility and quality constructs that are particularly appropriate for qualitative data. Trustworthiness as a qualitative criterion of quality has to do with the credibility of the evaluator to the people being interviewed or observed. Why should they trust the evaluator with their story? For example, in the evaluation of the residence for chronic alcoholics, the evaluator shared the fact that she came from an alcoholic family as part of establishing rapport and credibility. When you send out a questionnaire, who you are may not matter as much as the validity and reliability of the instrument. But when you're face-to-face for an hour or two interviewing a chronic alcoholic, a battered woman, a person in poverty, or a homeless person, who you are matters to them and affects what they are willing to tell you. Trust is an issue; thus, trustworthiness is a criterion of quality and credibility for qualitative outcomes evaluations.

Generalizability is another concept common in research that has been changed to fit qualitative inquiries. Generalizability is a statistical construct based on probability sampling that doesn't apply to qualitative data. In qualitative analysis, researchers extrapolate findings that are transferrable. Transferability has to do with establishing the relevance of the findings for other settings by identifying key factors that may apply elsewhere, examining how context matters in understanding and interpreting findings, and formulating principles (rather than using empirical generalizations) to guide action in other settings.

An example of this approach in human services is Lisbeth Schorr's (1989) classic study of effective programs for families in poverty, *Within Our Reach: Breaking the Cycle of Disadvantage*. Schorr did case studies of programs that achieved positive outcomes and extracted lessons. For example, she found that "successful programs see the child in the context of the family and the family in the context of its surroundings" (p. 257). This is not an empirical generalization. It is a lesson extrapolated from exemplary cases that can be transferred to new settings and interventions. Likewise, she found that successful programs are outcomes driven, but not in a narrow, rigid manner. Successful programs for children and families "adapt or circumvent traditional professional and bureaucratic limitations when necessary to meet the needs of those they serve" (p. 258). Thus, successful programs work on mandated outcomes but also address additional needs as they arise. The case studies provide the data for these transferrable extrapolations.

Another key issue affecting the credibility of qualitative data is the sample of cases studied. Because of the intensity of labor involved and relatively high costs of gathering qualitative data (compared with administering questionnaires and tests), qualitative samples tend to be small, far too small for empirical generalizations based on statistical probability samples. Perhaps nothing better captures the difference between quantitative and qualitative methods than the different logics that undergird sampling approaches. Qualitative inquiry typically focuses in depth on relatively small, purposefully selected samples. Quantitative methods typically depend on larger, randomly selected samples. The logic and power of qualitative purposeful sampling lie in selecting information-rich cases for in-depth study. Information-rich cases are those from which one can learn a great deal about issues of central importance to the purpose of the inquiry, thus the term *purposeful sampling* (also sometimes called *purposive sampling*). Studying information-rich cases yields insights and in-depth understanding rather than empirical generalizations. For example, if the purpose of an evaluation is to increase the effectiveness of a program in attaining outcomes among families from lower socioeconomic groups, one may learn a great deal more by studying in depth a small number of carefully selected families than by gathering standardized information from a large, statistically representative sample of all participating families.

There are several different strategies for purposefully selecting information-rich cases (Patton, 2002, ch. 5). The point is that for outcomes evaluation, you pick cases for study that provide insights into the meaning and context of the outcomes documented. Picking successful cases is one such approach; studying drop-outs and failures is another. Alternatively, studies of "average" cases may be constructed to provide insights into what the average means in terms of people's lives and put faces on the numbers. The sample used in the residence for chronic alcoholics was a maximum-diversity sample designed to see what core themes cut across diversity. Understanding and appreciating purposeful sampling, including both the strengths and limitations of such small samples, is critical to the credibility of qualitative outcomes evaluation.

Finally, triangulation is a way of addressing quality and increasing credibility. The logic of triangulation is based on the premise that any single method or data source has limitations. In contrast, multiple methods of data collection and analysis provide more grist for the outcomes evaluation mill. Combinations of interviewing, observation, and document analysis are now expected in much fieldwork. Studies that use only one method are more vulnerable to errors linked to that particular method (for example, loaded interview questions, biased or untrue responses) than studies that use multiple methods in which different types of data provide cross-data consistency checks. Triangulation includes mixed-methods studies that combine qualitative and quantitative data.

Four kinds of qualitative triangulation can contribute to verification and validation of qualitative outcomes analysis: (1) *methods triangulation*: examining the consistency of findings generated by different data collection methods (interviewing and observation); (2) *source triangulation*: examining the consistency of different data sources within the same method (interviewing staff, program participants, and participants' family members); (3) *analyst triangulation*: using multiple analysts to code and generate patterns; and (4) *theory/perspective triangulation*: using multiple perspectives or theories to interpret the data.

Case Example of Qualitative Evaluation: Residence for Persons with Chronic Alcohol and Substance Use Conditions

The San Marco is a residence for persons with chronic alcohol and substance use conditions, most of them homeless, aimed at providing a safe environment in which residents can achieve increased health, mental health, and quality-of-life outcomes. Ten of the 30 residents were selected for evaluation case studies using a *criterion-based maximum variation sample*, in which participants are as different as possible from one another. This means selecting both male and female participants, younger and older participants, participants from different racial and ethnic backgrounds, and participants with different health and mental health histories. This kind of qualitative sample permits documentation of diversity as well as identification of any common patterns in experiences and outcomes that cut across diverse populations.

Participants signed an authorization form that covered standard informed consent and voluntary participation issues. They were interviewed initially to establish a baseline, then again after six months. A focus group was also conducted to clarify and validate the individual interviews. Participants were given a stipend for each interview and for the focus group. Interviews were recorded, transcribed, and used to create participant case studies. Major themes and outcomes patterns were identified through cross-case analysis of individual and focus group interviews. Sample quotations are included to illustrate the outcome themes.

1. Participants reported more stable lives: "I'm eating better, have medical care, and a roof over my head. I have a family here that I didn't have out on the streets."

2. Participants reported feeling safe at the San Marco: "On the street you have to be real vigilant. You could get jumped in the middle of the night, or if you're coming back from the liquor store you could get jumped for money or liquor." "I feel safe because I don't have to worry about my friends getting me evicted. I have a little contact with old friends by cell phone. A couple of them showed up here. I wasn't drinking and the staff just got rid of them."

3. Participants reported being members of a community that feels like a family: "The San Marco is like a little community. I know a lot of people in this building, so I feel like I'm with friends that are more like a family, a big family. We get along like families do. There are some differences but nothing that can't be handled. We have parties and celebrate holidays together."

4. Participants feel supported and cared for: "The staff here is excellent. They're helpful, courteous, and treat residents like family. I get along with them well. They help me with my personal needs like appointments and shopping. They worry about me. I went to see a friend for three or four days and they put out an APB. It showed they really care."

5. Participants have a place to live that feels like home: "Best of all, I have my own place. I've fixed it up the way I want it, fixed it up like a home. It's just a room, but, still, I can come home here and they always wonder if I'm doing okay when I walk in."

6. Most participants report drinking less: "I drink less here. There is alcohol all around the building, but I still drink less. Out on the street I drank to keep warm and to drown out feelings. Around here I have people I can talk to. I don't drink every day. Some weeks I take two or three days off. I now drink maybe ten beers at a time and three screwdrivers. I'm not waking up sick every morning and not passing out at night. I'm remembering to take pills, remembering to eat right, and I'm more sociable."

7. Participants report looking beyond survival and short-term goals: "I'd like to stop drinking and move to the other side of the San Marco. Staff knows I can do it. When I'm sober, I do wood burning. I don't open my door or answer my phone. I'm very artistic, and I can sit all day long and listen to my favorite music. I would like more of it.

People knock on my door and want this and want that. I say, 'just get away from me for awhile, please.' I burn a little sage and I'm content."

8. Participants have maintained or increased contact with family: "I'm going to my dad's on weekends. He picks me up after work. We have a car project. I don't drink when I'm with my dad. He has invited me to his house for a month, but there's nothing to do there."

In addition to documenting and illustrating outcomes, the qualitative evaluation findings provided feedback about patterns of program effectiveness. The feedback at the program level both affirmed key elements of the human services model being pilot tested and identified areas to be engaged for improvement:

- Theme 1: Staff play an important role in parenting/nurturing the residents.

- Theme 2: The visitation rules are important to creating a sense of safety.

- Theme 3: People like being able to come and go as they please. They don't want to be institutionalized. They like being treated with respect and as adults and don't like being cooped up. They like to be outdoors.

- Theme 4: People need additional support to maintain sobriety.

These findings were used by program staff to improve the program and by funders, both government and philanthropic, to determine the merit and worth of the pilot project.

Conclusion: Implications of Increased Attention to Outcomes Evaluation

The question facing human services is no longer whether to do outcomes evaluation, but how to do it. Outcomes evaluation is expected. It comes with the territory of funding and implementing human services programs of all kinds. The issue then is how to do it, and how to do it well. The evidence from studies of evaluation use has shown that outcomes evaluation is more likely to be useful—and actually used—if key stakeholders are involved in the process from beginning to end (Patton, 2008). This means that the outcomes evaluation is designed with involvement of staff, program administrators, program participants, funders, and key policymakers. This group of key stakeholders then prioritizes evaluation questions, identifies critical outcomes to be evaluated, and determines the methods appropriate for evaluating those outcomes. Evaluators facilitating such decision making need to be able to offer and explain methodological and data options, which include qualitative outcomes approaches.

Because the focus on outcomes has become so dominant, attention to process has received correspondingly less emphasis. But how outcomes are achieved matters. Consequently, qualitative outcomes evaluation should include data on processes and on outcomes. Future developments in evaluation should incorporate systems thinking and complexity constructs into outcomes evaluation. As noted earlier, most outcomes evaluations are conceptualized with linear models that assume simple cause–effect attribution. Systems thinking and complexity challenge these simple linear constructions of how outcomes are attained. For example, early in the 20th century, the narrow focus on eradicating polio worldwide competed with scarce funds for basic health infrastructure. Polio vaccines aren't sufficient. A health infrastructure must be in place to support vaccination campaigns and achieve disease-prevention goals. Thus, the cutting edge for outcomes evaluation involves applying systems and complexity insights to outcomes evaluation (Patton, 2010). Qualitative data are especially important in this regard because qualitative fieldwork is particularly appropriate for identifying and analyzing unintended outcomes, emergent outcomes, and nonlinear relationships. An unintended outcome of the highly visible, well-funded polio eradication campaign was to weaken basic health infrastructure by pulling resources and personnel out of basic health care and focusing their efforts on one outcome. The resulting and unintended weakening of the overall health system in many developing countries where polio was targeted actually reduced the sustainability of the targeted long-term polio eradication outcome.

Family systems approaches are another example of moving away from targeting individuals for outcomes such as increased health to targeting the entire family as the foundation for the health of its individual members. We know, for example, that sustaining sobriety requires not only changes in an individual, but changes in the family and support systems in which they live. This is also true for sustaining health and mental health outcomes. Qualitative outcomes evaluation can document the relationships and interactions among individual family members that affect health outcomes in ways that go beyond quantitative measures of individual health outcomes. A qualitative study of a family system captures and describes the family dynamics (norms, interactions, relationships) that affect outcomes, both qualitative and quantitative.

Technology and communication developments are also changing what is available as data. Social networking technology and interactions are becoming an increasingly important source of qualitative data in human services, including outcomes documentation. As the Internet becomes more accessible to people in poor communities and students in traditionally under-resourced schools, the possible interactions will affect how outcomes are identified, tracked, documented, and evaluated.

Finally, we comment on some of the major issues facing the future of outcomes evaluation.

Standardization of Outcomes Measures

Standardization is the hallmark of statistics and the bane of qualitative evaluation. Outcomes measurement focuses on central tendencies, statistical averages, and bottom-line indicators. Qualitative evaluation emphasizes particularity, complexity, context, and holistic understanding. In the ongoing debate about the relative contributions of quantitative and qualitative approaches to evaluation, the mixed-methods approach counters simple (and often simplistic) outcome measures with more in-depth qualitative data about what those numbers mean in context. For example, one can measure youth strengths and assets on a standardized scale that generates a number and ranking. Qualitative inquiry adds information about what those young people's lives are like, the qualitative dynamics of their interpersonal relationships, and how they make sense of their world. By asking these more in-depth, holistic questions, qualitative outcomes evaluation resists standardization and the myth that everything that matters can be quantified and scaled. Individuality, particularity, and context also matter.

Common Language for Types of Evaluation and Outcome Measures

The language of evaluation is diverse and chaotic—we predict it to remain so. There are regular attempts by U.S. federal agencies, international organizations, and professional associations to impose universal definitions and create standard measures. But there aren't agreed-on definitions of even the most basic terms, such as *evaluation* and *outcomes*. One program's outcome is another program's input. For example, access to health care is considered by some to be an outcome, so they aim to increase access, but others view access as an input and reserve the language of outcomes for actual health status indicators. What this illustrates, from a qualitative perspective, is that language has to be defined and understood in context. Language is inherently cultural; the meanings of terms are culturally embedded and particular. The implications of these premises have been examined in depth in a special issue of *New Directions for Evaluation* titled "Why and How Language Matters" (Hopson, 2000). The variation in contextual meanings of common terms is a major area of qualitative inquiry. This won't keep people from generating and trying to impose standardized language. But that very phenomenon will assure qualitative researchers of future work studying why such efforts inevitably fail.

Shift toward Prevention and Wellness as Important Directions in Health Care Reform

This is an excellent and important issue with which to end this chapter. Quantitative measurement will, appropriately, seek standardized measures of prevention and wellness. Qualitative evaluators will continue to emphasize the importance of placing prevention and wellness in context and including larger systems understandings in any analysis. As noted earlier, measuring the incidence and prevalence of polio was critical to eradicating polio worldwide. However, it is also important to ask how the campaign to eradicate polio affected the larger health system and infrastructure, both positively and negatively. The history of many well intentioned interventions is that they can lead to unanticipated consequences that may, in the long run, be as bad as or worse than the original problem. As just one example, the huge emphasis on a low-fat diet in the United States over the past two decades, as a way of preventing heart disease, appears to have contributed to increased consumption of corn syrup and simple carbohydrates, which appears to be part of the reason for the diabetes epidemic now of great concern. Concepts like wellness, a strength-based approach, and prevention-focused interventions will mean different things over time and take on new meanings in different contexts. As discussed in the preceding discussion on language, this variance in meaning is part of the task implications of these approaches. The notion of wellness is exemplary in this regard. Some will define wellness in strictly physiological terms, some will insist on including psychological and mental health, and still others will insist on a spiritual dimension. Many will want to include cultural, social, and community outcomes such as a sense of belonging, strong family support, or sense of community as essential to wellness. The notion of wellness as a health outcome is relatively recent and may, as it is politicized and measured through standardized scales, pass away and be replaced by new concepts of what it means to be healthy.

Qualitative researchers and evaluators will track and elucidate the concepts of wellness, prevention, strengths, and health outcomes; document their implications for both intervention models and results; and place the findings in a larger context of time, place, culture, and complex adaptive systems.

References

Hopson, R. (Ed.). (2000). How and why language matters in evaluation [Special issue]. *New Directions for Evaluation*(86).

Mathison, S. (2005). *Encyclopedia of evaluation.* Thousand Oaks, CA: Sage Publications.

Patton, M. Q. (2002). *Qualitative research and evaluation methods* (3rd ed.). Thousand Oaks, CA: Sage Publications.

Patton, M. Q. (2008). *Utilization of focused evaluation* (4th ed.). Thousand Oaks, CA: Sage Publications.

Patton, M. Q. (2010). *Developmental evaluation: Applying complexity concepts to enhance innovation and use.* New York: Guilford Press.

Schorr, L. (1989). *Within our reach: Breaking the cycle of disadvantage.* New York: Anchor Books.

Williams, B., & Iman, I. (Eds.). (2007). *Systems concepts in evaluation: An expert anthology.* Point Reyes, CA: Edge Press of Inverness.

CHAPTER 4

Quantitative Approaches to Outcomes Measurement and Evaluation:
A Commentary

Brian T. Yates

Quantitative measurements of outcomes now routinely help determine the nature and funding of programs offered by human service organizations (HSOs) in private and public sectors and at state and federal levels. Outcomes are distinct from program performance and management, which commonly are assessed along with outcomes by the Performance Assessment Rating Tool (PART; see chapter 1 of this volume) and which also can result in continued or terminated program funding (Office of Management and Budget, 2010). Not only are client, program, and service outcomes viewed as more important than ever, but monetary outcomes—or savings in social resources such as those that might be devoted to unmet needs—have become primary considerations in treatment choice and funding decisions (APA Presidential Task Force on Evidence-based Practice, 2006; Washington State Institute for Public Policy, 2010).

Quantification has gone beyond simple numerics and data collection methods: The research evidence base for cost-effectiveness analyses (in which costs of services are compared with nonmonetary outcomes of those services), cost–benefit analyses (in which costs of services are compared with monetary outcomes), and cost–utility analyses (in which costs of services are compared with a common nonmonetary outcome such as quality-adjusted life years or disability-adjusted life years) is increasing (Yates, 1999, 2009).

Although the increased focus on quantitative outcomes (that are both monetary and nonmonetary) helps to meet the demands for accountability in the human services, many issues associated with the capacity to meet such demands, and to deal with the fallout of doing so, will continue to persist. For example, examining only the outcomes and costs of HSO programs potentially risks committing two additional errors: First, the potential to integrate the strengths of social science theory is excluded from human services work, and therefore the capacity to bridge theory, research, practice, and policy is weakened. Second, the humaneness of services is potentially diminished by relegating efforts into a static list of specific practices with assigned costs and outcomes that may not reflect the diversity of needs, backgrounds, and challenges that HSO clientele present.

Having spent more than 35 years researching and evaluating HSO programs, activities, and organizational outcomes (Yates, 1979, 1996, 2009), I offer the reader a guide to issues that are common to measuring outcomes quantitatively across HSOs during this challenging point in time, in which we will need to continue to do more with less (Talbott, 1988).

Twentieth-Century Standard Methods for Quantifying Outcomes Still Apply in the 21st Century, but New Approaches Are Emerging to Measure and Compare Outcomes Quantitatively

Over the past three decades, there has been a growing push in the human services to construct comprehensive models of human services that can be evaluated by means of quantitative modeling strategies (Rodgers, 2010). Traditional statistical tests of the null hypothesis and significance testing are but a subset of this more comprehensive modeling approach to arriving at a quantitative understanding of the key elements of a human service system (Rodgers, 2010; Yates, 1980). Why construct such a model, and why with numbers? Because inclusion in a quantitative model of the key elements of the service system allows easy manipulation of the model to discover how to optimize it, for example, how to deliver the most effective treatment or prevention services for the largest number of clients while not exceeding any of the limits on available resources, from building space to the time of different service providers (Yates, 1994). In particular, operations research, a science of solutions in search of problems (Ackoff, 1956), is extended to new domains.

Operations research has developed models that identify key features that need to be measured quantitatively to solve common, if daunting, problems in managing complex systems. Such problems range from maximizing positive outcomes in the context of multiple budget constraints to optimizing the flow of clients through networks of social services, minimizing waiting times for services, and optimizing diagnostic decision making (cf. Yates, 1980). However, can models of operations research developed for industrial, military, and business applications be applied to human services? Aren't the mechanisms entirely different? Actually, the general framework of the social learning model proposed in the 20th century by Rotter (1954; see also Bandura, 1986; Mischel, 1973) provides an approach to understanding the origins and modification of human behavior, cognition, and affect that is readily amenable to operations research models (Yates, 1979, 1997). The family of cognitive social learning models allows a variety of internal psychological, social, and even biological processes to be specified as being caused by observable activities in the interpersonal sphere (such as using self-instructions and reframing to help a client learn how to resist urges to relapse to tobacco or other substance use), and as in turn causing observable changes in clients' subsequent behaviors, cognitions, and affects.

One type of cognitive social learning model, the Resource/Activity/ Process/Outcome Analysis (RAPOA) model (Yates, 1980, 1996), takes into account the entire service process, including description of resources and outcomes that also matter to the public at large. The RAPOA framework extends the cognitive social learning model by adding quantitative measurements of the types and amounts of resources consumed in providing services to clients and quantitative measures of the changes in societal resources made available as a result of provider activities. In other words, RAPOA adds numeric descriptions of both the costs and the benefits (that is, the monetary outcomes) to accepted models of human services. The addition of both costs "in" and monetary outcomes "out" of the service system makes RAPOA models particularly useful when deciding whether to continuing funding specific services and, perhaps more constructively, how to systematically improve a service system so it can survive and flourish in a resource-poor environment (for example, reduced budgets for human services).

RAPOA typically measures the following:

- Resources that make human services possible (for example, the time of providers, the space in which services are provided)

- Activities engaged in by providers, clients, family, and others such as case management, group and individual therapy, mentoring, assertiveness, and relapse prevention training

- Changes in clients' knowledge, skills, thoughts, feelings, and other bio-psychosocial processes (for example, refusal scripts, condom use, self-efficacy expectancies, cognitive transformation, and resulting changes in depression and anxiety)

- Observable changes in client behavior (for example, reduced risky sexual activity, reduced substance abuse, reduced abuse of others)

- Changes in outcomes such as decreases in clients' and family members' use of other human services, including future health, mental health, substance abuse, and criminal justice services

- Increases in clients' creativity and productivity, and in employment wages and business profits.

Activities measurement, outcomes measurement, and outcomes evaluation are different but complementary activities that are a necessity for HSOs to conduct on a regular basis. Measuring the activities of a program (what it does on a day-to-day basis) is notably different from measuring the outcomes of a program (what happens after program activities), which in turn is different from evaluating outcomes of a program (understanding what the program accomplished as a result of its activities), There has been a gradual increase in understanding of the differences between measures of program activities and program outcomes. Several decades ago, a program often was considered "evaluated" if it did what was thought to be the best thing to do, despite the absence of any evidence that the program actually achieved its objectives! A program for preventing unwanted teen pregnancies might, for example, be judged a success if it reached a specific number or percentage of teenagers, delivering a message (and, perhaps, pregnancy risk reduction devices) that had been deemed appropriate and that seemed likely to result in a reduction in unwanted pregnancies. Similarly, a needle exchange program for reducing HIV transmission might be evaluated according to the number of needles distributed. Adherence by the program to specific, targeted activities was measured in this earlier form of quantitative evaluation, and if adherence exceeded a mandated threshold (such as attendance at sex education classes or percentage of users approached who exchanged old needles for new), the program's outcomes were judged satisfactory.

Presently, use of and quantitatively assessed adherence to specific, research-validated practices is necessary and sometimes sufficient for programs. That is, a program will receive funding only if it uses techniques from a list of evidence-based activities or practices. Actual outcomes of implementing those practices in a particular setting may or may not be evaluated. Although not all funders require a service to be on a list of evidence-based practices before funding, most are increasingly pressured to do so. Often in conflict with requirements that a service use evidence-based activities are strong personal, spiritual, and sometimes political preferences for particular services, and even stronger prejudices against inclusion of other services. These service preferences and prejudices are expressed by politicians, providers, and persons receiving services, particularly services involving reproduction, drug abuse, mental health, and education, even in the face of evidence that some preferred programs are ineffective (Trenholm et al., 2008) or even iatrogenic (Yates, 2002), although some disapproved programs appear to work (Belani & Muenning, 2008).

Issues Concerning the Reliability and Validity of Quantitative Outcomes Are No Longer Based Only on Science

Although most reliabilities and many validities of outcome measurement in the human services are improving (Kazdin, 2003; Meyer et al., 2001), what might be called the "cultural validity" of many measures—especially for decisions that will determine the appearance of human services in the next decades—is increasingly questioned (Guba & Lincoln, 1989). There is a growing awareness that many measures that have been long considered "scientific" have also been created in the context of specific cultures, interest groups, and other value sets (Seigart & Brisolara, 2002). Although some stakeholders believe that the entire Western European framework for quantitative measurement and testing should be challenged (LaFrance, 2004), others believe that the essential framework for quantitative measurement and research can be modified, taking into account that multiple perspectives on what is important to measure are essential to maximizing the validity of assessment and of decisions that use those assessments. For example, if reduction of illness is valued, how much a program reduces depression or anxiety might be measured. What needs to be kept in mind is that particular perspectives usually promote their own measures and too often ignore others. In order to create fair and normative measures, it is necessary to better understand how a complete web of quantitative measures can be developed that balances needs and interests.

Quantifying outcomes that are comparable between HSO programs remains a chronic challenge even with recent consensus about direction. The initial hope that quantifying outcomes for different types of human services would allow them all to be compared, judged, and decided upon fairly suffered early disappointment when it was realized that the many specific service outcomes, such as pregnancy prevention and adolescent obesity reduction, could not all be measured in the same type of units. In the past few decades, however, several strategies for comparing outcomes of different HSOs have emerged.

For example, a cognitive–behavioral therapy (CBT) for seasonal affective disorder (SAD) may reduce the number of days with severe depression, and a substance abuse treatment may increase drug-free days, but how are the two to be compared for outcomes, and thus funding? Many used to say that, here, we would have reached the limits of the quantitative approach, because these units (decreased depression days, increased drug-free days) were clearly incompatible and not comparable. For quantitative cross-program comparisons, outcomes can be quantified by using a measure that is sufficiently general to capture the essential outcomes of both programs for clients, such as levels of functioning (Martin & Kettner, 2010). By describing the outcomes of all programs with a more general but hopefully still valid measure, it was hoped that the impact of interventions as different as CBT for SAD and treatment for substance abuse could be compared, as has been done successfully by a variety of therapy researchers (for example, Lambert, Okiishi, Finch, & Johnson, 1998).

This approach to such standard measures has been viewed as rather "blunt" and unlikely to detect differences between outcomes of different programs (Siegert & Yates, 1980). More satisfactory to some, but unacceptable to more, was translation of the specific outcomes of different programs into common monetary units (Strupp, 1981). This benefits assessment solution summed, for example, increased earnings by clients with reduced use of health and criminal justice services. This method of quantifying monetary outcomes of HSOs has provided especially convincing evidence for the cost benefit of psychotherapies (Kraft, Puschner, Lambert, & Kordy, 2006). The result was the common metric of monetary outcomes (that is, benefits) such as "service X saved taxpayers between $X and $X per day per client."

Some, however, have disliked this "lowest common denominator" of outcome measures, proposing that the most important outcomes of services were not monetary and could not be transformed into monetary units. Well-being and quality of life were promoted as outcomes that were of tantamount importance but impossible to monetize (Strupp, 1981). Defenders of the common outcome metric of money have noted that many people pay a premium of one sort or another for higher quality of life or feelings of well-being, but others have been reluctant to place a price on improving quality of living or well-being (Weinstein & Skinner, 2010).

More recently, quantitative measures of outcomes of diverse programs have been compared by means of common nonmonetary units (Gold, Siegel, Russell, & Weinstein, 1996). For example, outcomes of depression treatments from Beck Depression Inventory scores can be translated into quality-adjusted life years (QALYs; Freed, Rohan, & Yates, 2007) by asking individuals familiar with depression at what point they would see as equivalent a year being depressed and a portion of a year having a high quality of life (including not being depressed). Although not without its critics, there is a growing literature on how to transform program-specific measures into common units by which different programs can be compared (Gold et al., 1996). Many researchers, and some managers and providers of physical health care, have gone further: They have measured and compared the cost per QALY attributable to different treatments (Drummond, Sculpher, Torrance, O'Brien, & Stoddard, 2005). Treatment funding is increasingly dependent on the cost per QALY found through quantitative research: The maximum acceptable cost per QALY is debated intensely when it is used to decide whether to fund treatment (Towse, 2009).

The Process of Selecting and Quantifying Outcomes for Funders and Other Stakeholders (Including Clients) Is Not Standardized

If one stakeholder perspective is deemed more important than another—and this certainly can be the case in some funding situations—the measure reflecting each perspective can be combined after weighting each for importance. There is no rational reason that different stakeholder perspectives cannot be reflected in the choice of different outcome measures—quantitative ones, qualitative ones, or both. The quantitative approach to assessing HSO outcomes acknowledges that some stakeholder groups may be so different that they may advocate entirely different measures. And what's wrong with that, especially if it is the truth? If a more global perspective is desired, different stakeholders' measures can be combined into a single composite measure by using a variety of quantitative techniques to make equivalent the scales and units of different measures (see Yates, Haven, & Thoresen, 1979). For example, decision makers can be surveyed to obtain importance weightings for each perspective's favored measure, arriving at a statistical consensus on those weights. Thus, by using concrete, quantitative measures that are integrated in quantitative ways, decisions may be made that represent multiple, even conflicting, perspectives that can be replicated when new data become available.

Attitudes about Quantifying Outcomes of HSOs Will Continue to Vary among Stakeholders

Ultimately, numbers have a better reputation than words among funders, managers, and other decision makers. In contrast, many providers and managers prefer not to measure program or client progress in numbers because the delivery of social and other human services is sometimes a subjective process that it is difficult to distill into a few numbers. For example, it can be difficult to quantify the results of one counseling session for a young parent, or to create an index to measure the multiple activities that a case manager performs. Some providers and managers would prefer that money and time spent on turning outcomes into numbers be spent making better outcomes happen for more clients.

Clients, their advocates, and even the communities in which clients reside also may fear that the numbers might not turn out the way they want them to. Numbers are more difficult to control than words, and in the politically charged climate of reduced funding and jobs for human services, numbers can be especially threatening. In addition, as noted earlier, numbers can instill unfounded confidence in decisions based on them. Numbers are only as accurate and free of bias as the instruments used to obtain them, and may be only as free of prejudice as the people who developed, administered, and responded to the instruments.

Moreover, many providers, program managers, and the communities in which they operate become concerned about outcome measures that quantify the impact of their work, because only a few of the numerous possible outcomes of their work with clients are measured in the typical HSO evaluation. Outcome measures may not be able to capture the spectrum of effects that result from the provider–client relationship. Likewise, decisions about what to measure may only include a few indicators, and therefore may also not reflect the broad spectrum of impacts that services may have had.

Looking toward the Future

In summary, quantifying outcomes can help providers, managers, funders, and clients and their advocates choose what should be the most effective, beneficial programs and approaches for preventing or treating a wide range of problems. However, decisions about human services, based on their outcomes, may be wrong if the research, modeling, and evaluation are wrong. That is, decisions can only be as good as the data on which they are founded. To increase the chances of making the best possible decisions, HSOs, funders, and other stakeholders need to become increasingly consumer oriented and interdisciplinary in the choice of measures and approaches. In particular, they need to work with stakeholders using approaches like RAPOA, so that they can define outcomes, and costs, in more inclusive ways that address concerns of all those who work in and/or are served by the field of human services.

References

Ackoff, R. L. (1956). The development of operations research as a science. *Operations Research, 4,* 265–295.

APA Presidential Task Force on Evidence-based Practice. (2006). Evidence-based practice in psychology. *American Psychologist, 61,* 271–285.

Bandura, A. (1986). *Social foundations of thought and action: A social cognitive theory.* Englewood Cliffs, NJ: Prentice-Hall.

Belani, H. K., & Muenning, P. A. (2008). Cost-effectiveness of needle and syringe exchange for the prevention of HIV in New York City. *Journal of HIV/AIDS & Social Services, 7,* 229–240.

Drummond, M. F., Sculpher, M. J., Torrance, G. W., O'Brien, B. J., & Stoddard, G. L. (2005). *Methods for economic evaluation of health care programs.* Oxford, England: Oxford University Press.

Freed, M. C., Rohan, K. J., & Yates, B. T. (2007). Estimating health utilities and quality adjusted life years in seasonal affective disorder research. *Journal of Affective Disorders, 100,* 83–89.

Gold, M. R., Siegel, J. E., Russell, L. B., & Weinstein, M. C. (Eds.). (1996). *Cost-effectiveness in health and medicine.* New York: Oxford University Press.

Guba, E. G., & Lincoln, Y. S. (1989). *Fourth generation evaluation.* Newbury Park, CA: Sage Publications.

Kazdin, A. E. (2003). Clinical significance: Measuring whether interventions make a difference. In A. E. Kazdin (Ed.), *Methodological issues and strategies in clinical research* (3rd ed., pp. 691–710). Washington, DC: American Psychological Association.

Kraft, S., Puschner, B., Lambert, M. J., & Kordy, H. (2006). Medical utilization and treatment outcome in mid- and long-term outpatient psychotherapy. *Psychotherapy Research, 16,* 241–249.

LaFrance, J. (2004). Culturally competent evaluation in Indian Country. *New Directions for Evaluation, 102,* 39–50.

Lambert, M. J., Okiishi, J. C., Finch, A. E., & Johnson, L. D. (1998). Outcome assessment: From conceptualization to implementation. *Professional Psychology: Research and Practice, 29,* 63–70.

Martin, L. L., & Kettner, P. M. (2010). *Measuring the performance of human service programs* (2nd ed.). Thousand Oaks, CA: Sage Publications.

Meyer, G. J., Finn, S. E., Eyde, L. D., Kay, G. G., Moreland, K. L., Dies, R. R., et al. (2001). Psychological testing and psychological assessment: A review of evidence and issues. *American Psychologist, 56,* 128–165.

Mischel, W. (1973). Toward a cognitive social-learning reconceptualization of personality. *Psychological Review, 80,* 252–283.

Office of Management and Budget. (2010). *ExpectMore.gov: Expect federal programs to perform well, and better every year.* Retrieved from http://www. white house.gov/mob/expectmore/about.html

Rodgers, J. L. (2010). The epistemology of mathematical and statistical modeling: A quiet methodological revolution. *American Psychologist, 65,* 1–12.

Rotter, J. B. (1954). *Social learning and clinical psychology.* Englewood Cliffs, NJ: Prentice-Hall.

Seigart, D., & Brisolara, S. (2002). Feminist evaluation. *New Directions for Evaluation, 96,* 123–152.

Strupp, H. (1981). Psychotherapy—The question of evidence. *Monitor on Psychology, 12*(3), 2.

Talbott, J. (1988). The chronically mentally ill: What do we know, and why aren't we implementing what we know? *New Directions for Mental Health Services, 37,* 43–53.

Towse, A. (2009). Should NICE's threshold range for cost per QALY be raised? Yes. *British Medical Journal, 338,* 181.

Trenholm, C., Devaney, B., Fortson, K., Clark, M., Bridgespan, L. Q., & Wheeler, J. (2008). Impacts of abstinence education on teen sexual activity, risk of pregnancy, and risk of sexually transmitted diseases. *Journal of Policy Analysis and Management, 27,* 255–276.

U.S. Department of Education. (2010). *Doing what works: Research-based practices online.* Retrieved from http://dww.ed.gov/index.cfm

Washington State Institute for Public Policy. (2010). *Topic: Costs and benefits.* Retrieved from http://www.wsipp.wa.gov/topic.asp?cat=18&subcat=0.

Weinstein, M. C., & Skinner, J. A. (2010). Comparative effectiveness and health care spending: Implications for reform. *New England Journal of Medicine, 362,* 460–465.

Yates, B. T. (1979). Three basic strategies for improving the cost-effectiveness of social services. In G. Landsberg (Ed.), *Evaluation in practice: A sourcebook of program evaluation studies from mental health care systems in the United*

States. Washington, DC: National Institute of Mental Health, Government Printing Office.

Yates, B. T. (1980). *Improving effectiveness and reducing costs in mental health.* Springfield, IL: Charles C Thomas.

Yates, B. T. (1994). Toward the incorporation of costs, cost-effectiveness analysis, and cost–benefit analysis into clinical research. *Journal of Consulting and Clinical Psychology, 62,* 729–736.

Yates, B. T. (1996). *Analyzing costs, procedures, processes, and outcomes in human services.* Thousand Oaks, CA: Sage Publications.

Yates, B. T. (1997). Formative evaluation of costs, cost-effectiveness, and cost–benefit: Toward cost/procedure/process/outcome analysis. In L. Bickman & D. Rog (Eds.), *Handbook of applied social research methods* (pp. 285–314). Thousand Oaks, CA: Sage Publications.

Yates, B. T. (1999). *Measuring and improving cost, cost-effectiveness, and cost–benefit for substance abuse treatment programs* (NIH Publication No. 99-4518). Bethesda, MD: National Institute on Drug Abuse.

Yates, B. T. (2002). Roles for psychological procedures, and psychological processes, in cost-offset research: Cost/procedure/process/outcome analysis. In N. A. Cummings, W. T. O'Donohue, & K. E. Ferguson (Eds.), *The impact of medical cost offset on practice and research: Making it work for you* (pp. 91–123). Reno, NV: Context Press.

Yates, B. T. (2009). Cost-inclusive evaluation: A banquet of approaches for including costs, benefits, and cost-effectiveness and cost–benefit analyses in your next evaluations. *Evaluation and Program Planning, 32,* 52–54.

Yates, B. T., Haven, W. G., & Thoresen, C. E. (1979). Cost-effectiveness analysis at Learning House: How much change for how much money? In J. S. Stumphauzer (Ed.), *Progress in behavior therapy with delinquents* (pp. 186–222). Springfield, IL: Charles C Thomas.

CHAPTER 5

Outcomes Measurement in the Human Services:

The Role of Evidence-based Practice

Bruce A. Thyer

As several chapters in this second edition of *Outcomes Measurement in the Human Services* describe, many factors in the past two decades have increased attention to outcomes measurement and performance assessment at many different governmental and societal levels (Mullen & Magnabosco, 1997). Legislative mandates like the Government Performance and Results Act (GPRA) have had significant ramifications for the human services, most notably by moving government toward funding programs that demonstrate effectiveness. Implementation of the GPRA has been uneven and has met with some resistance (Bruel, 2007; Davis, 2002; Darby & Kinnevy, 2010; Ho, 2007; Julnes, 2006).

One potentially worrisome response has been the emerging practice of federal funding agencies, foundations, and other funders to predetermine what outcome measures must be used in program evaluations of intervention programs in which they are interested: Selecting such measures may sometimes be made on the basis of nonscientific considerations. The practice of determining, in advance, what outcome measures may or may not be appropriate for a given study or reporting requirement is inconsistent with the process of evidence-based practice; although both "practices" are geared toward developing usable and meaningful knowledge, the latter is typically based more on objective scientific methods.

In brief, evidence-based practice (EBP) possesses the potential to dramatically and positively impact the human services, as it has the field of medicine, by focusing greater attention on scientific considerations in the selection of outcome and assessment measures, as well as interventions. Regardless of who makes decisions about measurement, funding, or interventions to be implemented, it is commonly accepted that the process of EBP is a useful, and at times utterly necessary, approach that can drive and/or enhance decision making on many levels.

Despite this acceptability, the methods by which knowledge is assessed within an evidence-based context are often not mainstreamed enough in teaching curriculums, agency work, public policy decision making, assessment of human service programs or agencies, advocacy efforts, or health promotion activities. This chapter reviews the process of EBP, its relationship to outcomes measurement, and misconceptions about the process and makes recommendations for its use as pressures to produce evidence-based measures and programs, and outcome and performance measures, continue to increase in the United States and abroad. The focus of this chapter is the measurement decisions made by individual practitioners, although some implications of the EBP approach for agency and policy practice are also discussed.

The EBP Process

The term *evidence-based practice* typically refers to a five-step process used to help clinicians make decisions about the care of individual clients. These decisions include what initial assessment or diagnostic measures should be used, what interventions should be offered, and what possible outcomes of intervention are appropriate to measure. Although the EBP model originated within the field of medicine, it is not explicitly a medical model. For example, there is no assertion in EBP that client dysfunction has a biological etiology and no assumption that intervention requires biological treatments such as drugs or surgery, nor does it maintain the default position that medical doctors are the primary providers of care. This largely atheoretical model has been widely adopted across virtually all the health care and human service professions, including macro-level practice—

such as supervision, administration, management, community intervention, and the formulation of public policy (Thyer, 2008)—which also belies any concern that the approach is somehow tainted via its origins in medicine. It is more properly seen as a generic scientific model for good practice.

In order to convey an accurate description of EBP, it is important to rely on a few of the model's primary source documents. For example, Guyatt and Rennie (2002) defined EBP as the

> *conscientious, explicit, and judicious use of current best evidence in making deci-sions about the care of individual patients. The practice of evidence-based medicine requires integration of individual clinical expertise and patient preferences with the best available external clinical evidence from systematic research. (p. 412)*

Similarly, Straus et al. (2005) defined *evidence-based medicine* (EBM) as requiring "the integration of the best research evidence with our clinical expertise and our patient's unique values and circumstances" (p. 1).

Definitions of EBP or EBM make an important point clear: EBP or EBM does not tell clinicians or others involved with an EBP or EBM process what to do. That is, EBP is a systematic process of integrating credible research evidence, with myriad other important factors, to arrive at initial decisions about what to do. In fact, the creation of any list of approved evidence-based treatments would be anathema to the process of EBP because such a list would omit consideration of the other significant elements of EBP such as clients preferences and situation, professional ethics, available resources, and individual clinical expertise. Properly deciding what course of action to offer can only be made by taking into account these myriad factors.

Because the focus of this chapter is on the relationship between the EBP process and outcomes measurement, the steps of EBP as they pertain to out-comes can be outlined as follows, drawing on Straus et al. (2005):

1. Convert the need for information about assessment and outcome measures into answerable questions.

2. Track down the best evidence with which to answer those questions.

3. Critically appraise that evidence for its reliability, validity, impact, and applicability.

4. Integrate this critical appraisal with clinical expertise and the client's unique values and circumstances.

5. Evaluate the effectiveness of carrying out steps 1 through 4, and seek ways to improve outcomes assessment methods.

Answerable questions, as noted in step 1, have several components, those pertaining to a given client population, a given assessment measure, possibly a comparison measure, and a clinical state. Here are some examples:

- "In frail elderly people who appear depressed, is the Beck Depression Inventory or the Pleasant Events Schedule most accurate in detecting depression?"

- "In work with children suspected of being sexually abused, does using anatomically correct dolls result in a more accurate determination of a history of sexual abuse than using standard age-appropriate clinical interviews?"

- "Do the Beck Depression Inventory scores accurately discriminate between clients subsequently diagnosed with major depression and those without?" (Gambrill & Gibbs, 2009, p. 1123)

Straus et al. (2005) provided detailed expositions on each of these steps, some of which (critically appraising research evidence) will be familiar to many human service professionals, especially social workers. Additional questions pertaining to evaluating the potential usefulness of an outcomes assessment measure include the following:

- Is this evidence about the accuracy/validity of a given assessment measure/diagnostic test valid?

- Does this credible evidence demonstrate an important ability to distinguish persons who do or do not have a specific disorder/condition/problem?

- Can I apply this valid assessment measure with a specific client?

The next section discusses approaches to answering these questions.

EBP: Locating and Assessing Credible Evidence

The process of EBP involves two major ways of summarizing and collecting evidence (Mullen, 2006). The first can be called a *bottom-up search*, whereby clinicians personally locate and evaluate individual pertinent psychometric evidence relating to the selection of measures, usually by locating individual published studies. The second is commonly referred to as a *top down* search, wherein the clinician locates a recently published and high-quality article that summarizes the evidence on the validity of a particular outcome measure.

Bottom-up Searching

Straus et al. (2005) and Rubin and Parrish (2009) provide excellent guidelines on locating primary research studies in the journal literature. In EBP, peer-reviewed journal articles are a preferred source of information, relative to books, book chapters, conference papers, unpublished dissertations, blogs, and other resources, given that journals usually vet their articles through blind peer review and screen out obviously misleading papers. This peer-reviewing process, while by no means without flaws, provides a level of quality control absent from most other forms of scholarship. A second advantage of relying on journals is that they are often (but not always) more current than other sources of information. A third advantage of journals is their relative ease of accessibility, with most being readily available via library or other institutional electronic subscriptions, often permitting off-site access, downloading, and printing.

The process of comprehensively tracking down primary research studies related to one's answerable question can be an arduous one, however, particularly when reviewing research studies on well known outcomes assessment methods. Apart from individual studies, articles that provide a comprehensive review of existing research related to the reliability and validity of a particular assessment measure can be a useful professional resource. It is important to conduct comprehensive searches because there are very many assessment methods that, although widely used, are either lacking in credible research support or have actually been shown to be useless or inaccurate (Thyer & Pignotti, in press).

Sometimes one can locate review articles that focus, not on a particular instrument, but on a particular psychosocial problem. For example, Joiner et al. (2005) wrote an article titled "Evidence-based Assessment of Depression in Adults," which any clinician working with depressed clients would profit from reading. They summarized their recommendations as follows:

> *On the basis of available knowledge, our recommendation for the optimal evidence-based depression assessment in clinical settings includes (a) the SCID [Structured Clinical Interview for the DSM–IV] to establish formal mood disorder diagnoses; (b) the MINI [MINI International Neuropsychiatric Interview] module on melancholic features to supplement the SCID; (c) the Seasonal Pattern Assessment Questionnaire…to assess the possibility of a seasonal component to any diagnosed mood disorder; (d) the BDI-II [Beck Depression Inventory II] to assess severity of depressive symptoms; and (e) the LIFE [Longitudinal Interview Follow-Up Evaluation] to formally assess remission of disorder once BDI-II scores are stably low for many weeks. For mass screening situations, the CES-D [Centers for Epidemiological Depression Scale] and BDI-II seem to be wise choices. (Joiner et al., 2005, p. 275)*

Such a summary is pure gold for the time-pressed clinician seeking concrete and specific advice about the best array of outcomes assessments for clients with particular disorders (for example, affective disorders).

In another example, Antony and Rowa (2005) published an analogous article titled "Evidence-based Assessment of Anxiety Disorders in Adults" and arranged their recommended assessment measures according to various domains, giving as one example a client suffering from panic disorder with agoraphobia and recommendations on an array of outcome measures. Again, a succinct summary of credible recommendations is of exceptional value to clinical social workers and other providers. Finding articles containing such recommendations can be a great time-saver, providing the information is accurately presented and complete. More comprehensive overviews of outcome measures relevant to specific disorders can be found in certain books that have such a focus (see chapter 10 in this volume; see also Antony, Orsillo, & Roemer, 2001; Nezu et al., 2000; Kelley, Reitman, & Noell, 2002).

Top-down Searching

A second, and sometimes more efficient, method of locating summaries of information relating to risk assessment, diagnostic, screening, and outcomes measurement is for the clinician to access the findings of systematic reviews prepared by qualified groups such as the Cochrane and Campbell Collaborations. The Cochrane Collaboration is a large organization associated with EBP whose primary function is to commission, appraise, and publish systematic reviews (SRs) related to the general field of health care. An SR is a review of a clearly formulated question that uses systematic and explicit methods to identify, select, and critically appraise relevant research and to collect and analyze data from the studies that are included in the review. Statistical methods (meta-analysis) may or may not be used to analyze and summarize the results of the included studies.

A Cochrane Review is a "systematic, up-to-date summary of reliable evidence of the benefits and risks of health care" (see http://www.cochrane.org). SRs are typically conducted by a multidisciplinary and international research team that tracks down relevant research studies, with special efforts made to locate unpublished and non–English-language works. All critical judgments are conducted by two or more independent appraisers and must reach acceptable levels of interrater agreement. Additional efforts are made to reduce bias in these appraisals as much as possible.

A special review group within the Cochrane Collaboration, the Diagnostic Test Accuracy Working Group, is devoted to screening and diagnostic tests (see http://srdta.cochrane.org/welcome) and offers training events to design and conduct SRs in this area. The working group publishes the *Cochrane Handbook for Systematic Reviews of Diagnostic Test Accuracy*, which represents the state of the art methodological practice, along with the *Standards for Reporting Diagnostic Accuracy* (*STARD;* Bossuyt et al., 2003). The STARD initiative is a 25-item checklist of recommended features to be included in any report on diagnostic test accuracy.

Among the protocols for completed assessment or screening reviews to be found in the Cochrane Library are screening and case finding instruments for depression, screening women for intimate partner violence in health care settings, domestic violence screening and intervention programs for adults with dental or facial injury, antenatal psychosocial assessment for reducing perinatal mental health morbidity, comprehensive geriatric assessment for older adults admitted to hospital, and alcohol and drug screening of occupation drivers for preventing injury

The Campbell Collaboration (Schuerman et al., 2002) is purposed similarly to the Cochrane Collaboration, with a focus on publishing SRs in the areas of social welfare, criminal justice, and education. Although most completed reviews focus on appraising the effects of interventions, a number of protocols describing SRs in preparation deal with the assessment of outcomes and risk (see http://www.campbellcollaboration.org), including

- The recurrence of child maltreatment: Predictive validity of risk assessment

- Screening and assessment tools used to assess juvenile/young offenders for admission to a prison/secure institution

- Risk assessment strategies for the prevention, treatment, and management of contact with the forensic mental health services or the criminal justice system.

Littell, Corcoran, and Pillai (2008) and Littell and Corcoran (2009) are excellent resources prepared by social workers on the topic of systematic reviews.

Other Stakeholder Approaches to Outcomes Measurement: Implications for Human Services and EBP

The Problem of Mandated Outcomes Measures

The process model of EBP relies on individual clinicians to make decisions about assessment methods and interventions. Sometimes, however, policymakers, agency administrators, or program directors decide, unilaterally or with staff input, on the regularized or required use of particular outcome assessments as a mandated aspect of agency functioning. The reasoning is something like (for example): "Because the BDI is so well-regarded as a scientifically supported and clinically useful measure, we will require that all our clinicians use it in appraising outcomes of practice with depressed clients." Such reasoning and practices would actually be at variance with EBP because they unduly promote research considerations above other equally compelling factors, such as client preferences and values, individual clinical skills, the client's situation and environment, costs, and ethical aspect of decision making. There is something to be said for making selected, empirically supported assessment measures available or even suggested, but certainly not mandated. If the client does not read English well, and only English translations of the BDI are available, then it would be inappropriate to require the clinician to use the BDI. If the client is in an acute state of suicidal crisis, then an agency protocol requiring the clinician to immediately administer the BDI to a client is also clearly inappropriate. If the assessment measure is normed on one group (White men and women) if may be inappropriate to use it with clients for whom appropriate normative data are not available, and particularly problematic to compare the non-White client's scores with the existing normative data derived from Whites and to make decisions about that non-White client in part on this basis. This illustrates how a managerial mandate to use a particular outcomes measure, or even a particular intervention, is not compatible with EBP.

Similar problems arise at the federal level. A recent SAMHSA request for proposals (RFP) contained the following language, which is very similar to that of RFPs issued by other governmental agencies:

> *All SAMHSA/CASP grantees are required to collect and report certain data so that SAMHSA can meet its obligations under the Government Performance and Results Act (GPRA). Applicants must describe their current capacity for collecting and reporting direct service and community level data as appropriate for their project, as well as plans for ensuring that SAMHSA's National Outcome Measures (NOMs) can be collected and reported at the participant and community level in time for the implementation phase of the proposed project.*

This is a mandate that a particular set of outcome measures be adopted by agencies that receive federal funding for various service programs. Like the BDI example, this leaves clinicians with the issue of what to do if the approved measures are clearly inappropriate for a given client.

The Problem of Mandated Treatments

Regrettably, many human service professionals have confused the empirically supported treatments (ESTs) project of Division 12 (Clinical Psychology) of the American Psychological Association (APA) with EBP. The ongoing EST project consists of two initiatives. The first is to establish some level of scientific evidence that could be used to justify designating a psychosocial assessment method or treatment as empirically supported. The second is to apply this evidentiary standard to existing treatments and designate them as empirically supported or as promising. The standard adopted by the EST movement requires that a given intervention meet the following criteria in order to be judged as empirically supported (see the APA Division 12 Web site: http://www.psychology.sunysb.edu/eklonsky-/division12/index.html):

> *The treatment is supported by at least two good randomized controlled trials showing that the target intervention is (a) superior (statistically significantly so) to pill or psychological placebo or to another treatment; (b) equivalent to an already established treatment in experiments with adequate sample size. The target treatment must also be conducted using treatment manuals, the characteristics of the client samples must be clearly specified, and the effects must have been demonstrated by at least two different investigators or investigating teams.*

If a given treatment meets the above criteria it is designated as a "well-established treatment," whereas those that meet a somewhat lesser evidentiary standard could be called "probably efficacious." In due course, lists of such ESTs were published, and they are regularly updated. Most of the publications and lists of ESTs can be found on the Internet. There are problems with designating certain interventions or measures as an EBP, however. First, there are no such things as EBPs in themselves. There is the process of EBP, and there are lists of ESTs, but these are quite distinct initiatives, with the latter being inconsistent with viewing EBP as a process and not a set of mandates. Thus, because cognitive behavior therapy is labeled on the APA site as an EST for clients with depression, such listing could lead to the impression that one should provide CBT (or another EST) for clients who are depressed. But suppose one's client has an intellectual disability and is unable to comply with the requirements of CBT? Then, obviously, CBT is an inappropriate therapy to attempt with this given client, even though it is designated an EST. Or suppose a client simply does not wish to engage in a given EST? There is little room within the practices of EST or of mandating selected outcome measures for clinicians to adapt to client wishes, values, ethical considerations, personal situations, and available resources. There is ample room with EBP for these vitally important factors to be considered.

Although the foregoing paragraphs have focused on treatments, analogous arguments can be made with respect to the selection of outcome measures. However, no matter how much evidence accrues that a given outcome measure is reliable and valid, it is inappropriate (by the tenets of EBP) to label that measure as an evidence-based assessment technique. One can decide the appropriateness of an outcomes assessment measure only in light of all the factors that go into the EBP process, not simply by reviewing the scientific evidence alone, or by selecting from a list of endorsed assessment measures (Antony & Rowa, 2005; Joiner et al., 2005). These latter methods can be useful guides to the EBP process but are not necessarily the primary determinants in clinical decision making related to selecting outcomes assessment.

Future Directions: Balancing Approaches to Outcomes Measurement and EBP

Human service professionals who wish to learn about the process of EBP should begin by becoming familiar with the primary source documents outlining this model. Clinicians, agency administrators, and the federal government should certainly conduct bottom-up and top-down systematic reviews of the credible research literature pertaining to a particular outcome measure, or of literature relevant to measuring outcomes in clients with a particular problem. However, the results of these appraisals should consist of statements of fact (for example, "the XYZ child abuse risk assessment measure has sufficiently strong reliability and validity characteristics to recommend its use with clients who read and write English"). With such summaries of the research literature, clinicians and agencies can take research information, integrate it with the other significant factors that go into EBP, and make a professional decision about what measures to use with a given client. This approach helps to maintain the integrity of EBP as a process to facilitate individual decision making on the part of clinicians and their clients. It was not developed as a tool for administrators and funders to direct human services professionals on how they should take care of their clients.

The tension between identifying valid versus invalid outcome measures and how this information is subsequently used in the human services will remain for the foreseeable future. At one extreme, policymakers, funders, or managers will likely continue to predetermine which outcome measures are to be used in a given program, with little consideration given to cultural appropriateness or local conditions. The converse, in which individual clinicians have complete latitude in determining which, if any, outcome or performance measures he or she will use in evaluating program outcomes (Hudson & Thyer, 1986), will not likely be the case.

The approach taken by the Cochrane and Campbell Collaborations provides one model for helping resolve this tension. However, both collaborations eschew publishing lists of approved or endorsed interventions, outcome measures, or risk assessment instruments, and they do not provide practice guidelines or assessment algorithms. They do provide, in as comprehensive a manner as possible, up-to-date information, and both avoid dictating practices. The emerging *Cochrane Handbook of Systematic Reviews of Diagnostic Test Accuracy* will likely prove to be a definitive resource for use in deciding what measures to adopt or exclude.

Professional training programs in the human services can also help to address this tension by educating students in the process of evaluating and selecting outcome measures for use in clinical practice and program evaluation, in a manner similar to that being applied (albeit modestly) to the selection of interventions. EBP has already been adopted as a curriculum-organizing framework within a number of academic social work (Howard, McMillen, & Pollio, 2003), psychology, medicine, and other programs. Professional accreditation bodies such as the Council on Social Work Education and the APA need to move in this direction also.

Lastly, consumer advocacy groups can take leading roles in promoting the adoption of EBP by service providing agencies, nongovernmental organizations, and state agencies. Issues of both scientific credibility and professional ethics strongly suggest that EBP is a positive development in improving care to clients and their families. Proposed legislation in the human services can be prospectively analyzed to assess its compatibility with EBP, and appropriately critiqued or promoted depending on how the analysis fares.

References

Antony, M. M., Orsillo, S. M., & Roemer, L. (2001). *Practitioner's guide to empirically based measures of anxiety.* New York: Kluwer Academic/Plenum Press.

Antony, M. M., & Rowa, K. (2005). Evidence-based assessment of anxiety disorders in adults. *Psychological Assessment, 17,* 256–266.

Bossuyt, P. M., Reitsma, J. B., Bruns, D. E., Gatsonis, C. A., Glasziou, P. P., Irwig, L. M., et al. (2003). Towards complete and accurate reporting of studies of diagnostic accuracy. The STARD initiative. *British Medical Journal, 326,* 41–44.

Breul, J. D. (2007). GPRA—A foundation for performance budgeting. *Public Performance and Management Review, 30,* 312–331.

Darby, K., & Kinnevy, S. C. (2010). GPRA and the development of performance measures. *Journal of Evidence-Based Social Work, 7*(1/2), 5–14.

Davis, T. S. (2002). The federal GPRA evaluation mandate: Is social work ready? *Social Policy Journal, 1*(3), 51–74.

Gambrill, E., & Gibbs, L. (2009). Developing well-structured questions for evidence-based practice. In A. R. Roberts (Ed.), *Social workers' desk reference* (2nd ed., pp. 1120–1126). New York: Oxford University Press.

Guyatt, G., & Rennie, D. (Eds.). (2002). *Users' guides to the medical literature: Essentials of evidence-based clinical practice.* Chicago: American Medical Association.

Ho, A. (2007). The governance challenges of the Government Performance and Results Act: A case study of the Substance Abuse and Mental Health Administration. *Public Performance and Management Review, 30,* 369–397.

Howard, M. O., McMillen, C. J., & Pollio, D. E. (2003). Teaching evidence-based practice: Toward a new paradigm for social work education. *Research on Social Work Practice, 13,* 234–259.

Hudson, W. W., & Thyer, B. A. (1986). Research measures and indices in direct practice. In A. Minahan (Ed.), *Encyclopedia of social work* (18th ed., Vol. 2, pp. 487–498). Washington, DC: NASW Press.

Jerrell, J. M. (2006). Psychometrics of the MHSIP Adult Consumer Scale. *Journal of Behavioral Health Services and Research, 33,* 483–488.

Joiner, T. E., Walker, R. L., Petti, J. W., Perez, M., & Cukrowicz, K. C. (2005). Evidence-based assessment of depression in adults. *Psychological Assessment, 17,* 267–277.

Julnes, P. D. (2006). Performance measurement: An effective tool for government accountability: The debate goes on. *Evaluation, 12,* 219–235.

Kautz, J. R., Neting, F. E., Huber, R., Borders, K., & Davis, T. S. (1997). The Government Performance and Results Act of 1993: Implications for social work practice. *Social Work, 42,* 364–373.

Kelley, M. L., Reitman, D., & Noell, G. H. (2002). *Practitioner's guide to empirically based measures of school behavior.* New York: Kluwer Academic/Plenum Press.

Littell, J. H., & Corcoran, J. (2009). Systematic reviews and evidence-based practice. In A. R. Roberts (Ed.), *Social worker's desk reference* (2nd ed., pp. 1152–1156). New York: Oxford University Press.

Littell, J. H., Corcoran, J., & Pillai, V. (2008). *Systematic reviews and meta-analysis.* New York: Oxford University Press.

Martin, L. L., & Kettner, P. M. (1997). Performance measurement: The new accountability. *Administration in Social Work, 21*, 17–29.

Mullen, E. J. (2006). Facilitating practitioner use of evidence-based practice. In A. R. Roberts & K. R. Yeager (Eds.), *Foundations of evidence-based social work practice* (pp. 152–159). New York: Oxford University Press.

Nezu, A. M., Ronan, G. F., Meadows, E. A., & McClure, K. S. (2000). *Practitioner's guide to empirically based measures of depression.* New York: Kluwer Academic/Plenum Press.

Royse, D., Thyer, B. A., & Padgett, D. (2010). *Program evaluation: An introduction* (5th ed.). Belmont, CA: Brooks/Cole.

Rubin, A., & Parrish, D. (2009). Locating credible studies for evidence-based practice. In A. R. Roberts (Ed.), *Social workers' desk reference* (2nd ed., pp. 1120–1126). New York: Oxford University Press.

Schuerman, J., Soydan, H., Macdonald, G. Forlund, M., deMoya, D., & Borich, R. (2002). The Campbell Collaboration. *Research on Social Work Practice, 12,* 309–317.

Straus, S. E., Richardson, W. S., Glasziou, P., & Haynes, R. B. (2005). *Evidence-based medicine: How to practice and teach EBM* (3rd ed.). New York: Churchill-Livingston.

Thyer, B. A. (2008). Evidence-based macro-practice: Addressing the challenges and opportunities for social work education. *Journal of Evidence-Based Social Work, 5,* 453–472.

Thyer, B. A., & Pignotti, M. (in press). Science and pseudoscience in clinical assessment. In C. Jordan & C. Franklin (Eds.), *Clinical assessment for social workers: Quantitative and qualitative approaches* (3rd ed.). Chicago: Lyceum Press.

CHAPTER 6

Building Capacity for Outcomes Measurement in Human Service Organizations:

The Getting to Outcomes Method

Joie D. Acosta and Matthew Chinman

Implementing any type of high-quality human service organization (HSO) program requires a significant amount of knowledge and skills, including needs assessment, planning, priority setting, program selection and delivery, evaluation, outcomes and/or performance measurement, continuous quality improvement (CQI), and strategies for sustainability. Many HSOs are chronically challenged in their efforts to effectively complete these critical program tasks because of myriad factors, including decreases in funding, little time for staff training, changes in client base (for example, demographic shifts or natural disasters), physical infrastructure needs, and lack of access to materials and guidance that can be helpful in growing and sustaining their HSO.

To help HSOs build the organizational capacity (that is, the knowledge, attitudes, and skills necessary to complete tasks critical to the success of any type of human service program such as decision making, planning, implementing, evaluating, and sustaining best practices or evidence-based programs) to improve performance of critical organizational tasks, Chinman and colleagues (Chinman, Hunter, et al., 2008; Chinman, Imm, et al., 2001; Chinman, Tremain, Imm, & Wandersman, 2009) developed a 10-step intervention model called Getting to Outcomes (GTO). GTO is based on several beliefs (for example, participation in a model like GTO can lead to a greater sense of competency and effectiveness, or self-efficacy, in performing GTO-related activities such as process and outcomes evaluation) and theories (for example, social cognitive theories of behavioral change, Bandura, 2004; workforce competencies needed for work performance, Hoge, Tondura, & Marielli, 2005). GTO is also based on the specific operationalization of empowerment evaluation theory, which states there will be a greater probability of achieving positive results when evaluators (who are part of HSOs or hired outside HSOs) collaborate with program implementers (managers and/or practitioners) and provide them with both the tools and the opportunities to better plan and implement programs, evaluate outcomes, and develop a CQI system themselves (Fetterman & Wandersman, 2005).

HSOs that implement high-quality programs are using approaches like the 10-step GTO model or comprehensive models that go beyond outcomes measurement to account for the steps HSOs need to achieve outcomes, not just measure them. GTO focuses on many aspects of organizational capacity and performance, with heavy emphasis on outcomes measurement and the use of assessment (for example, traditional evaluation methods; Rossi, Freeman, & Lipsey, 1999), as well as total quality management techniques (Deming, 1986). Steps 1 through 6 focus on planning, including strategies to help HSOs identify and use best practices and evidence-based programs; steps 7 and 8 focus on process and outcome evaluation; and steps 9 and 10 focus on the use of data to improve and sustain HSO programs. If HSOs implement all 10 steps they will have a well-defined program and the kind of comprehensive implementation plan needed to achieve realistic, specific, and measurable outcomes, as well as a high-quality evaluation design that will allow them to measure program outcomes.

GTO is a unique model that is more than just a process; it is also an intervention that builds the capacity of users to use outcome data for CQI, not just performance measurement. There are three strategies used to intervene with HSOs as they implement the GTO process (Chinman, Imm, & Wandersman, 2004): adaptation of the generic GTO manual and CD-ROM materials for user purposes (for example, specialized GTO manuals have been developed to help address underage drinking and teen pregnancy prevention, and promote positive youth development), face-to-face training and on-site *technical assistance* (TA), defined here as a process in which an intermediary assists HSOs to implement GTO, tailoring support to address specific gaps in capacities and capitalize on existing strengths. TA ensures that organizations are proactively making progress on one or more of these steps. Although the amount of TA can vary by project, GTO TA providers typically meet biweekly with organizations.

To date, GTO has been used, disseminated, and evaluated widely in a variety of domains. Since its inception in 2004, almost 80,000 GTO manuals have been purchased or downloaded from the Internet, and more than 80,000 additional visits have been made to two Web sites where the GTO model is described. Thirteen states have used the GTO model in efforts to reduce teen pregnancy and substance abuse. For example, GTO was used in South Carolina as a catalyst for significant improvement in substance abuse prevention at the state and local level. In California, GTO helped staff improve the mechanics of their coalition-building process, their HSO's CQI process, and the use of evaluation data for decision making (Chinman et al., 2008).

In absence of the capacity or resources to implement GTO full-scale (including biweekly TA), program implementers have used peer-to-peer support to facilitate implementation by troubleshooting issues relating to implementation of GTO model in a peer network, often using technology to facilitate the peer-to-peer support. The benefits of peer-to-peer sharing have also been documented in literature on *communities of practice*, or "groups of people who share a concern or a passion for something they do and learn how to do it better as they interact regularly" (Wegner, McDermott, & Snyder, 2002, p. 12; Wegner & Snyder, 2000).

The rest of this chapter will describe the GTO process in detail and discuss a real-life example of how GTO is being used to help adolescent health coalitions in Maine improve their program outcomes.

The GTO 10-Step Model

As described, the GTO model consists of 10 steps. The steps outline 10 accountability questions and provide tools for HSOs to answer them. They are designed to help practitioners systematically diagnose community problems, locate and apply best practices or evidence-based programs to those problems, and then self-evaluate those practices/programs in order to continually improve their outcomes. GTO manuals contain guidance and tools to walk organizations through these steps.

An important feature of the GTO model is its cyclical nature; HSOs are expected to continually apply the 10 steps of GTO to design, implement, and evaluate programs, and in turn to apply evaluation data to achieve CQI in the design, implementation, and evaluation of programs. GTO promotes outcomes measurement as a routine part of program implementation. Depending on existing capacity, each step of GTO takes varying lengths of time for HSOs to complete. Some organizations may have already implemented a needs and resources assessment (step 1) and thus can begin with developing a logic model that lays out their goals and objectives (step 2). GTO is flexible enough for HSOs to use regardless of their current level of capacity, and because it is cyclical, each step will be revisited over time, consequently building capacity among users. HSOs that continually use all 10 steps of GTO and their associated GTO manual worksheets (for example, needs assessments tools, evidence-based practice checklists, evaluation and data collection methods pros and cons) will develop high-quality programs.

HSO staff can use the GTO model independently or collaborate with outside evaluators or other stakeholders to implement GTO. When thinking about who to engage in GTO, HSOs should plan to include individuals with a significant role in program design, implementation, or evaluation. The 10 steps of GTO and the associated accountability questions and tools from the GTO manual are described in the following sections.

Step 1: Needs/Resources—What Are the Needs, Risks, Resources, and Conditions to Address?

Step 1 helps HSOs choose the community problem to target and assess needs and resources that are needed to do so. Information on community needs can include an assessment of the prevalence, incidence, or causes of a problem. Community resources can include policies, programs, volunteers, facilities, local expertise, and financial support. Knowing as much as possible about the problem and resources available will help set realistic goals and objectives in step 2. During this step, HSOs can create a workgroup to lead the needs and resources assessment, develop a plan for data collection that identifies the critical types of data needed, and collect and analyze the data.

Step 2: Goals—What Are the Goals and Desired Outcomes?

During this step, HSOs set goals, identify participants, and create a set of objectives. Goals are broad statements that describe the long-term impact of what the HSO hopes to accomplish. Goals indicate overall direction, whereas objectives describe specific measurable changes that occur as a result of a specific action or set of actions. Objectives represent the desired outcomes that contribute to the overall goal and can include changes in individuals' knowledge, attitude, skills, or behaviors, or broader changes in community awareness or mobilization, policies, laws/ordinances, or collaboration among community organizations. Measuring changes in each objective will help HSOs determine whether they have met their overall goals. This step helps HSOs to develop a basic set of priorities and specific outcomes that can facilitate an optimal evaluation design.

Step 3: Effectiveness—How Can Goals Be Achieved Effectively?

The emphasis of this step is on finding and emulating existing practices and programs that are considered effective or have been proven to work, as demonstrated by a research study published in a peer-reviewed publication. These can include specific evidence-based programs or broad best practices. HSOs are more likely to achieve the results they want if they use practices or programs that have been shown, through research, to work.

Step 4: Fit—How Does the Program Fit with Existing Programs and Communitywide Initiatives?

In step 4, HSOs assess the congruence between goals and objectives created in step 3 and community needs to determine whether the goals and objectives need to be modified or adapted. The purpose of this step is to increase the chances that the program will be appropriate to and accepted by the target audience and the community, and to reduce redundancy by complementing other programs and contributing to communitywide initiatives.

Step 5: Capacities—What Organizational Capacities Are Needed to Implement the Program?

In step 5, HSOs assess whether they have the operational infrastructure needed to direct and sustain the program. The core functions of an operational infrastructure are planning, decision making, and governance; accessing resources; convening, networking, and organizing committed leaders; communicating within the HSO or the community about the work of the HSO; providing tools, training, and technical assistance that can help HSOs with their program; and initiating and/or coordinating formal documentation, assessment, and evaluation. Different types of programs will require different core functions from the operational infrastructure.

Step 6: Plan—What Is the Plan for this Program?

HSOs make a plan to implement the program in step 6, which includes outlining activities, staffing, locations, and timelines, as well as expected attendance, duration of activities, and resources needed. Clearly laying out the steps for implementation will make it easier to determine what to measure with the process and outcomes evaluations in steps 7 and 8.

Step 7: Process—How Will the Quality of Implementation Be Assessed?

In step 7, HSOs assess the quality of program implementation by evaluating how the overall process is working. A process evaluation can involve tracking attendance of participants, monitoring fidelity for each program session or participant interaction, and conducting satisfaction surveys to assess the experience of program participants. Process evaluation allows organizations to make midcourse corrections to address challenges to program implementation, and add valuable information needed to explain why (or why not) and how the programs activities resulted in desired outcomes (Karachi, 1999).

Step 8: Outcomes—How to Determine Whether the Program Is Working

This step helps HSOs evaluate whether their programs are meeting their goals, reaching their target audience, and achieving their desired outcomes. An outcome evaluation measures changes that result from program implementation, such as changes in participants' knowledge, attitudes, skills, and behaviors.

Step 9: Continuous Quality Improvement— What Continuous Quality Improvement Efforts Are Needed to Improve the Program over Time?

In step 9, HSOs apply what has been learned from steps 1 through 8 to improve future organizational efforts. During this step, HSOs revisit whether needs and resources have changed (step 1); update goals and objectives (step 2); review the literature to ensure the HSO is using up-to-date best practices (step 3); determine whether the program still fits with existing programs (step 4); decide whether additional resources are needed to implement the program (step 5); assess how well the program was planned (step 6) and implemented (step 7); and determine whether the program achieved its goals and desired outcomes (step 8). By understanding what works well, organizations can repeat successes and avoid repeating mistakes or missteps. CQI also helps HSOs to capitalize on their investments in evaluation by encouraging them to use the findings for improvement. Each time process or outcome evaluation data are collected, HSOs should use the data to make improvements and refine their program and increase its effectiveness.

Step 10: Sustain—If the Program Is Successful, How Will It Be Sustained?

HSOs consider what is needed to sustain successful programs in step 10. The likelihood of continued support and funding depends on many factors; however, steps 7 through 9 can help provide information organizations can use to judge whether the efforts should be continued (that is, using evaluation data to determine whether the program is successful). This step urges HSOs to plan for sustainability at the beginning of the program; forge new partnerships and create shared leadership opportunities with other organizations to implement the program; and look creatively at what resources exist to support the program, suggesting that sustainability is about more than just funding.

In order to be successful in diffusing a model such as GTO, it is helpful to be guided by an implementation model and dissemination strategies. This is because there is now wide recognition that such models and strategies are needed to support local implementation (Fixsen, Naoom, Blase, Freidman, & Wallace, 2005). One such model is the Simpson Transfer Model (STM), in which diffusion happens in the four stages: exposure, adoption, implementation, and practice (Simpson, 2002). Organizations must first be exposed to an innovation (for example, face-to-face training on GTO), then build the capacity needed to adopt the innovation (for example, TA needs assessment to determine areas where capacity building are needed to begin implementation of GTO, designation of persons responsible for carrying out the specified actions). Once organizations have the capacity to implement the innovation, they begin early implementation, followed by practice of the innovation until it becomes institutionalized (for example, include evaluation as part of staff job descriptions, structure organization meetings to discuss outcome measures and progress on them).

To illustrate the use of GTO, the next section will describe how RAND is currently implementing and evaluating the model with 12 adolescent health coalitions (AHCs) in Maine. AHCs offer a useful example to show the broad scope of GTO because, similar to HSOs, they provide a range of prevention, intervention, and treatment services.

GTO in Action: An Example from AHCs in Maine

Twelve AHCs in Maine used GTO to improve their implementation of positive youth development programs run by program staff at each AHC. At the time of this writing, RAND was completing an evaluation of how GTO affects program success. In this study, the GTO approach was called Assets–Getting To Outcomes (A-GTO). It was a blend of GTO (a process-focused model which seeks to enhance AHC capacity for program planning, implementation and evaluation) and Developmental Assets (assets) (Fisher, Imm, Chinman, & Wandersman, 2006), a content-specific model designed to improve community mobilization and collaboration for positive youth development. The decision to combine GTO and Assets was based on previous research findings. For example, evaluation studies have shown that programmatic approaches that are narrowly focused on reducing or preventing adolescent risk behaviors (for example, substance abuse, delinquency) have been less effective than efforts to mobilize multiple community sectors to collaboratively meet young people's broad developmental needs (for example, Roeser, 2001; Roth, Brooks-Gunn, Murray, & Foster, 1998; Seligman & Csikszentmihalyi, 2000).

Consistent with the GTO model, three strategies were used to implement the blended A-GTO model with AHC program staff. AHC program staff were provided with an A-GTO manual and trained on the A-GTO model, and an ongoing technical support system consisting of two full-time TA providers and two part-time TA supervisors was put in place to support the implementation of A-GTO. During step 1, TA providers helped AHC program staff assess the needs and resources of each positive youth development program and identified that programs were part of a larger community context and participated in a broad accountability structure run by the AHC. In order for program staff to get support to conduct all 10 steps of the A-GTO model, they needed to engage AHC leadership. Therefore, TA providers were asked to work with both individual programs and AHC leadership. To make it easier for programs to implement A-GTO, TA providers worked with AHCs to align their organizational structure with the 10 GTO steps. For example, two of the AHCs used a mapping exercise to help identify what their coalition was doing on each A-GTO step. Coalition members were asked to identify target audience, needs, activities, and outcomes, as well as evaluation activities that were being conducted. Once the coalitions established an initial baseline of information about who was working on which steps of A-GTO, they included updates from each member in coalition meetings. This has promoted the sharing of evaluation activities and data across coalition members.

The following two sections provide a description of how A-GTO was used by AHC program staff to improve individual programs, and by AHC leadership to improve the AHCs or organizations.

Program-Level Support

After the needs and resources assessment (step 1), TA providers worked with AHC program staff to more clearly define program goals and objectives (step 2). Program staff, with support from TA providers, developed a logic model that showed how the program activities were tied to needs and resources, as well as to desired outcomes. TA providers also utilized the logic model to work with program staff on selecting process and outcome evaluation measures that captured the quality of program activities and desired outcomes, respectively (steps 7 and 8).

Process evaluations (step 7) were designed to capture program participant characteristics, assess participant satisfaction, and monitor program fidelity (for example, one program developed a rating form to be used in determining whether program implementers were adhering to the program curriculum). TA providers used tools from the A-GTO manual to help programs select process evaluation questions, determine the data needed to answer the questions, and weigh the expertise and time needed to collect the process evaluation data. Outcome evaluations (step 8) were designed to capture participant outcomes. Sample program-level outcomes and outcome measures identified for the AGTO project in Maine are included in Table 6-1 on page 82. Youths were the target population for each program. To define outcomes and outcome measures, TA providers worked with program staff to answer a series of questions:

1. Who and what do they expect to change?
2. Are these reasonable changes to expect, given program activities and the target population?
3. What percentage of the target population do they expect to change? By how much? When do they expect the change?

These questions helped to elicit some general information about program outcomes, similar to the information in Table 6-1. TA providers then used this information to help program staff create specific and measurable outcomes. Specific outcomes generally begin by identifying the target population (for example, sixth-graders at one middle school), then the specific amount and type of change expected (for example, a 10 percent increase in their level of school connectedness [as measured by the self-report School Connectedness Scale]), and finally the amount of time it will take for the change to occur (for

Table 6-1: Sample Adolescent Health Coalition Program-Level Outcomes and Outcome Measures

General Outcome	Outcome Measure
Increase developmental assets	Percentage of youths who improve from having a low or fair number of developmental assets to a high or excellent number of developmental assets (Developmental Assets Profile)
Improve school connectedness	Percentage of youths who show significant increases in overall school connectedness (School Connectedness Scale)
Delay sexual activity	Percentage of youths who self-report they delayed initiating sexual activity(National Longitudinal Study of Adolescent Health)
Improve youth involvement in community activities	Percentage of youths who show significant increases in civic participation (Civic Participation Scale)
Enhance youth antidrug attitudes	Percentage of youths who show significant increases in antidrug attitudes (Project Alert Outcome Evaluation Tool)
Improve healthy peer relationships	Percentage of youths who show significant increases in healthy peer relationships (Inventory of Peer Attachment)

example, by the end date of the program). After outcomes were drafted, TA providers walked through a brief checklist with program staff to ensure that their outcomes were realistic, specific, matched to at least one measure each, and formatted appropriately using the aforementioned guidelines.

Once outcomes were defined, TA providers worked with program staff to select an appropriate evaluation design that fit their program and defined outcomes, and chose a method of measurement and data collection. The GTO manual was used to help program staff compare common evaluation designs (for example, post only, pre–post with comparison group, pre–post with control group) to select an appropriate evaluation design that could be accomplished using program staff expertise and available resources. For example, program staff with minimal resources and limited experience conducting program evaluation could choose a post-only evaluation design, which is low in cost and easy to implement; however, it cannot measure change in participant outcomes. Program staff with more resources and experience conducting program evaluation could select a pre–post with control group design which is costly and requires program staff to address ethical issues associated with withholding program services from control participants; however, it provides a high level of confidence that the program caused positive changes in participant outcomes.

TA providers also worked with program staff to select an appropriate data collection method (for example, focus groups, telephone surveys, self-administered surveys, archival trend data) for their evaluation. For example, TA providers worked with program staff of a teen pregnancy prevention program to develop an evaluation to capture changes in knowledge, attitudes, and behaviors, as well as overall participant satisfaction. Participants in the program are teens and their parents. During the first session of this program and three months after the program ends, parents are given a short survey that assesses how likely they are to talk with their teen about sexual behaviors and set rules around sexual and dating behaviors (for example, boyfriend/girlfriend have to be of the same age). Teens and parents are also asked about their knowledge of the risks associated with sexual behavior as part of the pretest survey and upon completion of the program to determine changes in knowledge. A process evaluation of this program captured the lessons taught during each session and attendance at the program. Program staff distributed a satisfaction survey assessing the usefulness and clarity of the session content and materials distributed to participants at the end of the program.

This teen pregnancy prevention program used these data for CQI, making changes to their curriculum (for example, no longer using a video that was unclear, incorporating some conversation starters for parents to talk with their teens) to better meet the needs of the teens and parents they serve. Other AHC programs in Maine also used evaluation data for CQI. For example, after evaluation data showed that the one youth advocacy program did not come close to reaching its desired outcomes, program staff calibrated their goal by reducing the percent change they anticipated as a result program activities (step 2: Goals).

Organizational-Level Support

Similar to their work in program-level support, TA providers assisted the 12 AHCs with developing coalitionwide logic models and helping to determine whether they had the appropriate evaluation support to assess coalitionwide outcomes. Questions similar to those used with the individual programs were used with the coalitions when developing outcomes and selecting outcome evaluation measures. For example, AHCs considered who and what they expected to change; unlike programs, this was often more focused at a broad community level (for example, AHCs were trying to improve adolescent health across a city, county, or region) rather than a specific group of individuals.

AHCs would then review their profile of programs and activities to determine whether the changes were reasonable to expect. Many of the AHC's activities and programs were focused on increasing youth's developmental assets, and AHCs could look across specific program outcomes to help determine what types of changes to expect across the city, county, or region they were targeting. For example, if the AHC was running three programs that all anticipated a 10 percent improvement in developmental assets among the youth they were targeting, and these programs reached 75 percent of the AHCs total target population (for example, 75 percent of youth in one Maine city), the AHC could craft their overall desired outcome to be a 10 percent improvement in developmental assets among 75 percent of youth in one Maine city.

At the time of this writing, TA providers were also coaching the AHCs on how to negotiate with local schools to gain access to their survey data, which can be helpful in evaluating the coalition's overall impact. To help identify local schools to target for survey data, TA providers worked with coalition leadership to identify which grades at each school they were targeting and what steps were needed to obtain the data from school officials. For example, some schools required that the AHC leadership sign an agreement stating that they would not publish school-level estimates of substance abuse or teen pregnancy, sensitive data that may be used to label schools as problem areas.

Conclusion

We recognize that increasing expectations among HSO leaders, funders, and other stakeholders to demonstrate accountability, implement sound programs, and achieve positive outcomes set the bar high for many organizations. To achieve successful outcomes, HSOs must have the skills and knowledge needed to implement high-quality programming (that is, using the 10 steps of GTO in a continuous cycle); build their organizational capacity (that is, knowledge and skills) to complete critical program tasks (for example, choosing, planning, implementing, evaluating, and sustaining evidence-based practices), including outcomes measurement; and improve program performance. To help HSOs navigate the barriers and challenges to conducting outcomes measurement, we have used our experience implementing GTO with HSOs to compile a list of barriers and challenges and how GTO helps HSOs address them (see Table 6-2).

GTO provides a standardized, yet flexible, process to develop high-quality programs that can be implemented within a single program, across an entire organization, or across an entire state, regardless of current program capacity. Developing standards and defining measures for quality comparisons between

Table 6-2: Common Barriers and Challenges to Outcomes Measurement and How Getting to Outcomes (GTO) Can Help Navigate Them

Barrier or Challenge	How GTO Can Help
Programs within HSOs not well-defined, making parameters of evaluation unclear	GTO helps HSOs focus their program design. Step 2 (Goals) helps programs identify their goals. Step 8 (Outcomes) helps programs more clearly define outcomes.
Lack of expertise in evaluation design	GTO teaches HSO staff skills in evaluation design. Step 7 (Process) and step 8 (Outcomes) describe how to design an evaluation, select data collection methods, and identify relevant outcome measures. Step 9 (Continuous Quality Improvement) teaches how to apply what was learned through evaluation to improve future implementation.
Limited collection of data and dissemination of findings	GTO helps HSOs define outcomes and outcome measures and highlights opportunities for sharing data. As part of step 7 and step 8, GTO asks HSO staff to describe how data will be used and who they will be shared with. Dissemination is built into evaluation planning. GTO also provides the tools to help HSO staff decide what type of evaluation to use given their time, resources, and expertise.
Limited use of data once collected	GTO helps HSOs link process and outcome evaluation data to more fully understand how what they are doing is linked to outcomes. Step 9 also walks users through a series of steps to help them interpret and apply the lessons learned from evaluation to program improvement.

Note: HSO = human services organization.

HSOs will not be possible without a standardized process. The human services would realize systemwide benefit from using an approach like GTO to improve quality of services and to encourage CQI. We hope this chapter has provided a useful illustration of the ways in which GTO may be helpful in achieving these goals, especially outcomes measurement.

References

Bandura, A. (2004). Swimming against the mainstream: The early years from chilly tributary to transformative mainstream. *Behaviour Research & Therapy, 42,* 613–630.

Chinman, M., Hunter, S, Ebener, P., Paddock, S., Stillman, L., Imm, P., & Wandersman, A. (2008). The Getting to Outcomes demonstration and evaluation: An illustration of the Prevention Support System. *American Journal of Community Psychology, 41,* 206–224.

Chinman, M., Imm, P., Wandersman, A., Kaftarian, S., Neal, J., Pendleton, K.T., & Ringwalt, C. (2001). Using the Getting to Outcomes (GTO) model in a statewide prevention initiative. *Health Promotion Practice, 2,* 302–309.

Chinman, M., Imm, P., & Wandersman, A. (2004, January). *Getting to Outcomes™ 2004: Promoting accountability through methods and tools for planning, implementation, and evaluation.* Santa Monica, CA: RAND Corporation. Retrieved from http://www.rand.org/pubs/technical_reports/TR101

Chinman, M., Tremain, B., Imm, P., & Wandersman, A. (2009). Strengthening prevention performance using technology: A formative evaluation of interactive Getting to Outcomes. *American Journal of Orthopsychiatry, 79,* 469–481.

Deming, W. E. (1986). *Out of the crisis.* Cambridge, MA: MIT Press.

Fetterman, D. M., & Wandersman, A. (Eds.). (2005). *Empowerment evaluation principles in practice.* New York: Guilford Press.

Fisher, D., Imm, P., Chinman, M., & Wandersman, A. (2006). *Getting to Outcomes with developmental assets.* Minneapolis: Search Institute.

Fixsen, D. L., Naoom, S. F., Blase, K. A., Friedman, R. M., & Wallace, F. (2005). *Implementation research: A synthesis of the literature* (FMHI Publication No. 231). Tampa, FL: University of South Florida, Louis de la Parte Florida Mental Health Institute, National Implementation Research Network.

Hoge, M. A., Tondora, J., & Marielli, A. F. (2005). The fundamentals of workforce competency: Implications for behavioral health. *Administration and Policy in Mental Health, 32,* 509–531.

Karachi, T. (1999). Opening the black box: Using process evaluation measures to assess implementation and theory building. *American Journal of Community Psychology, 27,* 711–731

Roeser, R. W. (2001). To cultivate the positive. *Journal of School Psychology, 39,* 99–110.

Rossi, P., Freeman, H., & Lipsey, M. (1999). *Evaluation: A systematic approach* (6th ed.). Thousand Oaks, CA: Sage Publications.

Roth, J., Brooks-Gunn, J., Murray, L., & Foster, W. (1998). Promoting healthy adolescents: Synthesis of youth development program evaluations. *Journal of Research on Adolescents, 8,* 423–459.

Seligman, M.E.P., & Csikszentmihalyi, M. (2000). Positive psychology: An introduction. *American Psychologist, 55,* 5–14.

Simpson, D. D. (2002). A conceptual framework for transferring research to practice. *Journal of Substance Abuse Treatment, 22,* 171–182.

Wegner, E., McDermott, R., & Snyder, W. (2002). *Cultivating communities of practice: A guide to managing knowledge.* Boston: Harvard Business School Press.

Wegner, E., & Snyder, W. (2000, January–February). Communities of practice: The organizational frontier. *Harvard Business Review,* 139–145.

CHAPTER 7

Leadership in the Human Services:
Models for Outcomes-driven Organizational Cultures

Thomas Packard and Richard H. Beinecke

Effective leadership is critical to the delivery of high-quality human services, human services outcomes, and the development of human services professionals. Strong human services leadership is especially needed now, as major social, cultural, economic, political, and demographic factors are creating rapid changes in human service delivery systems. Pressures to measure and improve organizational performance (for example, the Government Performance and Results Act of 1993), budget cutbacks in the governmental and human services sector, the rise of managed care, performance-based contracting, expectations for collaborations and partnerships with clients and communities, and growing immigrant and refugee communities represent particular challenges and opportunities (Lewis, Packard, & Singh, 2007; Patti, 2009; Smith, 2010). Accenting the importance of the "outcomes movement", Martin and Kettner (2010) pointed to initiatives of leading organizations such as the United Way, the American Red Cross, and Good Will Industries that emphasize performance accountability. For example, health reform is introducing new management, service delivery, and outcomes measurement challenges for our human services workforce, and new participatory leadership challenges for consumers who are trying to forge a client-driven health and behavioral health system.

Concurrent with such transformational circumstances are additional transitionary challenges facing our main human services resource: Human service workers continue to move up from practitioner positions into management or leadership positions with limited experience and training, and minimal advanced training in topical areas (for example, health, mental health, and child and family services). Likewise, many human service leadership positions are being filled by business and public administration professionals who have little knowledge of human services fields (Beinecke, 2009, 2010). With more than 40 percent of the U.S. workforce over age 40, and as many as 40 percent of senior managers in the human services and public administration expected to retire in the next five years (Waymunya, 2003), leadership in the human services is headed for a crisis if we do not develop a better understanding of how to develop effective leaders, measure leadership effects and its impacts on human service outcomes at multiple levels, and integrate knowledge and lessons learned across disciplines.

Meeting such challenges cannot be done without attention to leadership at all levels in our human services system, and without attention to the undeniable impact that leadership has on implementing organizational change and achieving positive human services outcomes. As other chapters in this volume and its first edition (Berman & Hurt, 1997) describe, developing an outcomes and/or performance-based organizational acumen continues to be an utmost priority for human services organizations (HSOs). This chapter will describe conceptual models of leadership; discuss the relationship between leadership and HSO outcomes; and offer recommendations on how leaders and managers in HSOs can develop, implement, and sustain an outcomes- and/or performance measurement–based culture.

Outcomes Measurement: A Wicked Problem for HSO Leadership and Management

Effective leadership is integral to the initial decision to adopt an approach to integrate outcomes and/or performance measurement into organizational culture; to define what are appropriate outcomes; to implement outcomes measurement systems, and to develop the plans, activities, and programs that can lead to successful outcomes at all levels (for example, clinical, management, organizational, and systems). In the 21st century, this menu of activities is increasingly perceived to include a "shift…in leadership and management style [that] embraces a partnership approach that empowers staff, users, and managers to participate in developing creative solutions, developing positive, supportive behaviors and environments to sustain leadership and management development" (Leadership and Management Sub-Group, 2005, p. 5).

In brief, developing and implementing outcomes measurement systems in HSOs requires personal as well as professional and organizational change. Staff need to believe that outcomes measurement is being implemented not just because funders require it, but because it contributes positively to their human services practices and to their clients' outcomes. Staff may resist these changes for a variety of reasons, including concerns about how the outcomes data will be collected (for example, will client and provider information be kept confidential? will additional time be required of already over worked line staff to learn about outcomes measurement and to collect, analyze, report, and respond to the data?) and how and whether they will be used fairly (Fisher, 2005). As organizations move toward outcomes-based cultures, time, funding, and other resources will be needed to create and implement outcomes systems that can be used to improve clinical and administrative practice within a broader continuous quality management system. We discuss this in more depth later in this chapter.

Hence, implementing an outcomes measurement culture in HSOs is a "wicked" problem as it has not been faced before by many of those who must address it, and is entwined with other problems. The search for solutions never stops. Solutions are not good or bad or limited, but are judgment calls and are often difficult to measure. Wicked problems often crop up when organizations have to face constant change or unprecedented challenges (Camillus, 2008, p. 100). According to Heifitz (1994) such problems require new leadership skills and competencies, and a dynamic problem-solving process that emphasizes the need for quality, flexibility, adaptability, speed, and experimentation (Kanji & Moura E Sa, 2001).

Although these perspectives help to frame some of the context and identify some of the organizational components that are core to developing and implementing an outcomes-based culture in HSOs, they are only starting points from which to assess the great variation in the leadership knowledge base for HSOs and other organizations. Journals such as *Leadership Quarterly* publish articles that typically address narrowly focused research questions with limited practice implications, whereas books on leadership range widely in terms of models and variables studied. Most of the books on leadership in the popular press are written by or about well-known corporate chief executives or by consultants who have worked with organizations, most commonly in the business sector, using a limited evidence base.

We now turn to a discussion of leadership models and the literature regarding empirical relationships between leadership and HSO outcomes.

Leadership, Management, and Outcomes

Leadership and Management Defined

There are countless definitions of leadership. Northouse (2010) defined leadership as "a process whereby an individual influences a group of individuals to achieve common goals" (p. 3).

Although on the surface it appears that leadership is easy to define, controversy remains over what constitutes leadership and what constitutes management. Kotter (1990) made a distinction between management and leadership: Whereas a leader motivates and inspires, a manager controls situations and solves problems. With regard to HSOs, Packard (2004) defined administration as a combination of leadership (for example, visioning, change management, strategy development, organization design, culture management, community collaboration, ethics, and advocacy) and management (for example, program design, financial management, information systems, human resource management, program evaluation, and project management). In HSOs, both leadership and management skills are needed.

In the 21st century, leadership has also come to be defined in relation to evidence-based practices (EBPs). For example, leaders may use *evidence-based programming* (Briggs & McBeath, 2009), choosing an evidence-based intervention for implementation as an entire program rather than leaving the use of EBPs as a method to be used by an individual worker. Leaders may use *evidence-based management* (Pfeffer & Sutton, 2006) principles to assess leadership theories, models, and practice guidelines to inaugurate leadership activities. Leaders may also use *evidence-based process models* (Briggs & McBeath, 2009) or applications of EBPs that help create a learning culture in HSOs.

We now turn to a discussion of leadership theories and models, and research that highlights the relationship between leadership and organizational outcomes.

Leadership Models and Organizational Outcomes

Leadership can result in several types of outcomes at several different levels (for example, dyad, group, team, program, agency, community, and society/country). Specifics vary on the basis of the setting in which leadership is conducted, and range from the accomplishments of program objectives, to results of program evaluations, to client outcomes. For example, at the individual or team level, outcome variables such as job satisfaction or commitment can be measured; at the organizational level, leadership can affect HSO culture or climate.

The earliest research on leadership in the 20th century focused on *traits*, which were originally seen as innate characteristics of leaders. This area of study broadened to include skills and competencies, as well as the evolution of leadership styles and the notion that there is no one best way of leading (*contingency theory*). Current theories commonly include elements of several of these earlier models (Northouse, 2010).

Trait Models. There has been recent renewed interest in the study of leadership trait theory, especially characteristics of effective leaders, albeit with the recognition that this perspective is limited. Although little is known about how combinations of traits may impact effectiveness or how traits affect organizational outcomes (Northouse, 2010), researchers do agree that traits are important only to the extent that they are relevant to a particular leadership situation.

In light of these limitations, traits associated with effective leaders include intelligence, self-confidence, determination (for example, desire to get the job done, including initiative, persistence, dominance, and drive), integrity, and sociability (Northouse, 2010), a high energy level and tolerance for stress, an internal locus of control orientation, emotional stability and maturity, personal integrity, emotional and social intelligence (including curiosity, inquisitiveness, open-mindedness, learning orientation intelligence), urgency (for example, extroversion, high energy level, and power orientation), conscientiousness, and agreeableness (Yukl, 2010). In addition to these traits, leadership effectiveness has recently been associated with being "authentic." Grounded in positive psychology, the authentic leader is "confident, hopeful, optimistic, resilient, moral/ethical, future-oriented,…gives priority to developing associates to be leaders…is true to him/herself…[and] exhibits behavior [that] positively transforms or develops associates into leaders themselves" (Luthans & Avolio, 2003, p. 243).

Skills and Competencies. Competencies are reflected in the style theories of leadership or the notion that certain behaviors—for example, task, relationship, or change-oriented behaviors (Yukl, 2010), make leaders more effective, and that these behaviors or styles (for example, participative or autocratic leadership) can by and large be learned and improved. Mackay (1997) described competencies as

> *individual characteristics which must be demonstrated to provide evidence of superior or effective performance in a job.…The complete competency set or model for*

an individual role identifies all the knowledge, skills, experiences, and attributes a person should display in their behaviour when they are doing the job well.

Although the "competency movement" (Zenger & Folkman, 2002) has not yet produced a strong evidence base to relate lists of competencies to leadership effectiveness in specific situations, or to challenge the assumption that all competencies are equal, the literature shows that certain competencies are mandatory (to a greater or lesser degree) for effective leadership. For example, Zenger and Folkman (2002) found that business leaders with strengths in multiple competencies were most effective and, significantly, that particular combinations of competencies seemed to be more powerful predictors of effectiveness.

In their reviews of the leadership literature, leadership training programs, and competency models in eight countries, Beinecke (2009) and Beinecke and Spencer (2007) found that core leadership competencies are universal and do not differ for mental health, health, public administration, or business professionals, or by country. The five priority leadership competency areas that reflect this universality are illustrated in Figure 7-1.

Beinecke and Spencer (2007) used these domains to create the Leadership and Competency Skill Set Self-Assessment Tool for HSO leadership training

Figure 7-1: Leadership and Management Skill Set

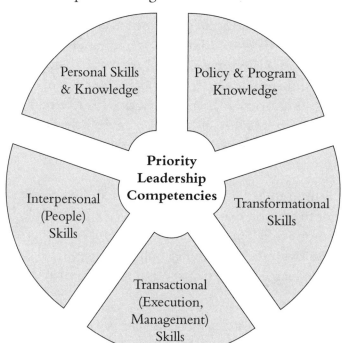

workshops and graduate leadership classes. This type of tool is consistent with current thinking that stresses a strengths perspective, in which administrators work to build upon their strengths in particular areas (Buckingham & Clifton, 2001) and also work on fixing flaws (Zenger & Folkman, 2002) so that the most can be learned from mistakes. All of the competencies and skills depicted in Figure 1 are important for leaders and managers in accomplishing organizational goals. (We encourage readers to conduct their own self-assessments. For example, we suggest that readers review a set of generic management competencies that have been developed by the National Network for Social Work Managers [see http://www.socialworkmanager.org/].)

Transformational and Transactional Leadership. One model of leadership with a broader evidence base contrasts transformational and transactional leadership styles. According to Avolio and Bass (2002), the best leaders use more transformational leadership than transactional leadership, but both used together (in different amounts in different situations) are optimally effective and important, and contribute to leader effectiveness and follower satisfaction (Beinecke, 2009; Boaden, 2006; Trottier, Van Wart, & Wang, 2008; Van Wart, 2005).

Transactional leadership is the more common leadership style and is critical to program implementation. In transactional leadership, an exchange process involves the leader and followers agreeing to do or provide things to accommodate each others' needs. A strong transactional leader stresses efficiency, planning and goal setting, competency, structure, and maintenance of the organization. Transactional leadership is especially useful for getting tasks done and implementing a vision or a new program.

In transformational leadership, the leader "transforms and motivates followers by (1) making them more aware of the importance of task outcomes, (2) inducing them to transcend their own self-interest for the sake of the organization or team, and (3) activating their higher-order needs" (Yukl, 2010, p. 275). This type of leader emphasizes personal relationships and development, teamwork, communication, autonomy and creativity, an empowering culture, honesty/integrity, humility and generosity, and continuous learning (Alimo-Metcalfe & Alban-Metcalfe, 2008; Bass & Avolio, 1993). By engaging followers' higher needs, transformational leaders move followers beyond their self-interest to work for the greater good and collective whole, thereby enhancing commitment and acceptance of responsibility and increasing follower effort and leadership

Summarizing research over the past 20 years, Bass and Avolio (2006) concluded that transformational leadership is positively related to organizational performance in various sectors: business, military, educational, government, and nonprofit. A number of other reviews have shown that transformational leadership has a strong positive relationship with objective measures such as work unit performance; subjective measures such as job satisfaction; measures of organizational culture, change, and performance (Alimo-Metcalfe & Alban-Metcalfe, 2008; Boaden, 2006; Mary, 2005); culture and change (Tucker & Russell, 2004); and hospital setting effectiveness and satisfaction (Gellis, 2001).

Yukl (2010) has offered several guidelines for the use of transformational leadership: articulate a clear and appealing vision and explain how it can be attained, act confident and optimistic, express confidence in followers, support the vision through resource allocations and emphasizing key values, and lead by example.

Exemplary Leadership. This model is based on five leadership practices and ten commitments articulated by Kouzes and Posner (2002). These are articulating one's personal values and aligning actions with them, inspiring a shared vision of the future, finding opportunities to innovate and change, fostering collaboration and trust, sharing power, and showing appreciation.

A number of studies in HSOs and other organizations have shown significant positive relationships between the five practices and a range of employee attitudes (Elpers & Westhuis, 2008; Kouzes & Posner, 2002; McNeese-Smith, 1996); outcome measures of performance are often missing or weak.

Participative Leadership/Decision Making. The literature on leadership styles, often characterized as the extent to which the leader focuses on task and relationship behaviors (Northouse, 2010), offers guidance to HSO leaders. A common term to describe a preferred style is participative decision making (PDM). For HSOs, PDM has been defined as "actual staff involvement, whether formal or informal, direct or indirect, in decision processes regarding issues affecting the structure, funding, staffing, or programming" (Ramsdell, 1994, p. 58) of the organization. This concept is often represented as a leader's decision making style on a continuum from *autocratic*, in which the leader makes all or nearly all decisions, to *participative*, in which subordinates have major involvement in sharing decision making with the leader.

Yukl (2010) has reported that there are often positive effects from PDM. For example, employee empowerment—and in turn, PDM—can be enhanced if several factors are present in HSOs, such as a culture of shared leadership and meeting chairing, team problem solving and decision making, flexible job designs, effective communication, rewards for employee initiatives, mutual (two-way) feedback, and employee development (Shera & Page, 1995). Packard (1989) found that child protective services units whose supervisors were seen as more participative had higher performance and job satisfaction than those with less PDM. Interestingly, these supervisors felt that workers were capable of much more PDM than they were currently allowed, suggesting that this is an underused approach (Packard, 1993).

Contingency Theories of Leadership. Contingency theory suggests that there is no one best way to lead, that different behaviors are appropriate in different situations, and that the effectiveness of leadership styles depends to a great extent on the situation (Hersey, Blanchard, & Johnson, 2001). As is the case with several leadership theories, the complexity of contingency theories makes them difficult to precisely implement and test (Northouse, 2010), with research having produced mixed results (Yukl, 2010). Regardless, applying principles of contingency theories and models to leadership practice requires leaders to engage in an assessment process of various factors (for example, the subordinates' skill and motivation levels) and subsequent selection of mixes of task and relationship behaviors and leadership approaches (for example, transformational or participative) that are appropriate for the situation at hand.

Diversity and Leadership Effectiveness. Although diversity issues in organizations have received increasing attention over the past three decades, specifics regarding leadership aspects of diversity have not yet been as fully addressed. Thomas (2006) has suggested that current notions of diversity need to be broadened to focus on *diversity management,* or "making quality decisions in the midst of difference, similarities, and related tensions" (p. 50). He added that leaders will need to acknowledge the challenges in making decisions in diverse organizations; "become more comfortable with tension and complexity" (Thomas, 2006, p. 51); and be more strategic in their thinking, considering diversity issues in the context of mission, vision, and strategy.

Results from a few studies highlight some of the challenges associated with meeting this goal. For example, with regard to gender, Northouse (2010) reported that "although quite similar to men in behavior and effectiveness, women leaders tend to be more participative and less autocratic, a pattern that is well suited to 21st-century global organizations" (p. 273). Gill (2006) noted that "several studies have suggested that male and female leaders tend to behave differently but are equally effective" (p. 310). Eagly and Carli's (2003) meta-analyses of the research on leadership and gender revealed that "on the average, contemporary female managers manifest a small advantage in leadership style but can face disadvantage from prejudicial evaluation of their competence as leaders, especially in male-dominated leadership roles" (pp. 851–852). With regard to race, Romero (2005) found that Hispanic leaders were perceived as equivalent to Euro-American leaders in effectiveness, that a leader-subordinate style match was important, and that participative approaches led to higher satisfaction.

Leadership and Organizational Change: Toward Outcomes-based Cultures in HSOs

As noted above, pressure to measure and improve outcomes in HSOs represents a continuing challenge. HSO administrators, as change leaders, can have a major impact in helping their agencies rise to this challenge. After a brief discussion of the various dimensions of organizational effectiveness, including client outcomes, principles of organizational change will be presented as a way to move HSOs toward the development of an outcomes-based culture.

In recent years, leadership and organizational change have been increasingly seen as inextricably linked (Fernandez & Pitts, 2007; Kotter, 1996), with leadership being viewed as a key factor in coordinating and aligning organizational processes (Lewis et al., 2007) and outcomes. From this perspective, organizational outcomes can be measured in terms of goal accomplishment, efficiency or cost effectiveness, acquisition of key resources (for example, funding), environmental adaptation, and satisfaction of key stakeholders (for example, funding sources). Client outcomes, of course, vary on the basis of field of practice, and generally involve recipients of services achieving some desired level of improved or optimal functioning. Outcomes could include families safely reunifying after child abuse or neglect, persons with mental illnesses living in the least restrictive facilities, former substance abusers living independently and substance free, homeless persons obtaining affordable and permanent housing, and former foster youth living independently with living-wage jobs.

Many factors need to be present and in alignment in an organization for them to achieve positive client outcomes. With so many measurement possibilities for HSO outcomes, it is helpful to consider how leadership and organizational factors relate in one conceptual model. Figure 7–2 illustrates a model of how leadership relates to organizational performance. At its far left are inputs, including staff characteristics, leadership and management competencies, and agency resources. Throughputs in the model are clustered into program capacity (including service delivery technologies and the use of evidence-based models) and management capacity (including management processes such as the management information system and organizational culture; Sowa, Selden, & Sandfort, 2004). In this model, a leader must assess contingency factors in the environment, in staff, and in the situation, considering staff characteristics and using leader–member processes to shape organizational climate and culture. Other factors, including program capacity (for example, the service delivery model), client characteristics, and the use of EBPs in program design, can affect ultimate outcomes. Outputs—or more precisely for purposes of this chapter,

Figure 7-2: Leadership and Other Key Organizational Factors Related to Human Service Organization Performance

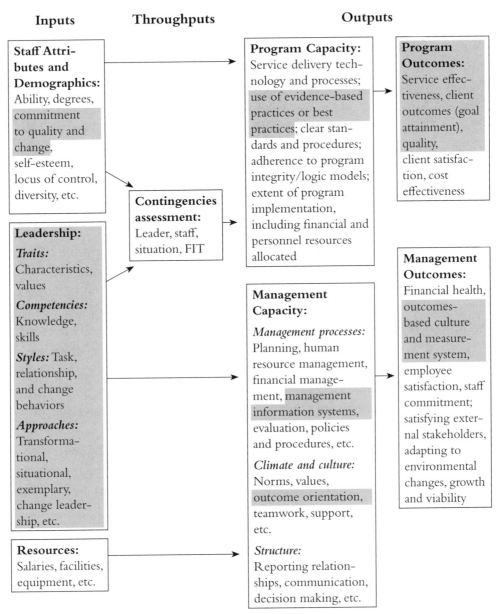

Inputs   **Throughputs**   **Outputs**

Staff Attributes and Demographics: Ability, degrees, commitment to quality and change, self-esteem, locus of control, diversity, etc.

Leadership:
Traits: Characteristics, values
Competencies: Knowledge, skills
Styles: Task, relationship, and change behaviors
Approaches: Transformational, situational, exemplary, change leadership, etc.

Resources: Salaries, facilities, equipment, etc.

Contingencies assessment: Leader, staff, situation, FIT

Program Capacity: Service delivery technology and processes; use of evidence-based practices or best practices; clear standards and procedures; adherence to program integrity/logic models; extent of program implementation, including financial and personnel resources allocated

Management Capacity:
Management processes: Planning, human resource management, financial management, management information systems, evaluation, policies and procedures, etc.
Climate and culture: Norms, values, outcome orientation, teamwork, support, etc.
Structure: Reporting relationships, communication, decision making, etc.

Program Outcomes: Service effectiveness, client outcomes (goal attainment), quality, client satisfaction, cost effectiveness

Management Outcomes: Financial health, outcomes-based culture and measurement system, employee satisfaction, staff commitment; satisfying external stakeholders, adapting to environmental changes, growth and viability

Notes: Based on Packard (2009) and Packard (2010). Shaded factors indicate the main focus of the model in this chapter.

outcomes—include client outcomes and program outcomes such as effectiveness, quality, efficiency, and client satisfaction, as well as management outcomes such as financial health of the agency. For a more complete description of this model please see Packard (2009, 2010).

After reviewing considerations in leadership, program and management capacity, and the importance of focusing on client outcomes, we will now examine tactics of organizational change that can be used to improve HSO functioning, with particular attention to moving an organization to an outcomes-based culture. This will begin with a brief discussion of organizational culture. Although the information presented here can apply to any HSO change goal or effort to measure organizational effectiveness, our particular interest is in creating outcomes-based cultures in HSOs.

Organizational culture has been defined simply as "the shared values, beliefs, and behavioral norms in an organization" (Glisson, 2009, p. 121). Leaders play an essential role in defining an organization's culture, and changing an organization's culture typically takes years. Schein (2004) suggests that creating a new culture requires leaders who have vision, persistence, patience, flexibility, and readiness regarding change, ability to perceive the problem, insight and self awareness about their strengths and limitations, strong motivation for change, emotional strength to handle the inevitable anxiety and criticism, the ability to bring to the surface and change existing culture assumptions, and the ability to involve others in the change process. Regarding HSOs, Latting et al. (2004) found that if nonprofit "organizational leaders create a work environment supportive of learning and innovation, supervisors may support their staff's empowerment, and staff may respond with increased trust and perceive service quality as higher" (p. 30). Gibson and Barsade (2003) listed themes in effective organizational culture change that are very consistent with the organizational change principles discussed below.

Our discussion of organizational change begins with a review of some literature regarding creating outcomes-based culture, followed by more detail on organizational change tactics that can be used to encourage an organization to adopt such a culture.

The importance of outcomes measurement in HSOs is receiving increasing attention in the literature (Poertner, 2009; Wilson, 2009). Yeager and Saggase (2008) addressed overcoming resistance to moving to an outcomes-based culture. Fisher (2005) summarized staff concerns about moving to outcomes measurement and showed how transformational leadership could be used with a team to develop an outcomes measurement system. Neuman (2003) presented the steps for developing an outcomes management program. Glisson (2007) summarized current knowledge regarding assessing and changing cultures to increase service effectiveness. There is also a growing literature in an area closely related to outcomes measurement: organizational change to adopt evidence-based practices (Austin & Claasen, 2008b); and implementation issues in these two areas are similar.

There is a vast literature on organizational change and a smaller literature on organizational change in HSOs. There are at least two models for organizational change designed for use specifically in HSOs (Lewis et al., 2007; Proehl 2001).

Fernandez and Rainey's (2006) comprehensive review of the literature identified eight "propositions," essentially principles or tactics associated with successful organizational change in both business and public settings, with an emphasis on governmental organizations. Their overall propositions, with additions based on other research, will be used here to represent generic principles that a change leader can use throughout a planned change process such as moving an HSO toward an outcomes-based culture.

Assess Existing Conditions, Readiness, and Resistance

Before initiating a major change, an agency's administrator as a change leader should ensure that the organization has a basic level of management competence and, ideally, a participative management philosophy. Management and employee readiness to engage in change and possible sources of resistance can be assessed through general observations and can be augmented through formal analysis (Austin & Claasen, 2008a; Fernandez & Pitts, 2007)

Ensure the Need and Demonstrate a Sense of Urgency

Change leaders must persuasively communicate the need for change, including demonstrating a sense of urgency that suggests that not changing would create significant problems for the agency and its staff. The need to change to an outcomes-based culture must be demonstrated in this era of increased demands for accountability and results. Multiple methods should be used to communicate the need for change, including stating the benefits and risks that are associated with making such a shift.

Provide a Plan

Change leaders should develop a course of action or strategy for implementing change, such as details for forming teams to implement outcomes measurement systems.

Use Widespread Participation in the Change Process

Participative decision making can be used to involve employees in change planning and implementation, including ongoing opportunities for communication about concerns and progress.

Ensure Top Management Support and Commitment

Executive leaders need to show ongoing support. A specific individual or group within the organization should be appointed to "champion" the cause for change.

Build External Support

Managerial leaders can gain support from outside groups such as boards and funding agencies who are interested in outcomes measurement.

Provide Resources

Adequate staff support, training, and time for employees to participate in change activities should be provided.

Institutionalize Change

After new outcomes systems are implemented, they should be formalized through policies and procedures. Moving to an outcomes-based culture will also require changes to the agency's management information systems, monitoring and evaluation processes, reward systems, and perhaps job descriptions. Leaders need to continually support the new culture.

Conclusions, Challenges, and Opportunities

Research has shown that leadership does make a difference in the ability of HSOs to achieve their goals. In the 21st century, effective leadership has become increasingly important for HSOs to successfully meet the myriad of challenges that exist today. As HSOs continue to respond to demands for accountability on several levels (for example, achieving organizational effectiveness and optimal outcomes for groups served), strong leadership and management is needed if successful client-based, outcomes-based cultures, measurement, and outcomes measurement systems are to be developed and implemented.

Leaders and managers need to work together to develop better outcome measures, service delivery methods, and organizational capacities that include the adoption of strengths-based approaches. Inspiring staff to higher levels of performance will be especially difficult in an era of declining resources and huge policy reforms such as health care. The conscious use of leadership principles to enhance prospects for success is crucial to responding to these external pressures and to the internal HSO pressures involved in delivering human services. In particular, change leadership skills will be useful in addressing these challenges and in the changing of organizational cultures.

Although a good deal has been learned about leadership, much more needs to be explored. Measuring the complexities of leadership and its effects is a daunting challenge. Overall, Yukl (2010) has concluded that research regarding styles and behaviors has been mostly inconclusive, but "the overall pattern of results suggests that effective leaders use a pattern of behavior that is appropriate for the situation and reflects a high concern for task objectives and a high concern for relationships" (p. 81). Some themes related to leader traits, competencies, and behaviors can be considered informal guidelines for leadership, management, clinical practice, and policy making.

For example, with regards to leader traits, higher levels of intellectual, emotional, and social intelligence should enhance prospects for success as a leader, as will high energy, tolerance for stress, self-confidence, an internal locus of control, self-regulation, systems thinking, self-awareness, and emotional stability and maturity. HSO leaders who want to improve their effectiveness should consider which of these could be developed, given their own characteristics. Leaders should work to understand their followers and address their strengths and concerns, and attend to task, people, and change behaviors, adapting to the unique needs of a situation. Regarding the move to an outcomes-based culture, change leaders should pay special attention to their agency's existing culture and the concerns that staff may have regarding a radical culture change, and work closely with staff to address concerns and areas of resistance, while educating them to the ultimate value of such a change.

One final implication warrants attention here: the need to develop new leadership for the HSOs of the future. Both *leader development*, "the expansion of a person's capacity to be effective in leadership roles and processes" (Van Velsor, McCauley, & Ruderman, 2010, p. 2), and *leadership development*, "encompassing the development of collective leadership beliefs and practices in addition to individual development" (McCauley, 2008, p. 6), are needed, with the latter especially important in changing an entire organization's culture.

Beinecke and Spencer (2007) found that

> *in most countries that we have studied, the United States being a prime example, leadership training is scattered and only partially covers many of these areas [see*

Figure 7-1]. It is not well organized or coordinated. Program availability varies greatly depending upon where one lives. There is no central site to find such programs. Most university programs that train human service workers focus on clinical skills, and few do an adequate job of training students in communication and analytical and management and leadership competencies, as well as outcomes assessment, evidence-based practices, and shared decision making. We are not doing an adequate job training the next generation of leaders. (p. 164)

Formal leader development programs (Hernez-Broome & Hughes, 2004; McCauley et al., 2010) are available through specialized training organizations, in-house programs for a particular organization, and consortia in which similar organizations pool resources. Leskiw and Singh (2007) found that

six key factors were found to be vital for effective leadership development: a thorough needs assessment, the selection of a suitable audience, the design of an appropriate infrastructure to support the initiative, the design and implementation of an entire learning system, an evaluation system, and corresponding actions to reward success and improve on deficiencies. (p. 444)

McCauley (2008) concluded that "the effectiveness of leader development programs varies widely, although effect sizes were positive across all criteria" (p. 26; see also Austin, Weisner, Schrandt, Glezos-Bell, & Murtaza, 2006; Packard, Gibson, Finnegan, & Coloma, 2008).

Agencies that recognize the need to move to outcomes-based cultures should assess their own training and development programs, the academic programs supplying staff for their agencies, and free-standing programs that provide training in leadership and information systems development (including a focus on outcomes measurement), and then, with reference to existing best practices (Riggio, 2008, p. 390), assess the extent to which our field is adequately addressing these needs. All opportunities for improvement, from changing university curricula to adapting existing programs (with particular thought to custom designing interdisciplinary programs to meet local and regional needs), should be considered.

The study of leadership and its effects on outcomes can be advanced by the use of increasingly refined and comprehensive models and measurement tools to assess current conditions and design and implement change and development processes to ultimately improve leader, worker, program, and agency effectiveness.

References

Alimo-Metcalfe, B., & Alban-Metcalfe, R. J. (2008). *Engaging leadership: Creating organisations that maximize the potential of their people.* London: CIPD.

Austin, M., & Claasen, J. (2008a). Impact of organizational change on organizational culture: Implications for introducing evidence-based practice. *Journal of Evidence-Based Social Work, 5,* 321–359.

Austin, M., & Claasen, J. (2008b). Implementing evidence-based practice in human service organizations: Preliminary lessons from the frontlines. *Journal of Evidence-Based Social Work, 5,* 271–293.

Austin, M., Weisner, S., Schrandt, E., Glezos-Bell, S., & Murtaza, N. (2006). Exploring the transfer of learning from an executive development program for human services managers. *Administration in Social Work, 30,* 71–90.

Avolio, B. J., & Bass, B. M. (2002). *Developing potential across a full range of leadership: Cases on transactional and transformational leadership.* Mahwah, NJ: Lawrence Erlbaum Associates.

Bass, B. M., & Avolio, B. J. (1993). Transformational leadership and organizational culture. *Public Administration Quarterly, 17*(8), 112–122.

Bass, B. M., & Avolio, B. J. (2006). *Transformational leadership* (2nd ed.). Mahwah, NJ: Lawrence Erlbaum Associates.

Beinecke, R. H. (2009). *Leadership training programs and competencies for mental health, health, public administration and business in seven countries.* Auckland, New Zealand: International Initiative for Mental Health Leadership.

Beinecke, R. H. (2010). Social work leadership and management development: Comparable approaches. In Z. van Zwanenberg (Ed.), *Leadership in social care* (pp. 162–177). London: Jessica Kinglsey.

Beinecke, R. H., & Spencer, J. (2007). International leadership competencies and issues. *International Journal of Leadership in Public Services, 3*(3), 3–14.

Berman, W., & Hurt, S. (1997). Developing clinical outcomes systems: Conceptual and practical issues. In E. J. Mullen & J. L. Magnabosco (Eds.), *Outcomes measurement in the human services* (pp. 81–97). Washington, DC: NASW Press.

Boaden, R. J. (2006). Leadership development: Does it make a difference? *Leadership & Organization Development Journal, 27*(1), 5–27.

Briggs, H., & McBeath, B. (2009). Evidence-based management: Origins, challenges, and implications for social work administration. *Administration in Social Work, 33,* 242–261.

Buckingham, M., & Clifton, D. O. (2001). *Now, discover your strengths.* New York: Free Press.

Camillus, J. C. (2008). Strategy as a wicked problem. *Harvard Business Review, 86*(5), 98–106.

Eagly, A., & Carli, L. (2003). Finding gender advantage and disadvantage: Systematic research integration is the solution. *Leadership Quarterly, 14,* 851–859.

Elpers, K., & Westhuis, D. (2008). Organizational leadership and its impact on social workers' job satisfaction: A national study. *Administration in Social Work, 32,* 26–43.

Fernandez, S., & Pitts, D. W. (2007). Under what conditions do public managers favor and pursue organizational change? *American Review of Public Administration, 37,* 324–341.

Fernandez, S., & Rainey, H. (2006). Managing successful organizational change in the public sector: An agenda for research and practice. *Public Administration Review, 66*(2), 1–25.

Fisher, E. (2005). Facing the challenges of outcomes measurement: The role of transformational leadership. *Administration in Social Work, 29,* 35–49.

Gellis, Z. (2001). Social work perceptions of transformational and transactional leadership in health care. *Social Work Research, 25,* 17–25.

Gibson, D., & Barsade, S. (2003). Managing organizational culture change: The case of long-term care. *Journal of Social Work in Long-Term Care, 2*(1/2), 11–34.

Gill, R. (2006). *Theory and practice of leadership.* Thousand Oaks, CA: Sage Publications.

Glisson, C. (2007). Assessing and changing organizational culture and climate for effective services. *Research on Social Work Practice, 17,* 736–747.

Glisson, C. (2009). Organizational climate and culture and performance in the human services. In R. Patti (Ed.), *The handbook of human services management* (pp. 119–141). Thousand Oaks, CA: Sage Publications.

Heifetz, R. A. (1994). *Leadership without easy answers.* Cambridge, MA: Harvard University Press.

Hernez-Broome, G., & Hughes, R. (2004). Leadership development: Past, resent, and future. *Human Resource Planning, 27*(1), 24–32.

Hersey, P., Blanchard, K., & Johnson, D. (2001). *Management of organizational behavior: Leading human resources* (8th ed.). Upper Saddle River, NJ: Prentice-Hall.

Kanji, G. K., & Moura E Sa, P. (2001). Measuring leadership excellence. *Total Quality Management, 12,* 701–718.

Kotter, J. P. (1990). A force for change: How leadership differs from management. New York: Free Press.

Kotter, J. P. (1996). *Leading change.* Boston: Harvard Business School Press.

Kouzes, J., & Posner, B. (2002). *The leadership challenge* (3rd ed.). San Francisco: Jossey-Bass.

Latting, J., Beck, M., Slack, K., Tetrick, L., Jones, A., Etchegaray, J., & Da Silva, N. (2004). Promoting service quality and client adherence to the service plan: The role of top management's support for innovation and learning. *Administration in Social Work, 28,* 29–48.

Leadership and Management Sub-Group. (September 2005). *21st century social work: Strengthening leadership and management capacity across social work services.* Retrieved from http://www.SocialworkScotland.org.uk/resources/Cp-Im/Leadershipand ManagementSubGroupReport.pdf

Leskiw, S., & Singh, P. (2007). Leadership development: Learning from best practices. *Leadership & Organization Development Journal, 28,* 444–464.

Lewis, J., Packard, T., & Lewis, M. (2007) *Management of human service programs* (4th ed.). Belmont, CA: Thomson–Brooks/Cole.

Luthans, F., & Avolio, B. J. (2003). Authentic leadership development. In K. S. Cameron, J. E. Dutton, & R. E. Quirm (Eds.), *Positive organizational scholarship* (pp. 241–261). San Francisco: Barrett-Koehler.

Mackay, P. (1997, January) *Competencies and competence: What are they and what part do they play?* Retrieved from http://www.ldc.govt.nz/?/information/publications.

Martin, L., & Kettner, P. (2010). *Measuring the performance of human service programs* (2nd ed.). Thousand Oaks, CA: Sage Publications.

Mary, N. L. (2005). Transformational leadership in human service organizations. *Administration in Social Work, 29,* 105–118.

McCauley, C. (2008). *Leader development: A review of research.* Retrieved from http://www.shrm.org/about/foundation/research/Documents/McCauley-%20Leader%20Dev%20Lit%20Review.doc.

McNeese-Smith, D. (1996). Increasing employee productivity, job satisfaction, and organizational commitment. *Hospital & Health Services Administration, 41,* 160–175.

Neuman, K. (2003). Developing a comprehensive outcomes management program: A ten step process. *Administration in Social Work, 27,* 5–23.

Northouse, P. (2010). *Leadership: Theory and practice* (5th ed.). Thousand Oaks, CA: Sage Publications.

Packard, T. (1989). Participation in decision making, performance and job satisfaction in a social work bureaucracy. *Administration in Social Work, 13,* 59–73.

Packard, T. (1993). Managers' and workers' views of the dimensions of participation in organizational decision making. *Administration in Social Work, 17,* 53–65.

Packard, T. (2004). Issues in designing and adapting an administration concentration. *Administration in Social Work, 28,* 5–20.

Packard, T. (2009). Leadership and performance in human service organizations. In R. Patti (Ed.), *The handbook of human services management* (pp. 143–164). Thousand Oaks, CA: Sage Publications.

Packard, T. (2010). Staff perceptions of variables affecting performance in human service organizations. *Nonprofit and Voluntary Sector Quarterly, 39,* 971–990.

Packard, T., Gibson, C., Finnegan, D., & Coloma, J. (2008, November). *Workplace outcomes of a leadership development initiative in human service organizations.* Philadelphia: Association for Research on Nonprofit Organizations and Voluntary Action Annual Conference.

Patti, R. (2009). Management in the human services: Purposes, practice, and prospects in the 21st century. In R. Patti (Ed.), *The handbook of human services management* (pp. 3–27). Thousand Oaks, CA: Sage Publications.

Pfeffer, J., & Sutton, R. (2006). *Hard facts, dangerous half-truths, and total nonsense: Profiting from evidence-based management.* Boston: Harvard Business School Press.

Poertner, J. (2009). Managing for service outcomes: The critical role of information. In R. Patti (Ed.), *The handbook of human services management* (pp. 165–182). Thousand Oaks, CA: Sage Publications.

Proehl, R. (2001). *Organizational change in the human services.* Thousand Oaks, CA: Sage Publications.

Ramsdell, P. (1994). Staff participation in organizational decision-making: An empirical study. *Administration in Social Work, 18,* 51–71.

Riggio, R. (2008). Leadership development: The current state and future expectations. *Consulting Psychology Journal: Practice and Research, 60,* 383–392.

Romero, E. (2005). The effect of Hispanic ethnicity on the leadership process. *International Journal of Leadership Studies, 1,* 86–101.

Schein, E. (2004). *Organizational culture and leadership* (3rd ed.). San Francisco: John Wiley & Sons.

Shera, W., & Page, J. (1995). Creating more effective human service organizations through strategies of empowerment. *Administration in Social Work, 19,* 1–15.

Smith, S. (2010). The political economy of contracting and competition. In Y. Hasenfeld (Ed.), *Human services as complex organizations* (2nd ed., pp. 139–160). Thousand Oaks, CA: Sage Publications.

Sowa, J., Selden, S., & Sandfort, J. (2004). No longer unmeasurable? A multidimensional integrated model of nonprofit organizational effectiveness. *Nonprofit and Voluntary Sector Quarterly,* 711–728.

Thomas, R. (2006). Diversity management: An essential craft for future leaders. In F. Hesselbein & M. Goldsmith (Eds.), *The leader of the future* (2nd ed., pp. 47–54). San Francisco: Jossey-Bass.

Trottier, T., Van Wart, M., & Wang, X. (2008). Examining the nature and significance of leadership in government organizations. *Public Administration Review, 68,* 319–333

Tucker, B., & Russell, R. (2004). The influence of the transformational leader. *Journal of Leadership and Organizational Studies, 10*(4), 103–111.

Van Velsor, E., McCauley, C. D., & Ruderman, M. N. (Eds.). (2010). *The Center for Creative Leadership handbook of leadership development* (3rd ed.). San Francisco: Jossey-Bass.

Van Wart, M. (2005). *Dynamics of leadership in public service: Theory and practice.* Armonk, NY: M.E. Sharpe.

Wamunya, W. (2003, March 10). Uncle Sam wants...workers; retirements to cause employee shortage. *Boston Herald,* p. 37.

Wilson, S. (2009). Proactively managing for outcomes in statutory child protection—The development of a management model. *Administration in Social Work, 33,* 136–150.

Yeager, J., & Saggase, M. (2008). Making your agency outcome informed: A guide to overcoming human resistance to change. *Families in Society, 89,* 9–19.

Yukl, G. A. (2010). *Leadership in organizations* (7th ed.). Upper Saddle River, NJ: Prentice-Hall.

Zenger, J., & Folkman, J. (2002). *The extraordinary leader.* New York: McGraw-Hill.

PART II

Outcomes Measurement in Health

CHAPTER 8

The Patient-centered Medical Home:
Implications for Behavioral Health and the Measurement of Integrated Care

John Bartlett

With the passage of the Patient Protection and Affordable Care (PPAC) Act into law in March 2010, a number of important and, frankly, sometimes competing changes have been set into motion for American health care. There is, however, one modification to the organization and delivery of health care codified in the PPAC Act that has been demonstrated empirically to produce both cost savings and improved results at the national level. This powerful intervention is the reestablishment of the primary care (PC) sector as the central and most important component of the overall health care delivery system, a situation that has come about because the American primary care system is, according to most knowledgeable commentators, "horribly broken—the victim of underinvestment, misaligned incentives, and malign neglect" (Dentzer, 2010, p. 757). This situation affects many of the very areas that the PPAC Act is designed to impact, including access, quality, and cost of care.

Evidence repeatedly shows that systems of care, including national systems, that are built around a strong PC focus produce better outcomes at lower cost than systems, such as the one found in the United States now, that are specialty care dominated. In fact, the lack of a robust PC focus within the American health care delivery system is cited as one of the major factors contributing to the nation's failure to produce both better health outcomes for its overall population and significant variations in outcomes across different subgroups (Phillips & Bazemore, 2010).

But how can health care built around a strong, lasting relationship with a PC provider be such a powerful intervention, one might legitimately ask. The evidence from multiple sources shows that when people have a long-lasting, trusting relationship with a health practitioner that is accessible, comprehensive, and coordinated across all aspects of their health care needs—in other words, with a PC provider irrespective of his/her discipline or specialty—that many good things come to pass. They access needed treatment earlier, have fewer visits to emergency rooms and hospital stays, and get fewer tests and procedures. They also have better health outcomes, including reduced mortality and improved quality of life (Phillips & Bazemore, 2010). They also receive more preventive services than those people who lack such a regular source of care and support (Dietrich & Goldberg, 1984). However, with a three-fold difference in income over a career between specialists and PC doctors, less than 10 percent of current American medical school graduates plan a career in PC, this at a time when, because of the impending aging of the baby boomers and the expansion of access to insurance under the PPAC Act, the need for PC practitioners will greatly increase (Bodenheimer & Pham, 2010).

The PPAC Act contains explicit language supporting investment in the reinvention of PC in numerous ways. These include additional funding in the form of increased Medicaid payments under both fee-for-service and managed care plans to PC physicians (specified in the legislation as family medicine, general internal medicine or pediatric providers); a 10 percent bonus payment to PC physicians in Medicare for five years beginning in Fiscal Year 2011; the increase in the number of graduate training positions through the redistribution of currently unused slots, primarily to PC and general surgery; and finally, training and financial support for innovative ways of organizing and delivering PC, such as the patient-centered medical home.

Importance of Integrating Primary Care and Behavioral Care: The Need to Build Bridges

But what, one might ask, does all this mean for those who work and/or receive care in the behavioral health care (BHC) sector? On an individual level, of course, it means that, if one is fortunate enough to have good health insurance coverage, one should try to establish and maintain a meaningful and lasting relationship with a PC provider. Having such a relationship will greatly increase our likelihood of living a long and healthy life. But for those individuals in society who live with a mental condition or an addiction, either acute or chronic, it has perhaps even greater significance for their health and well being.

Behavioral health conditions, including depression, anxiety, and substance abuse, among others, are widespread among the general population. Recent epidemiological estimates of the prevalence of these conditions in the U.S. population reveal that in any given year, 25 percent of the population will have a diagnosable mental illness or addiction (Kessler, Chiu, Demler, & Walters, 2005). Just as important, however, is that the level of unmet need for treatment remains very high. More than 50 percent of people never get any formal treatment, and on average, people struggling with depression go for almost 10 years before getting treatment. And, not surprisingly, this prevalence is reflected in the PC setting. In fact, studies show that about one in four individuals seen in PC has a comorbid behavioral condition that either accounts for that individual's seeking services or greatly complicates his or her medical presentation (Schulberg & Burns, 1988). More important is the fact that more than 50 percent of those people who receive treatment for depression get their care solely in the PC setting (Katon & Schulburg, 1992). The stakes, both in terms of cost and quality, of this fact have been greatly magnified by the passage of the Mental Health Parity and Addiction Equity Act of 2008 (MHPAEA), which prevents discriminatory application of behavioral health care benefits and therefore increases access to and affordability of appropriate treatment—if it can be made to happen

The need for addressing behavioral health conditions wherever treatment can be provided stems not only from their prevalence alone, but also from their impact. Depression alone affects more than 20 million U.S. children and adults every year and is the leading cause of disability in the U.S. and other developed nations for people ages 15 to 45 (World Health Organization, 2004). The direct and indirect cost of anxiety disorders in the U.S. each year amounts to an estimated 42 billion dollars (Greenberg et al., 1999). In addition, mental illnesses and addictions are highly comorbid with chronic medical illnesses and, when untreated, can lead to higher health care costs, worse outcomes, and even higher mortality rates (Katon & Ciechanowski, 2002). Studies show that patients with comorbid medical and mental health conditions die earlier than the general population. In fact, one study found that patients with heart disease and depression were twice as likely to die within 2 years of diagnosis as their peers suffering from heart disease alone (Lichtman et al., 2008).

One additional fact only further underscores the importance of the relationship between PC care and BHC. Recent data from a study supported by the National Association of State Mental Health Program Directors showed that individuals living with severe and persistent mental illnesses had vastly increased mortality rates compared with other people their age, dying on average some 25 years earlier (Colton & Manderschied, 2005). This shortened life span is due in large part to unhealthy life styles and poor access to treatment for medical problems such as heart disease, diabetes (often linked to psychotropic medications, such as the atypical antipsychotics), and respiratory conditions, as well as to such social determinants of health as the social isolation, poverty, and stress found in these individuals.

It is clear from this body of evidence that behavioral health problems and lifestyle choices play a significant role in the incidence, prevalence, and cost of care of a wide variety of conditions in both the PC and specialty settings. In fact, the data suggest that PC may well be the most important component in terms of volume of the overall mental health and addiction delivery system in the United States (Unützer, Schoenbaum, Druss, & Katon, 2006). Quite surprising to many BHC clinicians, the PC setting is the de facto frontline mental health delivery system. It is reasonable then to ask how well the PC sector does in the recognition and treatment of behavioral issues such as depression, anxiety, and substance abuse. Unfortunately, the evidence shows that, despite the existence of effective interventions, such as medications and practice guidelines, treatment for behavioral conditions within the PC setting produces little real clinical improvement in the vast majority of patients. In fact, only about 30 percent of patients treated for depression in PC show clinically significant improvement, meaning that despite targeted treatment, millions of patients in PC remain depressed (Williams et al., 2007) and tens, if not hundreds of millions of dollars are wasted on ineffective courses of treatment. And, although less research exists on the diagnosis and treatment of anxiety and substance abuse disorders, similar studies have shown significant gaps in the effectiveness of the treatment received by PC patients who have been accurately diagnosed with anxiety disorders (Stein et al., 2004).

On the basis of the above body of evidence, the case for the closer and more effective collaboration between the fields of PC, BHC, and even health promotion/disease prevention (HP/DP) is clear.

Evidence Base for Approaches to the Integration of PC and BHC

The case for just such closer functional integration of PC and BHC has been an identified public policy priority since the publication of the Surgeon General's Report on Mental Health in 1999 (U.S. Department of Health and Human Services, 1999). Since that time, a significant body of research has evolved that addresses the issue of effectively integrating BHC into PC. And the message from this evidence base is clear: It matters not only that integration is done, but also how it is done.

Through the implementation of large demonstration projects (Grypma, Haverkamp, Little, & Unützer, 2006; Oftedahl, Solberg, & Trangle, 2009) over the last decade, numerous studies exist on what elements make up the best field practices in integrated care, again largely focusing on the recognition and treatment of depression. A recently published meta-analysis has shown that "sufficient randomized evidence had emerged by 2000 to demonstrate the effectiveness of collaborative care beyond conventional levels of statistical significance" (Gilbody, Bower, Fletcher, Richards, & Sutton, 2006, p. 2320). What has, in fact, developed over time is this concept of collaborative care, in which PC providers, including physicians, nurses, mental health clinicians, and care management specialists, work in a team-based approach with patients to recognize and treat depression and anxiety. The roles and responsibilities for the various team members are well defined and stratified according to case severity. This model has proven to represent both a cost-effective and a patient-centered approach to integration. In this approach, many patients are managed successfully without direct contact with a mental health specialist; all are followed closely by a designated case manager, who may be a professional, such as a nurse or a social worker or even a nonprofessional, such as a peer specialist with appropriate training; and only those patients who have very complex presentations (for example, medical conditions that complicate pharmacotherapy with antidepressant medications) are seen face-to face by a psychiatrist.

In these collaborative care models, patients are closely monitored; treatment outcomes are tracked with evidence-based rating scales, such as the nine-item depression scale of the Personal Health Questionnaire (the PHQ-9); and both patient and provider adherence to treatment recommendations are supported through the active care management function. Treatments are systematically adjusted for patients who do not improve as expected, using evidence-based medication guidelines and/or the addition of psychotherapy. Such collaborative care programs can double or even triple the effectiveness of usual care for depression (Gilbody et al., 2006). Moreover, collaborative care models have proven to be as effective for those patients who suffer a comorbid condition as for those who do not (Felker & Chaney, 2006; Katon, Roy-Byrne, Russo, & Cowley, 2002).

A critical component of this kind of effective depression care that has evolved over the past decade has been the concept of *measurement-based practice*, in which physicians carefully follow outcomes and adjust treatments as needed. This emerged as a crucial element in the largest depression treatment trial conducted to date, the Star-D trial (Trivedi & Daly, 2007). Measurement-based practice, combined with the adaptation and modification of clinical interventions based on the ongoing measurement of the patient's response to treatment ("stepped care," which begins with less aggressive interventions and increases in intensity if the patient fails to respond adequately), has also proven to produce effective outcomes at lower cost (Unützer et al., 2006). These practices rely on systematic and consistent care, which is rare in the contemporary PC setting because of a number of factors, including fragmentation, lack of time, and lack of provider knowledge. These factors can be remedied under a collaborative approach, in which staff are trained to monitor patients and physicians work in teams with mental health specialists and care managers.

Implementation Status of Evidence-based Approaches to Integrated Care

The evidence base for an approach to integrated care clearly exists. Yet, during a conference cosponsored by the National Center for Primary Care at the Morehouse School of Medicine and the Carter Center Primary Care Initiative in November 2008 titled "Making It Real: Integrating Primary Care and Behavioral Health in Community-Based Settings," it was estimated that well less than 10 percent of PC patients have access to this type of "best practice" collaborative care. This striking gap between knowledge and practice, and the associated waste and suffering, call for clear and decisive action.

Is it possible, then, with the passage of health care reform legislation, with its emphasis on reinvestment and reinvention in PC, to expect that in the near future evidence-based approaches to integrated care will become more widespread? One hopeful note is that, at the same time that best practices for integrated care have become more clearly defined, a conceptual model for the reinvention of and reinvestment in PC has emerged. This model for PC reform is the patient-centered medical home (PCMH). The PCMH has been embraced by 17 specialty societies, most Fortune 500 companies, all of the leading national health plans, the Veterans Administration, and many consumer groups (Rittenhouse & Shortell, 2010). The concept of the PCMH, initially introduced by the American Academy of Pediatrics in 1967 and expanded on in 2002, is built around providing comprehensive, cost-effective, and patient-oriented PC (Kellerman & Kirke, 2007). It describes a model of practice redesign centered on four overarching themes: PC, patient centeredness, new-model practice, and payment reform (Rittenhouse & Shortell, 2010). Through these cornerstones, the PCMH addresses the gaps in the current health care delivery system, shifting its focus from highly specialized, fee-for-service, illness-oriented care to primary, patient-oriented, and preventative care.

In 2007, members of the American Academy of Family Physicians, the American Academy of Pediatrics, the American College of Physicians, and the American Osteopathic Association (totaling approximately 333,000 physicians) agreed on a set of joint principles for the PCMH with the goal of further defining the model (Kellerman & Kirke, 2007). One major principle put forth defines the role of the personal physician in the PCMH as the first contact for care, working closely and comprehensively with the patient. The primary physician directs a team that assumes collective responsibility for the patient, who, as the name of the model suggests, forms the focus around which care is oriented. The team must attend to the health of the whole patient in consultation with appropriate specialists as needed, addressing all aspects of health: chronic, acute, behavioral, and preventative (Kellerman & Kirke, 2007).

In keeping with one of the major goals of the Institute of Medicine's (IOM) seminal work, *Crossing the Quality Chasm,* in this model the patient is central, not merely a passive agent around whom health is coordinated, but rather an active participant in treatment planning, monitoring, and even feedback to improve the practice itself. Information technology, especially the electronic medical record, plays a fundamental role in decision support for both the patient and the treatment team and in the ongoing assessment of quality by tracking patient and practice health outcomes through online databases.

Payment reform represents one of the more critical and challenging principles of the PCMH. Without altering incentives, moving from a fee-for-service model to one that takes into account quality and consumer satisfaction, integrating care will fail to be an attractive option for providers. Recommendations, as outlined by the joint principles, include compensating the work of staff outside of the patient's visit and allowing physicians to benefit from savings brought about by reduced hospitalization and effective preventive care, thereby incentivizing quality outcomes (Kellerman & Kirke, 2007). Although smaller institutions may lack the resources to revise care systems on the basis of the principles outlined for the PCMH, studies show that savings can be expected from the decreases in hospitalizations, serious procedures, and emergency care that are associated with this model (Shi et al., 2003). A further challenge linked to payment reform is that of reduced human capital in PC caused by the lack of reimbursement when compared with other, more specialized practice areas (Cronenwett & Dzau, 2010).

In 2009 alone, there were 22 pilot projects involving the PCMH, allowing for some assessment of its efficacy (Cronenwett & Dzau, 2010). One recent study of a PCMH pilot project implementation, from Group Health Cooperative, examines patient experiences, quality, burnout of clinicians, and total costs up to 2 years after implementation. The results show improvements in patient experiences, quality, and clinician burnout and satisfaction. Moreover, compared with other Group Health clinics, patients in the PCMH experienced 29 percent fewer emergency visits and 6 percent fewer hospitalizations (Reid et al., 2010). In addition to pilot projects, in 2009, 20 bills addressing this concept across 10 states had been put forth (Rittenhouse & Shortell, 2010).

Thus, there appears to be a consensus developing around the best approaches to the integration of PC and BHC and the ascendancy of a strong model for the reinvention of PC, one that defines the PC setting as both the first point of contact and the coordinating focus for all patient care, including BHC and HP/DP activities. The question remains, however, whether the PCMH will be able to deliver on this promise. The Carter Center Mental Health Program, through its Primary Care Initiative, brought together a group of thought leaders in the summer of 2009 from the three fields (PC, BHC, and HP/DP). Out of that summit meeting, a number of recommendations to support the scaling up of evidence-based approaches to integrated care arose (The Carter Center Mental Health Program, 2009), which were subsequently prioritized and are in the process of being implemented. For many professionals, however, effective collaboration in the PC environment will require different skills and techniques than those normally used in the clinical practice of their behavioral health specialty.

There is reciprocal interest and activity in the development of PCMHs in the specialty behavioral health care sector for persons living with serious mental illness. The need for closer integration of PC into the specialty behavioral care sector is clear from the elevated cohort mortality rates for these individuals (Colton & Manderschied, 2005). The National Council for Community Behavioral Healthcare has advanced a four-quadrant model that, at a conceptual level, determines the best site for any given individual's medical home on the basis of the severity of his or her medical and behavioral issues. What is lacking to date are the "rules of engagement" that would allow this concept to be operationalized in clinical practice; the Carter Center Mental

Health Program is in discussions with both representatives of PC and BHC to initiate a process to define these rules. As to the design of the PCMHs located in the specialty behavioral sector, significantly fewer studies have been performed around best practices for addressing PC needs in the specialty mental health setting. However, the evidence base to date supports the importance of managing care and reducing fragmentation (Druss et al., 2010).

Implications for Performance Measurement

The challenges associated with the implementation of evidence-based approaches to the integration of BHC, HP/DP, and PC are numerous. They include several topics that are also covered in other chapters of this book, such as differences in culture between the various sectors, different operational workflows, lack of capital and manpower to support the implementation, and a historical schism between the various sectors, among others. It is precisely because of these challenges, however, that monitoring the adoption of these approaches and, more important, their effect on clinical, administrative, and financial outcomes, is so crucial. Although the measurement of outcomes might well be the ultimate desired goal for such monitoring efforts on the part of policymakers and others, experience has shown that the sound measurement of true clinical outcomes is difficult in the clinical practice environment. Its requirements for data that measure important components of health status both pre- and postintervention, as well as for case-mix adjustment (that is, the stratification of individuals by level of risk or severity) are difficult to operationalize in busy clinical organizations. Therefore, efforts at performance measurement should weigh both the importance and the feasibility of actually collecting good data quite heavily in selecting potential measures. The goal is to design and implement measures that rigorously monitor processes of care (for example, the rate or penetration of a particular evidence-based intervention) that are in turn linked to good outcomes by the research base (McLellan et al., 2007).

Structural approaches to the determination of performance, such as accreditation or licensing standards, which look at the presence or absence of certain defined characteristics or attributes of a health care provider or entity, can be useful supplements to the establishment of process-based performance metrics. With regard to the PCMH, the National Committee for Quality Assurance (NCQA) promulgated a set of accreditation standards in early 2008. In their initial form, they looked at 10 important aspects of the structure, organization, and clinical functions of PC practices consistent with the 2007 Joint Principles of the PCMH (American Academy of Family Physicians, American Academy of Pediatrics, American College of Physicians, &

American Osteopathic Association, 2007). These areas included such functions as patient tracking and registry, electronic prescribing, and care management, among others. The standards have the potential for considerable impact in the clinical practice environment, especially in the context of the numerous demonstration projects, both public and private, that are beginning around the country after the passage of the PPAC Act.

Despite such beginning foundations, the original set of PCMH standards promulgated by NCQA in January 2008 made no explicit mention of either BHC or HP/DP activities. Therefore, in one of the major tools defining the functional characteristics of the PCMH, there was no acknowledgment of the importance of BHC issues to the PC setting and no reference to the functions and/or the interventions that have been shown to yield greatly improved clinical outcomes in the treatment of depression and substance use in the PC setting. It was for this reason that one of the major initiatives arising from the Carter Center Medical Home Summit in July 2009 was an effort to have these standards adapted to better reflect both the importance and the realities of integrated care within the context of the PCMH. Fortunately, in December 2009, NCQA announced the formation of an advisory group to "evolve" the PCMH standards. The resulting draft standards, which were made available for public review in late May 2010, do show considerable progress in better reflecting the importance of integrated care, in that they include numerous explicit references and requirements addressing both BHC and HP/DP activities. However, in their draft form as of July 2010, they do not adequately reflect the findings from the evidence base about what kind of interventions are effective in integrated care. The concern here is that, without specific reference to these interventions, such as measured care and stepped care (see above), outdated interventions such as colocation might be adequate to meet the standards, but ultimately prove ineffective in clinical practice.

The evolved PCMH standards also reflect the fact that approaches to the reinvention of PC, specifically the PCMH, have both internal and external needs for measuring their performance in a variety of domains, both financial and nonfinancial. The external requirements clearly center on the need for innovations such as the PCMH to demonstrate their superiority (both clinical and financial) over traditional approaches to the organization and delivery of PC; the internal needs, reflected in the NCQA standards, support ongoing organizational efforts at quality improvement. There are in the standards specific structural and functional requirements that support the establishment of a quality improvement culture within the PC practice, one that collects and analyzes data about a variety of its functions in order to identify opportunities for improvement. Therefore, although standards themselves are not part of any performance measurement initiative, because they define structures and processes rather than measure them, they can be used to help establish the infrastructure and organizational culture that support performance measurement.

With the support of these kinds of structural and process standards, it will prove easier in the future to measure the impact and performance of the PCMH. The key question remains, however, "What exactly do we measure?" Traditional approaches to the measurement of the impact of the PCMH have looked at measures of utilization such as reduced numbers of hospitalizations and emergency room visits. They have also attempted to measure reductions in total cost per patient for those individuals enrolled in a PCMH. Of increasing interest are measures that look at the experiences in the PCMH environment of both the patient and the provider; early results have shown increases in satisfaction for both (Reid et al., 2010). However, there still remains widespread concern about the current ability to measure all the important components of quality improvements associated with the PCMH (Holmboe, Arnold, Weng, & Lipner, 2010). And when it comes to the measurement of the impact of integrated approaches to the delivery of BHC in the PC setting, traditional metrics have largely focused on the reduction in symptoms, especially in the treatment of depression or the reduction of high-risk behaviors such as smoking.

An optimal strategy for answering some of the questions raised at the beginning of this section, one which balances the tension between importance and feasibility in the clinical practice environment, would be to develop process metrics that evaluate the interventions linked to better outcomes by the evidence base, such as the use of valid, reliable tools to monitor response to treatment for depression (Löwe, Kroenke, Herzog, & Gräfe, 2004), or tracking the process of stepped interventions in response to nonimprovement. Measurement of the use of the PHQ-9 to follow response to treatment in depressed patients would require two relatively simple things: a registry of all patients with depression and a data element, such as a specific procedure code, recording the administration of the instrument. These two alone would allow for the development of a relatively simple metric showing the number of depressed patients who had taken the PHQ-9 (the numerator) in relation to the total number of depressed patients in the practice from the registry (the denominator).

With the additional ability to record actual PHQ-9 scores for individual patients over time (that is, with a history file of scores by date), true clinical outcomes for depression treatment could be followed. And finally, with the implementation of an electronic health record with the appropriate scalar and narrative data elements, the ability to monitor stepped responses to nonimprovement in PHQ-9 scores in individual patients could also be tracked, by linking the response of the provider (for example, a change in antidepressant dosage, a change of medication, the addition or substitution of an evidence-based psychotherapy, and so forth) to patient outcomes. This capability is important because the evaluation of how an innovation such as the PCMH is functioning requires not only the measurement of how many people get the appropriate intervention, but also some understanding of the quality of that intervention.

The widespread use in PC of similar brief, valid, and reliable tools to follow treatment response in anxiety and substance abuse would greatly expand the ability to monitor the scope and impact of integrated care (please see chapter 15, by Corcoran and Hozack, in this volume). The ideal would be the development of a brief (for example, eight to 10 question) tool that would screen for all highly prevalent behavioral health conditions such as anxiety, depression, substance abuse, and trauma, and then monitor treatment response for the identified condition, perhaps through a condition-specific but slightly expanded tool. In addition, if clinicians could track the medical costs of patients with both a medical illness and a comorbid behavioral health condition, they could begin to measure the direct cost savings associated with the improvement in clinical outcomes brought about by evidence-based approaches to integrated care. Linkage to nonmedical cost databases, such as those tracking disability and absenteeism expenditures, would potentially allow for the tracking of indirect cost savings as well.

Through all of these efforts to monitor the performance of both the PCMH and an evidence-based integrated care component within it, however, providers should always keep in mind the reasons for the reinvention of both PC and its relationship to BHC. The goals of these efforts are to address in a substantive manner the issues of poor access, high cost, and poor outcomes that the current American health system (or, rather, "nonsystem") produces year after year. Therefore, as the PC sector is strengthened through reinvestment and improved through reengineering, the ultimate measure of the success of these efforts will be changes in macro-level measures such as per capita annual expenditures and population health statistics such as reduced burdens of disease. Burden of disease is a time-based measure that combines years of life lost as a result of premature mortality and years of life lost as a result of time lived in states of less than full health. Currently, according to the World Health Organization, depression accounts for the greatest burden of disease in high-income places such as the United States and Europe; alcohol abuse accounts for the fifth highest burden.

Ultimately, therefore, as innovative approaches to PC such as the PCMH; associated evidence-based interventions in integrated care such as measured care, stepped care, and case management; and HP/DP activities are implemented widely, the key metrics of success will begin to focus on the overall health status of the PC caseload of patients and be viewed in a broader public health context. As our reinvented and reengineered PC organizations aggregate into truly accountable health care organizations, with their wider range of services and broader geographic reach within communities, the focus of measurement will shift to the health status of broader populations (within Standard Metropolitan Statistical Areas, for example, or even within states). It will be through the measurement of performance—cost, quality and patient experience—at the population level that the real value of a reinvigorated PC sector, and our overall health care system—one which pays full attention to the reduction of risk and the recognition and treatment of BHC conditions—will be ultimately recognized.

References

American Academy of Family Physicians, American Academy of Pediatrics, American College of Physicians, & American Osteopathic Association. (2007). *Joint principles of the patient centered medical home.* Retrieved from http://www.pcpcc.net/content/joint-principles-patient-centered-medical-home

Bodenheimer, T., & Pham, H. H. (2010). Primary care: Current problems and proposed solutions. *Health Affairs, 29,* 799–805.

The Carter Center Mental Health Program, Primary Care Initiative. (2009). *Carter Center's Medical Home Summit: Proceedings.* Retrieved from http://www.cartercenter.org/resources/pdfs/health/mental_health/Proceedings-MedicalHomeSummit-DCapproved.pdf

Colton, C. W., & Manderschied, R. W. (2005). Congruencies in increased mortality rates, years of potential life lost, and causes of death among public mental health clients in eight states. *Preventing Chronic Disease, 3,* 37–47.

Cronenwett, L., & Dzau, V. (2010). *Who will provide primary care and how will they be trained?* Presented at the Josiah Macy, Jr. Foundation Conference, Durham, NC.

Dentzer, S. (2010). Reinventing primary care: A task that is far too important to fail. *Health Affairs, 29,* 757.

Dietrich, A. J., & Goldberg, H. (1984). Preventive content of adult primary care: Do generalists and sub-specialists differ? *American Journal of Public Health, 74,* 223–227.

Druss B. G., von Esenwein, S. A., Compton, M. T., Rask, K. J., Zhao, L., & Parker, R. M. (2010). A randomized trial of medical care management for community mental health settings: The primary care access, referral, and evaluation (PCARE) study. *American Journal of Psychiatry, 167*, 151–159.

Felker, B., & Chaney, E. (2006). Developing effective collaboration between primary care and mental health providers. *Journal of Clinical Psychiatry, 8*(1), 12–16.

Gilbody, S., Bower, P., Fletcher, J., Richards, D., & Sutton, A. J. (2006). Collaborative care for depression: A cumulative meta-analysis and review of longer term outcomes. *Archives of Internal Medicine, 166*, 2314–2321.

Greenberg, P. E., Sisitsky, T., Kessler, R. C., Finkelstein, S. N., Berndt, E. R., Davidson, J. R., et al. (1999). The economic burden of anxiety disorders in the 1990s. *Journal of Clinical Psychiatry, 60*, 427–435.

Grypma, L., Haverkamp, R., Little, S., & Unützer, J. (2006). Taking an evidence-based model of depression care from research to practice: Making lemonade out of depression. *General Hospital Psychiatry, 28*, 101–107.

Holmboe, E. S., Arnold, G. K., Weng, W., & Lipner, R. (2010) Current yardsticks may be inadequate for measuring quality improvements from the medical home, *Health Affairs, 29*, 859–866.

Katon, W., & Ciechanowski, P. (2002). Impact of major depression on chronic medical illness. *Journal of Psychosomatic Research, 53*, 859–863.

Katon, W. J., Roy-Byrne P., Russo J., & Cowley, D. (2002). Cost-effectiveness and cost offset of a collaborative care intervention for primary care patients with panic disorder. *Archives of General Psychiatry, 59,* 1098–1104.

Katon, W., & Schulberg, H. (1992). Epidemiology of depression in primary care. *General Hospital Psychiatry, 14,* 237–247.

Kellerman, R., & Kirke, L. (2007). Principles of the patient-centered medical home. *American Family Physician, 15,* 774–775.

Kessler, R. C., Chiu, W. T., Demler, O., & Walters, E. E. (2005). Prevalence, severity, and co-morbidity of twelve-month DSM–IV disorders in the National Co-morbidity Survey Replication (NCS-R). *Archives of General Psychiatry, 62,* 617–627.

Lichtman, J. H., Bigger, J. T., Jr., Blumenthal, J. A., Frasure-Smith, N., Kaufmann, P. G., Lespérance, F., et al. (2008). Depression and coronary heart disease; recommendations for screening, referral, and treatment. A science advisory from the American Heart Association Prevention Committee of the Council on Cardiovascular Nursing, Council on Clinical Cardiology, Council on Epidemiology and Prevention and Interdisciplinary Council on Quality of Care and Outcomes Research. *Journal of the American Heart Association.* doi:10.1161/CIRCULATIONAHA.108.190769

Löwe, B., Kroenke, K., Herzog, W., & Gräfe, K. (2004). Measuring depression outcome with a brief self-report instrument: Sensitivity to change of the Patient Health Questionnaire (PHQ-9). *Journal of Affective Disorders, 81,* 61–66.

McLellan, A. T., Chalk, M., & Bartlett, J. (2007). Outcomes, performance, and quality—What's the difference? *Journal of Substance Abuse Treatment, 32,* 331–340.

Oftedahl, G., Solberg, L., & Trangle, M. (2009). *DIAMOND initiative: Depression improvement across Minnesota offering a new direction* [PowerPoint slides]. Retrieved from www.icsi.org/colloquium_-_2007/diamond_panel.html

Phillips, R. L., & Bazemore, A. W. (2010). Primary care and why it matters for US health system reform. *Health Affairs, 29,* 806–810.

Reid, R. D., Coleman, K., Johnson, E. A., Fishman, P. A., Hsu, C., Soman, M. P., et al. (2010). The Group Health medical home at year two: Cost savings, higher patient satisfaction, and less burnout for providers. *Health Affairs, 29,* 835–843.

Rittenhouse, D. R., & Shortell, S. M. (2010). The patient-centered medical home: Will it stand the test of health reform? *JAMA, 301,* 2038–2040.

Schulberg, H. C., & Burns, B. J. (1988). Mental disorders in primary care: Epidemiologic, diagnostic, and treatment research directions. *General Hospital Psychiatry, 10,* 79–87.

Shi, L., Macinko, J., Starfield, B., Wulu, J., Regan, J., & Politzer, R. (2003). The relationship between primary care, income inequality, and mortality in US states, 1980–1995. *Journal of the American Board of Family Medicine, 16,* 412–422.

Stein, M. B., Sherbourne, C. D., Craske, M. G., Means-Christenson, A., Bystritsky, A., & Roy-Byrne, P. P. (2004). Quality of care for primary care patients with anxiety disorders. *American Journal of Psychiatry, 161,* 2230–2237.

Trivedi, M. H., & Daly, E. J. (2007). Measurement-based care for refractory depression: A clinical decision support model for clinical research and practice. *Drug and Alcohol Dependence, 88*(Suppl. 2), S61–S71.

Unützer, J., Schoenbaum, M., Druss, B. J., & Katon, W. J. (2006). Transforming mental health care at the interface with general medicine: Report for the President's Commission. *Psychiatric Services, 57,* 37–47.

U.S. Department of Health and Human Services, Substance Abuse and Mental Health Services Administration. (1999). *Mental health: A report of the Surgeon General.* Retrieved from http://www.surgeongeneral.gov/library/mentalhealth/home.html

Williams J., Gerrity M., Holsinger T., Dobscha S., Gaynes B., & Dietrich A. (2007) Systematic review of multifaceted interventions to improve depression care. *General Hospital Psychiatry, 29,* 91–116.

World Health Organization. (2004). *The world health report: Changing history.* Geneva: Author.

CHAPTER 9

Health and Quality-of-Life Outcomes:
The Role of Patient-reported Measures

Dasha Cherepanov and Ron D. Hays

This chapter discusses key issues in the use of patient-reported outcome (PRO) measures, with special emphasis on health-related quality of life (HRQoL) and patient evaluations of care, as well as their applications for population surveillance, research, and clinical practice. A discussion of patient evaluation of care measures from the Consumer Assessment of Healthcare Providers and Systems (CAHPS) program is then presented as an example. We conclude with comments on the future of PRO measures and long-term implications for achieving positive health outcomes in the United States and globally.

PRO AND HRQoL MEASURES

PROs

The U.S. Food and Drug Administration (FDA, 2009) refers to PROs as "any report of the status of a patient's health condition that comes directly from the patient, without interpretation of the patient's response by a clinician or anyone else" (p. 2). PRO measures encompass a broad range of dimensions, including symptoms (for example, pain, fatigue, energy); functioning and well-being in physical, mental, and social domains of life (that is, HRQoL); health behaviors (for example, adherence to medicines, tobacco use, participation in exercise programs); patients' preferences for different types of care and their desire to participate (or not to participate) in care; and evaluation of their care that can include reports about patient–clinician communication, coordination of care, and access to care. This chapter focuses on PROs that encompass HRQoL and patient evaluations of care.

Since the publication of the first edition of *Outcomes Measurement in the Human Services* in 1997, PROs have been increasingly used in clinical and research settings, and many more measures have been developed. In clinical settings, these measures are used to evaluate and screen patients and to aid in medical decision making. In research, they are often used to study group-level comparisons of health and care. PROs are important in tracking the health of populations and establishing national norms. Importantly, these measures are now commonly included in clinical trials and are essential to economic and policy analysis (for example, cost-effectiveness analysis). Many new disease-targeted measures have been developed (for example, Hays et al., 2003; Khanna et al., 2007), and existing measures that focus on PROs have been refined, translated, and evaluated in different languages (for example, Bullinger, 1998; Ware et al., 1998). These significant contributions to the development, delivery, and study of PRO measures have led to various publications (for example, Fryback, Palta, Cherepanov, Bolt, & Kim, 2010; Hays et al., 1989, 2009; see also http://www.rand.org) examining relationships among measures, mode effects, readability, minimally important differences, responsiveness and measurement error, reliability and validity, population norms, and health condition disutilities for cost-effectiveness analyses.

The rapid development of PROs has motivated the creation of three major databases: (1) Patient-Reported Outcome and Quality of Life Instrument Database (proqolid.org) currently has descriptions of approximately 700 PRO measures. This database library aims to identify and describe PRO measures to aid researchers and users in accessing the appropriate measure(s) for their goal of study or application; (2) Patient-Reported Outcomes Measurement Information System (PROMIS; see http://www.nihpromise.org) was created to establish a national resource for accurate and efficient measurement of patient-reported symptoms and other health outcomes in clinical practice and research (Cella et al., 2007); and (3) Consumer Assessment of Healthcare Providers and Systems (CAHPS; see http://www.cahps.ahrq.gov), commonly used for various purposes by researchers, patients/consumers, quality monitors/regulators, purchasers, provider organizations, and health plans.

HRQoL Measures

HRQoL refers to how health affects an individual's ability to function and his or her perceived well-being in physical, mental, and social domains of life. The functioning part of HRQoL includes basic activities of self-care (for example, bathing and dressing), work-related activities (for example, housework and career), and social functioning or the extent to which one is able to interact with family and friends. Measuring functioning is thought to be a relatively objective activity because self-report of information can be compared with other sources of data such as observations or performance measures. Measuring well-being is more of a subjective activity because a respondent is most often the exclusive source of information about his or her well-being (for example, type of pain, level of energy). Comprehensive HRQoL measures try to assess all domains of life that are deemed important for health.

There are two types of HRQoL measures: generic and disease targeted. Generic measures are designed to be applicable to anyone, assess multiple aspects of HRQoL (for example, physical functioning, mental health), and yield person scores that can be compared with one another if produced from the same questionnaire. Generic HRQoL measures can be further subdivided into profile measures and preference-based summary measures: Profile measures yield separate scores on multiple aspects of HRQoL, whereas preference-based measures yield a single score that summarizes multiple domains of HRQoL. Disease-targeted measures are designed for a population with a particular condition and assess health-related aspects of that condition. Selected generic and disease-targeted measures are summarized in Tables 9-1 and 9-2 on pages 132 and 133 (for more detail, see Coons et al., 2000; Fryback et al., 2007).

HRQoL measures can be used to achieve a range of goals at the individual, organizational, community, and system levels. Clinicians often use HRQoL measures to screen patients' health status (for example, Table 9-1, Dartmouth COOP charts) in daily clinical settings to monitor progression or onset of a disease and improve patient–provider communication (McDowell & Newell, 1996). Disease-targeted measures are important for clinical research. Although these measures are primarily used in research rather than in clinical settings, one result of clinical research findings is their translation into clinical practice to aid in decision making at the patient-provider level. Generic profile HRQoL measures (for example, Table 9-1, CDC HRQoL14, SF-36) are critical in tracking population health in national surveys, evaluating health disparities, and comparing burden of disease across different subgroups of the population, as well as differentiating the effectiveness of health care treatments

Table 9-1: Domain Content of Selected Generic (Profile- and Preference-based) Measures

Generic Profile Measures				
SF-36 Health Survey	NHP	SIP	Dartmouth COOP Charts	CDC HRQOL-14
Physical functioning	Physical mobility	Physical dimension:	Physical fitness	Healthy days
Role limitation due to physical problems	Energy level	Ambulation	Daily activities	Physically unhealthy days
Bodily pain	Pain	Mobility	Social activities	Mentally unhealthy days
Vitality	Sleep	Body care and movement	Quality of life	Activity limitation
Social functioning	Social isolation	Psychology dimension:	Overall health	Pain
Role limitations due to emotional problems	Emotional reactions	Communication	Change in health	Sad/blue/depressed
Mental health		Alertness behavior	Pain	Anxious
Health transition		Emotional behavior	Feelings	Sleepless
General health perceptions		Social interation	Social support	Full of energy
		Independent categories:		
		Sleep and rest		
		Eating		
		Work		
		Home management		
		Recreation and pastimes		

Generic Preference-based Measures of Summary HRQoL				
QWB	HUI2	HUI3	EQ-5D	SF-6D
Physical activity	Mobility	Ambulation	Mobility	Physical functioning
Self-care/mobility	Emotion	Emotion	Anxiety/depression	Mental health
Self-care/usual activities	Cognition	Cognition	Pain/discomfort	Bodily pain
Acute and chronic symptoms	Pain	Pain	Self-care	Role limitation
	Self-care	Vision	Usual activities	Social functioning
	Sensation	Hearing		Vitality
		Speech		
		Dexterity		

Note: SF = Short Form; NHP = Nottingham Health Profile; SIP = Sickness Impact Profile; COOP = Primary Care Cooperative Information Project; CDC = Center for Disease Control and Prevention; HRQoL = health-related quality of Life; QWB = Quality of Well-Being Scale; HUI = Health Utilities Index; EQ = EuroQol..

Table 9-2: Domain Content of Selected Disease-targeted Measures

Disease-targeted Measures			
KDQOL	**NEI-VFQ-25**	**NEI-RQL**	**SSC-GIT 1.0**
Symptom/problems	General health	Clarity of vision	Reflux/indigestion
Effects of kidney disease on daily life	General vision	Expectations	Diarrhea
Burden of kidney disease	Ocular pain	Near vision	Constipation
Work Status	Near activities	Far vision	Pain
Cognitive function	Distance activities	Diurnal fluctuations	Emotional well-being
Quality of social interaction	Driving	Activity limitations	Social functioning
Sexual function	Color vision	Glare	
Sleep	Peripheral vision	Symptoms	
Social support	Vision specific	Dependence on correction	
Dialysis staff encouragement	Social function	Worry	
Patient satisfaction	Mental health	Suboptimal correction	
Eight SF-36 scales	Role difficulties	Appearance	
Overall health rating	Dependency expectations	Satisfaction with correction	

Note: KDQOL = Kidney Disease Quality of Life; NEI-RQL = National Eye Institute Refractive Error Quality of Life; NEI-VFQ = National Eye Institute Visual Functioning Questionnaire; SSC-GIT = Scleroderma Gastrointestinal Tract.

on health and well-being (Centers for Disease Control and Prevention [CDC], 2000; http://www.sf-36.org). Generic preference-based measures of HRQoL (for example, Table 9-1, SF-6D) are especially important for cost-effectiveness analysis and regulatory analyses (Miller, Robinson, & Lawrence, 2006) used to judge cost acceptability of new interventions.

Although all HRQoL measures profile a wealth of information over multiple domains, it can be difficult to determine effects of an intervention and/ or to make an overall conclusion about HRQoL because some HRQoL scales may show improvement and others may not. In research, attrition of subjects as a result of mortality poses a unique problem for profile measures because results can be biased if those who die are dropped from the analysis. Although some proposals for imputing HRQoL scores for deceased patients have been made (for example, Diehr et al., 1995), generic preference-based summary measures of HRQoL provide an explicit basis for incorporating deceased patients in summarizing different aspects of HRQoL into a single score.

Preference-based summary measures of HRQoL are designed to integrate across domains of health to produce a single summary score for each health state. The summary score is anchored relative to "dead" (score of 0) and "perfect" or "full" health (score of 1) by means of weighted preference-based scoring algorithms, specific to each measure, developed by valuation techniques that represent community- or population-based preferences for health states. Table 9-1 shows the most widely used preference-based measures: the Quality of Well-Being Scale (QWB), the Health Utilities Index Mark 2 (HUI2) and Mark 3 (HUI3), the EuroQol–5D (EQ-5D), and the Short Form–6D (SF-6D; for more detail, see Coons et al., 2000; Fryback et al., 2007).

The QWB assesses health across four domains (Physical Activity, Self-Care/Mobility, Self-Care/Usual Activities, Acute and Chronic Symptoms) over the past 3 days. The HUI2 and HUI3 define health status on the basis of ability in six domains (Mobility, Emotion, Cognition, Pain, Self-Care, and Sensation) and disability in eight domains (Ambulation, Emotion, Cognition, Pain, Vision, Hearing, Speech, and Dexterity) over the past week, and are scored from the same 40-item questionnaire. The five EQ-5D questions refer to "your health today" and define health on the basis of five domains (Mobility, Anxiety/Depression, Pain/Discomfort, Self-Care, and Usual Activities). Both EQ-5D and QWB also have a visual analogue scale rating of overall health ranging from 0 to 100.

A British research group developed the SF-6D (Brazier, Roberts, & Deverill, 2002) using 11 SF-36 items and seven SF-12 items (sf-36.org) to summarize health on the basis of six domains: Physical Functioning, Mental Health, Bodily Pain, Role Limitations, Social Functioning, and Vitality. This preference-based version of the SF-36 is being increasingly used in research studies. For example, Kaplan et al. (2011) administered the five preference-based measures (Table 9-1) to a sample of cataract patients before and after surgery and found statistically significant improvements in HRQoL 1 month after surgery for all indexes except the SF-6D. The mean differences in HRQoL ranged from 0.00 (for the SF-6D) to 0.06 (for the HUI3). Considering the minimally clinically important difference for generic preference-based measures—accepted as 0.03 (Kaplan, 2005)—these findings indicate the possibility of substantial variation in scores produced by different preference-based measures despite being anchored on a common theoretical metric. This highlights the need for further work to document and explain these differences to improve validity and comparability of HRQoL measures.

Depending on which measure is selected, different conclusions about the change in HRQoL might be reached. Hence, regardless of use in clinical practice or research, there are factors one should consider when choosing

HRQoL measures, such as study objective, population of interest, length of the questionnaire, and the measure's susceptibility to ceiling effects and varying sensitivity to different aspects of health. For example, the QWB is the only preference-based measure with a long list of self-reported symptoms, whereas the HUIs have unique domains of sensation. The QWB and EQ-5D are the only measures with U.S.-derived preference-based scoring functions. It is recommended that HRQoL scores from different preference-based indexes not be mixed in the same cost-effectiveness analysis. Comparisons of the different HRQoL scores within the same population should be done with consideration of the HRQoL measure-specific construction and health-related structure. Comparison of studies should be limited to those that have the same mode of administration (for example, telephone surveys tend to lead to more positive HRQoL estimates than self-administered surveys; Hays et al., 2009), and measures should be chosen by carefully weighing their pros and cons.

Disease-targeted measures, compared with generic measures, have the potential to be more sensitive to smaller differences and changes over time in HRQoL because they are selected to be relevant to a given condition. In a study that examined men treated for localized prostate cancer, there were no differences in the SF-36 scores between those treated with surgery, radiation, or watchful waiting and an age- and zip-code matched control group (Litwin et al., 1995). However, disease-targeted measures that assessed function and distress in three organ systems (sexual, urinary, and bowel) revealed worse HRQoL among the treatment groups (that is, radiation, surgery). In another study, among 598 persons with chronic eye diseases, the National Eye Institute Visual Functioning Questionnaire scales were found to have low correlations with the SF-36 scales (Mangione et al., 1998). Although the SF-36 was not associated with self-rated severity of gastrointestinal tract involvement, disease-targeted scales in the Scleroderma Gastrointestinal Tract 1.0 survey were sensitive to differences in disease severity (Khanna et al., 2007).

Choice of measure (generic, disease-targeted) for a particular study depends on project aims, methodological concerns, and practical constrains. Patrick and Deyo (1989) recommend using a combination of generic and disease-targeted items in studies examining particular diagnostic groups to produce both generic measurements that can be compared across populations and interventions and disease-targeted measurements that assess the states and concerns of the disease of interest. For example, the 134-item Kidney Disease Quality of Life measure (Hays, Kallich, Mapes, Coons, & Carter, 1994) includes the SF-36 as its generic core plus 11 kidney disease–targeted domains that assess symptoms and problems such as general burden of disease and specific effects of the disease on daily activities, work, quality of social interaction, sexual function, and sleep. Including disease-targeted measures in tandem with generic scores can greatly improve the sensitivity and effectiveness of health assessment in clinical studies by providing important and unique information about HRQoL.

Applications of HRQoL Measures

HRQoL measures used in research and clinical studies can help achieve a wide range of goals in public policy and in everyday clinical practice. HRQoL measures are often used to study some aspect of population health, the association of self-reported health with health care utilization, or quality of care delivery. The most common application of HRQoL measures in research has been to examine health disparities or to compare the health of different disease groups. Following are examples of applications of HRQoL measures in research (population and clinical studies) and clinical practice.

Use of HRQoL Measures in Population Studies

In a study of U.S. Medicare managed-care beneficiaries, Bierman, Bubolz, Fisher, and Wasson (1999) found that responses to self-reported general health status measures predicted subsequent health care utilization. Age- and gender-adjusted annual expenditures in the year after a self-rating of health varied from $8,743 for those who rated their health as poor to $1,656 for those who rated their health as excellent. Bierman et al. (1999) concluded that self-reports of fair or poor health identified a group of patients who may benefit from targeted interventions. But health plans may place greater priority on maximizing profits by disproportionally enrolling beneficiaries with good health status, and minimize any disadvantage by not enrolling beneficiaries who view themselves as sick (Bierman et al., 1999). Another example is the administration of the SF-36 in the Medical Health Outcomes Survey (see http://www.hosonline.org) to managed care Medicare beneficiaries to monitor health plan performance and accountability, stimulate quality improvement, and assess and improve health of the Medicare population.

HRQoL measures are also critical for assessment of population health in national surveys. HRQoL questionnaires have been administered in several large national studies to produce utility scores for cost-effectiveness analyses, assess and track the health of populations, and provide national data for a range of research studies. The National Health Measurement Study, a national computer-assisted telephone survey, simultaneously administered several commonly used HRQoL measures, including the EQ-5D, SF-36, HUI2/3, QWB, and three CDC Healthy Days questions, to adults 35 to 89 years old residing in the continental United States to produce population norms of HRQoL (Fryback et al., 2007). Consequently, these national data were used to examine a number of research questions, such as variation of HRQoL by gender, race, socioeconomic status, body mass index, and disease groups (for example, Cherepanov, Palta, Fryback, & Robert, 2010).

Use of HRQoL Measures in Clinical Studies

HRQoL measures are often used in clinical studies to compare disease groups and evaluate the impact and health improvement associated with different treatments at a point in time or longitudinally. In a national cohort study of HIV patients, surveyed in 1996 and 1998, additional symptoms at follow-up were associated with worsened overall health and overall quality of life ratings (Lorenz, Cunningham, Spritzer, & Hays, 2006). In the Medical Outcomes Study, the association between physical activity/exercise and HRQoL was examined at baseline and indicated those who exercised more had better physical functioning two years later (Stewart et al., 1994).

Use of HRQoL Measures in Clinical Practice

HRQoL measures are used in daily clinical practice to measure patients' health status and progress, screen patients to determine treatments and health outcome goals, and improve patient and provider communication. In a study that compared physicians who used the Dartmouth Primary Care Cooperative Information Project (COOP) charts to a control group of physicians who used no measure of health status to assess the HRQoL of their adult patients during a single clinical encounter (Wasson et al., 1992), the ordering of tests and procedures for women was increased by exposure to the COOP charts, whereas the effect in men was not as significant. Although women reported no change in satisfaction with care received, men claimed that the clinician helped in the management of pain. This indicates the use of the COOP charts had a mixed but potentially positive impact on delivery of health care.

Despite some encouraging results in the use of HRQoL measures in clinical practice, and support for their use in research studies (for example, Velikova et al., 2004; Wasson et al., 1992), Greenhalgh et al. (2005) has argued that the use of PRO measures, particularly HRQoL measures, has little influence on clinical decision making. The influence of HRQoL data on clinical decision making seems to depend on a large number of factors such as design of the treatment intervention, patients' and clinicians' attitudes toward HRQoL measures (for example, desire to discuss HRQoL issues within the consultation), and clinicians' views of the clinical relevance and accuracy of HRQoL measures. While further research is needed to understand the ways in which clinicians incorporate HRQoL information within patient care, Greenhalgh, Long, and Flynn (2005) propose that the impact of HRQoL information on clinical decision making may be maximized if two actions take place: Well-developed patient-centered measures are used; and a data exchange throughout the treatment decision making and care process is facilitated by including HRQoL data that is accessible, interpretable, and available in a clinically relevant format.

Patient Evaluation of Care Measures and Applications

Measures

Patient satisfaction refers to the extent to which a patient is satisfied with the health care he or she receives. Because patient satisfaction is measured by self-report, it is considered a PRO measure (Fung & Hays, 2008). The focus can be on health care provided by health plans, provider groups, individual physicians, or a variety of care settings. Patient satisfaction data are important for improvement of health care quality because they provide the patient's perspective on the care delivered and are associated with adherence to medical recommendations, allegiance to health care providers, and utilization of health care services (Fung & Hays, 2008). Patient-reported measurement of technical quality of care should be avoided because patients are typically not a good source of this information, and more appropriate methods developed by the RAND Corporation and University of California, Los Angeles (Shekelle, 2004) should be used instead. The important domains of care for which patients are a good source of information can vary depending on the setting; however, the core elements across settings include access to care, providers' communication, and courtesy and respect of office staff. Although there are many patient satisfaction measures in the health care field, we focus on the surveys developed as part of CAHPS program, the largest national effort to measure and report patients' experiences with health care services.

The Agency for Healthcare Research and Quality launched the CAHPS program (see http://www.cahps.ahrq.gov) in 1995 to measure, report on, and improve the quality of health care from consumers' and patients' perspectives. The CAHPS program has two goals: to develop comprehensive standardized, evidence-based surveys that can be used to compare patients' and consumers' experiences with health care across sponsors and over time, and to generate and support tools and resources that sponsors can use to produce understandable and usable comparative information for both consumers and health care providers (cahps.ahrq.gov). A number of surveys have been developed to investigate ambulatory care (for example, health plan, clinician, and group), facility care (for example, hospital, in-center hemodialysis, nursing home), and behavioral health services (mental health treatment and substance abuse counseling services). The program established a set of principles to guide the development of CAHPS surveys and tools, and has maintained the CAHPS database, a national repository for CAHPS data that includes the Health Plan Survey data submitted each year by health plans, government agencies, and purchasers (see http://www.cahps.ahrq.gov).

The CAHPS surveys measure patients' experiences across domains of care using two types of measures, global ratings of care and reports of specific domains of care. The surveys ask patients to rate the care received on a 0 to 10 response scale, where 0 is the worst possible care and 10 represents the best possible care, thereby eliciting numeric evaluations rather than descriptions of satisfaction with care (although satisfaction and ratings of care are highly correlated and provide similar information). CAHPS surveys elicit reports about domains of care by asking how often positive and negative aspects of care occurred. For example, in the Health Plan Survey, the question, "How often was it easy to get an appointment with a specialist?" measures access to needed care, and, "How often did your personal doctor explain things in a way that was easy to understand?" measures how well doctors communicate. Similarly, in the In-Center Hemodialysis Survey, the question, "How often did your kidney doctor listen carefully to you?" measures nephrologists' communication and caring, and, "How often did the dialysis center staff explain things in a way that was easy to understand?" evaluates dialysis center care and operations.

CAHPS surveys are available for use in multiple ambulatory/outpatient and institutional settings. Ambulatory care surveys measure consumers' and patients' experiences with care and services delivered by health plans, clinicians and their staff, managed behavioral health care organizations, dental plans, medical groups, and home care providers. The widely-used CAHPS Health Plan Survey, launched in 1997, is currently a national standard for measuring and reporting enrollees' experiences with their health plans (see http://www.cahps.ahrq.gov). Health care facility surveys measure patients' experiences with care in hospitals, hemodialysis centers, and nursing homes. Hospitals across the United States are using the CAHPS Hospital Survey (H-CAHPS), which is designed to capture experiences of inpatient adults with hospital care and services, and are voluntarily reporting data to the Centers for Medicare and Medicaid Services (see http://cahps.ahrq.gov).

Patients' experiences with physicians and their staff can be measured by the CAHPS Clinician and Group Survey, which asks respondents about their experiences with a doctor in the past 12 months across three domains of care (getting appointment and health care when needed, how well doctors communicate, courteous and helpful office staff) and a single general rating question: "Using any number from 0 to 10, where 0 is the worst doctor possible and 10 is the best doctor possible, what number would you use to rate this doctor?" (see http://cahps.ahrq.gov). Other versions of the CAHPS Clinician and Group survey are under development, such as one that assesses care received from providers other than a physician (for example, nurse practitioners and physicians' assistants). The CAHPS program also includes the ECHO Survey, a survey of behavioral health services that measures the experience of consumers (adults or children) of mental health and substance abuse treatment and counseling services, covering managed care organizations and managed behavioral health care organizations.

Applications

Data from patient evaluations of care are used to compare health plans, physician groups, individual physicians, hospitals, nursing homes, and other providers of care with one another for a variety of purposes: to help inform patients about health care provider options, to help providers improve the quality of care they deliver, to help sponsors (for example, health plans, Center for Medicare and Medicaid Services) monitor care delivery to their overall and subgroup populations, and to help groups (for example, National Committee for Quality Assurance) complete accreditation processes of plans or pay-for-performance initiatives. Similar to HRQoL measures, CAHPS measures have been used to investigate a range of topics. We discuss several below.

Disparities in Health Care: Reported Differences. Several studies have recently examined racial and ethnic disparities in consumer experiences of health care using the CAHPS Health Plan Survey across five domains: Getting Needed Care, Getting Care Quickly, How Well Doctors Communicate, Courteous and Helpful Office Staff, and Customer Service. Ratings represent respondents' assessments of their providers (personal doctor, nurse, or specialist seen most often), health plan, and overall health care (Onstad, 2005).

Racial and ethnic minorities report worse care than whites, with greater racial and ethnic disparities associated with care experiences rather than with ratings of care (Onstad, 2005). Blacks, compared with whites, report better ratings of personal providers (doctor/ nurse), their plans, and better experiences with provider communication and customer service. However, blacks have worse experiences than whites with getting care quickly.

Hispanics/Latinos as a group reported similar experiences and ratings as whites, yet when subdivided by language, both English- and Spanish-speaking

Hispanics/Latinos reported worse experiences with getting care quickly and courteous and helpful office staff. Hispanics/Latinos consistently rated their health plan better than whites regardless of language, and Spanish-speaking Hispanic/Latinos gave more positive ratings in all care areas. Asians/Pacific Islanders, especially non-English speakers, had the most negative perceptions of care of all racial/ethnic subgroups. English-speaking Asians/Pacific Islanders tended to provide similar or more positive reports and ratings of care, whereas non–English-speaking Asians/Pacific Islanders provided worse experiences and ratings with care across all domains compared with white English speakers (Onstad, 2005). On the basis of these data, three primary strategies were identified: Devise different strategies for meeting the needs of the respective affected populations; stratify ongoing quality improvement activities where appropriate; and tailor health education and outreach efforts to affected populations.

Response Tendencies. A tendency to respond systematically to questions on the basis of some aspect other than what the questions were designed to measure is referred to as a *response style* or *response tendency* (Weech-Maldonado et al., 2008). A recent study using the CAHPS survey data found that Hispanics exhibited a greater tendency toward extreme responding to a 0 to 10 rating scale than non-Hispanic whites; in particular, they were more likely than whites in commercial plans to endorse a 10, and often scores of 4 or less, compared with an omitted category of 5 through 8 (Weech-Maldonado et al., 2008). Elliott, Haviland, Kanouse, Hambarsoomians, and Hays (2009) found that Medicare beneficiaries with greater educational attainment were less likely to use both extremes of the 0 to 10 rating scale than those with less education. The studies recommend several approaches to limit the influence of response tendency, including pooling responses of the response scale or stratifying the sample (for example, by education level) when making group comparisons. These findings suggest the need for caution in interpreting disparities in patient experience of care assessed by central tendency measures and the proportion of 10 ratings.

Methodological Issues. PRO data are collected using different modes of administration (for example, self-administered, telephone/face-to-face interviewers, Internet). As with HRQoL measures, reports and ratings of care tend to be more positive when an interviewer is involved in the data collection because the presence of an interviewer may create a socially desirable response bias (Hays, Hayashi, & Stewart, 1989). Because of potential mode effects, the same mode should be used consistently whenever possible, but in hard-to-reach subgroups such as Medicaid beneficiaries, it is necessary to use a mixed mode (for example, mail followed by phone) measurement to maximize the participation rate (Brown, Nederend, Hays, Short, & Farley, 1999). Likewise, when comparing different providers of care, it is important to adjust for differences in the kinds of patients they treat (for example, case mix models) to avoid producing differences in reports and ratings of care that are unrelated to the quality of care delivered (Elliott, Swartz, Adams, Spritzer, & & Hays, 2001). The goal of case-mix adjustment of consumer reports and ratings is to eliminate response bias, and hence potentially provide more appropriate data for comparing quality of care delivered (Elliot et al., 2001, 2009).

Last, proxy reports may be useful when a patient is too ill or too young to provide his or her own evaluation. A proxy-reported outcome is defined by the FDA (2009) as "a measurement based on a report by someone other than the patient reporting as if he or she is the patient" (p. 32). Elliot, Beckett, Chong, Hambarsoomians, and Hays (2008) found that proxy respondents, such as family members, tend to provide less positive evaluations of beneficiary health care experiences, especially for ratings of care (for example, on a scale of 0 to 10). When a proxy assists the target respondent in completing a survey, the differences in reports are similar but approximately half as large. Reports from spouses as proxy respondents are more positive than those from other proxies and are similar to what would have been reported by the beneficiaries themselves. Interestingly, Hays and Ware (1986) found that an individual's own ratings of care are more favorable than perceptions of care by other people in general, a result due in part to socially desirable response bias. Hence, all proxy responses to subjective ratings in evaluation of health care should be treated cautiously. In a case when a high proportion of respondents are expected to use a proxy, it is recommended to use more specific and objective reports rather than subjective ratings and to perform adjustments that incorporate the relationship of proxies to respondents.

Conclusions and Future Directions

HRQoL and patient evaluation of care measures are increasingly being used in the United States and other countries to monitor outcomes of health and care. Recent national efforts to develop and support PROs (for example, PROMIS, CAHPS) underscore the growing impact of these measures on societal health. There is also a growing movement toward application of more complex psychometric methods to develop, examine, and administer PRO measures, for example, item response theory to assess these measures and use of computer-adaptive testing to implement efficient and accurate assessment for use in clinical practice and research (for example, PROMIS).

The future importance of PRO measures is further assured with the recent passage of H.R. 3590, the Patient Protection and Affordability Care Act (see http://www.opencongress.org), and the establishment of the Patient-Centered Outcomes Research Institute, whose duties will be to identify research priorities and establish research project agendas with the purpose to "assist patients, clinicians, purchasers, and policymakers in making informed health decisions by advancing the quality and relevance of evidence concerning the manner in which diseases, disorders, and other health conditions can effectively and appropriately be prevented, diagnosed, treated, monitored, and managed through research (Section 6301)." As such, PRO measures, in their various forms, may gain special significance in the time of U.S. health care reform, when the focus of health care delivery will shift from diagnosis and consequent treatment of a health problem to disease prevention and wellness of the U.S population, highlighting the importance of tracking PROs on a national level.

References

Bierman, A. S., Bubolz, T. A., Fisher, E. S., & Wasson, J. H.. (1999). How well does a single question about health predict the financial health of Medicare managed care plans? *Effective Clinical Practice, 2*, 56–62.

Brazier, J. E., Roberts, J., & Deverill, M. (2002). The estimation of a preference-based measure of health from the SF-36. *Journal of Health Economics, 21*, 271–292.

Brown, J. A., Nederend, S. E., Hays, R. D., Short, P. F., Farley, D. O. (1999). Special issues in assessing care of Medicaid recipients. *Medical Care, 37*, MS79–MS88.

Bullinger, M., Alonso, J., Apolone, G., Leplège, A., Sullivan, M., Wood-Dauphinee, S., et al. (1998). Translating health status questionnaires and evaluating their quality: The IQOLA Project approach. *Journal of Clinical Epidemiology, 51*, 913–923.

Cella, D., Yount, S., Rothrock, N., Gershon, R., Cook, K., Reeve, B., et al. (2007). The Patient-Reported Outcomes Measurement Information System (PROMIS): Progress of an NIH Roadmap cooperative group during its first two years. *Medical Care, 45*(5, Suppl. 1), S3–S11.

Centers for Disease Control and Prevention. (2000). *Measuring healthy days.* Atlanta: Author.

Cherepanov, D., Palta, M., Fryback, D. G., & Robert, S. A. (2010). Gender differences in health-related quality-of-life are partly explained by sociodemographic and socioeconomic variation between adult men and women in the US: Evidence from four US nationally representative data sets. *Quality of Life Research, 19,* 1115–1124.

Coons, S. J., Rao, S., Keininger, D. L., & Hays, R. D. (2000). A comparative review of generic quality-of-life instruments. *Pharmaeconomics, 17*(1), 13–35.

Diehr, P., Patrick, D., Hedrick, S., Rothman, M., Grembowski, D., Raghunathan, T., & Beresford, S. (1995). Including deaths when measuring health status over time. *Medical Care, 33,* AS164–AS172.

Elliott, M. N., Beckett, M. K., Chong, K., Hambarsoomians, K., & Hays, R. D. (2008). How do proxy responses and proxy-assisted responses differ from what Medicare beneficiaries might have reported about their health care? *Health Services Research, 43,* 833–848.

Elliott, M. N., Haviland, A. M., Kanouse, D. E., Hambarsoomians, K., & Hays, R. D. (2009). Adjusting for subgroup differences in extreme response tendency in ratings of health care: Impact on disparity estimates. *Health Services Research , 44,* 542–561.

Elliott, M. N., Swartz, R., Adams, J., Spritzer, K. L., & Hays, R. D. (2001). Case-mix adjustment of the National CAHPS® Benchmarking Data 1.0: A violation of model assumptions? *Health Services Research, 36,* 555–573.

Fryback, D. G., Dunham, N. C., Palta, M., Hanmer, J., Buechner, J., Cherepanov, D., & Herrington, S. (2007). U.S. norms for six generic health-related quality-of-life indexes from the National Health Measurement Study. *Medical Care, 45,* 1162–1170.

Fryback, D. G., Palta, M., Cherepanov D., Bolt, D., & Kim, J. S. (2010). Comparison of 5 health-related quality-of-life indexes using item response theory analysis. *Medical Decision Making, 30*(1), 5–15.

Fung, C., & Hays, R. D. (2008). Prospects and challenges in using patient-reported outcomes in clinical practice. *Quality of Life Research, 17,* 1297–1302.

Greenhalgh, J., Long, A. F., & Flynn, R. (2005). The use of patient reported outcome measures in routine clinical practice: Lack of impact or lack of theory? *Social Science Medicine, 60,* 833–843.

Hays, R. D., Hayashi, T., & Stewart, A. L. (1989). A five-item measure of socially desirable response set. *Educational and Psychological Measurement, 49,* 629–636.

Hays, R. D., Kallich, J. D., Mapes, D. L., Coons, S. J., & Carter, W. B. (1994). Development of the Kidney Disease Quality of Life (KDQOL) instrument. *Quality of Life Research, 3,* 329–338.

Hays, R. D., Mangione, C. M., Ellwein, L., Lindblad, A. S., Spritzer, K. L., & McDonnel, J. P. (2003). Psychometric properties of the National Eye Institute Refractive Error Quality of Life instrument. *Ophthalmology, 110,* 2292–2301.

Hays, R. D., Kim S., Spritzer, K. L., Kaplan, R. M., Tally, S., Feeny, D., et al. (2009). Effects of mode and order of administration on generic health-related quality of life scores. *Value Health, 12,* 1035–1039.

Hays, R., & Ware, J. E. (1986). My medical care is better than yours: Social desirability and patient satisfaction ratings. *Medical Care, 24,* 519–525.

Kaplan R. M. (2005). The minimally clinically important differences in generic utility-based measures. *COPD: Journal of Chronic Obstructive Pulmonary Disease, 2,* 91–97.

Kaplan, R. M., Tally, S., Hays, R. D., Feeny, D., Ganiats, T.G., Palta, M., & Fryback, D.G. (2011). Five-preference-based indexes in cataract and heart patients were not equally responsive to change. *Journal of Clinical Epidemiology, 64,* 497–506.

Khanna, D., Hays, R. D., Park, G. S., Braun-Moscovici, Y., Mayes, M. D., McNearney, T. A., et al. (2007). Development of a preliminary scleroderma gastrointestinal tract 1.0 (SSC-GIT 1.0) quality of life instrument. *Arthritis Care and Research, 57,* 1280–1286.

Litwin, M., Hays, R. D., Fink, A., Ganz, P.A., Leake, B., Leach, G. E., & Brooke, R. H. (1995). Quality of life outcomes in men treated for localized prostate cancer. *JAMA, 273,* 129–135.

Lorenz, K.A., Cunningham, W. E., Spritzer, K. L., & Hays, R. D. (2006). Changes in symptoms and health-related quality of life in a nationally representative sample of adults in treatment for HIV. *Quality of Life Research, 15,* 951–958.

Mangione, C. M., Lee, P. P., Pitts, J., Gutierrez, P., Berry, S., & Hays, R. D. (1998). Psychometric properties of the National Eye Institute Visual Function Questionnaire, the NEI-VFQ. *Archives of Ophthalmology, 116,* 1496–1504.

McDowell, I., & Newell, C. (1996). *Measuring health: A guide to rating scales and questionnaires.* New York: Oxford University Press.

Miller, W., Robinson, L.A., & Lawrence, R. S. (Eds.). (2006). *Valuing health for regulatory cost-effectiveness analysis.* Washington, DC: National Academies Press.

Onstad, K. (2005). *Research brief: Racial and ethnic disparities in the experiences of health care consumers. The National CAHPS Benchmarking Database* (AHRQ Contract Number 290-01-0003). Rockville, MD: AHRQ.

Patrick, D. L., & Deyo, R. A. (1989). Generic and disease-specific measures in assessing health status and quality of life. *Medical Care, 27,* S217–S232.

Shekelle, P. (2004). The appropriateness method. *Medical Decision Making, 24,* 228–231.

Stewart, A. L., Hays, R. D., Wells, K. B., Rogers, W. H., Spritzer, K. L., & Greenfield, S. (1994). Long-term functioning and well-being outcomes associated with physical activity and exercise in patients with chronic conditions in the Medical Outcomes Study. *Journal of Clinical Epidemiology, 47,* 719–730.

U.S. Food and Drug Administration. (2009). *Guidance for industry: Patient-reported outcome measures: Use in medical product development to support labeling claims.* Silver Spring, MD: Author.

Velikova, G., Booth, L., Smith, A. B., Brown, P. M., Lynch, P., Brown, J. M., & Selby, P. J. (2004). Measuring quality of life in routine oncology practice improves communication and patient well-being: A randomized controlled trial. *Journal of Clinical Oncology, 22,* 714–724.

Ware, J. E., Kosinski, M., Gandek, B. G., Aaronson, N. K., Apolone, G., Bech, P., et al. (1998). The factor structure and content of the SF-36 Health Survey in 10 countries: Results from the International Quality of Life Assessment (IQOLA) Project. *Journal of Clinical Epidemiology, 51,* 1159–1165.

Wasson, J., Hays, R., Rubenstein, L., Nelson, E., Leaning, J., Johnson, D., et al. (1992). The short-term effect of patient health status assessment in a health maintenance organization. *Quality of Life Research, 1,* 99–106.

Weech-Maldonado, R., Elliott, M. N., Oluwole, A., Schiller, K. C., & Hays, R. D. (2008). Survey response style and differential use of CAHPS rating scales by Hispanics. *Medical Care, 49,* 963–968.

CHAPTER 10

Outcomes Measurement and Gerontology:
What the United States Needs as It Grows Older

Barbara Berkman and Daniel B. Kaplan

The global realities of a rapidly aging population cannot be denied, nor should the health, mental health, and social service needs of these older adults be underestimated. People are living longer because of advances in public health, health care technology, and improved treatments and service delivery. Thus, life expectancy has risen significantly. By 2030, one fifth of the U.S. population will be 65 and older (Administration on Aging [AOA], 2007), with the greatest rate of increase being in the oldest and most vulnerable: those 85 years and older. The older population is also becoming more diverse in race, ethnicity, language, and culture. By 2050, members of racial and ethnic minorities will constitute almost two fifths of the U.S. population age 65 and older (Federal Interagency Forum on Aging-Related Statistics, 2008). Although the majority of older adults enjoy well-being into late life, vulnerable, chronically ill older adults will represent an increasing percentage of persons living with significant physical and daily activity impairments and other threats to quality of life. This population shift will require increased help from a variety of human service professionals, policymakers, and advocates, including social workers (Burnette & Kang, 2003; Gonyea, Hudson, & Curley, 2004). Developing effective and efficient care models to meet the needs of the older population is vital, and the evaluation of the outcomes of these services is equally important.

The context of delivery of care to older adults has been evolving rapidly. For example, the work of Carl Rogers and Tom Kitwood has recently inspired gerontological practitioners to promote person-centered care for older adults with chronic disabilities such as dementia (Brooker, 2006), and the Pioneer Network has been advocating for the adoption of culture change within long-term care institutions (Rahman & Schnelle, 2008). Efforts such as these have fostered important improvements in geriatric care, but they have also altered the ways in which we conceptualize and evaluate outcomes related to quality of care and quality of life for older adults. Most recently, the adoption of healthcare reforms by the 111th Congress, through the Patient Protection and Affordable Care Act (H.R. 3590, 2009), brings urgent attention to the use of clinical health outcomes measures for older adults. This legislation mandated changes aimed at improving the quality of health care for older adults and created the Patient-Centered Outcomes Research Institute.

With their unique set of values, skills, resources, and roles in multiple locations within health and mental health systems, social workers are ideally suited to facilitating interventions and supportive services to older adults and to their family members and caregivers (Kaplan & Berkman, in press). In the last decade, the context of social work practice and research in gerontology has experienced significant positive change that affects the ability of social workers to confront the considerable need for geriatric care in the coming years. These changes include an expanding knowledge base and a growing base of practitioners and scholars interested in aging-related issues. Academic and research interest in gerontological social work has been stimulated by the support of the Hartford Geriatric Social Work Initiative, which was created and funded to address the deficiencies in geriatric social work manpower and education (John A. Hartford Foundation, 2009). Concomitantly, there have been significant additions to the gerontology-specific social work and research literature, such as the *Handbook of Social Work in Health and Aging* (Berkman, 2006), *Social Gerontology: A Multidisciplinary Perspective* (Hooyman & Kiyak, 2008), and *Assessing Older Persons: Measures, Meaning, and Practical Applications* (Kane & Kane, 2000). Social work practitioners and researchers are now better equipped to understand substantive issues related to aging and measurement of outcomes.

To meet the challenges of care for older adults and their families, interventions will be required to ensure that access to and utilization of social and health care systems are achieved effectively and equitably. Practitioners will be increasingly expected to identify the most compelling data and utilize the strongest scientific evidence in defining client problems, collaborating with clients to select appropriate treatments, and monitoring the effects of interventions. Researchers and practitioners in all health and human services domains will be challenged to understand and study outcomes related to these interventions. Therefore, reliable and valid outcome measures are absolutely vital and at the very core of evidence-based practice.

Outcomes Measurement Challenges for Older Adults

Measurement of outcomes in older adults is frequently, if not always, challenged by the complex multidimensionality of their physical, psychological, and social needs. Thus, measuring outcomes of interventions usually cannot be limited to a single factor or dimension. For example, older clients experiencing cognitive impairment may simultaneously confront significant psychological, social, and physiological impairments, and measuring outcomes of treatment activities may require an array of measures across multiple domains both during the assessment process and after the intervention. The high rates of co-occurring health and mental health conditions among older adults further complicate the assessment of outcomes to determine the effectiveness of interventions. With multiple conditions and providers, and interacting treatments, the study of specific outcomes is driven by such questions as: Is the phenomenon being measured the result of one intervention or is it the result of an intervention by another involved therapist, or the interactions between the two?

The study of outcomes with older adults presents an ongoing struggle to create, test, and refine measures to use with those who lack ability or are limited in communication skills. For example, the inability of dementia patients to contribute valuable information in advanced stages of the disorder remains a serious challenge when attempting to measure the outcomes of care services or psychodynamic interventions in this population. In addition to cognitive impairments, numerous other conditions may present measurement challenges when working with older adults. Age-associated vision and hearing impairments, as well as sensory disorders not related to aging, can have a profound impact on the health, mental health, and quality of life of older adults (Stuen, 2006). These impairments also interfere with participation in surveys and interviews as well as with the administration of assessment-based instructions. In addition, Parkinson's disease and other neurological disorders complicate written and oral responses

(Horowitz, 2006). Careful attention to sensory and functional capacities of older adults should be ensured in practice and research settings.

Another challenge in research with older adults is in outcome satisfaction surveys frequently conducted in hospitals and health centers. Particularly problematic in measuring the satisfaction of older adults is their reluctance to respond negatively because they fear service repercussions from their providers (Hsieh & Essex, 2006). In addition, low expectations of health outcomes may influence assessment responses among older adults (Atherly, Kane, & Smith, 2004), and those who become overwhelmed by feelings of grief, sadness, or anger pose additional challenges to be addressed by assessors (Geron, 2006). Confronting these measurement challenges is now an urgent priority as social service providers and researchers race to identify reliable and valid instruments to aid in the care of a rapidly aging clientele.

Meeting Outcomes Measurement Challenges for the Elderly: The National Institutes of Health Priority Areas

Much of social work practice focuses on improving the social and behavioral priority areas for older adults that the National Institutes of Health (2003) have identified: changing lifestyle behavior for better health, maintaining health and functioning, improving the quality of life for persons with chronic conditions, enhancing the end-of-life experience, and reducing health disparities. These priority areas offer a useful roadmap for both social work practitioners and researchers to identify domains for the development of social work interventions and the measurement of outcomes that help to build the evidence base upon which practitioners and managers can rely (Raveis, Gardner, Berkman, & Harootyan, 2010).

Throughout the remainder of this chapter, we will discuss considerations for outcome measures in gerontological practice and research, placing them in the context of these National Institutes of Health priority areas. Although many assessment tools are used in clinical practice with older adults (Kane & Kane, 2000), some also have been used as outcome measures in research studies when they meet psychometric standards for reliability and validity. Because we base this chapter on the premise that health and mental health outcomes in social work practice and research with older adults are significantly intertwined, examples of measures from both domains will be discussed, and we will highlight specific measures used in the evaluation of outcomes in social work research with older adults.

Changing Lifestyle Behavior for Better Health

Research has shown that lifestyle and other social environmental influences can affect outcomes in late life (Rowe & Kahn, 1997). We also know that remaining relatively healthy and emotionally vital into very advanced age is a realistic expectation. The view that illness is a chronic process raises the questions of whether an acute episode can be prevented and whether a disease process can be delayed, placing great importance on individuals' abilities to anticipate their own health care needs (Berkman, 1996). The focus of care thus moves from symptom management to disease prevention and health promotion. The new healthcare reform act has incentives for such preventive care (H.R. 3950, 2009).

In practice and research efforts focused on improving lifestyle behaviors for older adults, tracking adherence to a prescribed regimen of activities, while offering indications of success in facilitating intervention compliance, does not measure meaningful outcomes. Constructs of greater complexity and multidimensionality need to be incorporated into such studies. Unfortunately, such constructs tend to be more methodologically challenging to measure. Social support is a good example of a complex construct for outcomes measurement.

Social support is an important and often-studied construct, which, according to Vaux et al. (1986), comprises social network resources, specific supportive acts, and subjective appraisals of support. Social support has been described as a buffer for stress as well as a moderator of psychological and physical well-being (Berkman & Syme, 1979). Social ties, social networks, and social supports can be framed as important outcomes of lifestyle-oriented and behavioral interventions aimed at bolstering this domain in the lives of older adults. We discuss here three examples of measures of social support available for studies of older adults: the Social Support Appraisal Scale (SS-A), the Social Support Behaviors Scale (SS-B), and the UCLA Loneliness Scale.

The SS-A is a brief measure of subjects' appraisals of their social relationships (Vaux et al., 1986). Perception of the availability of social support is one component of the larger social support construct as defined by Vaux et al. (1986), but it is thought to be the most prominent component in terms of believing one is meaningfully and reliably connected to others, esteemed and valued, cared for and loved (O'Reilly, 1995). The SS-A assesses these appraisals across a 23-item scale with four-point Likert-type responses that gauge the extent to which participants feel they are loved by, esteemed by, and involved with family, friends, and others. This measure is well suited to intervention studies focused on social support outcomes in older adults, as well as those designed to build social skills or enhance social networks.

The SS-B is a 45-item measure of five modes of social support, including emotional support, socializing, practical assistance, financial assistance, and advice/guidance. The SS-B assesses the participants' perceptions of the availability of support by asking them to report the likelihood that family or friends would perform each specific supportive behavior (Vaux, Reidel, & Stewart, 1987). With its focus on the actual supportive behaviors of family members and friends, the SS-B is a useful instrument for comparisons of support received by older adults and the different types of problems they face, as well as for studies of the caregiver/care recipient dyadic relationship across distinct supportive modes.

The UCLA Loneliness Scale, a 20-item measure using four-point Likert-type items, has been used to gauge the outcome of a cognitive enhancement intervention to build social support networks for institutionalized older adults (Winningham & Pike, 2007). This scale unpacks the construct of social support into distinct measures of (a) participant appraisals of the extent of availability of support, (b) the likelihood of supportive behaviors from family and friends, and (c) the current extent of feelings of loneliness. This measure is a more useful instrument for evaluating the multidimensional construct of social support in older adults than those focused only on a single aspect of the target construct.

Maintaining Health and Functioning

Innovative models of service delivery are now being developed by social workers and other human services professionals to affect the environmental and psychosocial factors that impede older adults' functional independence, and which can have detrimental effects on quality of life, morbidity, and mortality (Raveis et al., 2010). Intervention programs under evaluation are often aimed at improving functional capacity or alleviating the depression that can accompany poor health or diminished functional ability. Functional measurement instruments have typically been grouped into four broad categories (Pearson, 2000): (1) self-report questionnaires, (2) proxy report measures, (3) direct observation measures, and (4) performance-based measures. Although specific utility of each category varies, it is recommended that measurement instruments from multiple categories be used to achieve valid comprehensive assessment.

For example, in a hypothetical study of the effects of a psychosocial health behaviors intervention for octogenarians receiving care from formal care providers, validity and reliability of the study would likely be jeopardized if only self-reports of functional status were used. Despite the fact that these self-report measures can be more affordable and simple to administer, they have several weaknesses. These include participant sensitivity to change in functional ability; inflation of reported ability caused by a strong desire to remain independent; or, conversely, underreporting of functional limitations caused by a desire to retain supportive services (Pearson, 2000). Potential threats to validity are compounded by the presence of any conditions of cognitive impairment, dementia, or delirium at the time of assessment. Triangulating information from the participant, the formal care provider, and perhaps from direct obser- vation can help increase the likelihood of capturing significant, accurate, and subtle degrees of change during and after the intervention period.

Numerous standardized measures are useful for the evaluation of the older person's functional capacity, such as the Functional Independence Measure, the Lawton Instrumental Activities of Daily Living Scale (1969), the Functional Status Index (FSI), and the Physical Performance Test. For example, the FSI (Deniston & Jette, 1980) was originally created for a pilot study of arthritis in older adults and consists of 45 items that measure the degree of help or assis- tance a person needs to perform an activity (dependence), how hard or easy it is to perform an activity (difficulty), and the degree of discomfort experienced during the activity (pain). An 18-item, self-report version of the FSI takes only 15 minutes to complete and may spare study participants undue burden dur- ing each measurement session in a research study. The FSI provides measures for multiple summary score indexes, including mobility, personal care, home chores, and interpersonal activities. Totaling sums of scores across indexes is not appropriate, but summary functional scores for dependence, difficulty, and pain are averaged across indexes during scoring.

Improving Quality of Life in Chronic Conditions

Despite concerted efforts to maintain health and functional capacities as they advance into old age, chronic diseases threaten quality of life for a great many older adults. Today, people are living longer with complex, chronic physical and mental health conditions. Most older Americans have at least one chronic health condition (AOA, 2008), and 69 percent have multiple physical and/or mental health conditions (Berkman, Silverstone, Simmons, Howe, & Volland, 2000). Many older adults are living with chronic illnesses such as hypertension (48 percent), heart disease (29 percent), cancer (20 percent), and diabetes (16 percent; AOA, 2008). These conditions are long term or permanent, often requiring monitoring and management for extended numbers of years. The presence of mental health disorders further complicates the management of chronic physical conditions as a result of challenges associated with treatment compliance, sparse social support, and limited self-advocacy within the health care arena. Similarly, the identification and treatment of mental disorders can be obscured by the presence of chronic physical illness. For example, older people with serious medical problems are significantly more likely to experi- ence major depressive disorder than older adults in the general population

(Zarit & Zarit, 2007). Such depression often goes unreported, undiagnosed and untreated (Gellis, McGinty, Horowitz, Bruce, & Misener, 2007).

Social workers are actively involved in developing and testing interventions to help diagnose and alleviate geriatric depression. For example, Gellis and colleagues conducted a pilot randomized clinical trial to compare brief problem-solving therapy in home care to usual care for a sample of older medically ill home-care patients with severe depression (Gellis et al., 2007). The Beck Depression Inventory and the Geriatric Depression Scale Short Form were used to evaluate outcomes related to depressive symptom severity; both have been widely used in research in clinical settings and offer suitable sensitivity and specificity for assessment or screening efforts.

In addition to comorbidities, older adults often have significant physical and daily living activity impairments that are due to chronic health conditions and contribute to decline in their quality of life (Burnette & Kang, 2003; Gonyea et al., 2004). Community-based or institutional long-term care is required for those whose physical and mental disorders have eroded their ability to sustain independent functioning. Research related to outcomes in home- and community-based long-term care has focused primarily on physical health. Although these physical health foci surely suggest important outcomes to be studied, a primary goal of long-term care is to preserve quality of life in the face of chronic illness and functional decline (Robert, 2003). Thus, quality-of-life measures should be incorporated into long-term care evaluations.

In order to better understand how best to mobilize community-based and institutional long-term care services for the elderly, researchers in the field of social work and other human service domains are studying the relationship between quality of life (as an outcome), access to and utilization of long-term care services (Ai & Carrigan, 2006), and long-term care innovations (Kane, Boston, & Chhilvers, 2007). Although quality of life is an extremely broad construct with numerous conceptualizations (Frytak, 2000), standardized health-related quality-of-life (HRQoL) indicators offer uniform conceptual definitions and measurements that are closely aligned with client priorities, and, in turn, allow social workers and social scientists to evaluate those dimensions of health-related interventions most relevant to practice (Berkman, 1996; see also other chapters in this volume).

One such group of measures comes from the Medical Outcomes Study (Ware & Sherbourne, 1992) which was conducted in the early 1990's. This Study created one of the most widely used and validated HRQoL measures, the 36-item Short Form Health Survey (SF-36). The SF-36 consists of a set of scales that assess functional capacity and perceptions of health for adults with chronic health conditions. Domains measured by the SF-36 include physical and social functioning, role limitations caused by physical and mental problems, bodily pain, mental health, vitality, and general health perceptions. Markowitz, Gutterman, Sadik, and Papdopoulos (2003) used the short version of the SF–36, the SF–12, to assess the relationship between caregivers' HRQoL and the burden of caring for persons with Alzheimer's disease. They demonstrated that behavioral problems and depressive symptoms among patients, lower levels of caregiver support, more hours of caregiving, and perceptions of poor quality of patient medical care are significantly associated with reduced caregiver quality of life. This study showed important implications for the design of health and psychosocial interventions for older adults with Alzheimer's disease and their caregivers, but it also highlights one of the many essential uses of quality-of-life outcome measures in gerontological research, namely, the quality of life of family caregivers, who are known to assume the lion's share of caregiving responsibilities in our society.

Enhancing the End-of-Life Experience

Despite the fact that the evidence base in this arena remains limited, there is now growing interest in building knowledge of the death experience in both acute and long-term care settings where most deaths occur. Psychosocial challenges associated with death and dying include anxiety and depression, caregiving needs, and the need for social support and communication among family members and providers (Morrison & Meier, 2003). Although psychosocial outcomes at the end of life can be difficult to quantify for those actually dying, social scientists from several disciplines are leading the way forward in research and practice. In particular, social workers provide a uniquely valuable perspective about care, intervention, and research (see Waldrop, 2008) as they promulgate the values of families, communication, and a focus on the person-in-environment.

Intervention research in this arena may focus on any number of relevant outcomes, such as satisfaction with end-of-life care (Ringdal, Jordhoy, & Kaasa, 2002), quality of life (Corner et al., 2003), social adjustment (Tudiver, Hildich, Permaul, & McKendree, 1992), compliance with patient and family preferences for place of death (Ratner, Norlander, & McSteen, 2001), and specific issues and dynamics associated with the end of life. Studies that focus on these types of outcomes have generally used a combination of standardized and nonstandardized measures and established instruments that assess the more broadly evaluated constructs such as depression, anxiety, and quality of life.

For example, Aday and Shahan (1995) evaluated anxiety about death, as well as depression and life satisfaction with regard to patient views of death, following a seven-session death education program offered to small groups of nursing home residents. The researchers chose the Templer Death Anxiety

Scale, which is a widely used measure of death orientation composed of 15 true–false items related to feelings, thoughts, and fears of death (Templer, 1971). Other sufficiently validated instruments specific to end-of-life issues are the Caregiving at Life's End Questionnaire, the Death Depression Scale, and the Sense of Symbolic Immortality Scale.

Reducing Health Disparities

Health disparities are population-specific differences in health outcomes in which the quality of and access to health care vary by gender, race/ethnicity, sexual orientation, education or income, geographic location, and disability (U.S. Department of Health and Human Services, 2000). A major demographic trend that affects health care services and social work practice is the increased cultural diversity among the older adult population. By the year 2050, the proportion of Hispanic individuals age 65 or older is expected to triple, representing an estimated 18 percent of the population. At the same time the percentage of elderly Whites in the U.S. population will have decreased by 20 percent (Federal Interagency Forum on Aging-Related Statistic, 2008). Disease risk factors, as well as responses to treatment, caregiving, and overall quality of life, may be affected by race, ethnicity, gender, and socioeconomic status through discrimination and stigmatization. Thus, there is a vast array of factors that may affect the health care of older adults, including emotional reactions, health beliefs, health care utilization, health risks, and patterns of relationships with family members (Maramaldi & Guevara, 2003).

In order to address the service challenges associated with heterogeneity and demographic changes in the older adult population, social workers and other human service professionals must develop more effective outcome measures to help deepen our knowledge about the interaction between culture and health, and how health beliefs that are grounded in culture effect self-care and other dimensions of well-being and health care delivery. The field of social work brings significant expertise to meet such needs (Chadiha, Adams, Phorano, Ong, & Byers, 2004; Mui, Kang, Chen, & Dietz Domanski, 2003). Much of this work has centered on developing a better understanding of the culture-specific meanings that underlie constructs such as depression and pain (Horowitz, 2006). Despite the availability of several resources for finding measures to use in the study of older adults, there remains a significant need to understand the fit of existing measures for research with members of ethnic minorities (Horowitz, 2006). For example, how do culture, linguistics and other modes of expression vary among older adults of different ethnicities? How do these differences affect their answers to questions in measurement instruments?

Culture-specific adaptation to established measures is an area of significant progress in recent decades but which still requires considerable further development. Contemporary examples of culturally adapted measures for use with older adults include the Chinese translation of the six-item De Jong Gierveld Loneliness Scale, the Arabic translation of the 15-item Geriatric Depression Scale, and the Korean translation of the Caregiving Satisfaction Scale. The Uniform Data Set—clinical, behavioral, and neuropsychological measures used by the Alzheimer's Disease Centers of the National Institute on Aging across the country for diagnostic assessment and treatment evaluation (Acevedo et al., 2009; Morris et al., 2006)—is also being translated and adapted to meet variations among Spanish-speaking groups in the United States. However, adequate language translation alone does not necessarily make for valid and reliable instruments. For example, when assessment instruments are created within the context of Western culture, essential constructs tapped by the questions in the instrument may have significantly different interpretations in Eastern cultures (Mouton & Esparza, 2000). Thus, when seeking outcome measures to evaluate interventions addressing health disparities, researchers and practitioners would do well to identify instruments that have had both linguistic translations of questions and instructions as well as sociocultural translations of constructs and symptoms.

Conclusion

In 1931, the General Director of Massachusetts General Hospital, Dr. Richard Cabot, speaking at an annual meeting of social work health professionals, said

> *I appeal to you to do far more often the thing that since 1923 you have been saying you were going to do: measure, evaluate, estimate, appraise your results in some form, in any terms that rest on anything beyond faith, assertion, and the "illustrative case."*

As human services providers and researchers address many of the social and behavioral priority areas that the National Institutes of Health have developed for research in aging, they strive to meet Cabot's appeal. These professionals must rethink health outcomes in geriatrics, which have been defined narrowly in the past to focus on the biological component of the biopsychosocial model. Accordingly, the new Patient-Centered Outcomes Research Institute, in its mandate to build data capacity for comparative clinical effectiveness research, will need to go beyond traditional physiological outcomes to include psychological and social outcomes of social behavioral interventions in clinical health. Research using outcome measures will continually be needed to show how the use of human services, including social work services, can provide valuable, cost-effective care. The systematic study of intervention outcomes in gerontological practice is and will continue to be an important means of informing principles of practice by developing evidence-based knowledge.

References

Acevedo, A., Krueger, K. R., Navarro, E., Ortiz, F., Manly, J. J., Padilla-Vélez, M. M., et al. (2009). The Spanish translation and adaptation of the Uniform Data Set of the National Institute on Aging Alzheimer's Disease Centers. *Alzheimer Disease and Associated Disorders, 23*(2), 102–109.

Aday, R. H., & Shahan, D. R. (1995). Elderly reactions to a death education program in a nursing home setting. *Gerontology & Geriatrics Education, 15*(3), 3–18.

Administration on Aging. (2007). *Older population by age: 1900 to 2050. Persons 65 and over.* [Excel file]. Retrieved from http://www.aoa.gov/AoARoot/Aging_Statistics/future_growth/future_growth.aspx

Administration on Aging. (2008). *A statistical profile of older Americans aged 65+.* Washington, DC: Author.

Ai, A., & Carrigan, L. T. (2006). Older adults with age-related cardiovascular disease. In B. Berkman, (Ed.), *Handbook of social work in health and aging* (pp. 19–27). New York: Oxford University Press.

Atherly, A., Kane, R. L., & Smith, M. A. (2004). Older adults' satisfaction with integrated capitated health and long-term care. *Gerontologist, 44,* 348–357.

Berkman, B. (1996). The emerging health care world: Implications for social work practice and education. *Social Work, 41,* 541–553.

Berkman, B. (Ed.). (2006). *Handbook of social work in health and aging.* New York: Oxford University Press.

Berkman, B., Silverstone, B., Simmons, W. J., Howe, J., & Volland, P. (2000). Social work gerontological practice: The need for faculty development in the new millennium. *Journal of Gerontological Social Work, 34*(1), 5–23.

Berkman, L. F., & Syme, S. L. (1979). Social networks, host resistance and mortality: A year follow-up study of Alameda County residents. *American Journal of Epidemiology, 109,* 186–204.

Brooker, D. (2006). *Person-centered dementia care: Making services better.* London: Jessica Kingsley.

Burnette, D., & Kang, S.-Y. (2003). Self-help care by urban, African American elders. In B. Berkman & L. Harootyan (Eds.), *Social work and health care in an aging society* (pp. 123–148). New York: Springer.

Cabot, R. C. (1931). Treatment in social casework and the need for tests of its success and failure. *Proceedings of the National Conference of Social Work.*

Chadiha, L. A., Adams, P., Phorano, O., Ong, S. L., & Byers, L. (2003). Cases from the field: Stories told and lessons learned from black female caregivers' vignettes for empowerment practice. *Journal of Gerontological Social Work, 40*(1/2), 135–144.

Corner, J., Halliday, D., Haviland, J., Douglas, H. R., Bath, P. L., Clark, D., et al. (2003). Exploring nursing outcomes for patients with advanced cancer following intervention by Macmillan specialist palliative care nurses. *Journal of Advanced Nursing, 41,* 561–574.

Deniston, O., & Jette, A. (1980). A functional status assessment instrument: Validation in an elderly population. *Health Services Research, 15*(1), 21–34.

Federal Interagency Forum on Aging-Related Statistics. (2008, March). *Older Americans 2008: Key indicators of well-being.* Washington, DC: U.S. Government Printing Office.

Frytak, J. R. (2000). Assessment of quality of life in older adults. In R. L. Kane & R. A. Kane (Eds.), *Assessing older persons: Measures, meaning, and practical applications* (pp. 200–236). New York: Oxford University Press.

Gellis, Z. D., McGinty, J., Horowitz, A., Bruce, M. L., & Misener, E. (2007). Problem-solving therapy for late-life depression in home care: A randomized field trial. *American Journal of Geriatric Psychiatry, 15,* 968–978.

Geron, S. M. (2006). Comprehensive and multidimensional geriatric assessment. In B. Berkman (Ed.), *Handbook of social work in health and aging* (pp. 721–727). New York: Oxford University Press.

Gonyea, J., Hudson, R., & Curley, A. (2004, Spring). The geriatric social work labor force: Challenges and opportunities in responding to an aging society. *Institute for Geriatric Social Work Issue Brief,* 1–8.

Hooyman, N. R., & Kiyak, H. A. (2008). *Social gerontology: A multidisciplinary perspective* (8th ed.). Boston: Pearson Education.

Horowitz, A. (2006). Issues in conducting social work research in aging. In B. Berkman (Ed.), *Handbook of social work in health and aging* (pp. 989–1000). New York: Oxford University Press.

Hsieh, C.-M., & Essex, E. (2006). Measuring client satisfaction among older adults and families. In B. Berkman (Ed.), *Handbook of social work in health and aging* (pp. 1009–1017). New York: Oxford University Press.

John A. Hartford Foundation. (2009). *2009 annual report.* New York: Author.

Kane, R. L., Boston, K., & Chhilvers, M. (2007). Helping people make better long-term care decisions. *Gerontologist, 47,* 244–247.

Kane, R. L., & Kane, R. A. (Eds.). (2000). *Assessing older persons: Measures, meaning, and practical applications.* New York: Oxford University Press.

Kaplan, D., & Berkman, B. (in press). Dementia care: A global concern and social work challenge. *International Social Work.*

Maramaldi, P., & Guevara, M. (2003). Cultural considerations in maintaining health related quality of life in older adults. In B. Berkman & L. Harootyan (Eds.), *Social work and health care in an aging society* (pp. 297–318). New York: Springer.

Markowitz, J. S., Gutterman, E. M., Sadik, K., & Papadopoulos, G. (2003). Health-related quality of life for caregivers of patients with Alzheimer disease. *Alzheimer Disease & Associated Disorders, 17*(4), 209–214.

Morris, J. C., Weintraub, S., Chui, H. C., Cummings, J., DeCarli, C., Ferris, S., et al. (2006). The Uniform Data Set (UDS): Clinical and cognitive variables and descriptive data from Alzheimer disease centers. *Alzheimer Disease & Associated Disorders, 20*(4), 210–216.

Morrison, R. S., & Meier, D. (2003). Introduction. In R.S. Morrison & D. Meier (Eds.), *Geriatric palliative care* (pp. xxi–xxix). New York: Oxford University Press.

Mouton, C. P., & Esparza, Y. B. (2000). Ethnicity and geriatric assessment. In J. J. Gallo (Ed.), *Handbook of geriatric assessment* (3rd ed., pp. 13-27). Gaithersburg, MD: Aspen Publishers.

Mui, A., Kang, S.-Y., Chen, L. M., & Dietz Domanski, M. (2003). Reliability of the Geriatric Depression Scale for use among elderly Asian immigrants in the USA. *International Psychogeriatrics, 15*(3), 253–271.

National Institutes of Health. (2003). *NIH plan for social work research.* Retrieved from http://obssr.od.nih.gov/pdf/SWR_Report.pdf

O'Reilly, B. K. (1995). The Social Support Appraisals Scale: Construct validation for psychiatric patients. *Journal of Clinical Psychology, 51*, 37–42.

Patient Protection and Affordable Care Act, H.R. 3590, 111th Cong. (2009). Retrieved from http://www.govtrack.us/congress/bill.xpd?bill=h111-3590

Pearson, V. I. (2000). Assessment of function in older adults. In R. L. Kane & R. A. Kane (Eds.), *Assessing older persons: Measures, meaning, and practical applications* (pp. 17–48). New York: Oxford University Press.

Rahman, A. N., & Schnelle, J. F. (2008). The nursing home culture change movement: Recent past, present, and future directions for research. *Gerontologist, 48*, 142–148.

Ratner, E., Norlander, L., & McSteen, K. (2001). Death at home following a targeted advance-care planning process at home: The kitchen table discussion. *Journal of the American Geriatrics Society, 49*, 778–781.

Raveis, V. H., Gardner, D. S., Berkman, B., & Harootyan, L. (2010). Linking the NIH strategic plan to the research agenda for social workers in health and aging. *Journal of Gerontological Social Work, 53*, 77–93.

Ringdal, G. I., Jordhoy, M. S., & Kaasa, S. (2002). Family satisfaction with end-of-life care for cancer patients in a cluster randomized trial. *Journal of Pain and Symptom Management, 24*(1), 53–63.

Robert, S. A. (2003). Home and community-based long-term care policies and programs: The crucial role for social work practitioners and researchers in evaluation. In B. Berkman & L. Harootyan (Eds.), *Social work and health care in an aging society* (pp. 531–376). New York: Springer.

Rowe, J. W., & Kahn, R. L. (1997). Successful aging. *Gerontologist, 37*, 433–440.

Stuen, C. (2006). Older adults with age-related sensory loss. In B. Berkman (Ed.), *Handbook of social work in health and aging* (pp. 65–77). New York: Oxford University Press.

Templer, D. I. (1971). Death anxiety as related to depression and health of retired persons. *Journal of Gerontology, 26*, 523–531.

Tudiver, F., Hilditch, J., Permaul, J. A., & McKendree, D. J. (1992). Does mutual help facilitate newly bereaved widowers? Report of a randomized controlled trial. *Evaluation and the Health Professions, 15*(2), 147–162.

U.S. Department of Health and Human Services. (2000). *Healthy people 2010: Understanding and improving health* (2nd ed). Washington, DC: U.S. Government Printing Office.

Vaux, A., Phillips, J., Holly, L., Thomson, B., Williams, D., & Stewart, D. (1986). The Social Support Appraisals (SS-A) Scale: Studies of reliability and validity. *American Journal of Community Psychology, 14*(2), 195–219.

Vaux, A., Riedel, S., & Stewart, D. (1987). Modes of social support: The Social Support Behaviors (SS-B) Scale. *American Journal of Community Psychology, 15*(2), 209–237.

Waldrop, D. P. (2008). Chapter 11: Treatment at the end of life. *Journal of Gerontological Social Work, 50*, 267–292.

Ware, J. E., & Sherbourne, C. D. (1992). The MOS 36-item short-form health survey (SF-36). *Medical Care, 30*, 473–483.

Winningham, R. G., & Pike, N. L. (2007). A cognitive intervention to enhance institutionalized older adults' social support networks and decrease loneliness. *Aging & Mental Health, 11*, 716–721.

Zarit, S. H., & Zarit, J. M. (2007). *Mental disorders in older adults: Fundamentals of assessment and treatment* (2nd ed). New York: Guilford Press.

CHAPTER 11

Complementary Alternative and Integrative Medicine:
Current Challenges for Outcomes Measurement

Ian D. Coulter and Raheleh Khorsan

Increasingly, individuals have been using complementary alternative medicine (CAM) and integrative medicine (IM) approaches to improve their wellness and treat their illnesses (Coulter & Willis, 2007). In the United States, CAM and/or IM have been increasingly seen as part of health care and have been reimbursed by managed care entities, insurance carriers, and hospital providers (Pelletier, Marie, Krasner, & Haskell, 1997). A national survey of adults established that 34 percent used at least one unconventional therapy to treat back problems, insomnia, headaches, anxiety, depression, and cancer. Costs for such care were estimated at $425 million compared with $338 million in costs for visits to primary care physicians. Expenditures for CAM/IM were estimated at $11.7 billion; of this, $10.3 billion in out-of-pocket expenditures exceeded those for hospital care ($12.8 billion) and represented half of all physician out-of-pocket expenses (Eisenberg et al., 1993). Today, it is estimated that the prevalence of CAM use is 38 percent for adults and 11.8 percent for children in the United States (Nahin, Barnes, Stussman, & Bloom, 2009). More than

30 billion dollars ($33.9) are spent on out-of-pocket CAM visits and CAM products, with chiropractic services noted as the most frequently used therapy among manual modalities. In 2003, a national survey of 1,007 U.S. hospitals documented that 16 percent provided IM and more than 27 percent offered some form of CAM (Larson, 2005).

Although the percentage of CAM/IM use is dependent on how CAM and IM are defined (Bhattacharya, 1998), continued, and likely increased, use of CAM/IM is considered more fact than speculation. Studies estimate that 30 percent to 40 percent of medical patients in North America will use some form of alternative health care in the future (Nahin et al., 2009). In the United States, integration of CAM and biomedicine (traditional medicine as practiced in Western cultures) is being led by patients as they combine both approaches to treatment (that is, they typically seek out a biomedical provider before or concurrent to seeking CAM care; Barnes, Powell-Griner, McFann, & Nahin, 2004; Eisenberg et al., 2001; Ni, Simile, & Hardy, 2002) on a daily basis to address their physical and mental health needs (Astin, 1998; Eisenberg et al., 1998). In 2003, a national survey of 1,007 United States hospitals documented that patient demand was the most significant factor (83 percent) for incorporating CAM/IM (Larson, 2005).

In addition to a propensity to seek out multiple treatment modalities, the most predictive demographic factors associated with CAM use appear to be gender (women use CAM more than men), age (18 to 65 years old), race/ethnicity (whites use CAM more than other groups), education level (higher level of education), and geographic region (rural more than urban (Barnes et al., 2004; Eisenberg et al., 1998; Graham et al., 2005).

In this chapter, we continue to discuss how additional empirical, philosophical, and theoretical underpinnings surround the measurement and assessment of CAM/IM. It is not our purpose to suggest specific outcomes or assessment measures but to review some of the main research and measurement approaches being used and their associated challenges, and to make recommendations that offer promising approaches for the future.

Definitions and Integrated Paradigms: The Journey toward Consensus

General Definitional Issues

CAM modalities are thousands of years old (Whorton, 1999). Despite this well known fact, modern day definitions of what constitutes CAM /IM in the United States vary considerably with no agreed-upon uniform definition of what constitutes CAM.

The diversity and range of practices included under the rubric of CAM lessen the usefulness of establishing a definition. They range from focused therapy approaches (modalities) such as reflexology to systems of comprehensive treatment that focus on all aspects of the health of the patient and all the systems/organs of the body, such as traditional Chinese medicine. In the United States, this range includes such therapies as chiropractic medicine, naturopathy, homeopathy, and aromatherapy. Although these modalities share commonalities and are different, none are part of biomedicine.

The issue of what to call the CAM/IM group of approaches also has important social and political ramifications. To term the group of modalities *alternative* may be to claim too much for their role in health care, but to term them *complementary* may make their role seem secondary to primary medical care (Coulter, 2004). But, overall, to define them in terms of "otherness," that is, by what they are not (as in "not taught in medical schools" or "not practiced by conventional medicine") is also somewhat useless (Eisenberg et al., 1998). That being said, The National Center for Complementary and Alternative Medicine (2000) defines CAM as those

> *healthcare practices that are not an integral part of conventional medicine. As diverse and abundant as the peoples of the world, these practices may be grouped within five major domains: alternative medical systems; mind–body interventions; biologically-based treatments; manipulative and body-based methods; and energy therapies. (p. 7)*

As CAM is increasingly included in the teaching programs in medical schools and in medical practice, these distinctions are becoming increasingly problematic (Bhattacharya, 1998).

Like those of CAM, definitions of IM can range from simply incorporating CAM into conventional medicine to the notion that integrative health care constitutes a new form of medical practice. A single definition or set of definitions for IM has been difficult to establish even by leading entities that shape health care policy and practice. For example, in one of their recent reports on IM, the Institute of Medicine referred to "integrative medicine" in one section and "integrated medicine" in another, even though integrative medicine and integrated medicine are generally not considered the same thing (Ullman, 2009). Maizes, Schneider, Bell, and Weil (2002) defined the term *integrative medicine* as "medicine that reemphasizes the relationship between patient and physician, and integrates the best of complementary and alternative medicine with the best of conventional medicine" (p. 852). Boon, Verhoef, O'Hara, and Findlay (2004) defined "integrative health care" as the combination of an interdisciplinary, nonhierarchical blending of both CAM and conventional medicine that uses a collaborative team approach, is guided by consensus building and mutual respect, and shares a vision of health through a partnership of patient and practitioners to treat the whole person.

Currently, organizations that define themselves as IM health care centers or include IM or CAM as part of their care differ in the type of staff that primarily deliver and manage the care (for example, physicians, nurses, specially trained CAM providers); sources of revenues (for example, fee-for-service, health insurance, philanthropy, research grants); type of delivery setting (for example, teaching hospital, nonprofit or for-profit hospital, community clinic); type of care they provide (for example, primary care, adjunctive, maintenance care after conventional medical care is not effective); and in strategic approaches to integrating CAM into biomedicine (for example, incorporating only those CAM therapies and providers that are already credentialed or licensed). The result is that IM care can be delivered in vastly different ways and in vastly different settings and with vastly different therapies. In this chapter, we define IM as a process in which integration or convergence between biomedicine and CAM occurs without implying a degree of integration, the nature of the integration, or the process by which it is achieved.

Paradigms of Health

Before we discuss empirical work and approaches to outcomes measurement for CAM/IM, it is necessary to understand the paradigms that underlie both: Developing, selecting, using, and monitoring outcome measures that represent any dimension of health involves the philosophical and theoretical paradigms on which such measures are based. Actual measures will differ depending on what these assumptions are (Khorsan, Coulter, Hawk, & Choate, 2008). Biomedicine and CAM paradigms have distinct philosophical foundations, a priori assumptions, and metaphysical beliefs that are considered by many to be incommensurable, incomparable in a Kuhnian sense, and contradictory (Kuhn, 1962). Given such differences, many challenges remain to unify these paradigms into one without doing great harm to one or transforming the other (Coulter, 1990). While we would like to share full arguments to support these premises here, space permits only a brief discussion. We encourage the reader to consult references provided in this section for more detail.

The Biomedical Paradigm. Biomedicine in the West can trace its roots to the germ theory of disease, which helped to transform medicine from an art to a science by bringing together the practice of medicine and the scientific method of investigation. This move to a more scientific approach resulted in a reductionist approach to illness. In this paradigm, the search for external, microscopic causes of disease reduced the consideration of illness to a primary focus on pathology. This shift also elevated the concept of biological determinism. That is, causes of diseases were looked for internally, in the biological structure of the patient (Coulter, 2001). Health came to be seen as an absence of disease, with disease explained in materialistic terms, and a focus on acute illness and trauma taking precedence over chronic illness.

The CAM/IM Paradigm. Although CAM/IM is extremely heterogeneous in practice, many CAM practices arose, or at least developed, in reaction to the biomedical paradigm, in particular the germ theory of disease. Although this reaction took many forms, it was seldom an outright rejection of the theory but more a recognition of its limitations. The most serious opposition concerned the germ theory's "inability" to account for the distribution of disease (Coulter, 1990).

Most supporters of the CAM paradigm postulate that the origin of disease, or health, comes not simply from external causes but from within the body. When disease occurs, it does so because of predisposing factors in the individual. According to this view, germs may be the initiating factor, but lowered resistance is the predisposing factor. The body, when functioning properly, is able to successfully combat disease, and illness is a failure in the body's natural restorative power. Germs by themselves do not cause illness. Biomedicine, in this view, attacks the effects or symptoms of disease but not the cause.

This fundamental a priori difference between CAM and biomedicine leads to a different logic for approaches to treatment. In CAM, the focus is on treating the patient, whose body then will initiate the healing. Whereas in biomedicine the intent of the provider is to cure patients, in CAM the intent is to assist patients in healing themselves. In this approach, diseases are symptoms of a more fundamental underlying cause. Disease here means "dis-ease," or lack of ease in the body, not pathology.

Integration of the Two Paradigms. As we briefly mentioned at the beginning of this chapter, the move to CAM by the public is changing the framework in which medicine is viewed. As Bausell and Berman (2002) state,

> *What we are observing is really nothing less than a genuine Kuhnian paradigmatic shift in world views [that] may represent a consumer-driven variant of George Engel's call for an actual reformulation of what is meant by the practice of medicine itself (p. 31).... As it truly evolves, truly integrative medicine [will] depend on its philosophical foundations and patient-centered approach on systems of CAM that emphasize healing the person as a whole. (p. 134)*

Bell et al. (2002) assert that IM that simply combines biomedicine with CAM

> *is not integrative. Integrative medicine represents a higher order system of care that emphasizes wellness and healing of the entire person (bio-psycho-socio-spiritual dimension) as primary goals, drawing on both conventional and CAM approaches in the context of a supportive and effective physician–patient relationship. (p. 133)*

These assertions, and current events in the health care field, imply that there are three possible scenarios that might describe paradigm integration between CAM and biomedicine: (1) CAM will be adopted (co-opted) into biomedicine itself as largely adjunctive therapy without its philosophical elements; (2) CAM will bring about a surreptitious transformation of medicine that will result from integrating CAM into biomedicine; and (3) a meta-paradigm will be formulated that will allow for both paradigms, and approaches to care, to coexist. A recent article examining the IM curricula in academic health science centers suggests that the first option more accurately describes what is happening in the university-based centers (Benjamin et al., 2007). Likewise, three approaches of integration of IM into biomedicine can be considered: Incorporate into biomedicine those CAM therapies that have (1) passed rigorous scientific scrutiny, (2) passed the test of time, and/or (3) are credentialed or licensed.

Although the chances of the first scenario for integrating CAM and bio-medicine paradigms are probably greater than those of the second or third, the most prominent question is whether therapies, from either approach, will have the same success if they are stripped of the paradigm from which they originated. It may be the case that CAM approaches are effective because they are incorporated in a broad-based wellness paradigm. That is, dismantling each individual paradigm and rebuilding aspects of each paradigm into a new scenario may not produce results that are as effective. Regardless of the pathways that the integration of CAM/IM will continue to take, some sort of "whole systems framework" (for example, a broad focus that goes beyond the disease and interventions of clinical studies to include the total organization of the care delivery) is necessary to build upon (Jonas et al., 2006). As such, several issues associated with this process will need to continue to be addressed, including historical professional animosity, changes in work environment infrastructure, culture and relationships, economic competition, the lack of clearly agreed upon principles on which to base integration at organizational and health care system levels, and the variation in organizational models that exist.

CAM, IM, and Outcomes Measurement: Measurement and Research Challenges

Overall, measurement of outcomes for biomedicine and CAM tend to be based on different underlying philosophies, such as objective versus subjective measurement. Objective measures (for example, physiological states) are derived from the philosophy of logical positivism (which sees the world as largely material in nature and which can be subjected and measured empirically) and are based on the view that the human body in health and illness can likewise be studied by material factors and measured in much the same way as the purely physical world of nature Subjective measures (for example, behavior and quality of life) are derived from such philosophies as existentialism and phenomenology (which evolved and challenged logical positivism and empiricism) and are based on the notion that human beings are agents of their own behavior (Hunt & McEwen, 1980). Regardless of these distinctions, biomedicine and CAM can share some elements in common (Khorsan et al., 2008). With regard to CAM, existential and phenomenological approaches (that is, approaches that are grounded in the meanings held by the patient for their illness or well being) are key aspects of instruments that are likely to collect information about the sick role; the concept of illness as opposed to disease; social/psychological, and in some cases spiritual, aspects of illness; and patient-centered measures (or example, patients perception of daily activities, functioning and disability, quality of life); they also may collect more qualitative than quantitative data. The SF 36 (Garratt, Ruta, Abdalla, & Russell, 1994) and the Health-Related Quality-of-Life (Zahran et al., 2005) are examples. Research approaches to measuring outcomes in biomedicine and CAM/IM also are based on different philosophies and methodological traditions, with some overlap depending on topic. We will touch briefly on some of these methodological approaches and the challenges they pose for CAM/IM, within the context of health services research (HSR), and encourage the reader to consult sources for additional approaches.

HSR is defined as the investigation of the relationship between social structure (for example, personnel, facilities, services available, organizational features, and financing), process (for example, the transaction that occurs between the provider and the patient), and outcomes for personal health services. The strength of HSR is the breadth of its focus, which goes beyond the disease and interventions of clinical studies to include the total organization of care delivery. This is also its major contribution to evidence-based practice (Coulter & Khorsan, 2008). As part of the goal to be as evidence based as possible, HSR also strives to build and classify its hierarchy of evidence (Linde

& Coulter, in press), which includes the following (from highest to lowest strength): evidence provided by at least one appropriately designed randomized clinical trial (RCT); evidence provided by a controlled trial that is not randomized; evidence provided by a well-designed cohort or case-control study; evidence provided by a multiple time series; descriptive studies, case reports, and opinions of experts or respected authorities (Evidence-Based Medicine Working Group, 1992). Three research approaches that are broadly used within HSR have significance for CAM: studies of efficacy and effectiveness, systematic reviews, and descriptive/observational studies.

The real importance of HSR is its focus on such things as utilization, costs, appropriateness, and outcomes in real settings (Coulter & Khorsan, 2008). In this regard, descriptive studies are extremely significant. Herman, D'Huyvetter, and Mohler (2006) note that of the 84 abstracts they investigated related to HSR and CAM, the majority (30) were from surveys of CAM users and their reasons for using CAM. To design studies that can investigate a fuller range of outcomes in real settings, more CAM studies need to be conducted that build the evidence base on scope of practice, patient characteristics, utilization rates, and patient profiles.

Thus, more studies that measure the efficacy (that is, the causal connections between an intervention and specific outcomes, with the RCT as the most rigorous approach) and effectiveness (that is, studies that measure how well an intervention is working or has worked and the associated outcomes with this) of CAM modalities can follow. Although biomedicine uses RCT as its preferred research model (Luce, Kramer, & Goodman, 2009), several problems arise in applying this approach to CAM/IM. First, the use of controls in RCTs results in a situation that is not like normal practice, in which therapies ultimately will be delivered (Coulter, 2007). That is, many areas of CAM (for example, spirituality, chi, and multi-complex therapies that combine unique combinations of herbs so that no two patients get the same combination) are not amenable to inclusion in RCTs without significantly compromising the very therapy being studied, thereby removing aspects of the holistic therapeutic approach that CAM promulgates (Coulter, in press). Second, exclusion criteria for the subjects in RCTs may ensure that the very subpopulations the provider wants to treat in a CAM situation may not be included in the trial. And third, RCTs require a sham treatment such as placebo. In many areas of CAM/IM, it has proved to be impossible to develop a true sham treatment (for example, for acupuncture). So RCTs, for all their strengths and acceptability as the gold standard in traditional medicine, are not an appropriate methodology for assessing the relevance of CAM/IM to the real world of practice.

Like RCTS, there are several challenges associated with conducting *systematic reviews* (that is, formal assessments of the quality of studies that results in a research synthesis or meta-analysis) about CAM/IM. Compared with other fields of practice in health, the number of studies that exist to include in systematic reviews for CAM, and particularly IM, is far lower. Most systematic reviews are based only on the literature in English. This is a problem, as much of CAM research is not published in English, and publications in English and other languages do not often turn up in the refereed literature found in MEDLINE and PubMed. Most of CAM/IM practice is also not located in the universities or the standard research institutes and is not typically part of scholarly interchanges in mainstream health conferences, faculty exchanges, or joint research projects. Consequently, it has been difficult to establish and use a hierarchy of evidence to assess the scope of knowledge that has been generated. Although systematic reviews privilege certain forms of data and knowledge over others (with the expert or specialist getting the lowest rating), the very studies that are privileged are those that are lacking in CAM/IM. This is complicated further by the fact that whole areas of evidence, such as HSR and program evaluation, tend to be left out of systematic reviews (Linde & Coulter, in press).

As one would expect, then, systematic reviews have established the lack of high-quality, rigorous trials in CAM. Such studies have also shown that some of the so-called quality differences that arise when comparing CAM/IM and whole systems research (which are not RCTs) with approaches to drug research (where the gold standard is rigorous RCTs) are not actually differences in quality but differences in research methodology, which make it inappropriate to use such terms as *superior* or *inferior*. The methodologies are simply different (Coulter, 2006).

For CAM/IM, then, the assessment of quality is laden with methodological and other challenges (Feinstein & Horwitz, 1997). To help address these issues, observational study approaches are often used to develop and assess the data needed for clinical practice decisions and programming (Coulter, 2003). Although there is increasing evidence that observation studies compare favorably to RCTs (Benson & Hartz, 2000), there have been several major strikes against the use of observation studies in systematic reviews. The first is that, because all observational studies lack randomization, true assessment of efficacy is not possible. Furthermore, it is not possible to determine whether provider and patient biases may have influenced the results. Results from observation studies cannot be pooled without caution in a meta-analytic sense; however, qualitative data analysis approaches such as content and thematic analyses can be employed to synthesize data in a similar fashion.

The Way Forward: Systems Model and Comparative Effectiveness Research

It is clear that the use of CAM/IM will continue to grow (Coulter & Willis, 2007). The number of CAM providers is growing, recognition of CAM through licensure is increasing, and coverage of CAM by insurance plans is expanding. However, as we have discussed, the challenge to developing research approaches and measures that are most relevant to CAM/IM involves the acknowledgement, compromise, and integration of philosophical, scientific, political, and social issues.

Two pertinent questions arise. First, what type of theoretical or conceptual model is most appropriate to capture the holistic nature of CAM/IM? We suggest the use of a systems paradigm, general systems theory (Beckman, Fernandez, & Coulter 1996). This theory has several features that make it the appropriate theory for CAM/IM, as it posits multilevel structures (mutually dependent organizational levels in which any changes in any one of the subsystems has impacts throughout the system: a holistic model) within an entire system; an ecological view of the relationship between the system and the environment in which both synchronously affect each other; nonlinear causality, in which self-reinforcing feedback plays a significant role in self-maintenance and self-transformation; self-organization, which recognizes the body's ability to return to a balanced state (homeostasis) and to heal itself (vitalism); self-transcendence, or emergent properties (the whole is greater than the sum of its parts); the belief that the mind is characteristic not only of the individual but of social, cultural, and ecological systems; and a rejection of the concept of dualism between the mind and the body.

The second question is what does this mean for CAM/IM outcome measures? The application of systems theory to CAM/IM is still in its infancy, but it implies that measurement must be done at multiple levels: biological, psychological, social, cultural, and ecological. Consequently, a systems approach to outcomes measurement for CAM/IM will help achieve the following:

- Elevate the notion of person-centered care and patient-centered outcome measures, thereby recognizing the value of patient-focused evidence and aligning with efficacy, effectiveness, and efficiency studies of health care services (Khorsan et al., 2008, 2009)

- Elevate the importance of health measures (for example, health-related quality of life), as opposed to disease measures, and the acceptance that health is not just the absence of disease

- Keep CAM/IM outcomes measurement approaches in HSR centered on practice (Coulter & Khorsan, 2008), with a focus on both patient and provider measures, as seen in recent work on IM (Hsiao et al., 2005)

- Turn attentions to evaluations of programs so that assessments and outcomes are also performed at an aggregate level.

Given the importance of CAM/IM in the health care of the American public, it is somewhat surprising that the amount of funding available for research in this area is miniscule in relation to what is spent on biomedicine. In 2009, the National Institutes of Health spent a total of $29,835,000,000 on biomedical research while it spent a total of $584,000 on CAM research (Center for Complementary Alternative Medicine, personal communication, May 22, 2010). That represents 0.02 percent of the Institute's budget. It is therefore not surprising that the development of outcome measures for CAM/IM has lagged considerably behind that in other areas of health. However, given the recent allocation of $1.1 billion to fund comparative effectiveness research (CER: the "generation and synthesis of evidence that compares the benefits and harms of alternative methods to prevent, diagnose, treat, and monitor a clinical condition or to improve the delivery of care. The purpose of CER is to assist consumers, clinicians, purchasers, and policymakers to make informed decisions that will improve health care at both the individual and population levels" [Sox & Greenfield, 2009, p. 203]) from the American Recovery and Reinvestment Act of 2009; other allocations, such as $300 million for the Agency for Healthcare Research and Quality, $400 million for the National Institutes of Health, and $400 million at the discretion of the Secretary of Health and Human Services; and a request for research proposals by the National Centre for Complementary Alternative Medicine for CER Studies of Complementary and Alternative Medicine, it is safe to say that both CER (Conway & Clancy, 2009) and CAM/IM outcomes research have entered a new era.

In many ways, the emphasis on CER should be beneficial for CAM research. CER solves two historical concerns for CAM/IM researchers: It focuses on effectiveness, not efficacy, and tests holistic approaches to care. CER allows providers to care for patients in any way they choose (Coulter, in press), thereby setting the stage for trials that are more in alignment with a whole systems research approach rather than with RCT (Jonas et al., 2006). This approach also allows for variability in the way individuals are treated in the trial, thereby coming closer to personalized medicine (Garber & Tunis, 2009).

Because CER will allow studies to focus on those who are receiving care normally, it includes populations and subpopulations that are normally seen in practice, which makes results more clinically relevant. The focus will also largely be on what concerns providers and patients (that is, effectiveness) and not as much on what has traditionally concerned scientists (for example, efficacy). CER's focus on observational studies also harmonizes well with the CAM field (Coulter, 2007), broadening the definition of acceptable evidence.

So, then, what is the future for outcome measures in CAM/IM? Like all the health professionals, both CAM/IM providers will be increasingly asked to substantiate what significant outcomes their approach achieves, at what cost, and how these outcomes compare to other available therapies. To achieve this, we would suggest the following agenda:

- Establish clarity about what CAM/IM is. This is a descriptive task and will involve qualitative and observational methods. This type of study must identify what is actually done in the practice of various CAM providers and in IM. For the latter, there is such variability at the moment about which CAM therapies are part of IM that at best there exist only exemplars of IM clinics. There is no one dominant form yet.

- Base outcome measures on what has meaning to the patients and what the providers set out to achieve.

- Develop comprehensive measures that capture the multi-disciplinary nature of IM and the large variability in CAM, by which patients receive highly personalized care.

- Develop outcome measures that capture context process and outcomes (program evaluation) and are sensitive to complexity (that is, whole-system measures).

- Adapt biomedical outcome measures and HSR measures that are appropriate to CAM/IM.

The challenge of this agenda is to make sure these measures are validated for CAM/IM populations. This is largely a psychometric task but does involve qualitative work to establish that these instruments have meaning for these patients. We are certain that this agenda can be achieved if a cadre of stakeholders (researchers, clinicians, patients, managers, policymakers, and advocates) commits to taking on these tasks together, with passion and vigor, and that research funding allocations continue to include CAM/IM as integral parts of health care reform.

References

Astin, J. A. (1998). Why patients use alternative medicine: Results of a national study. *JAMA, 279,* 1548–1553.

Barnes, P. M., Powell-Griner, E., McFann, K., & Nahin, R. L. (2004). Complementary and alternative medicine use among adults: United States, 2002. *Advance Data, 343,* 1–19.

Bausell, R. B., & Berman, B. M. (2002). Commentary: Alternative medicine: Is it a reflection of the continued emergence of the biopsychosocial paradigm? *American Journal of Medical Quality, 17*(1), 28–32.

Beckman, J. F., Fernandez, C. E., & Coulter, I.D. (1996). A systems model of health care: A proposal. *Journal of Manipulative and Physiological Therapeutics, 19,* 208–215.

Bell, I. R., Caspi, O., Schwartz, G. E., Grant, K. L., Gaudet, T. W., Rychener, D., et al. (2002). Integrative medicine and systemic outcomes research: Issues in the emergence of a new model for primary health care. *Archives of Internal Medicine, 162*(2), 133–140.

Benjamin, P. J., Phillips, R., Warren, D., Salveson, C., Hammerschlag, R., Snider, P., et al. (2007). Response to a proposal for an integrative medicine curriculum. *Journal of Alternative & Complementary Medicine, 13,* 1021–1033.

Benson, K., & Hartz, A. (2000). A comparison of observational and randomized, controlled trials. *New England Journal of Medicine, 342,* 1878–1886.

Bhattacharya, B. (1998). Programs in the United States with complementary and alternative medicine education: An ongoing list. *Journal of Alternative & Complementary Medicine, 4,* 325–335.

Boon, H., Verhoef, M., O'Hara, D., & Findlay, B. (2004). From parallel practice to integrative health care: A conceptual framework. *BMC Health Services Research, 4,* 15.

Conway, P. H., & Clancy, C. (2009). Comparative-effectiveness research: Implications of the Federal Coordinating Council's report. *New England Journal of Medicine, 361,* 328–330.

Coulter, I. D. (1990). The patient, the practitioner, and wellness: Paradigm lost, paradigm gained. *Journal of Manipulative Physiological Therapy, 13*(2), 107–111.

Coulter, I. D. (2001). Evidence-based dentistry and health services research: Is one possible without the other? *Journal of Dental Education, 65,* 714–724.

Coulter, I. D. (2003). Observational studies and evidence-based practice: Can't live with them, can't live without them. *Journal of Evidence-Based Dental Practice, 3,* 1–4.

Coulter, I. D. (2004). Integration and paradigm clash. In E. G. Tovey, P. J. Adams, & G. Easthope (Eds.), *The mainstreaming of complementary and alternative medicine: Studies in social context* (pp. 103–122.). London: Routledge.

Coulter, I. D. (2006). Evidence summaries and synthesis: Necessary but insufficient approach for determining clinical practice of integrated medicine? *Integrative Cancer Therapies, 5*, 282–286.

Coulter, I. D. (2007). Evidence based complementary and alternative medicine: Promises and problems. *Forsch Komplementmed, 14*(2), 102–108.

Coulter, I. D. (in press). Comparative effectiveness research: Does the emperor have clothes? *Alternative Therapies in Health and Medicine.*

Coulter, I. D., & Khorsan, R. (2008). Is health services research the holy grail of CAM research? *Alternative Therapies in Health and Medicine, 14*(4), 40–45.

Coulter, I. D., & Willis, E. (2007). Explaining the growth of complementary and alternative medicine. *Health Sociology Review, 16*(3/4), 214–225.

Eisenberg, D. M., Davis, R. B., Ettner, S. L., Appel, S., Wilkey, S., Van Rompay, M., & Kessler, R. C. (1998). Trends in alternative medicine use in the United States, 1990–1997: Results of a follow-up national survey. *JAMA, 280*, 1569–1575.

Eisenberg, D. M., Kessler, R. C., Foster, C., Norlock, F. E., Calkins, D. R., & Delbanco, T. L. (1993). Unconventional medicine in the United States. *New England Journal of Medicine, 328*, 246–252.

Eisenberg, D. M., Kessler, R. C., Van Rompay, M. I., Kaptchuk, T. J., Wilkey, S. A., Appel, S., et al. (2001). Perceptions about complementary therapies relative to conventional therapies among adults who use both: Results from a national survey. *Annals of Internal Medicine, 135*, 344–351.

Evidence-Based Medicine Working Group. (1992). Evidence-based medicine: A new approach to teaching the practice of medicine. *JAMA, 268*, 2420–2425.

Feinstein, A. R., & Horwitz, R. I. (1997). Problems in the "evidence" of "evidence-based medicine." *American Journal of Medicine, 103*, 529–535.

Garber, A. M., & Tunis, S. R. (2009). Does comparative-effectiveness research threaten personalized medicine? *New England Journal of Medicine, 360*, 1925–1927.

Garratt, A. M., Ruta, D. A., Abdall, M. I., & Russell, I. T. (1994). SF-36 health survey questions: II. Responsiveness to change in health status in four common clinical conditions. *Quality Health Care, 3*, 186–192.

Graham, R. E., Ahn, A. C., Davis, R. B., O'Connor, B. B., Eisenberg, D. M., & Phillips, R. S. (2005). Use of complementary and alternative medical therapies among racial and ethnic minority adults: Results from the 2002 National Health Interview Survey. *Journal of the National Medical Association, 97*, 535–545.

Herman, P. M., D'Huyvetter, K., & Mohler, M. J. (2006). Are health services research methods a match for CAM? *Alternative Therapies in Health and Medicine, 12,* 78–83.

Hsiao, A. F., Hays, R. D., Ryan, G. W., Coulter, I. D., Andersen, R. M., Hardy, M. L., et al. (2005). A self-report measure of clinicians' orientation toward integrative medicine. *Health Services Research, 40,* 1553–1569.

Hunt, S. M., & McEwen, J. (1980). The development of a subjective health indicator. *Sociology of Health and Illness, 2,* 231–246.

Jonas, W. B., Beckner, W., & Coulter, I. (2006). Proposal for in integrated evaluation model for the study of whole systems health care in cancer. *Integrative Cancer Therapies, 5,* 315–319.

Khorsan, R., Coulter, I. D., Hawk, C., & Choate, C. G. (2008). Measures in chiropractic research: Choosing patient-based outcome assessments. *Journal of Manipulative Physiological Therapy, 31,* 355–375.

Khorsan, R., York, A., Coulter, I. D., Wurzman, R., Walter, J. A., & Coeytaux, R. R. (2009). Patient-based outcome assessment instruments in acupuncture research. *Journal of Alternative & Complementary Medicine, 16,* 27–35.

Kuhn, T. (1962). *The structure of scientific revolutions.* Chicago: University of Chicago Press.

Larson, L. (2005). Integrating integrative medicine—A how-to guide. *Trustee, 58*(10), 14–16, 21–22, 1.

Linde, K., & Coulter, I. D. (in press). Systematic reviews and meta-analyses. In G. Lewith, W. Jonas, & H. Walach (Eds.), *Clinical research in complementary therapies.* Oxford, England: Elsevier.

Luce, B. R., Kramer, J. M., Goodman, S. N., Connor, J. T., Tunis, S., Whicher, D., & Schwartz, J. S. (2009). Rethinking randomized clinical trials for comparative effectiveness research: The need for transformational change. *Annals of Internal Medicine, 151,* 203–205.

Maizes, V., Schneider, C., Bell, I., & Weil. A. (2002). Integrative medical education: Development and implementation of a comprehensive curriculum at the University of Arizona. *Academic Medicine, 77,* 851–860.

Nahin, R., Barnes, P. M., Stussman, B. J., & Bloom, B. (2009). *Cost of complementary and alternative medicine (CAM) and frequency of visits to CAM practitioners: United States 2007* (National Health Statistics Reports No. 18). Hyattsville, MD: National Center for Health Statistics.

Ni, H., Simile, C., & Hardy, A. M. (2002). Utilization of complementary and alternative medicine by United States adults: Results from the 1999 National Health Interview Survey. *Medical Care, 40,* 353–358.

Pelletier, K. R., Marie, A., Krasner, M., & Haskell, W. E. (1997). Current trends in the integration and reimbursement of complementary and alternative medicine by managed care, insurance carriers, and hospital providers. *American Journal of Health Promotion, 12*(2), 112–123.

Ruta, D. A., Abdalla, M. I., Garratt, A. M., Coutts, A., & Russell, I. T. (1994). SF 36 health survey questionnaire: I. Reliability in two patient-based studies. *Quality in Health Care, 3*(4), 180–185.

Sox, H. (2010). Defining comparative effectiveness research: The importance of getting it right. *Medical Care, 48*(Suppl. 6), S7–S8.

Sox, H., & Greenfield, S. (2009). Comparative effectiveness research: A report from the Institute of Medicine. *Annals of Internal Medicine, 151,* 203–205.

Ullman, D. (2010). A review of a historical summit on integrative medicine. eCAM 2010: 7(4) 54-514. doi:10.1093/ecam/nep128

Whorton, J. C. (1999). The history of complementary and alternative medicine. In W. Jonas & J. S. Levine (Eds.), *Essentials of complementary and alternative medicine* (pp. 6–30). Philadelphia: Lippincott Williams & Wilkins.

Zahran, H. S., Kobau, R., Moriarty, D. G., Zack, M. M., Holt, J., & Donehoo, R. (2005). Health-related quality of life surveillance—United States, 1993–2002. *Morbidity and Mortality Weekly Report Surveillance Summaries, 54*(4), 1–35.

CHAPTER 12

Research-to-Practice Example:

Screening and Outcomes Assessments in Cancer Care

James R. Zabora

This chapter is one of three research-to-practice examples in the second edition of Outcomes Measurement in the Human Services. *Following in the spirit of the first edition, the three examples illustrate particular issues that are pertinent to integrating or translating research into practice in each of the human service domains featured in the book: physical health, behavioral health, and child and family services. This chapter describes an instrument and screening and outcomes assessment process for chronic care, specifically psychosocial distress associated with cancer.*

Despite health care reform having become a national priority, the United States continues on course in 2010 to have national health care expenditures reach 18 percent of the gross domestic product, with per capita spending exceeding $9,000 (Centers for Disease Control and Prevention, 2010). To a not inconsiderable extent, undetected and untreated psychological distress (that may be transformed into somatic complaints such as fatigue, pain, or sleep disorders) contributes to this economic burden. Given data that one third of the chronically ill experience a significantly elevated level of distress,

30 million patients would benefit from an integrated health care system that includes access to essential mental health services. If the net gain was only a $3,000 per capita savings after expenses related to the integration of mental health services, the total in savings would approximate $100 billion dollars. For example, brief psychosocial interventions that address significantly elevated levels of distress at the initiation of treatment may be far less costly than a series of medically inappropriate procedures and scans, or an avoidable hospitalization if physical complaints increase in severity (Zabora, 2009).

Estimates suggest that more than 10 million Americans live with some form of cancer, with a lifetime risk to develop cancer of 1 in 2 for men, and 1 in 3 for women. Medical costs related to cancer are staggering, but the psychological and social consequences of cancer are also great. However, the same is true of other chronic conditions such as cardiovascular disease, HIV/AIDS, renal disease, and diabetes. In fact, the Centers for Disease Control and Prevention estimate that at least 1 of every 3 people in the United States lives with a chronic illness (Centers for Disease Control and Prevention, 2010). Despite the development of Distress Management Guidelines by the National Comprehensive Cancer Network in 1999, availability of and access to formalized and structured psychosocial or mental health programs for patients, survivors, and families continue to be severely lacking. The integration of cancer care with high-quality psychosocial programs tends to occur only in National Cancer Institute–designated comprehensive cancer centers, which serve only a small fraction of cancer patients and survivors. Nearly 85 percent of all cancer patients do not receive treatment in comprehensive cancer centers, but rather through a range of community-based programs and settings (Institute of Medicine, 2007).

Likewise, for other chronic diseases, medical management seldom pays attention, let alone sufficient attention, to the critical need to integrate health and mental health care. Models of care are necessary that integrate mental health approaches with the delivery of care for chronic illnesses. Methods can be implemented to provide effective and rapid models of psychosocial screening (please also see chapter 15 in this volume) to identify high-risk patients in order to offer effective mental health interventions within communities. If this integration is successful, overall health care costs resulting from unnecessary and inappropriate medical utilization could be dramatically reduced (Zabora, 2009).

Interactions with patients suggest that all patients experience some level of distress as part of a process of normalizing early reactions to a diagnosis of a chronic condition. Of primary importance is *psychological distress*, an unpleasant emotional experience of a psychological, social, and/or spiritual nature that interferes with the ability to cope effectively with cancer and its treatments. Distress extends along a continuum, ranging from common normal feelings of vulnerability and sadness to problems that can be disabling, such as depression, anxiety, and social isolation. (National Comprehensive Cancer Network, 2010). If emotional distress is undetected and untreated, unhealthy behaviors can occur; satisfaction with life can decrease; and, as mentioned, inappropriate use of health care resources may increase (Allison et al. 1995; Zabora, Loscalzo, & Smith, 2000). Undetected emotional distress may be converted into multiple somatic complaints such as fatigue and pain, and health care providers may respond by ordering unnecessary evaluations, medications, and treatments. This type of approach also sets the stage for outcomes assessment. For example, patients with higher levels of distress can be targeted for appropriate evidence-based interventions. After screening and before intervention, additional standardized instruments could be completed to measure symptoms such as pain or fatigue or a critical item such as quality of life. In this way, a repeated measures system could assess and demonstrate the effectiveness of the interventions on items such as distress and quality of life. Of note, although much of the research related to psychological distress has been done with cancer patients and their families, the Institute of Medicine's report (2007) clearly stated that these approaches to psychosocial care are applicable to other chronic illnesses.

Although the aforementioned approaches to detecting psychological distress seem reasonable, studies indicate that physicians, nurses, and other health care clinical personnel often do not identify patients with elevated levels of anxiety and depression in a timely manner (Rainey, Wellisch, & Fawzy, 1983); this therefore affects the offering and delivery of psychosocial or mental health interventions at appropriate times in the course of care. To date, although many investigators have examined the concept of psychosocial screening among cancer patients, little progress has been achieved (despite the distress management guidelines established by the National Comprehensive Cancer Network) in demonstrating clinical feasibility, utility, and benefit of an early detection approach. This is distressing in and of itself, as psychological distress can be measured with a high level of reliability and validity. In fact, a series of studies from 1983 to 2001 indicates that one of three cancer patients experiences levels of distress that are two standard deviations above the mean (Zabora, BrintzenhofeSzoc, Curbow, & Piantadosi, 2001).

Screening questionnaires offer an excellent method for identifying people who are distressed, especially those who do not convey their distress when speaking to their health care providers or staff. The screening process, by the nature of its content, also communicates to the individual and his or her family that the health care team cares about and values quality of life. Although a variety of questionnaires are available, instruments such as the Brief Symptom Inventory-18 (Zabora, BrintzenhofeSzoc, Jacobsen, et al., 2001), and the

Problem Checklist (Zabora, Loscalzo, & Weber, 2003) offer a comprehensive examination of critical constructs that identify patients at risk. The following section describes these instruments and their application in practice.

The Brief Symptom Inventory-18 and Problem Checklist

The Brief Symptom Inventory–18 (BSI-18) requires only one to two minutes of patient time to complete, and even less staff time to score. The BSI-18 can easily be given during the initial visit to a cancer center, and can be repeated at appropriate intervals to monitor the effectiveness of mental health interventions. The Problem Checklist (PCL) also requires only about one minute to complete and lists 20 of the most common problems that cancer patients experience. Of particular note, given their disabling effects, fatigue and pain are the only two problems that appear in a visual analogue format.

The BSI-18 is scored by adding the numerical response each of the 18 items, which results in an overall distress score. There are also three separate subscores for anxiety, depression, and somatization. The results of the BSI-18 should be discussed with the patient and his or her caregivers, and treatment or further evaluation provided for those with elevated scores. The current cutoff scores that were used at the Sidney Kimmel Comprehensive Cancer Center at Johns Hopkins University to determine whether some type of mental health intervention was indicated are shown in Table 12-1.

If male and female patients score more than 10 or 13 respectively, they should be seen for a comprehensive assessment within 72 hours of completing these instruments. At the time of assessment, social workers, as focal members of the health care team (for example, social workers provide about 70 percent of all mental health care in the United States [Zabora, 1998]), can use specific responses from the BSI-18 that seem to be most important to the patient.

Table 12-1: Current Cutoff Scores for the Brief Symptom Inventory–18 Used at Johns Hopkins

	Low Distress		High Distress	
Domain	**Men**	**Women**	**Men**	**Women**
Depression	≤3	≤3	≥4	≥4
Anxiety	≤3	≤5	≥4	≥6
Somatization	≤3	≤4	≥4	≥5
Total Distress	≤9	≤12	≥10	≥13

These responses can further be understood with the PCL, a tool developed by the social work staff at Johns Hopkins, which is designed to be completed by each cancer patient along with the BSI-18.

The PCL assesses common problems experienced by patients receiving care in a cancer center. The checklist includes problems with fatigue, pain, management of emotions, and communication with family members, as well as practical problems such as transportation. This unique, tailored approach enables staff to provide a systematic approach to common problems. Results from the PCL also communicates to patients that problems are common and can be managed. That is, a plan of action can be developed in conjunction with knowledgeable health care professionals to instill a sense of hope, control, and optimism.

If the BSI-18 and the PCL are used for screening, critical decisions need to be made in advance about how to respond to elevated scores. One simple scheme is to offer a psychosocial assessment only to patients who score at or above the cutoff scores on the BSI-18. Psychosocial assessments should be provided by a trained mental health professional such as a social worker, psychologist, or psychiatrist. For the BSI-18, scoring norms have been developed specifically for cancer patients, and at Johns Hopkins, for example, an assessment is provided if a threshold score is attained or surpassed. At a minimum, the high-risk patients are covered. The relationships between levels of distress and appropriate psychosocial interventions are detailed in Figure 12-1, which also provides guidance for how social workers and other health care professionals can develop and provide comprehensive clinical approaches in the care of cancer patients and their families.

On the basis of the data from Johns Hopkins in Table 12-1, slightly more than one third of screened patients specifically requested assistance with fatigue, which was the most commonly endorsed problem on the PCL. With pain as the second most frequently endorsed problem, the importance of the ability for patients to maintain physical functioning is shown as being paramount. A meaningful quality of life is virtually impossible within the context

Figure 12-1: Psychosocial Distress and Psychotherapeutic Interventions

Table 12-2: Critical Outcome Assessment Domains and Elements

Domain	Element
Physical	Performance status, mental status, symptoms, physical imitations, sexuality, advance directive
Psychological	Level of distress, internal resources, problem-solving skills, quality of life
Social	External resources, adequacy of support, availability of support, employment history, family functioning
Financial	Insurance status, level of income, access to other financial resources, debts
Legal	Will, estate planning
Spiritual	Hope
Existential	Meaning of life, value of my life, helplessness versus worthlessness, life review

of untreated fatigue and pain. Attention to the effective management of acute and debilitating symptoms is essential to the comprehensive clinical care of cancer patients.

The BSI-18 and the PCL offer the foundation for assessments by providing the social worker with scores for overall distress, depression, anxiety, and somatization (physical symptoms caused by emotional distress), as well as a series of problems that are specifically relevant to the patient. In addition, a number of psychosocial programs add pain and fatigue to the PCL but display these symptoms on 10-point Likert scales. If additional time is available, other domains can be considered to complete a more comprehensive assessment (see Table 12-2). Such an assessment can then lead to recommendations for proven effective psychosocial interventions (Fawzy et al., 1995) that include psycho-educational, cognitive–behavioral, disease-management, and brief counseling/therapy modalities.

A few of these domains are important to highlight. Spirituality and sexuality continue to gain importance on the basis of results from patient-focused research findings among persons with various chronic illnesses. *Spirituality* can be defined as "the search for meaning, purpose, and connection with self, others, the universe, and the ultimate, however one understands it. This may or may not be expressed through religious forms or institutions" (Sheridan, 2009). Research findings indicate that spirituality or religious involvement acts as a protective mechanism, as evidenced by people experiencing lower rates of cardiovascular disease, hypertension, depression, elevated stress hormones, and social isolation. Correspondingly, high levels of religious involvement or spiritual beliefs result in higher rates of immune functioning, hope, optimism, and social support (Koenig, 2001). The HOPE Approach to Spiritual Assessment (Anandarajah & Hight, 2001) provides clear guidance to assess the religious/spiritual domain and integrate it into a problem-solving intervention.

Although sexuality should be addressed in a comprehensive psychosocial assessment, little information is available to assist professionals in approaching this domain of physical functioning. In addition, there is a lack of agreement as to whose responsibility is it to examine sexuality and intimacy within the health care team. Although a rationale can be put forward that the social worker is most appropriate in this regard, other members of the health care team might challenge this, as psychologists and nurses may be perceived as having higher levels of training needed to address these issues. Body image and self-concept, sexual functioning and desire, and relational concerns can all be barriers to patients—especially those with chronic illnesses—seeking and receiving the care they need (Cagle & Bolte, 2009).

Conclusions

Despite the apparent ease of screening for distress and related problems, there are clearly benefits, as well as barriers, to this process. Benefits include enhanced ability to allocate resources on the basis of patient data; streamlined intake assessment; awareness by the psychosocial team of patient concerns before initial assessment, and clear communication to patients regarding the importance of psychosocial care in the institution. Most often, these benefits facilitate the commitment of social workers and health care professionals, and support staff such as clinic registrants, who strive to enhance patient care. However, barriers may also be present, including increased institutional liability if high-distress patients are identified; increased workload for already overburdened social workers and other health care professionals; identification of who will assume the additional responsibility and tasks associated with screening; duplicated efforts of social work and nursing staff who already assess for emotional needs, and increased documentation time. Each of these barriers must be addressed with facts and data to decrease potential liability, make workloads more manageable, and recruit and motivate staff to participate in the screening process.

Accordingly, three critical points need to be emphasized. First, although the focus of this chapter has been cancer, the Institute of Medicine Report (2007) that focused on the needs of cancer patients presented evidence that psychosocial screening and early interventions would also benefit patients with other chronic illnesses. Other conditions such as cardiovascular disease, HIV/AIDS, renal disease, and chronic obstructive pulmonary disease equally challenge patients to emotionally respond their altered health status along with the management of difficult treatments and related symptoms. These types of chronic diseases generate symptoms such as anxiety, fatigue, and pain, which are amenable to these psychosocial approaches.

Second, use of a standardized instrument such as the BSI-18 to identify high-distress patients serves as the first measurement point for outcomes assessment. In a repeated measures design, distress could be measure every 3 or 6 months along with other measures of symptoms and quality of life. In this way, social workers could demonstrate the effectiveness of their interventions in both the short and long term.

Finally, the current trend in health care reform provides a unique opportunity for health care social workers and other health care professionals to, in turn, design new systems of care that focus on management of distress and symptom management. The approach detailed in this chapter enables oncology social workers to promote new methods within their clinical settings that are based on evidence and produce documentable outcomes. Although outcomes such as reductions in distress and increases in quality of life are desirable goals in themselves, the economic potential associated with this approach should result in strong support from members of the health care team and administrators. Health care social workers must seize this opportunity to demonstrate these skills and be active, direct participants in health care reform.

References

Allison, T. G., Williams, D. E., Miller, T. D., Patten, C. A., Bailey, K. R., Squires, R. W., & Gau, G. T. (1995). Medical and economic costs of psychologic distress in patients with coronary artery disease. *Mayo Clinic Proceedings, 70*, 734–742.

Anandarajah, G., & Hight, E. (2001). Spirituality and medical practice: Using the HOPE questions as a practical tool for spiritual assessment. *American Family Physician, 63*(1), 81–99.

Cagle, J. G. & Bolte, S. (2009). Sexuality and life-threatening illness: Implications for social work and palliative care. *Health & Social Work, 34,* 223–233.

Centers for Disease Control and Prevention. (2010). *Diseases & conditions.* Retrieved from http://www.cdc.gov/DiseasesConditions/

Fawzy, F., Fawzy, N., Arndy, L. A., & Pasnau, R. O. (1995). Critical review of psychosocial interventions in cancer care. *Archives of General Psychiatry, 52,* 100–113.

Institute of Medicine. (2007). *Cancer care for the whole patient: Meeting psychosocial health needs.* Washington, DC: National Academies Press.

Koenig, H. G. (2001). Religion, spirituality, and medicine: How are they related and what does it mean? *Mayo Clinic Proceedings, 76,* 1189–1191.

National Comprehensive Cancer Network. (2010). *NCCN clinical practice guidelines in oncology: Distress management.* Ft. Washington, PA: Author.

Rainey, L. C., Wellisch, D. K., & Fawzy, F. I. (1983). Training health care professionals in psychosocial aspects of cancer: A continuing education model. *Journal of Psychosocial Oncology, 1*(1), 41–60.

Sheridan, M. J. (2009, November 18). Spiritually-sensitive social work practice in healthcare. *Department of Social Work grand rounds.* New York: Mt. Sinai Hospital.

Zabora, J. R. (1998). Screening procedures for psychosocial distress. In J.C. Holland. (Ed.), *Psycho-oncology* (pp. 653–661). New York: Oxford University Press.

Zabora, J. R. (2009). *A white paper on health care reform in the United States: The need to integrate mental health services into health care delivery.* Washington, DC: Catholic University of America.

Zabora, J. R., BrintzenhofeSzoc, K., Curbow, B., Hooker, C., & Piantadosi, S. (2001). The prevalence of psychological distress by cancer site. *Psycho-oncology, 10,* 19–28.

Zabora, J. R., BrintzenhofeSzoc, K., Jacobsen, P., Curbow, B., Piantadosi, S., Hooker, C., & Derogatis, L. (2001). A new psychosocial screening instrument for use with cancer patients. *Psychosomatics, 42,* 241–246.

Zabora, J. R., Loscalzo, M. L., & Smith, E. D. (2000). Psychosocial rehabilitation. In M. D. Abeloff (Ed.), *Clinical oncology* (2nd ed., pp. 2845–2865). New York: Churchill Livingstone.

Zabora, J. R., Loscalzo, M. J., & Weber, J. (2003). Managing complications in cancer: Identifying and responding to the patient's perspective. *Seminars in Oncology Nursing, 19*(4, Suppl. 2), 1–9.

PART III

Outcomes Measurement in Mental and Behavioral Health

CHAPTER 13

New Directions for Outcome-oriented Mental Health System Transformation[1]

Timothy A. Kelly

America's mental health service delivery system is in shambles...[and] needs dramatic reform. (New Freedom Commission on Mental Health, 2003)

Less than half of all mental health care is supported by good evidence. It will take decades to conduct comparative effectiveness studies, modify laws and change practitioner behavior. (National Council for Community Behavioral Healthcare, 2008)

The current system of mental health and substance use care in America has been overly reliant on outdated treatments, quick to medicate and hospitalize, and stubbornly resistant to reforms such as the use of evidence-based practices and clinical outcome measurement systems. Despite recent pushes for "transformation," America's health care system has yet to commit to and implement a system of care that focuses on helping clients truly "recover" from serious

---

[1] Much of the material for this chapter was drawn from *Healing the Broken Mind: Transforming America's Failed Mental Health System* (Kelly, 2009), which contains additional references on the topic at hand. It is reused here with permission from NYU Press.

mental illness and substance use. Recovery does not mean perfect healing, but it does mean being able to succeed in one's home community by having a real home, a fulfilling job, and deep relationships. With effective treatments, this is an achievable goal.

There have been laudable presidential efforts made to reform mental health care over the past half-century, but with disappointing results. During the Kennedy administration, Community Mental Health Centers were launched with the hope of providing effective community care, especially for those who were deinstitutionalized or discharged from psychiatric hospitals. During the Carter and Clinton administrations, White House–level conferences were held to address mental health reform needs. During the Bush administration, the New Freedom Commission likewise evaluated the system of mental health care and offered prescriptions for improvement. In each case, systemic problems were correctly identified and corrective policies were proposed. Yet, somehow, America's fragmented, ineffective mental health system of care has stubbornly refused to yield to innovative, consumer-focused, outcome-oriented home- and community-based care that would readily facilitate recovery.

The 21st century is not the time to defer once again to the forces of the status quo. Rather, it is time to do whatever it takes to finally get it right, starting with a focus on the actual clinical outcomes of care in the lives of consumers. New policies and approaches to care must be implemented in order to promote an outcomes-oriented system of care that is evidence based, as less than 15 percent of consumers currently receive such mental health services (Merrens, 2005). Accordingly, this chapter addresses what it means to have an outcomes-oriented system of mental health care, and what it takes to get there.

Evidenced-based Practice and Measuring Clinical Outcomes

Until the 1970s, the question of the appropriateness and effectiveness of mental health treatment was seldom raised, and if ever it was, it was simply left up to the treating authorities in charge. From the 1970s on, mental health providers have been working hard to find ways to effectively treat those who come to them for care. Persons with mental illness and/or substance use and their families have been working hard to make the mental health and substance use system more consumer driven and humane. And third-party payers have been trying to find a mix of services and coverage that they think can achieve efficient treatments. But, despite all these efforts, the outcomes of mental health and substance use care in the United States remain bitterly disappointing:

Consumers continue to experience the vicious cycle of clinical crisis, hospitalization, and discharge to less-than-optimal community services (Kelly 2009; Mechanic, 2008). Why is this?

Since the 1990s, a steady and much-needed march toward the promotion of evidence-based practice (EBP) has been launched, with a growing number of researchers and policymakers calling for EBPs, especially in the United Kingdom. For example, The Cochrane Collaboration, dedicated to the promotion of EBPs and maintaining a library of current relevant research (for example, Clarke & Oxman, 1999; see also http://www.cochrane.org) was established in 1993, as well as the British journal, *Evidence-Based Mental Health* (see http://ebmh.bmjjournals.com). In the United States, the implementation of assertive community treatment has begun to demonstrate the value of using EBPs.

Over the past 15 years, a growing body of research literature has succeeded in establishing the definition, importance, and practical usefulness of evidence-based mental health practices (for example, Corrigan, McCracken, & McNeilly, 2005; Davies, Nutley, & Smith, 2000; Dixon & Goldman, 2003; Drake, Merrens, & Lynde, 2005; Kelly, 2003, 2009; Merrens, 2005; Roth & Fonagy, 1996). As a result, an increasing number of policymakers, insurers, and other funders are expecting that treatments or services offered for a person with mental illness and/or substance use will first be subjected to scientific outcomes-oriented testing and found to be effective. For instance, many insurers now require their mental health practitioners to identify modalities used with patients, and they expect to see evidence-based approaches such as cognitive–behavioral therapy included.

Testing to establish EBPs requires the use of clinical outcome data. In other words, one natural application of outcome data, as they accumulate, is to help identify EBPs. The hope is that by scientifically testing various approaches to care, all mental health treatments will eventually become truly evidence based, and in turn, those that are ineffective will be identified and replaced. It is likely that in the not-too-distant future mental health insurers will require that all covered services consist of EBPs.

Unfortunately, some providers are comfortable with using EBPs but not with using outcome surveys on a regular basis (for example, they are viewed as too burdensome, threatening, expensive, or unnecessary) even though it was those very surveys that identified EBP treatments in the first place. What could possibly be wrong with measuring the extent to which a person has been helped by mental health care? The answer depends on who you are, as stakeholders have different concerns regarding this matter.

Regardless of perspective, the question of clinical effectiveness has been the focus of much research and publication, especially over the last 15 years.

Clinical outcome research has established, for example, the effectiveness of cognitive and interpersonal therapy and antidepressant medications for treating depression, the effectiveness of cognitive and systematic-desensitization therapy and antianxiety medication for treating anxiety disorders, and the importance of the therapeutic relationship (Bickman, 2005; Seligman, 1994; Shadish, Navarro, Matt, & Phillips, 2000). (The science involved is known as either *efficacy research*, which is performed under controlled situations [usually through a university lab], or *effectiveness research*, which is performed in the field. Effectiveness research is more applicable, because it takes into account the multiple variables providers must address when working with actual patients in the field—for instance, many patients have more than one diagnosis [for example, depression and alcohol dependence]—whereas efficacy research typically focuses on only one diagnosis at a time.)

Because this research requires the use of clinical surveys, there is also a growing body of literature on standardized clinical outcome measures and their uses. In the mid-1990s, Martin Seligman (1995) demonstrated what has since become widely accepted: A survey (that focuses primarily on symptom reduction and functional life improvement) of those receiving care in the field is, in fact, the "gold standard" of data for establishing clinical effectiveness.

Drawing on this growing body of clinical effectiveness literature, several teams of researchers have developed core batteries of outcome questionnaires that meet the needs of researchers, clinicians, consumers, insurers, and policymakers alike (for example, Barkham et al. 1998). However, despite the availability of these scientifically proven and clinically useful outcome measures, many "are struck by how slow the field has been to deal adequately with the subtleties of outcome measurement" (Jacobson, Roberts, Berns, & McGlinchey, 1999, p. 306).

What is needed is for the field to adopt a scientifically credible and consumer-focused methodology with which mental health and substance use providers, and others, can assess and document their clients' clinical improvements. Such a methodology must be based on the consumer's self-report, because that is the most direct source of information. (Of course, there are some exceptions to this rule. Some consumers may be incapable of accurate assessment due to severity of illness, hypochondria, having another agenda requiring the need to "fake bad," and so on. In those cases, common sense requires a heavier reliance on the provider's assessment.) The methodology must also be scientifically sound. Fortunately, over the past 15 years, standardized, objective clinical outcome measures have been developed and tested for use with nearly every population and treatment setting, and for nearly any diagnosis (for example, Corcoran & Fischer 2000). These measures are basically questionnaires (instruments) designed to be minimally burdensome on those who fill them out, yet comprehensive enough to capture improvement in the most relevant areas. The questions (items) used on these instruments have been honed through research to be clear and concise, and to identify clinical improvements as well as areas where further needs must be addressed. For example, an item might read as follows: "During the past week I have felt down or depressed: (a) all the time, (b) frequently, (c) daily, (d) occasionally, (e) never." Assuming careful and honest responses, items like this yield important data that, when taken together, produce an accurate profile of the consumers' mental health status.

There are currently many reliable and valid standardized mental health outcome measures available, such as the Treatment Outcome Package and the CORE Outcome Measure, both developed for use in outpatient mental health clinics. These are sometimes referred to as *core batteries*, or *core measures*. The categories they address are the same covered in any doctor's office—symptoms (symptomatology) and level of functioning (functionality). The items must cover the range of symptoms normally seen with a given population, as well as how well one is functioning (at home, at work, or at school).

The Treatment Outcome Package is a 37-item instrument for measuring adolescent and adult clinical status that meets all scientific criteria (Kraus, Seligman & Jordan, 2005). It is designed to be appropriate for anything from solo practice to large networks of providers, and takes approximately 20 minutes for the client to complete. The items primarily cover four areas of concern: depression, anxiety disorders, suicidality, and violence. It is available from Behavioral Health Labs (http://www.bhealthlabs.com).

The CORE Outcome Measure has 34 items designed to measure common symptoms, subjective well-being, life/social functioning, and risk to self and others and is scientifically sound (Barkham et al., 2001). The instrument is designed to generate a "global level of distress" that is calculated as the mean score of all 34 items. This mean score, as well as individual items, can be tracked over the course of therapy as measures of clinical improvement. The measure was developed by England's Department of Health and has been in use there since 1998 (CORE System Group, 1998; see also http://www.coreims.co.uk)

Although symptomatology and functionality are usually sufficient for applied clinical outcome measurement, one other category is often included as well: the consumer's overall sense of satisfaction with services received. Satisfaction with care is of course a valid expectation for mental health consumers, just as it would be with customers of any service, and it should be fairly high from day one of treatment.

How often outcome measures are used depends upon the consumer's needs, the setting, and other factors. For instance, in an intense inpatient setting such as a psychiatric hospital acute ward, symptoms may need to be checked daily. In a typical outpatient setting where the consumer is coming for weekly services, once every other week (or even once every four weeks) may be sufficient. In every setting, the goal is to measure frequently enough to capture important changes early on, yet infrequently enough so as not to unnecessarily burden the consumer or the provider.

Given the strong psychometric properties of state-of-the-art clinical outcome measures, which mean that their results are reliable and valid, accuracy is not a concern so long as the questions are carefully and honestly answered. (*Reliable* means that the measure provides stable results over time, meaning that the resultant data are not random; *valid* means that the measure actually measures the issue intended.) The result is information that truly reveals how well the consumer is responding to care provided. The items have been honed through painstaking research so that they typically yield an accurate view of the respondent's actual clinical status and demographics. Consumers, providers, and insurers alike are usually pleasantly surprised at the extent to which clinical surveys provide accurate and revealing profiles of the patient's needs. For example, I have had patients who were relieved to acknowledge what a depression survey revealed: that they were still significantly depressed despite denying it to themselves and others.

At the same time, the potential for inaccuracies must be addressed. It is possible to imbed a "fake-bad scale" of improbable answers in the survey in order to detect those who may be trying to exploit the system (for example, as is done with the Minnesota Multiphasic Personality Inventory, which includes item profiles that are unrealistic or illogical and, thus, invalidate the survey). This is a group of questions that are designed to be sensitive to someone who is exaggerating difficulties. If the respondent is either unable or unwilling to provide careful, honest answers, then the results are invalid and will be indicated as such on the survey. Furthermore, a consumer who has difficulty with the reading level required or with the language (although most measures are available in multiple languages) may unintentionally provide inaccurate data. But this can usually be detected by the random nature of responses and can be corrected by having someone verbally walk through the items with the consumer.

If the respondent is unwilling to provide honest and accurate information for any reason (for example, not wanting to terminate care even though all treatment goals are met, or not wanting to be hospitalized), this will become clear by the pattern of data and by responses on the fake-bad scale (if used). Thus, it is possible to detect those who may try to take unfair advantage of the system by carefully analyzing the survey data and noting the improvement trajectory. For instance, if a person initially struggling with major depression has actually improved but tries to conceal progress (that is, "fake bad") in order to continue receiving services, he or she will typically generate a profile showing satisfaction with current services, yet no improvement. This would serve as a red flag because a consumer who is not getting better is usually (and understandably) dissatisfied with his or her current services. In such a case, the provider could be asked to resolve the discrepancy by carefully reviewing the consumer's clinical status. (As an additional administrative burden, the time required must be covered by the third-party payer.)

Stakeholder Views on EBPs and Outcomes Measurement

Unfortunately, even though there is a growing call for the use of EBPs and clinical outcome data to improve quality of care, there is also resistance to such changes on the part of many of the stakeholders in America's system of mental health care. This must be fully understood, and justifiable concerns overcome, if outcome-oriented reform is to take place.

Providers

Many mental health providers see the value of clinical outcome data in helping them do their best with each consumer and are willing to take reasonable steps in that direction. But there are others who feel that outcome measures constitute one more intrusion in the consumer–provider relationship, as well as an unpaid administrative drain on already-stretched time. They are simply not willing to administer, score, and track patient results unless and until third-party payers cover the time and effort required, a valid concern. Consequently, some researchers are pessimistic about how quickly the field will actually adopt outcome measures, because it would require a major change in clinical practice patterns.

In addition, there is concern that the resultant data could be used punitively by reviewers who may not take into account differences among consumer populations. For instance, although significant functional improvement at work, school, or home is the expected outcome for most patients who have had a physical illness, that is not so for all consumers who have had or have a chronic, mental health disorder. For those with the most severe cases of mental illness (for example, chronic paranoid schizophrenia), simple maintenance of current functioning may be an appropriate expected outcome. If these differences in consumer populations are not taken into account, then outcome data may make providers who work with persons who have the most severe cases of mental illness appear ineffective in contrast with other providers. Clearly, population and setting differences must always be carefully referenced when analyzing outcome data.

Furthermore, most mental health providers are very familiar with managed care procedures such as utilization review, wherein application is made to insurance reviewers in order to authorize coverage for continued treatment. Consequently, some providers fear that outcome measures may simply be used to add to the complexity and burden of utilization review.

It is certainly understandable that some providers may fear the misuse of clinical outcome data, or that punitive (rather than remedial) actions could be taken if their clients do not improve. It is also understandable that some providers are resistant to the idea of an additional unpaid administrative requirement. All of these concerns must be addressed. Indeed, it is critical that as outcome measures become required, the resultant data are used to support the good-faith clinical efforts of the mental health provider. If outcomes are not as expected, then remediation or referral, not punishment, is in order. If outcomes are consistently below expectations for a given provider or program, then perhaps further training would be in order. If further training is not successful, then and only then should consideration be given to shifting funds to a more effective program or provider.

It is also critical that the providers' administrative burden in managing the flow of outcome data be adequately reimbursed. If policymakers or insurers want to require the use of outcome measures, then they must realistically cover the cost of time and effort, without reducing pay for services. In other words, new funds will be required (for example, from increase in insurance premiums). Otherwise, compliance will be sporadic and begrudging at best. Fortunately, these problems are not unsolvable. They can and must be resolved in a fair manner, with give and take from both sides. It is surprising how collaborative and flexible opposing parties can be when they both have fiscal incentive to do so (for example, providers can improve care and demand for services; insurers can get better results for their funding).

Insurers

Third-party payers are very interested in the possibility of clinical outcome data improving the quality of funded care, as well as the opportunity to build results-oriented accountability into mental health services. Some insurance companies and governmental agencies are already requesting that providers use EBPs whenever possible. The use of clinical outcome measures takes that one step further by making sure that the treatment offered is not just statistically proven, but that it works well for each individual consumer. Third-party payers have a lot to gain by using outcome data. But at the same time, some insurers note that the collection of information is not without cost, and that the resultant data could be used to justify additional care beyond usual provisions. In other words, there is concern about having to pay for the cost of surveying, as well as for additional services if the data show further need. Furthermore, there is concern that outcome instruments could yield inaccurate measures of the consumer's actual clinical needs, or could perhaps be exploited by either consumers or providers to indicate need for services ad infinitum.

Insurers should welcome the use of outcome measures, as benefits would likely offset or even outweigh costs. Costs include the need for insurers to fund the administrative component and to authorize additional services when so indicated by the outcome data. Benefits include confidence that the consumer (and insurer) are getting what they are paying for: effective, evidence-based care. Surely it is better for insurers to know that their funded services are working well, even if it costs something to find that out, than to continue to pour money into ineffective treatments.

Consumers

Most consumers of mental health services like the idea of their improvement being monitored, taken seriously, and based on their own input. After all, it means that their assessment of treatment will be helping to shape their own care. This is the ultimate consumer-oriented and individualized treatment approach, because the outcome data used for case management are actually the voice of the one receiving care. Nonetheless, some consumers worry that filling out the surveys could be burdensome, that information may not be kept confidential, or that the results could be used to prematurely terminate care (once they show improvement). These are understandable concerns, but they can all be resolved fairly easily.

Regarding the question of burden, it is critical that clinical outcome measures/surveys used by providers take no more than 10 to 15 minutes to complete. This is a short enough time not to disrupt schedules, and may simply require that the consumer come in a little early, say, every fourth session. Consumers are likely to find that short surveys are more than worth the cost in time and effort. Persons with serious mental illness in inpatient settings will likely require more time, and perhaps some help, to complete the surveys. But this is time well spent, even if staff efforts are required.

Regarding confidentiality, it is of course imperative that all clinical outcome data be kept absolutely confidential, follow rules and regulations of the Health Insurance Portability and Accountability Act, and that only aggregated data (for example, averages, no identifying information) be used for program reporting. Individual data must only be used to authorize further care and must always remain strictly confidential.

As for using data to prematurely terminate care, significant reduction of the consumer's symptoms and return to a normal level of functioning provide a reasonable target for treatment termination, but only if relapse issues have been addressed as well. On-paper-only improvement is not acceptable, only real recovery as verified by both the provider and the consumer. Outcome data constitute but one source of information among many (for example, clinician's judgment, reports from family members or coworkers, and so on) to be included when considering termination, which is a decision point that should be reached collaboratively by both provider and consumer. Furthermore, appeals mechanisms and emergency measures must be in place so that consumers have options in cases where care is not meeting their actual needs.

Federal and State Government

Several states have begun moving in the direction of requiring clinical outcome data, as has the primary federal agency that helps fund mental health services, the Substance Abuse and Mental Health Services Agency (SAMHSA). SAMHSA has been developing national outcome measures (NOMs) for mental health services that include measures of symptomatology, functionality, and consumer satisfaction. NOMs also include other important service considerations such as use of hospitalization, use of EBPs, and overall program cost effectiveness. SAMHSA is encouraging state mental health agencies to begin using these key outcome measures, which include decreased symptomatology, improved functionality at work or school, improved stability/ functionality at home, client perception of care, abstinence from drug and alcohol abuse (if applicable), decreased criminal justice involvement (if applicable), reduced use of psychiatric inpatient beds (if applicable), use of EBPs, and cost effectiveness

NOMs are clearly a step in the right direction, as they represent the first time the federal government has successfully promoted a credible set of standardized clinical outcome measures for nationwide use. It is in fact a long-overdue action that many mental health researchers and advocates have been calling for and working towards for years (Corrigan et al., 2005; Drake et al., 2005; Evans et al. 2000; Grob & Goldman 2006; Kelly, 1997, 2000, 2003, 2009; Manderscheid, 1998, 1999; MHSIP Task Force, 1996; New Freedom Commission on Mental Health, 2003; U.S. Department of Health and Human Services, 1999).

SAMHSA's intention is for states to use NOMs (or equivalent measures) on a regular basis, thus generating detailed and comparative clinical outcome data that will help promote system improvements. If state mental health agencies were to implement these measures in a uniform manner, providers, policymakers, insurers, and consumers alike would be able to see clearly what works well and for whom. Likewise, in the private sector, if innovative mental health care providers were to implement standardized clinical outcome measures, they would reap the benefits of improved efficiency and quality of care.

In sum, certain stakeholders resist embracing clinical outcome measures. Their concerns, though understandable, can be addressed. It is well worth doing so, as the potential for outcome-oriented improvement in quality of care, and in real-life consumer recovery, will greatly benefit all parties.

Recommendations for Transformation to a National Outcomes-based Mental Health System: A Blueprint for Change

What steps might realistically be taken in order to promote much-needed outcome-based reforms in our mental health and substance use systems? Policymakers must recognize that now is the time to enact legislation to promote outcome-oriented mental health reform, even if doing so carries some political risk. Specifically (Kelly, 2009), I recommend that policymakers should implement legislation or regulations to achieve the following:

1. *Require the regular use of standardized, objective, and uniformly applied clinical outcome measures (such as NOMs), and link the availability of outcome data to continued funding.* In other words, codify the concept that programs being paid to provide mental health services should be accountable for the outcome of those services. Over time, this will reveal which programs and treatments are most effective for which consumers in which settings. The actual measures selected (for both inpatient and outpatient services) and the protocol for their use should be facilitated at the federal level (for example, SAMHSA) for uniformity, so that results can be compared both within and across states. The selection of these measures should result, not from arbitrary federal imposition, but from a collaborative process wherein all constituents are invited to the table to offer input and feedback.

2. *Require that the resultant transparent outcome data (aggregated and without any identifying information) are to be made available.* Data should be provided to policymakers and third-party payers for the purpose of reviewing the effectiveness of care across programs, and to consumers for making informed decisions regarding their own treatment options. At the same

time, guidelines for analysis must be developed so that differences in consumer populations and treatment settings (for example, in severe versus
mild-to-moderate mental illness) do not lead to misinterpretation of outcome data.

3. *Stipulate that outcome data are to be used in a remedial manner.* Specific programs or treatment services found not to be as effective as desired should
be offered help in technical assistance, training, and reassignment. Only
after such help fails to improve outcome should other options, such as
shifting funding to more effective care, be considered.

4. *Adequately fund the cost of implementing clinical outcome measures.* A sure way
for outcome measures to fail is to require them of providers without offering technical assistance and training, and without remuneration for the
added administrative costs entailed. Evaluation costs something; it must
be adequately funded, with realistic allowance for training and equipment
and extra time required, or it will not succeed. Furthermore, the funds
must not simply come from reduction of current service rates, because
this would be asking providers to pay for system transformation. States
will need access to federal grants to be able to launch systemwide mental
health outcome measurement initiatives, and counties will need access to
state grants. The more impoverished public systems will require even more
help, such as on-site consultation and technical assistance.

5. *Stipulate which agency or office will regularly review and analyze the resultant
clinical outcome data, and how that analysis will be used for quality improvement and system transformation.* In the public sector, this could involve the
states' departments of mental health and SAMHSA. In the private sector,
it could involve insurance industry groups and mental health professional
organizations.

6. *Put oversight in place, at both the federal and state levels, to ensure that the overall
result of all of the above is improved lives for persons with mental illness, especially
for those with serious mental illnesses.* The whole point of measuring clinical
outcomes is to make sure that those receiving care improve to the point
of recovery. Any treatments or programs found not to be effective should
be given opportunity to improve, but if improvement is not forthcom-
ing, funding should shift to more effective care. It is not compassionate to
continue to fund services that accomplish little in the lives of persons with
serious mental illness. It is compassionate, ethical, and rational to fund that
which works.

Conclusion

Promoting effective, cost-efficient clinical care is critical not only for mental health system reform, but also for the success of national health care reform. Many of the topics discussed above apply to both. It is hoped that as national health care reform advances, so too does mental health system transformation, in both cases guided by the actual outcome of care in the life of the consumer. In fact, for health care reform to succeed in the long run mental health reform must also be implemented since mental health services constitute a large portion of overall health care costs.

If correctly implemented, outcome data will improve life for all parties— providers, consumers and third-party payers alike. Social workers, psychologists, psychiatrists and other human services professionals who provide mental health and support services will find that the initial frustration of having to do "one more thing" as part of usual care will be more than compensated for by the resultant improvement in case management, consumer satisfaction, and clients mental health and well-being. Consumers will find that their feedback becomes a primary voice in determining care and promoting rapid improvement. Third-party payers will find their funded services becoming more effective and cost efficient.

Now is the time for America to roll up her sleeves and do what it takes to develop and implement an outcomes-oriented and evidence-based mental health care system that guarantees recovery for neighbors and family members who deal with mental illness and substance use in their daily lives. When that happens we will write not about a system in shambles, but about an integrated mental health system that works and enables those with mental illness and substance use to finally come home to their communities.

References

Barkham, M., Margison, F., Leach, C., Lucock, M., Mellor-Clark, J., Evans, C., et al. (2001). Service profile and benchmarking using the CORE-OM: Toward practice-based evidence in the psychological therapies. *Journal of Consulting and Clinical Psychology, 69,* 184–196.

Bickman, L. (2005). A common factors approach to improving mental health services. *Mental Health Services Research, 7,* 1–4.

Clarke, M., & Oxman, A.D. (1999). *Cochrane reviewers' handbook 4.0* [updated July 1999]. In Review Manager (Version 4.0) [Computer program]. Oxford, England: Cochrane Collaboration.

Corcoran, K., & Fischer, J. (2000). *Measures for clinical practice: A sourcebook* (3rd ed., Vol. 2). New York: Free Press.

CORE System Group. (1998). *CORE System (information management) handbook.* Leeds, England: Author.

Corrigan, P. W., McCracken, S. G., & McNeilly, C. (2005). Evidence-based practices for people with serious mental illness and substance abuse disorders. In C. Stout & R. Hayes (Eds.), *The handbook of evidence-based practices in behavioral healthcare: Applications and new directions* (pp. 153–172). New York: John Wiley & Sons.

Davies, H., Nutley, S., & Smith, P. (2000). *What works? Evidence-based practice in public services.* Bristol, England: Policy Press.

Dixon, L. B., & Goldman, H. H. (2003). Forty years of progress in community mental health: The role of evidence-based practice. *Australia and New Zealand Journal of Psychiatry, 37,* 668–673.

Drake, R. E., Merrens, M., & Lynde, D. (Eds.). (2005). *Evidence-based mental health: A textbook.* New York: John Wiley & Sons.

Drucker, P. F. (2003). *Peter Drucker on the profession of management.* Boston: Harvard Business Publishing.

Evans, C., Mellor-Clark, J., Margison, F., Barkham, M., McGrath, G., Connell, J., et al. (2000). Clinical outcomes in routine evaluation: The CORE-OM. *Journal of Mental Health, 9,* 247–255.

Grob, G. N., & Goldman, H. H. (2006). *The dilemma of federal mental health policy.* New Brunswick, NJ: Rutgers University Press.

Jacobson, N. S., Roberts, L. J., Berns, S. B., & McGlinchey, J. B. (1999). Methods for defining and determining the clinical significance of treatment effects: Description, application, and alternatives. *Journal of Consulting and Clinical Psychology, 67,* 300–307.

Kelly, T. A. (1997). A wake up call: The experience of a mental health commissioner in times of change. *Professional Psychology: Research and Practice, 28,* 317–322.

Kelly, T. A. (2000, January 7). Principled mental health system reform. *Heritage Foundation Backgrounder, 1341,* 1–12.

Kelly, T. A. (2002, March 7). A policymaker's guide to mental illness. *Heritage Foundation Backgrounder, 1522,* 1–16.

Kelly, T. A. (2003). Clinical outcome measurement: A call to action. *Journal of Psychology and Christianity, 22,* 254–258.

Kelly, T. A. (2009). *Healing the broken mind: Transforming America's failed mental health system.* New York: NYU Press.

Kraus, D. R., Seligman, D. A., & Jordan, J. R. (2005). Validation of a behavioral health treatment outcome and assessment tool designed for naturalistic settings: The Treatment Outcome Package. *Journal of Clinical Psychology*, *61*, 285–314.

Manderscheid, R. (1998). Addressing the crisis of quality in behavioral health care at the millennium. *Journal of Behavioral Health Services and Research*, *25*, 233–236.

Manderscheid, R. (1999, April). Untangling the accountability maze: Developing outcome measures, report cards and performance indicators. *Managed Behavioral Health News*, 6–7.

Mechanic, D. (2008). *Mental health and social policy: Beyond managed care* (5th ed.). Boston: Allyn & Bacon.

Merrens, M. (2005). *Evidence-based mental health practice*. New York: W. W. Norton.

MHSIP Task Force. (1996). *The mental health statistics improvement program consumer-oriented mental health report card*. Rockville, MD: Center for Mental Health Services.

New Freedom Commission on Mental Health. (2003). *Achieving the promise: Transforming mental health care in America*. Rockville, MD: Author.

Roth, A., & Fonagy, P. (1996). *What works for whom? A critical review of psychotherapy research*. New York: Guilford Press.

Seligman, M. (1994). *What you can change and what you can't*. New York: Knopf.

Seligman, M. (1995). The effectiveness of psychotherapy. *American Psychologist*, *50*, 965–974.

Shadish, W. R., Navarro, A. M., Matt, G. E., & Phillips, G. (2000). The effects of psychological therapies under clinically representative conditions: A meta-analysis. *Psychological Bulletin*, *126*, 512–529.

U.S. Department of Health and Human Services. (1999). *Mental health: A report of the Surgeon General*. Rockville, MD: Author.

CHAPTER 14

Toward Integrated Outcome Measurement for Mental Health and Substance Use Services and Systems

James Siemianowski and Thomas A. Kirk Jr.

The past decade has seen significant attention being placed on quality improvement and performance measurement in the fields of health and behavioral health. (*Behavioral health* refers to services that are focused on treating mental health and substance use problems. Mental health and substance use services may be provided within one setting or they may be provided separately.) A wide range of national and state efforts have focused on developing the science and knowledge base as it relates to outcomes and performance measurement. The Substance Abuse and Mental Health Service Administration (SAMHSA), Institute of Medicine (IOM), American College of Behavioral Health Leadership, Network for the Improvement of Addiction Treatment, the Washington Circle Group (WCG), National Committee for Quality Assurance, national mental health and addiction trade organizations, and advocacy groups have played roles in developing outcome and performance measures to evaluate service effectiveness. The Surgeon General's Report on Mental Health (U.S.

Department of Health and Human Services, 1999), the New Freedom Commission on Mental Health (2003), and IOM Reports (2001) have emphasized deficiencies in the mental health system and made recommendations for system transformation and renewed commitments to improving quality.

Although these efforts are prompting activities on the national, state, and local levels to transform mental health systems and have strengthened the ability to measure outcomes and performance—usually within one sector or the other (for example, mental health or substance use)—they have not generally promoted common measures for the entire behavioral health field. In other words, such efforts have not provided, to date, a full and well-integrated framework for outcomes and performance measurement for services provided to individuals simultaneously receiving care in both the mental health and substance use sectors of the behavioral health system.

What have been some of the unique historical influences that have shaped the lack of behavioral health integration? For one, the mental health and substance use service systems have evolved in separate and distinct ways as a result of ideological, professional, fiscal, and structural differences (Davidson & White, 2007). Key areas of variances include the following:

- Separate authorities on the federal, state, and local level to manage and regulate the mental health and substance use sectors, leading to competition for funding
- Independent service delivery systems with varying degrees of community support made available for long-term recovery and wellness
- Distinct treatment orientations and models
- Views of the potential for long-term recovery (Davidson & White, 2007)
- Roles played by people in recovery within the treatment system
- Emphasis placed on mutual supports and self-help.

Not surprisingly, the separate identities, funding streams, and regulatory authorities led to the development of parallel service systems that functioned autonomously. Coordination and integration between mental health and substance use service providers was limited and overlooked the fact that many individuals were receiving services in both systems. The growth of these autonomous systems of care ignored strengths within each system and failed to recognize the many commonalities they shared. In recent years however, the historical differences that have traditionally separated the fields are beginning to be bridged, and new influences are shaping a more integrated behavioral health field. For example, many integrated behavioral health networks—that offer both mental health and substance use services—are being established, largely as a response to Medicaid carve-outs of behavioral health services (Frank & Garfield 2007).

Impetus for Integrated Performance Measures

Recent developments in the behavioral health service system and lessons learned over the past few decades are accelerating the creation of a common vision for behavioral health outcome and performance measurement that is linked to the larger health care system. One primary impetus is the increased frequency and recognition of co-occurring disorders (CODs) among individuals who seek treatment from one or both service systems. In 2008, there were an estimated 9.8 million adults age 18 or older in the United States with serious mental illness during the past year, and 23.1 million persons age 12 or older needed treatment for an illicit drug or alcohol use problem (SAMHSA, 2010). Many of these individuals have been diagnosed with CODs. The prevalence of CODs among persons with serious mental illness is estimated to range from 30 percent to 60 percent (Regier et al., 1990). The growing prevalence of individuals with CODs and, too often, the ineffectiveness of our current treatments for CODs are leading to an increase in integrated service models and delivery systems.

As the prevalence of CODs has risen, so too has knowledge of the ineffectiveness of services that are delivered in parallel systems of care. Research on treatment of CODS over the past 10 years documents that treatment services like those in the United States that are typically provided in parallel but separate systems are ineffective (Drake et al., 2004). Treatment potentially unfolds in disconnected episodes of care that may require an individual to deal with their substance use issues before they can receive treatment for their mental health condition. Outcomes studies focused on the use of evidence-based practices such as integrated dual disorders treatment are reinforcing the importance of providing integrated behavioral health treatment to individuals with CODs. Integrated treatment, however, may be more costly in the short term. Although research clearly shows improved client outcomes and fewer repeated episodes of costly acute care services when integrated approaches are used, cost savings are more difficult to quantify and require further study (Drake et al. 2004).

Integration does not simply occur. Bridges must be built to join the mental health and substance use systems in support of highly effective care for persons with these disorders. At the state level, the National Association of State Mental Health Program Directors membership list shows that at least 30 states and territories have combined state behavioral health departments, with single state authorities for mental health and substance abuse services. Other states, in response to fiscal pressures, have combined behavioral health departments within a super agency. Although these consolidations may initially be generated by fiscal concerns, increased collaboration and integration are the desired outcomes.

At the philosophical and service delivery levels, the recovery movement and persons receiving behavioral health services are also building bridges (White & Davidson, 2006). The increased focus on recovery has created considerable momentum at the state and national levels for the development of integrated *recovery-oriented systems of care* (ROSCs), or systems of health and human services that affirm hope and recovery, exemplify a strength-based orientation, and offer a wide spectrum of services and supports aimed at engaging people with mental health and substance use conditions into care and promoting their resilience and long term recovery from which they and their family members may choose (Yale University Program on Recovery and Community Health, 2008). A number of federal and state initiatives are now focused on defining and developing ROSCs. As these develop and mature, states are committing resources to implement and sustain ROSCs, thereby also prompting a need for integrated outcomes that are compatible with recovery.

Although certain forces are pushing services within behavioral health treatment systems toward more integration, other forces are focusing attention on outcomes and quality in these systems. The national and state fiscal crises have raised questions about the cost, outcomes, and benefits of behavioral health services. Legislators, policymakers, and administrators have been forced to more carefully assess the cost effectiveness of care. They are mandating that behavioral health systems prove that the services yield positive outcomes at a reasonable cost.

A final factor influencing outcomes and integration is health care reform. The recently enacted Patient Protection and Affordable Care Act of 2010 places significant emphasis on quality and outcomes. This legislation has tremendous potential to reshape the medical and behavioral health care landscape. Integration under health care reform goes well beyond integration of mental health and substance use service systems. Further, the legislation establishes provisions that support the consolidation and linking of primary care and behavioral health care. The health care reform legislation is being closely linked to the Mental Health Parity and Addiction Equity Act of 2008. This federal law provides for equity in mental health and substance use insurance coverage.

Regulations have been recently published that will guide the implementation of the Parity Act and its relationship to the new health care legislation. The legislation, fiscal concerns, prevalence of CODs, recovery focus, and design and implementation of ROSCs are collectively propelling behavioral health systems toward integration. Common outcome measures must be developed and implemented to measure quality across these previously separated systems of care—a critical task if behavioral health is to be an essential and integral force in the evolving quality-driven health care environment.

Creating Integrated Outcomes and Performance Measures: Highlights from Major Efforts

Within the behavioral health field, efforts have been made to distinguish outcome measures from performance measurement. The demands placed on behavioral health systems to evaluate and implement performance measures and assess outcomes have led to confusion among service providers and policymakers about basic terminology (McLellan, Chalk, & Bartlett, 2007). *Outcome measures* are the results or effects that services, interventions or supports have on the status of individuals or communities (Garnick, Lee, Horgan, & Acevedo, 2009). In behavioral health, these are typically measured as improvements in functioning such as obtaining employment and stable housing, reduced arrests or substance use, and increased use of social supports. An outcome domain is an area of life function measured at the individual level that is expected to be positively influenced by a treatment or intervention. Positive function in most outcome domains may be indicative of degrees of recovery (McLellan et al., 2007).

Performance measurement refers to an organized way to report the outcomes that are achieved by a system or by behavioral health care providers. Outcome measures are part of the performance measurement system and may be used to evaluate how well service providers assist individuals receiving treatment to achieve outcomes. Coleman et al. (2007) define a quality management reporting system (QMRS) as one that measures the quality of behavioral health care; reports its results to consumers; and has the goals of quality improvement, management, and decision support. These measures are focused at the organizational level and evaluate the quality of care provided by an organization or system (McLellan et al., 2007).

Several recent SAMHSA initiatives have focused on the development of integrated performance and outcome measurement. As noted earlier,

SAMHSA (2004) has taken a lead role in recognizing the critical need for data to support performance measurement and management. It developed the National Outcome Measures (NOMs) in collaboration with states (see also chapters 13 and 24 in this volume). They are a set of 10 mental health and substance use domains or indicators that measure whether an individual has benefited in a practical way from treatment. The domains assess the use of evidence-based treatments, treatment retention, abstinence, employment, stable living, social supports, criminal involvement, satisfaction with services, access, and cost effectiveness. The domains are designed to embody meaningful, real-life outcomes for people who are striving to attain and sustain recovery (for example, building resilience, working, and participating fully in one's community). SAMHSA has applied the NOMs to persons with CODs, an important step in the development of integrated outcomes. Beginning efforts have focused on morbidity and abstinence, criminal involvement, social supports and the use of 12-step programs, and access and retention. The NOMs are also applicable to ROSCs, measuring a broad range of recovery indicators. This will be discussed later in this chapter.

SAMHSA, in another multistate project, convened in 1998 the WCG, with the goals of developing and disseminating performance measures for substance use services. Composed of researchers, care providers, health plan representatives, and public policymakers, the group specified and tested three performance process measures and originally applied them to private health plans because these plans have standardized data sets. The group then set about to determine the feasibility of applying these process measures (identification, treatment initiation, and treatment engagement) to the public sector. The WCG concluded that the initiation and engagement measures could be readily incorporated into public sector performance measurement systems using data that were already available in state systems (Garnick et al., 2009). These efforts are leading states to incorporate WCG measures into their performance measurement system.

States and behavioral health networks have also begun to refine performance measurement systems that evaluate the outcomes for individuals receiving care, as well as the effectiveness of the mental health and substance use system. Among other approaches, states are using dashboard reports, agency and program report cards, and balanced scorecards that incorporate many of the outcomes and measures described earlier. Building on the national initiatives that have been introduced over the past decade, these efforts are designed to improve the overall quality of services at a systemic level, improve outcomes at the individual client level, and increase accountability and performance measurement at the provider level.

Toward a Framework for Integrated Performance Measurement: The Connecticut Experience

Connecticut's efforts to create an integrated behavioral health care system began in 1995 when legislation was enacted to link the Department of Mental Health and a separate addiction service structure located within the Department of Public Health. The Department of Mental Health and Addiction Services (DMHAS) resulted. Early efforts to integrate services encountered an expected range of philosophical and systemic barriers as the new department began to blend organizational cultures, leadership, administrative procedures, service provider groups, and stakeholders. Over time, the barriers were eliminated and the department became more fully integrated. Connecticut's efforts to develop an integrated system of care that included a focus on quality improvement, and blended outcomes and performance measurement within an ROSC framework, were shaped by a number of external and internal factors:

Commitment to a Recovery-oriented System of Care

DMHAS is unique for its long-standing focus on promoting a recovery-oriented system of care within an integrated single state authority for mental health and substance use services. The new agency's original commissioner, the late Albert J. Solnit, emphasized that integration would be beneficial for both patient populations and would yield an organization greater than the sum of its parts. His strong leadership affected all levels of the newly formed state agency in those early years and was followed by strong leadership and executive teams from 2000 to date. DMHAS has also benefited from talented executive and middle management teams, by leveraging of state and federal funds, an active recovery and advocacy community, and a mature and strong service provider system.

Connecticut's consumer and advocacy communities and the DMHAS's desire to create a recovery-oriented system of care were the cornerstones for system development. Treatment was recognized as a tool for recovery, but also acknowledged was the need for nontraditional support services to extend and promote recovery. The approach emphasized that there were multiple pathways to recovery, and the DMHAS strategically set about to implement that vision. It developed a holistic view of recovery that went far beyond reducing symptoms, instead focusing heavily on real-life outcomes such as stable housing, work, relationships and social supports, abstinence, and community participation. This led to a multiyear system change effort that included the development of a Commissioner's Recovery Policy, Practice Improvement Collaboratives and Guidelines, and a Recovery Institute.

The department developed the Practice Guidelines in collaboration with the Yale University Program on Recovery and Community Health. The Guidelines integrated the IOM quality indicators and linked them to DMHAS' Practice Domains of recovery-oriented care. The final document (DMHAS, 2008) identified six Practice Guidelines that can be used as one set of potential qualitative indicators of an ROSC: person and family driven; timely and responsive: trustworthy and safe; effective, efficient, and equitable; person centered; and focused on the use of natural supports and recovery.

Creation of the General Assistance Behavioral Health Program

In 1998, a decision was made to carve out the behavioral health benefit of the State Administered General Assistance Program. The resulting General Assistance Behavioral Health Program (GABHP) targeted low-income adults who did not qualify for Medicaid support. Administrative control was transferred from the Department of Social Services to the DMHAS. A comprehensive behavioral health benefit package was designed that reimbursed service providers for a range of mental health and addiction services. The program served large numbers of individuals with CODs. A number of innovative practices were introduced, including intensive case management services for frequent service users; the implementation of opioid agonist treatment protocols; a four-step quality improvement/financing strategy, the Reinvestment, System Enhancement Cycle (Savings, Reinvestment, Innovation, Improved Outcomes); and the use of assistance such as short-term housing and transportation to help support recovery.

Continual Training and Technical Assistance

Throughout its 15-year history, DMHAS has continually emphasized through training and technical consultation the importance of delivering quality behavioral health services to individuals with CODs and sought grant funds to enhance that focus. Among the most important was a 2005 SAMHSA award of a five-year Co-Occurring State Incentive Grant (COSIG) that concentrated efforts on enhancing service provider's COD capabilities. Through this multiyear project, DMHAS introduced the Integrated Dual Disorders model and worked with service providers to incorporate the Dual Diagnosis Capability in Addiction Treatment Index into the system (McGovern, Matzkin, & Giard, 2007). DMHAS also introduced intensive outpatient and co-occurring residential programs to respond to the growing demand for this level of care, all with incentivized rate structures. SAMHSA's support for system change continued through several grant awards, among them the Mental Health Transformation and Access to Recovery awards, as well as various prevention grants that typically required participation from multiple stakeholders.

Focus on Development of Integrated Measurement and Data Systems

The vision for creating and maintaining an ROSC prompted review of outcomes that were compatible with recovery. Also, as the state increasingly recognized the growing number of individuals with CODs, it began to evaluate how outcomes and performance could be evaluated when individuals were simultaneously receiving both mental health and substance use services. Further, the budget crisis in Connecticut forced the Legislature to expand their focus on performance and accountability; they embraced Results-Based Accountability (RBA) as one of their tools and required agencies to report annually on their activities using the principles of RBA. These principles helped to shape Connecticut's new framework for outcomes and performance measurement. RBA sought to answer simple questions related to utilization, effectiveness, and value, and most important, whether clients improved as a result of the services provided (Friedman, 2005).

Integrated outcome and performance measures could not be implemented without major modifications to DMHAS's data and quality infrastructure. Although DMHAS had always emphasized quality and monitoring, it lacked a comprehensive vision for outcomes and performance measurement and needed to first improve the quality and data infrastructure. The actions that were taken to improve the infrastructure included the following:

- Initiated implementation of new information systems and a data warehouse
- Required service providers to report and update data at admission, six-month intervals, and discharge to allow for outcome measurement across an individual's treatment episode
- Standardized data elements to be reported, including new requirements for mental health providers to submit substance use data for individuals with CODs
- Established common outcome measures for all service providers
- Developed a vision for integrated performance measurement.

The primary objective of all of these infrastructure enhancements was to develop an integrated performance measurement system that represented three different outcome perspectives: the state or federal funder, the service provider, and the person/family in care. One overall goal was to develop common outcomes that measured an individual's response to treatment regardless of where they received services. Any outcome measures included in the integrated system must answer the question, "Do people get better as a result of the services they receive"?

Ten criteria or guiding principles informed the development of the new performance measurement system: offer regular feedback to providers and consumers; minimize provider reporting burden, where possible; inform decision making at all levels of the organization; serve as the foundation for improving quality in the behavioral health system; collect only data that support departmental quality and planning objectives; support other DMHAS cultural competency, co-occurring, and trauma initiatives; assist in measuring recovery and be compatible with department's vision of an ROSC; incorporate client-level outcome measures, and provider- and system-level performance measures; measure outcomes consistently regardless of whether an individual was receiving mental health or substance use services or both; and utilize or build upon existing reporting requirements such as NOMs and the federally required Treatment Episode Data Set (TEDS; SAMHSA, 2009). (For more information on TEDS, see http://www.oas.samhsa.gov/dasis.htm#teds2. TEDS is part of SAMHSA's Drug and Alcohol Service Information System, which compiles admission and demographic data for substance abuse.)

Development and Use of an Outcomes/ Performance Report Card

DMHAS introduced a provider report card performance evaluation system in 2009 to evaluate outcomes for individuals in care as well as agency and program performance by examining a wide range of state and regional indicators. Where DMHAS standards exist, service providers will be compared with the established standard. Report cards are issued on a quarterly basis, and DMHAS intends to publish the report cards on the agency Web site beginning in February 2011. The report card design and the indicators that were selected for measurement draw from a number of efforts previously discussed (for example, NOMs, IOM), including the Mental Health Statistical Improvement Pilot (MHSIP) Consumer Satisfaction Survey (Center for Mental Health Services, 1996), which DMHAS customized by adding a recovery domain to measure a person's satisfaction with his/her recovery. The current report card measures include the following domains and measures that DMHAS must report to federal funders and that can be used by service providers for routine tracking:

- Client Outcome Domain: Consumer Satisfaction: MHSIP with a DMHAS-specific domain for recovery; IOM Quality Domains: Care is accessible and patient centered; NOMs: Employment, living situation, social support, abstinence, arrests, and treatment completions.

- Provider Outcomes: Measures that evaluate the number served, hourly or daily service provision, residential bed use, and compliance with DMHAS-required data submissions (that is, admissions, discharges, claims data, TEDs data, co-occurring screenings, and periodic data updates).

- System Outcomes: Measures of readmission to same or more intensive level of care (30, 180 days) and of continuity of care that show how quickly clients receive follow-up care.

The above two indices represent a different orientation than the traditional ones (for example, treatment completion, drop-out and related retention measures). In accord with recommendations of a National Policy Council formed by Boston University's JoinTogether project (2003) and an earlier study (McCorry, Granick, Bartlett, Cotter, & Chalk, 2000), this measurement approach reinforces the fact that substance use and/or mental health disorders are chronic conditions best addressed by effective continuing care strategies. The GABHP described above included a format that identified persons who were being readmitted to the same or a higher level of care (for example, intensive residential) within 30 to 90 days from their last discharge. A protocol was introduced that linked such individuals with options that promoted greater continuity of care. This approach also allowed pre/post cost and service comparisons over a year for individuals and aggregate groups of persons in care, many with levels of co-occurring disorders. Comparison of Fiscal Year 2008 with Fiscal Year 2003 baseline aggregate data showed the average cost of care decreasing from $2,489 to $1,913 and several million dollars being available to be invested more effectively (DMHAS, 2009).

Similarly, the Continuity of Care measure tracks how quickly a person is linked to a confirmed admission and retention into a lower level of care after discharge from a higher level. It is not length of stay in one level of care that is critical, but retention in a continuum of care, especially for persons with CODs.

The report card project is becoming the foundation for evaluating individual and system outcomes across a range of variables and departmental priorities. First, it provides DMHAS with the capacity to measure outcomes for persons with CODs, regardless of where the person is receiving services. Further, individual/system outcomes can be assessed on the basis of race/ethnicity and other diagnostic criteria. This capability can be used to examine whether statewide disparities exist in outcomes for a particular racial/ethnic group and can also specifically identify program-level outliers. The performance management system has already improved data quality and reporting compliance. Each successive iteration of the report cards has shown improved data quality and reporting compliance. For example, the report card has not included all six IOM quality indicators. The measures of Access and Person-Centered Care have been introduced gradually and will likely be expanded as appropriate indicators for other IOM measures are developed.

Future Directions

Although considerable progress has been made in the area of outcomes and performance measurement for behavioral health and substance use, much work remains to be done. Connecticut's initiatives to develop integrated outcome and performance measures offer a beginning framework that may be built upon. The framework that DMHAS developed for the integrated performance measurement system above meets a number of system, quality improvement, and integrated outcomes and performance objectives that mental health and substance use services and systems can use in their transformation efforts. Even so, research must continue to focus on identifying best practices and validating and confirming measures that may be applicable to the expanding and increasingly diverse populations in need of multiple behavioral health and support services, including persons at earlier or lower levels of mental health or substance use severity, those in the child welfare and criminal justice systems, the military and their families, young adults transitioning between systems, newly released offenders, persons unnecessarily residing in nursing homes, and so on.

Concurrent with the focus on developing integrated behavioral health outcomes, health care reform will push the behavioral health system to consider how to integrate outcomes related to primary care and behavioral health. This is especially critical when one considers the lowered life expectancy for people with serious mental illness and substance use disorders and the comorbid medical conditions they frequently experience. The field is now challenged not only to further integrate behavioral health outcomes, but also to move beyond and develop performance measurement systems that look at the entire person. The behavioral health system may need to incorporate other tools or instruments and expand use of tools such as the World Health Organization's (2004) Quality of Life, a standardized instrument that measures an individual's satisfaction with the quality of his or her life in domains such as physical and psychological status, social relationships, and their environment.

Key elements of the health care legislation may stimulate the pace at which systems integrate. Stakeholders at all levels will be called on to identify new care models that meet new comparative effectiveness standards; medical and behavioral health homes are developed under health care reform. As new community- and home-based services become part of a Medicaid benefit package, outcomes must be adapted to measure the effectiveness of these services. What will define a "service" and an "episode of care" in an integrated behavioral and primary health system? How do we assess the efficacy of new combinations of quality improvement initiatives and indices of the growth rate of costs in these larger, integrated systems?

Certain outcomes may become increasingly important under health care reform. Measures such as abstinence, reduced legal involvement, social connectedness, stable housing, and employment will be key because of their recovery orientation and applicability to CODs. Other measures that assess health status such as connection to a medical home, recent physicals, compliance with follow-up medical visits, and participation in preventive care must be incorporated into integrated performance measurement systems. It may be necessary to use or develop scales to measure improvements in functioning (for example, depression, anxiety) for individuals with less serious mental health and substance use issues.

As reimbursements for more behavioral health services fall under Medicaid, attention must be focused on standardized data sets that will be required to measure quality. Medicaid and other private insurers that are typically claim driven often have more limited data requirements, which may decrease the ability to measure outcomes. Policymakers at all levels must give careful consideration to data reporting requirements in the developing health care system. If this is not attended to, progress that has been made in the area of outcomes and performance measurement may be eroded. Hence, the next decade of primary health and behavioral health service delivery offers considerable promise and significant challenges. Common outcomes and performance measures for the behavioral health field will continue to grow in importance as all stakeholders work to introduce national health care reform that is cost effective and produces positive results for all individuals.

References

Boston University School of Public Health (2003). *Join together action kit: Rewarding results: Improving the quality of treatment for people with alcohol and drug problems.* Boston and New York: Boston University School of Public Health and Partnership at Drugfree.org.

Center for Mental Health Services. (1996). *The final report of the Mental Health Statistics Improvement Project (MHSIP) Task Force on a consumer-oriented mental health report card.* Rockville, MD: Author.

Coleman, M., Strother, H., Hurwitz, D., & Hedberg, S. (2007). *Promising practices in behavioral health quality improvement: Summary of key findings and lessons learned.* Shrewsbury: University of Massachusetts Medical School Center for Health Policy Research.

Davidson, L., Tondora, J., O'Connell, M., Kirk, T., Rockholz, P., & Evans, A. (2007). Creating a recovery-oriented system of behavioral health care: Moving from concept to reality. *Psychiatric Rehabilitation Journal, 31,* 23–31.

Davidson, L. & White, W. (2007). The concept of recovery as an organizing principle for integrating mental health and addiction services. *Journal of Behavioral Health Services & Research, 34,* 109–120.

Drake, R., Muser, K., Brunette, M., & McHugo, G. J. (2004). A review of treatments for people with severe mental illnesses and co-occurring substance use disorders. *Psychiatric Rehabilitation Journal, 27,* 360–374.

Frank, R., & Garfield, R. (2007) Managed behavioral health care carve-outs: Past performance and future prospects. *Annual Review of Public Health, 28,* 303–320.

Friedman, M. (2005). *Trying hard is not good enough: How to produce measurable improvements for customers and communities.* Victoria, British Columbia, Canada: Trafford Publishing.

Gagne, C., White, W., & Anthony, W. (2007). Recovery: A common vision for the fields of mental health and addictions. *Psychiatric Rehabilitation Journal, 31*(1), 32–37.

Garnick, D. W., Lee, M. T., Horgan, C. M., & Acevedo, A. (2009). Adapting Washington Circle performance measures for public sector substance abuse treatment systems *Journal of Substance Abuse Treatment, 36,* 265–277.

Institute of Medicine. (2001). *Crossing the quality chasm: A new health system for the 21st century.* Washington, DC: National Academies Press.

Institute of Medicine. (2006). *Improving the quality of healthcare for mental and substance use conditions.* Washington, DC: National Academies Press.

Mant, J. (2001). Process versus outcome indicators in the assessment of quality of health care. *International Journal for Quality in Health Care, 13,* 475–480.

McCarty, D. (2007). Performance measurement for systems treating alcohol and drug use disorders. *Journal of Substance Abuse Treatment, 33*, 353–354.

McCorry, F., Granick D., Bartlett J., Cotter F., & Chalk M. (2000). Developing performance measures for alcohol and other drug services in managed care plans. *Journal on Quality Improvement, 26*, 633–643.

McGovern, M., Matzkin, A., & Giard, J. (2007). Assessing the dual diagnosis capability of addiction treatment services: The Dual Diagnosis Capability in Addiction Treatment (DDCAT) Index. *Journal of Dual Diagnosis, 3*(2), 111–123.

McLellan, A. T., Chalk, M., & Bartlett, J. (2007). Outcomes, performance, and quality—What's the difference? *Journal of Substance Abuse Treatment, 32*, 331–340.

National Committee for Quality Assurance. (2006). *The health plan employer data and information set (HEDIS)*. Washington, DC: Author.

New Freedom Commission on Mental Health. (2003). *Achieving the promise: Transforming mental health care in America. Final report* (DHHS Publication No. SMA-03-3832). Rockville, MD: U.S. Department of Health and Human Services.

Regier, D. A., Farmer, M. E., Rae, D. S., Locke, B. Z., Keith, S. J., Judd, L. L., & Goodwin, F. K. (1990). Co-morbidity of mental disorders with alcohol and other drug abuse: Results from the Epidemiological Catchment Area (ECA) study. *JAMA, 264*, 2511–2518.

Rosenberg, L. (2007). Quality as the cornerstone of behavioral health: Four critical issues *Journal of Behavioral Health Sciences and Research 34*, 353–356.

Substance Abuse and Mental Health Services Administration. (2004). *A report required by Congress on performance partnerships*. Retrieved from http://www.nationaloutcomemeasures.samhsa.gov/outcome/index.asp.

Substance Abuse and Mental Health Services Administration. (2009). *Drug abuse information systems: TEDS quick statistics—Summary tables*. Retrieved from http://www.oas.samhsa.gov/dasis.htm#teds2

Substance Abuse and Mental Health Services Administration. (2010). *Results from the 2009 National Survey on Drug Use and Health: Volume I. Summary of national findings* (Office of Applied Studies, NSDUH Series H-38A, HHS Publication No. SMA 10-4586). Washington, DC: Author.

U.S. Department of Health and Human Services. (1999). *Mental health: A report of the Surgeon General: Executive summary.* Rockville, MD: U.S. Department of Health and Human Services, Substance Abuse and Mental Health Services Administration, Center for Mental Health Services, National Institute of Mental Health.

White, W., & Davidson, L. (2006). Recovery: The bridge to integration? Part one. *Behavioral Healthcare, 226*(12), 24–26. Retrieved from http://www.

behavioral.net/ME2/dirmod.asp?sid=&nm=&type=Publishing&mod=
Publications%3A%3AArticle&mid=&id=275C497AD93D4F3AA4EB1
0C64B0D12E1&tier=4

World Health Organization. (2004). *The World Health Organization Quality of
Life (WHOQOL-BREF)*. Geneva: Author.

Yale University Program for Recovery and Community Health. (2008). *Practice guidelines for recovery-oriented care for mental health and substance use conditions* (2nd ed.). Hartford: Connecticut Department of Mental Health and
Addiction Services.

CHAPTER 15

Rapid Assessment Instruments as Outcomes Measures:
Past and Current Uses

Kevin Corcoran and Nikki Hozack

During the past three decades, exponential growth of psychometrically sound and clinically useful measurement tools has occurred. On the Internet alone, there are more than 10,000 instruments. This is a tremendous amount of instruments that can be used by clinical practitioners and researchers working with a particular mental health condition (for example, Brodsky & Smitherman, 1983; Fischer & Corcoran, 2007a, 2007b; Turk & Melzack, 2001), but this vast variety of tests does not come without pitfalls. Without the resources and understanding of where to find particular instruments such as Rapid Assessment Instruments (RAIs), or the ability to distinguish psychometrically sound instruments from those with less vigorous or no evidence, trying to find an appropriately researched measurement is overwhelming. However, we will show that gathering appropriate materials and using RAIs to further knowledge in research, inform policy and enhance clinical practice is not difficult, nor is understanding importance of their regular use and in times of the current health care reform.

RAIs are defined as surveys or questionnaires having fewer than 50 items or those that can be completed in less than 5 minutes. They are designed to be easily used within the context of clinical or research interviews and are meant to systematically quantify and provide numerical estimates of affect, cognition, or conduct over time. Because RAIs are quick to administer, score and interpret, they are particularly useful to clinicians as outcomes measures, as well as measures that can facilitate assessment, diagnosis, and monitoring of the mental health and/or substance use treatment process.

We posit that RAIs, like the increased use of evidence-based practice (EBP), has important utility in practice. We define EBP as problem-specific treatments that have been empirically supported by research and provide statistical evidence that the intervention is effective. The goal of EBP is to develop best-practice guidelines and involves not only the available information on a mental health problem, such as depression, but also patient characteristics, preferences, and environments, the latter of which are often ignored in the current health and mental health care system. EBP research goals are to enhance practice and increase practice knowledge; RAIs are already used to collect practice-based evidence in research. As such, the transference of psychometrically sound RAIs into evidence-based clinical practice should be viewed an important process in improving practice at the individual, community, or institutional levels of care. Yet, RAIs are only good supplements to—but never a substitute for—practice wisdom, clinical judgment, intuition and commonsense, which practitioners must always use to effectively meet their clients' needs. Proper use of appropriate RAIs not only informs practice, but may soon become a required part of practice as the current health care reforms begin.

As health and mental health care reform—and an emphasis on health promotion—increases the demand for accountability and feedback (Vandiver, 2009), RAIs are likely to become a standard for clinicians needing to demonstrate and document treatment outcome in practice. As RAI scores inform practice, so may empirical evidence in the form of RAIs inform policymakers in understanding therapist, agency, or intuitional effectiveness in treating mental health clients. Consumer feedback, as either qualitative (RAIs) or quantitative information, is an important component of mental health promotion, and it empowers the client to become a part of the therapeutic learning process (Vandiver, 2008). Both accountability and feedback are important components of individual, agency, and institutional responsibility in practice and in the advancement of mental health care reform.

To illustrate how RAIs can be used to meet some of the accountability demands associated with health care reform, this chapter focuses on two applications: RAIs as evidence of treatment necessity, and RAIs as treatment outcome measures, with particular attention given to using RAIs to estimate clinical significance, or the real-life effects (rather than the statistical significance) of treatment outcomes. Evidencing statistical significance by using changes in scores over the course of treatment has always been considered easier than being able to assert that the intervention actually worked (that is, clinical significance; Jayaratne & Levy, 1979). In this chapter, we discuss how to use RAI scores to determine treatment need and outcomes; how to determine clinical significance; and where to look for, and how to determine the psychometric soundness of, available measurements.

RAIs as Treatment Necessity Outcome Measures

As health care reform continues to move forward and inevitably affect ways in which clinical practices are delivered, it follows that methods for determining service need, or treatment necessity, will also be altered. This will likely be manifested by restricting services to those whose conditions are severe enough to warrant treatment. RAI scores can be used to effectively and efficiently demonstrate treatment necessity (Corcoran & Boyer-Quick, 2009). We are basing this notion on the assumption that persons who have mental health symptoms that are more severe are more likely to necessitate services; that is, severity and pervasiveness of symptoms tend to define the need for clinical services. Scores on RAIs provide a convenient way to quantify severity of symptoms. Interpreting severity is accomplished by comparing a client's pretreatment scores with norms from a general population; such comparisons are evidence that a client is sufficiently dissimilar from the general population and therefore warrants treatment. In addition, by comparing the client's score with the norms from a clinical sample, one is able to illustrate that the client is similar to those already receiving services. It is indisputable that if your client is similar to those who are in treatment and not like those in the general population, there is a need for treatment. This use of RAI scores in establishing treatment necessity requires norm-referenced comparisons.

Scores from an RAI may provide this persuasive evidence, so long as the instrument has a mean and standard deviation from a relevant population or sample. For example, the most precise comparison to a general population or a clinical sample is with a Z-score transformation. One simply subtracts the client score from the mean score of the population or sample, and divides by the standard deviation. The result converts the client's score to a matrix of -3

to +3 with a mean of 0. It can then be determined what percentage of the population of the sample is above and below the client's score by referring to standard statistical tables.

In essence, a Z-score allows the clinician to determine how much more or less severe the client's symptoms are compared with the general population and clinical sample. As stated earlier, if the client's score is similar to those of persons already receiving service and/or is dissimilar from that of the general population, then treatment necessity is persuasively averred. Consider a typical client whose payor requires proof of treatment necessity before authorizing payment for services. This may be a private insurance policy or a state requirement for public services. Oregon, for example, has a state statute requiring a particular evidence-based procedure, and private insurers require preauthorization. If your client has an RAI score that is similar to the scores of patient already receiving services, to deny him or her services would be negligence (Cicio v. Vytra Healthcare, 208 F. Supp. 2nd 288, 2001). This argument is strengthened if you are able to concomitantly illustrate that your client's condition or symptoms are noticeably different from those who do not need treatment, that is, the general population.

Another way to use norm-referenced comparison and treatment necessity is when an RAI has a cutting score. A *cutting score* is derived from a variety of psychometric research procedures; the result is a score that allows immediate interpretation in terms of whether or not the condition is sufficiently severe to suggest a clinical diagnosis and need for services. There are many clinical RAIs with cutting scores for most major mental health conditions and many codes from the *Diagnostic and Statistical Manual of Mental Disorders* (American Psychiatric Association, 2000), including the Beck Depression Inventory (Beck, 1967) and Hudson's clinical measure package (Hudson, 1997) which includes more than a dozen instruments to assess common problems seen by social workers and psychologists. By simply seeing that your client's score exceeds an established cutting score evidences that your client is similar or dissimilar to a known group with the same condition.

RAIs as Treatment Measures

In addition to their use to estimate treatment necessity, RAIs can be used to monitor client change over the course of treatment and to estimate goal attainment (Fischer & Corcoran, 2007b). That is, scores on RAIs, in effect, quantify whether the client actually changed. RAIs can be used to collect scores before, during, and after intervention and have been in use for more than 30 years (Jayaratne & Levy, 1979). In contrast to estimating treatment necessity by means of comparisons with general populations and clinical samples (that is, norm–referenced comparisons), using RAIs to measure individual client change is known as a *self-referenced comparison* (Fischer & Corcoran, 2007a, 2007b). One framework that is used to help breakdown and understand self-referenced comparisons is the AB [research] design (Fischer & Corcoran, 2007a). Scores during treatment (that is, B phase) are compared with scores before treatment (that is, A phase). Including a follow-up assessment after treatment termination allows one to see if the change has been stable or not.

For all of these reasons, RAIs can be particularly valuable as evidence of accountability in health care reform. This use of RAIs is easily integrated into routine practice because it has only three essential elements for monitoring progress over the course of treatment: (1) a simple research design that reflects the reality of the treatment process (that is, the B phase) for comparison with when treatment has not occurred (that is, A or follow-up assessments); (2) a systematic method to observe the client's problem or treatment goal, such as an RAI that is administrated routinely before, during, and after treatment; and (3) interpretation of the scores. Scores are easily interpreted by plotting them on a graph to help determine if they have changed over the course of treatment. Although more advance designs are available (Bloom, Fischer, & Orme, 2009), the simplicity of the AB design with a follow-up assessment makes its use more viable for busy practitioners. The AB design, which tracks client change with an RAI, provides valuable information for monitoring the course of treatment to observe whether progress is occurring or the presenting problems are getting worse or not changing at all. The inclusion of a follow-up assessment enables the client to assess whether the observed change has continued after treatment has ended or whether there may be a need for additional services.

RAIs as Evidence of Clinical Significance

Change that is clinically significant has been generally defined as changes in functioning that are meaningful to the individuals receiving psychosocial or medical treatments (Bauer, Lambert, & Neilson, 2004; Jacobson & Truax, 1991). Since the early introduction of empirical clinical practice, mere change in scores on a RAI is distinguishable from clinically significant change. This provokes the question, when considering the effects of treatment change, of whether the intervention produce a real and practical change in the everyday life of the client and the lives of the people with whom he or she interacts (Kazdin, 1999).

Asserting that change has occurred when it may not have is due chiefly to the degree of variability in scores. For example, the two-pack-a-day cigarette smoker who enters a cessation program and decreases the frequency of use to a pack and half has a statistically significant change. The client, however, is still at risk for lung cancer, heart disease, and a host of other health and social consequences.

Although there are different methods for calculating clinical significance, all seek to determine how close the individual who has received or is receiving treatment (that is, the intervention) has moved toward the mean of the functional population (Bauer et al., 2004). These calculations can determine "the percentage of clients who improved but did not recover, the percentage of clients who recovered, and the percentage of clients who remain unchanged or who deteriorated" (Jacobson, Roberts, Berns, & McGlinchy, 1999). We will illustrate this below.

Clinical significance is now commonly used in research studies to show intervention efficacy. The results of these studies can influence policy decisions, such as research funded by government agencies that reports the findings to Congress. Both practitioners and agency policymakers may use the research finding to fund some program and not others (Bauer et al., 2004).

In addition, clinical significance can be a practical and useful tool to assess and monitor the degree of change obtained by individuals in treatment and to measure the degree of success of the client intervention (Bauer et al., 2004). This is different from comparing client scores over the treatment process in that the scores are compared with those of persons considered functional and dysfunctional. That is, scores are compared with those of people who have and do not have the particular condition warranting treatment.

Though several methods are available for calculating clinical significance, the most frequently used in both research is the Jacobson-Truax model (Bauer et al., 2004). Jacobson and Truax formulated the reliable change index (RCI), which is in fact the same Z-score procedures used above to estimate treatment necessity (Jacobson & Truax, 1991). The RCI is based on measurement scores before treatment (X_{pre}), the scores post treatment (X_{post}), and the standard error of difference between the two scores (S_{diff}):

$$\frac{\text{RCI} = X_{post} - X_{pre}}{S_{diff}}.$$

When the RCI score is greater than 1.96, the change is considered statistically significant and it is unlikely to be an artifact of a measurement error. In other words, it can be reasonably assumed that the individual has improved (Ogles, Lunnen, & Bonesteel, 2001).

Like the procedures for establishing treatment necessity, this approach to using RAIs to estimate clinical significance is straightforward. In fact, if one simply reverses the logic for establishing treatment necessity, clinical significance may be deduced if RAI scores have changed from dissimilar from the general population at the beginning of treatment to similar to the general population at the end. With such a contrast in the client's condition, clinical significance may be reasonably and persuasively asserted. The question may very well be what degree of similarity to or dissimilarity from the general population mean is acceptable; the decision rests solely on clinical judgment.

The assertion of clinically meaningful change in a mental health or health condition is paramount in health care reform. It is increasingly becoming commonplace for government and other payers to restrict reimbursement to procedures that are evidence based. Practitioners of all health and allied services must master a variety of particular interventions with established procedures that may be implemented consistently. Often these interventions have a manual that guide the practitioner's use of the procedure, with the sole purpose of increasing the likelihood of successful change.

Limitations of RAIs and Conclusion

Although RAIs are useful outcomes measures, they are not without limitation. RAIs require time and resources to administer, score, and interpret. They are of little use for those clients who terminate treatment after a few sessions, or for human services that provide treatment that is designed to be very brief, such as such as crisis intervention or family mediation. In addition, RAI scores are meaningful only relative to other numbers.

Choosing a fitting measurement may also be challenging because of the easy availability of tests that may have irregularities in standardization, norming, reliability, and validity. *Standardization* refers to the ability of the test to be administered and scored in a consistent, predetermined manner. *Test norming* refers to distribution ranking of the test scores and is derived from the analysis of test scores drawn from sample of a population.

A common complaint about many assessments used in the behavioral science is that they are not standardized or normed appropriately to the populations they serve (Cicchetti, 1994) and that to be relevant they must be based on a systematic stratification of various criteria such as age, gender, education, and ethnic and cultural norms. There are many norm-referenced comparisons in practice, though this does not ensure that all measurements are adequately normed. Collecting normative data is expensive and, therefore, few data are available for many instruments, and they are rarely up-to-date. Further, the sample used may not be sufficiently similar to a particular client and therefore inappropriate for meaningful comparisons. For example, normative data often are not available for clients of color, immigrants, children, and members of low-income groups. Consequently, care needs to be exercised when using normative data that may lead to invalid conclusions.

Two other issues of concern in choosing the proper measurement have to do with test validity and test reliability. *Validity* is the degree to which the test is actually measuring what it intends to measure and also refers to the extent to which the test scores are appropriate and meaningful. *Test reliability* refers the consistency and stability in measuring what it is intended to measure. In other words, a test is reliable if the same results are approximately the same within itself and over multiple administrations..Validity and reliability are interrelated: One cannot have test reliability without validity, and having test reliability is unimportant if the test is not valid; that is, what does measurement consistency matter if one is not measuring what it is they are seeking to quantify?

With the vast array of measurements to choose from in assessing issues, it is important not only to find tests standardized and normed to your populations, but that those tests are also valid and reliable. Fortunately, with proper research and resources (for example, academic journals, books, measurement-specific publishing houses, the Internet), clinicians, researchers and others will most often find many appropriate measurements.

We end where we began, with the assertion that while RAIs are not a substitute for trained professional judgment and the human element in mental health care practice, they do provide valuable data on the need for services and the impact and outcome of services. We support the use of appropriate RAIs in clinical settings and encourage social workers and other human services professionals to promote the use of properly evidenced instruments.

References

American Psychiatric Association. (2000). *Diagnostic and statistical manual of mental disorders* (4th ed., text rev.). Washington, DC: Author.

Bauer, S., Lambert, M. J., & Nielsen, S. L. (2004). Clinical significance methods: A comparison of statistical techniques. *Journal of Personality Assessment, 82*(1), 60–70.

Beck, A. T. (1967). *Depression: Clinical, experimental and theoretical aspects.* New York: Harper.

Bloom, M., Fischer, J., & Orme, J. G. (2009). *Evaluating practice: Guidelines for the accountable professional* (6th ed.). New York: Allyn & Bacon.

Brodsky, S. L., & Smitherman, H. O. (1983). *Handbook of scales for research in crime and delinquency.* New York: Plenum.

Cicio v. Vytra Healthcare, 208 F. Supp. 2nd 288, 2001.

Corcoran, K. & Boyer-Quick, J. (2009). How clinicians can effectively use assessment tools to evidence medical necessity and throughout the treatment process. In A. R. Roberts (Eds.), *Social workers' desk reference* (2nd ed., pp. 317–324). New York: Oxford University Press.

Fischer, J., & Corcoran, K. (2007a). *Measures for clinical practice and research, Vol. 1: Adults* (4th ed.). New York: Oxford University Press.

Fischer, J., & Corcoran, K. (2007b). *Measures for clinical practice and research, Vol. 1: Couples, families and children* (4th ed). New York: Oxford University Press.

Hudson, W. W. (1997). *WALMYR Assessment Scales scoring manual*. Tallahassee, FL: WALMYR Publishing.

Jacobson, N. S., Roberts, L. J., Berns, S. B., & McGlinchey, J. B. (1999). Methods for defining and determining the clinical significance of treatment effects: Description, application, and alternatives. *Journal of Consulting and Clinical Psychology, 59*, 300–307.

Jacobson, N. S., & Truax, P. (1991). Clinical significance: A statistical approach to defining meaningful change in psychotherapy research. *Journal of Consulting and Clinical Psychology, 59*, 12–19.

Jayaratne, S., & Levy, R. L. (1979). *Empirical clinical practice*. New York: Columbia.

Kazdin, A. E. (1999). The meanings and measurement of clinical significance. *Journal of Consulting and Clinical Psychology, 67*, 332–339.

Ogles, B. M., Lunnen, K. M., & Bonesteel, K. (2001). Clinical significance: History, application and current practice. *Clinical Psychology Review, 21*, 421–446.

Turk, D. C., & Melzack, R. (2001). *Handbook of pain assessment*. New York: John Wiley & Sons.

Vandiver, V. (2009). *Integrating health promotion and mental health: An introduction to policies, principles and practices*. New York: Oxford University Press.

CHAPTER 16

Outcomes Measurement and the Mental Health Consumer Movement:

Research, Recovery, and Recognition in the Human Services

Jean Campbell

To persons with mental illness, "recovery" has always implied having hope for the future: living a self-determined life, maintaining self-efficacy, and achieving meaningful roles in society. The *National Consensus Statement on Mental Health Recovery* (Substance Abuse and Mental Health Services Administration [SAMHSA], 2005) defines *recovery* as "a journey of healing and transformation enabling a person with a mental health problem to live a meaningful life in a community of his or her choice while striving to achieve his or her full potential." The 10 fundamental components of recovery are self-direction, individualization, person centeredness, empowerment, holism, nonlinearity, strengths-based, peer support, respect, responsibility, and hope (Onken, Craig, Ridgway, & Cook, 2007).

This meaning of recovery is rooted in the rich history of the Mental Health Consumer/Survivor/Ex-Patient Movement and its foundation in organized peer support services (Bassman, 2006; Campbell, 2005; Chamberlin, 1990; Cook & Jonikas, 2002; Dain, 1989; Frese & Davis, 1997). Of the first 300 first-person accounts of madness that were published in the English language (Hornstein, 2002), most were written as a means to organize ex-patients in order to improve psychiatric services or offer alternatives. In the United States in the early 1970s, large numbers of psychiatric patients were discharged from psychiatric hospitals to find themselves adrift in uncaring communities. Throughout the next two decades, they organized small groups to provide mutual support through self-help approaches and to advocate for social justice (Campbell, 2005).

In the 1990s, people with mental illness began to more formally organize on a national level, championing the South African disability motto "Nothing About Us Without Us." (This motto relies on the principle of participation, and it has been used by disabled people's organizations throughout the years as part of the global movement to achieve the full participation and equalization of opportunities for, by, and with people with disabilities.) They also became involved in mental health services research that was defining new mental health measures related to recovery (for example, empowerment, well-being, perceptions of care, and needs and preferences) and conducting mental health services satisfaction assessments. Some acquired federal funding for national technical assistance organizations run by persons with mental illness, and others obtained State Mental Health Authority (SMHA) support for statewide networks of persons with mental illness and Offices of Consumer Affairs (Campbell, 2005). In the process, many of the small, independent self-help groups became bundled together as consumer-operated service programs (COSPs), an umbrella term for programs that are administratively controlled and operated by persons with mental illness and emphasize self-help as their operational approach in delivering peer support services.

By the turn of the 21st century, the push for recovery and the use of peer support services accelerated across the United States as COSPs matured, diversified, and increased in numbers. In 2002, the Survey of Organized Consumer Self-Help Entities was conducted by the Center for Mental Health Services to systematically identify and describe consumer organizations in the United States (Goldstrom et al., 2005). The first survey of its kind, it counted a total of 7,467 organizations: 3,315 were mutual support groups, 3,019 were self-help organizations run by and for persons with mental illness and/or family members of persons with mental illness, and 1,133 were COSPs. Mutual support groups reported that 41,363 people attended their last meetings; self-help organizations reported 1,005,400 members; and COSPs provided support to

534,551 participants. Approximately one-third (2,100) of the total provided services to other people with mental illness as their sole or partial purpose (Goldstrom et al., 2006).

Today, a wide range of peer support services are available to persons with mental illness through six primary COSP service delivery models:

1. *Organized self-help groups* of persons with mental illness typically offer assistance and encouragement through a small group dynamic. Such groups differ from naturally occurring social support because the process is intentional and includes "standard procedures, routines, and prescriptions for addressing problems and issues of everyday life" (Davidson et al., 1999, p. 168). Self-help groups expose members to successful role models and help them make sense of their experiences (Chamberlin, 1988).

2. *Drop-in centers* provide an open venue for persons with mental illness to receive a variety of peer support services as needed within a centralized location. Individuals participate in drop-in activities on a voluntary, noncoercive basis. Service components include self-help and activity groups, access to telephones, laundry facilities, and computers, as well as assistance with entitlements, medication education, clothing, bus or transportation passes, and moving. Drop-in centers provide information to their membership on coping, wellness, community resources, rights and advocacy issues, and leadership skills (Diehl & Baxter, 1999).

3. *Peer educator and advocacy programs* are based on the belief that persons with mental illness are best able to address their own recovery needs and to advocate for change within the mental health system when they have accurate and comprehensive knowledge about mental illness and psychiatric services and strategies to support wellness. Peer educator and advocacy programs use well-defined curricula to teach consumers this kind of information, sometimes in short-term classroom settings.

4. *Specialized peer support services* address a single problem such as psychiatric crisis, unemployment, or inadequate housing and homelessness. Supportive housing programs link affordable housing with supportive services, assisting persons with mental illness to live stable and independent lives in community settings. Supportive employment programs emphasize competitive employment and provide a place for persons with mental illness to gain skill and confidence, educate themselves about work and disability, and get help over the course of a career. Supportive crisis intervention or respite programs provide an informal, nonclinical environment where people can stabilize with the help of peer counselors.

5. *Peer-run multiservice agencies* assist persons with mental illness who are underserved to obtain vital social service benefits (for example, Social Security Disability Income, or SSDI). Through advocacy, outreach, case management, and related services, such agencies function as an open door to the mental health system by teaching people how to find and utilize community resources.

6. *Peer phone support lines or "warmlines"* are operated by volunteer or paid persons with mental illness in order to address gaps in the peer support service delivery system. They offer persons with mental illness a safe connection to other peers through the telephone when they experience social isolation or need information.

It is clear that while many of the details of these COSP service delivery models appear to be different, at the heart of the programs is a common set of operating structures, beliefs, and practices that recognize and nourish personal strengths and personhood; support quality lives for participating peers; and embrace the principles of choice, hope, empowerment, recovery, acceptance; and respect for diversity, spiritual growth, and self-help. Peer support practices encourage participants to tell their stories of illness and recovery, engage in formal and informal peer support, mentor and become mentors, learn self-management and problem-solving strategies, express themselves creatively, and advocate for themselves and other peers. (Systematic identification of cross-cutting elements common to all COSPs produced a list of "common ingredients" and an objective rating system to measure program fidelity and initiate quality improvements [Holter et al., 2004; Johnsen, Teague, & McDonel Herr, 2005].)

Certainly COSPs offer much-needed human resources and promote a sense of well-being among participating peers, but until recently mental health services research has focused primarily on the effectiveness of traditional mental health modalities and programs to treat mental illness, and has neglected to consider COSPs as valued service programs that can produce positive outcomes that lead to recovery. This neglect has had a profound effect on the quality, amount, and content of the research conducted on COSPs, and consequently, the uneven development of a COSP evidence base and the integration of peer support services into the continuum of care. Like the mental health consumer/survivor/ex-patient movement itself, consideration of COSPs as effective peer support service programs with a valid and reliable evidence base has had it its own evolution within mental health services research; only a few highlights from this history can be presented here.

Key to development of the COSP evidence base has been the continued support of the federal government, which began to promote self-help as part of a broader effort to reform psychiatry through patient self-advocacy. Involvement of persons with mental illness in mental health services was mandated by federal law and actively promoted by projects at the federal and state levels (National Institute of Mental Health, 1991). Increasing federal and state support of COSPs through block grants and other federal funding, such as research demonstration initiatives, produced a wealth of descriptive and quasi-experimental studies of peer support services.

Building on uncontrolled studies, demonstrations of feasibility, and preliminary findings, the successful collaboration between persons with mental illness and scientists produced a summary of peer support services in the 1999 *Surgeon General's Report on Mental Health* (U. S. Department of Health and Human Services, 1999). Researchers began to conduct more rigorous studies of COSPs with experimental and quasi-experimental designs and to include measures of empowerment, recovery, and other dimensions related to well-being and quality of life as part of their protocols. Such advances corroborated the claims of persons with mental illness to an important voice in transforming the content and character of community mental health services by promoting the hope of recovery.

Most notably, the 2003 New Freedom Commission on Mental Health *Final Report* (U.S. Department of Health and Human Services, 2003) statement that persons with mental illness had "a key role in expanding the mental healthcare delivery workforce and creating a system that focuses on recovery" (p. 37) brought increasing appreciation of peer support services. The report recommended that consumers be involved in a variety of appropriate service and support settings: "In particular, consumer-operated services for which an evidence base is emerging should be promoted" (p. 37).

Today, the mental health community better understands how peer support services work, the range of outcomes that persons with mental illness experience as a result of participating in COSPs, and the impact of COSPs on the recovery of persons with mental illness. However, no systematic assessment of the body of scientific knowledge about COSPs currently exists that would determine the quality, quantity, and consistency of the evidence base that supports (and has supported) COSPs. (*Quality* of evidence is the extent to which a study's design, conduct, and analysis minimize selection, measurement, and confounding biases. *Quantity* of evidence is the magnitude of effect, numbers of studies, and sample size or power. *Consistency* of evidence is the extent to which similar findings are reported using similar and different study designs.) Certainly, such knowledge is critical to a broad acceptance of COSPs as safe, effective, and a key partner in the shift of the mental health system to a recovery-based continuum of care. As a starting point, the remainder of this chapter will discuss work undertaken to systematically identify COSP outcome studies to date and apply an exploratory framework to score the quality of the COSP evidence base and grade the research conclusions. This is followed by further considerations regarding the future directions of peer support services and studies of their effectiveness.

An Exploratory Framework for Grading the COSP Evidence Base

With mental health care policy increasingly relying on evidence from empirical studies rather than on expert opinion or clinical experience alone for making health care decisions, a number of evidence scoring systems have emerged to consolidate and gauge evidence to grade conclusions drawn from systematic reviews of available studies of medical interventions (Adkins et al., 2004; Leff, Conley, & Elmore, 2005; West et al., 2002). Most of these systems modified the approach developed by the Agency for Healthcare Research and Quality (AHRQ, previously the Agency for Health Care Policy and Research), the federal agency directed by Congress to undertake the identification of methods to assess health care research results as part of the Healthcare Research and Quality Act of 1999. AHRQ standardized and provided cogent rules to appraise published research, determine its validity, and summarize its utility in practice (West et al., 2002). Over the past decade, its system of scoring a study by level of evidence from Ia (highest score) to IV (lowest score), and grading the strength of the body of evidence overall (conclusions) from A to C on the basis of these scoring levels became central to the definition of evidence-based practice. Therefore, the AHRQ evidence grading system was selected to grade the COSP evidence base, although features of other systems were also used as appropriate.

Although the AHRQ protocol for scoring study evidence and assigning grades is based almost entirely on research design type, its structural simplicity was particularly useful in grading the strength of the COSP evidence base because it allows for reviews of published COSP studies in which quantity and consistency of evidence are not always discussed. Clearly, more comprehensive approaches to scoring evidence and grading recommendations are optimum where time and resources are available. However, the goals of this effort were exploratory: to test the practicality and value of using a simple framework to evaluate the trustworthiness of COSP research conclusions in order to provide decision support to policymakers, providers, researchers, and the people they serve as the mental health community struggles to determine which mental health services are evidence based.

The systematic search of COSP studies produced 201 theoretical and empirical articles, book chapters, and reports from a computerized library search of PsycINFO, CINAHL, Current Contents, Social Services Abstracts, and Sociological Abstracts databases from 1970 to 2005. (I conducted the literature review of COSP studies and the application of the AHPR evidence grading system as part of a review of COSP evidence and other resources collected in conjunction with the production of the COSP Evidence-based Practices KIT sponsored by SAMHSA/CMHS [in federal clearance]. I was assisted by a core working group of leading mental health consumers with expertise in peer support services and staff at the COSP Coordinating Center, located at the Missouri Institute of Mental Health.) The search was performed by crossing *mental health*, *research*, and *evaluation* with the following key words: *peer*, *consumer*, *program services*, and *mutual support*. A second search was done by crossing *research* and *evaluation* with *self-help*, resulting in the identification of 606 additional citations. Sixty-six publications were also suggested by core group members and colleagues. After eliminating duplicate citations and articles outside the scope of the search, a database of 115 entries was selected on the basis of content relevance, appropriateness, and quality and sorted into the following categories: research (38), theory (10), description (23), historical (19) supplemental (17), and general (8). An additional three published outcome studies were recently located in the scientific literature from 2005 through 2010.

In the research category, 29 empirical studies were found that reported COSP outcomes. Each was assigned a score from I to IV, guided by determination of the type of evidence and use of study quality grids (West et al., 2002) to document the strengths and weaknesses of the different studies. A summary of COSP study scores, followed by a short description of selected study outcome results found at each scoring level and completion of the framework protocol with assignment of a preliminary grade to COSP research conclusions is provided in Table 16-1.

Level IV Evidence

Level IV, the lowest ranking of evidence quality, includes a sampling of evidence from five expert committee reports and opinions and/or experience of respected authorities. The bulk of COSP evidence at Level IV is written by people with mental illness who documented their self-help experiences in peer support services. Zinman (1986) wrote, "Self-help groups demystify our emotional life, giving back to us the knowledge and tools to help ourselves. Our emotional life is no longer somebody else's, the medical profession's specialty. We are the experts" (p. 11).

Table 16-1: Consumer-operated Service Program Study Scores

Score	Type of Evidence	Studies	Total
Ia	Evidence obtained from meta-analysis of randomized controlled trials		0
Ib	Evidence obtained from at least one randomized controlled trial	Campbell et al. (2006); Dumont & Jones (2002); Gordon, Edmunson, Bedell, & Goldstein (1979)	3
II	Evidence obtained from at least one well-designed controlled study without randomization or evidence obtained from at least one other type of well-designed quasi-experimental study	Galanter (1988); Hodges & Segal (2002); Kennedy (1990); Lucksted, McNulty, Brayboy, & Forbes (2009); Magura, Laudet, Mahmood, Rosenblum, & Knight (2002); Nelson et al. (2007); Roberts et al. (1999); Yanos, Primavera, & Knight (2001)	8
III	Evidence obtained from well-designed non-experimental descriptive studies, such as comparative studies, correlation studies and case control studies	Brown, Shepherd, Merkle, Wituk, & Meissen (2008); Carpinello, Knight, Videka-Sherman, Solka, & Markowitz (1996); Chamberlin, Rogers, & Ellison (1996); DeMasi et al. (1997); Kaufmann, Ward-Colasanate, & Farmer (1993); Kurtz (1988); Lewis (2001); Luke, Roberts, & Rappaport (1994); Mowbray & Tan (1993); Mowbray, Wellwood, & Chamberlain (1988); Raiff (1984); Trainor, Shepherd, Boydell, Leff, & Crawford (1997); Van Tosh & del Vecchio (2001)	13
IV	Evidence obtained from expert committee reports or opinions and/or clinical experience of respected authorities	Campbell & Schraiber (1989); Chamberlin (1979); Stroul (1986); Zinman (1986); Zinman, Harp, & Budd (1987)	5

Testimony about peer support services was also collected by persons with mental illness as part of the ground-breaking Well-Being Project (Campbell & Schraiber, 1989) to explore what promotes or deters well-being for adults in California with serious mental illness. Howie the Harp noted, "I've pretty much been able to stay out of the hospital with the help of self-help groups" (p. 43). Pierce related (about a drop-in center), "The biggest thing that has brought me a sense of empowerment is to be a member of CAPABLE" (p. 51). Kaplan observed (about a drop-in center), "I've seen people grow tremendously while they been at Spiritmenders. They come and find peers; they find friends.... Here they feel like they're human beings" (p. 45). Price concluded, "It's in the right direction.... People don't believe us, that we're capable of doing anything.... But the trouble is, self-help works" (p. 53).

Level III Evidence

Level III evidence includes 13 reports of from well-designed nonexperimental descriptive studies (for example, comparative, correlation and case control studies) that do not involve a comparison group and in which researchers were required to use other means to determine whether the program was effective. Most of the research at this level was done during the early development of COSPs to ascertain the characteristics of persons who chose to participate in peer support services, the services that led to personal change, and members' perspectives on benefits of peer support services. Positive impacts reported by study participants included improvements in quality of life, increased problem-solving skills; satisfaction with peer support services; growth of social connectedness; reduction in hospitalizations, manic depressive symptoms, and use of traditional treatments; and acquisition of coping skills.

Level II Evidence

Level II evidence includes eight well-designed controlled studies or evidence obtained from other types of well-designed quasi-experimental studies. Several studies of COSPs that used nonrandomized control groups or pretest scores as comparisons found that participation in COSPs reduces psychiatric symptoms and hospitalization, improves psychological and social adjustment, encourages goal advancement, and helps with adherence to psychiatric medication.

Level Ia and Ib Evidence

Because no meta-analysis of randomized controlled trials (RCTs) of COSPs has been performed, the highest evidence level scored for COSP studies was Ib for three RCTs, including a multisite study. The power and methodological rigor of these RCTs strengthened the quality of COSP evidence but also added methodological problems and analytical complexity to some study protocols, including issues of low engagement and selection bias (Campbell et al., 2006).

The COSP Multisite Research Initiative (1998 to 2006) is the most rigorous study of COSPs to date (Campbell et al., 2006), conducted under a stringent experimental design that included intent-to-treat (IT) analysis within a multisite randomized clinical trial. It is also the largest study of COSPs, with 1,827 participants interviewed at baseline, four months, and 12 months at eight sites nationwide: four drop-in centers, two organized self-help programs, and two educational/advocacy programs. Overall, the IT study findings support the conclusion that participation in COSPs by adults with serious mental illness as an adjunct to traditional mental health services leads to a significant increase in subjective well-being (a composite measure of hope, empowerment, meaning in life, self-efficacy, and goal attainment), increases that were greater than those achieved through participation in traditional mental health services alone. (Because outcomes were assessed over a relatively brief follow-up period of one year, significant differences in outcomes associated with greater durations of recovery such as employment and independent living were not anticipated.) Furthermore, researchers applied post hoc observational methods, including as-treated analysis, to estimate the effect of actual services use, examine differences in slopes, and examine the results by site. In the as-treated analysis, participants who used COSPs at least minimally (for example, at least one visit) were found to have greater average increases in well-being than those who did not use COSPs at all, and those who participated more in the COSPs had greater average increases in well-being than those who participated less.

COSP use was positively associated with increases in personal empowerment without significant variation across the study sites and supported the conclusion that COSPs in general have a positive additive effect on empowerment when the subjective construct is measured (Rogers, et al, 2007). Most important, the COSP multisite study provided a greater understanding of the relationship of outcomes and peer practices within COSPs. Researchers in collaboration with providers of peer support services identified and scored 46 common COSP structures, values, and processes at the study sites by administering the Fidelity Assessment Common Ingredients Tool (Johnsen, Teague & McDonel Herr, 2005). Results of this instrument correlated with differences in well-being, especially with regard to COSP environmental characteristics (for example, peer services provided free of charge; program rules developed by members ensure physical safety; no hierarchy, but rather a sense of freedom and warmth among members and staff; sense of community; and lack of coerciveness) and peer practices that encourage self-expression among members (for example, artistic expression, opportunities for sharing life experiences or telling one's story, and formal peer support activities). Such findings support the conclusion that the common ingredients of peer support services identified and scored in the COSP Multisite Research Initiative are critical to the delivery of effective COSPs, especially those that seek to promote the subjective well-being of their membership.

Grading the Evidence

The initial scoring of COSP studies included in the exploratory analysis was used to assign grades to the strength of COSP research conclusions:

- Evidence levels Ia and Ib were assigned an A grade because they met the following criteria: at least one RCT as part of the body of literature of overall good quality and consistency in addressing the specific conclusion. An example of the type of research conclusion evidence that was graded A includes: Participation in a COSP self-help group by adults with serious mental illness as an adjunct to coping skills training reduces psychiatric hospitalization and utilization of traditional mental health services and increases community tenure and feelings of independence (Gordon et al., 1979).

- Evidence levels IIa, IIb, and III were assigned a B grade because they met the following criteria: well-conducted studies, but no RCTs on the topic of the conclusion. An example of the type of research conclusion evidence that was graded B includes: Participation in COSPs by adults with mental illness promotes positive subjective wellness outcomes (increases in perceived quality of life, self efficacy, social connectedness, empowerment, goal attainment, community integration and enhanced coping skills) and positive clinical treatment outcomes (reduction in psychiatric hospitalization, symptoms, utilization of mental health services, and increased medication compliance).

- Evidence levels IV was assigned a C grade because they met the following criteria: evidence from expert committee reports or opinions and/or experience of respected authorities. This grade indicates absence of directly applicable studies of good quality. An example of the type of research conclusion evidence that was graded C includes: First-person accounts of adults with mental illness on the perceived effects of participation in COSPs describe enhanced meaning in life, self-efficacy, empowerment, and social connectedness.

The research conclusions at all three grade levels support the effectiveness of COSPs in promoting various subjective well-being factors such as hope, self-efficacy, empowerment, goal attainment, meaning in life, and social connectedness among adults with serious mental illness who receive peer support services. There is a smaller and weaker body of evidence supporting COSPs' positive effect on clinical outcomes such as reduced hospitalization, symptoms, and medication compliance when these outcomes are a primary focus of the peer support services that also received a grade of A. However, in most cases, the COSPs that were studied in this review functioned as an adjunct to traditional mental health services (rather than alternatives) both directly through linkages with the mental health system and indirectly through the utilization of clinical services by COSP participants. Overall, the exploratory effort to grade COSP research conclusions clarified questions regarding the strength of research justifications for clinical and policy decision makers to fund COSPs within the continuum of care.

The use of such an approach, especially among practitioners and researchers working with promising new practices, could also prove helpful in translating research into practice. Since different types of questions require different types of evidence, the inflexible use of current evidence grading system is not recommended. It is time to broaden the scope by which evidence is assessed, including evidence from qualitative studies. The best available evidence for each outcome of potential importance to service recipients is needed, and that requires evidence assessments to draw on a variety of types of research where persons with mental illness have brought their perspectives to the table.

Conclusion: From Deinstitutionalization to Recovery

This chapter brings to light some important understandings about recovery as concept and lived experience and the course that COSPs have taken in their journey from small, alternative self-help groups to promising best practices with a national constituency and resources from federal and state mental health agencies, as well as growing recognition within the scientific community as an evidence-based practice. The strongest research conclusions of COSP effectiveness refer to outcomes that are positive, profoundly subjective, and that promote wellness. This is not surprising, as the shift away from focusing on patienthood to celebrating personhood in the decades after deinstitutionalization marked a significant transformation in the consciousness of persons with mental illness that was not to be found within the traditional mental health system until very recently.

The timing of the COSP Multisite Research Initiative was especially opportune for advancing knowledge about peer support services and converting this knowledge into improving the effectiveness of COSPs in achieving valued outcomes. However, the application of the evidence-based practice paradigm to peer support services has generated concerns among persons with mental illness that the application of evidence-based peer practices will limit COSP program choices, and many factors important to members will be neglected. On the other hand, the thoughtful assessment of the strength of the COSP body of research conclusions, the practical application of these research conclusions to real-life situations, and the ongoing conversations that will follow will continue to define the possible. Through ongoing dialogue and negotiation, evidence-based peer practices have the potential to transform the relationships among COSPs, public and private mental health agencies, and local communities as recovery theory and practice become grounded in community-based partnerships. This occurs in an era in which new legislative directives, such as national health care reform and parity, have the potential to form partnerships that truly embody the idea of "nothing about us without us."

References

Adkins, D., Eccles, M., Flottorp, S., Guyatt, G., Henry, D., Hill, S., et al. (2004). Systems for grading the quality of evidence and the strength of recommendations 1: Critical appraisal of existing approaches. *BMC Health Services Research, 4,* 38.

Bassman, R. (2006). The evolution from advocacy to self-determination. In R. W. Manderscheid & J. T. Berry (Eds.), *Mental health, United States, 2004* (DHHS Pub No. SMA 06-4195) (pp. 14–22). Rockville, MD: Substance Abuse and Mental Health Services Administration.

Campbell, J. (1996). Towards collaborative mental health outcomes systems. *New Directions for Mental Health Services, 71,* 69–78.

Campbell, J. (1997). How consumers/survivors are evaluating the quality of psychiatric care. *Evaluation Review, 21,* 357–363.

Campbell, J. (1998). Consumerism, outcomes, and satisfaction: A review of the literature. In R. W. Manderscheid & M. Henderson (Eds.), *Mental health, United States, 1998* (pp. 11–28). Rockville, MD: U.S. Department of Health and Human Services, Substance Abuse and Mental Health Administration Center for Mental Health Services.

Campbell, J. (2005). Historical and philosophical development of peer-run programs. In S. Clay (Ed.), *On our own together: Peer programs for people with mental illness* (pp. 17–64). Nashville, TN: Vanderbilt University Press.

Campbell, J., & Johnson, J. R. (1995). Struggling to reach common ground. *Behavioral Health Tomorrow, 4,* 40, 45–46.

Campbell, J., & Leaver, J. (2003). Emerging new practices in organized peer support. In *Report to the National Technical Assistance Center for State Mental Health Planning (NTAC).* Alexandria, VA: National Association of State Mental Health Program Directors.

Campbell, J., Lichtenstein, C., Teague, G., Johnsen, M., Yates, B., Sonnefeld, J., et al. (2006). *The Consumer-Operated Service Programs (COSP) multisite research initiative: Final report.* Saint Louis: Coordinating Center at the Missouri Institute of Mental Health.

Campbell, J., & Schraiber, R. (1989). *In pursuit of wellness: The well-being project.* Sacramento: California Department of Mental Health.

Carpinello, S., Knight, E., Videka-Sherman, L., Sofka, C., & Markowitz, F. (1996). *Self-selection distinguishing factors: Participants and non participants of mental health self-help groups.* Unpublished manuscript, Center for the Study of Issues in Public Mental Health, Orangeburg, NY.

Chamberlin, J. (1979). *On our own: Patient-controlled alternatives to the mental health system.* New York: McGraw-Hill.

Chamberlin, J. (1988). *On our own: Patient-controlled alternatives to the mental health system.* Washington, DC: National Association of Mental Health.

Chamberlin, J. (1990). The ex-patient's movement: Where we've been and where we're going. *Journal of Mind and Behavior, 11,* 323–336.

Chamberlin, J., Rogers, E. S., & Ellison, M. (1996). Self-help programs: A description of their characteristics and their members. *Psychiatric Rehabilitation Journal, 19,* 33–42.

Cook, J., & Jonikas, J. (2002). Self-determination among mental health consumers/survivors: Using lessons from the past to guide the future. *Journal of Disability Policy Studies, 13,* 88–96.

Dain, N. (1989). Critics and dissenters: Reflections on "anti-psychiatry" in the United States. *Journal of the History of the Behavioral Sciences, 25,* 3–25.

Davidson, L., Chinman, M., Kloos, B., Weingarten, R., Stayner, D., & Tebes, J. (1999). Peer support among individuals with severe mental illness: A review of the evidence. *Clinical Psychology: Science and Practice, 9,* 165–187.

DeMasi, M., Carpinello, S., Knight, E., Videka-Sherman, L., Sofka, C., & Markowitz, F. (1997). *The role of self-help in the recovery process.* Unpublished manuscript, Center for the Study of Issues in Public Mental Health, Orangeburg, NY.

Diehl, S., & Baxter, E. (2001). Back from where I've been: Stories from the BRIDGES program of recovery from mental illness. Nashville: Tennessee Department of Mental Health and Development Disabilities.

Dumont, J., & Jones, K. (2002, Spring). Findings from a consumer/survivor defined alternative to psychiatric hospitalization. *Outlook,* 4–6.

Emerick, R. (1990). Self-help groups for former patients: Relations with mental health professionals. *Hospital and Community Psychiatry, 41,* 401–407.

Fisher, S. H. (1960). Rehabilitation of the mental hospital patient: The Fountain House programme. *International Journal of Social Psychiatry, 5,* 295.

Frese, F., & Davis, W. (1997). The consumer-survivor movement, recovery, and consumer professionals. *Professional Psychology: Research and Practice, 28,* 243–245.

Galanter, M. (1988). Research on social supports and mental illness. *American Journal of Psychiatry, 145,* 1270–1272.

Goertzel, V., Beard, J. H., & Pilnick, S. (1960). Fountain House Foundation: Case study of an expatient's club. *Journal of Social Issues, 16,* 54.

Goldstrom, I., Campbell, J., Rogers, J., Blacklow, B., Henderson, M., & Manderscheid, R. (2006). Mental health consumer organizations: A national picture. In R. W. Manderscheid & J. T. Berry (Eds.), *Mental health, United States, 2004* (DHHS Publication No. SMA-06-4195, pp. 247–255). Rockville, MD: Substance Abuse and Mental Health Services Administration.

Goldstrom, I., Campbell, J., Rogers, J., Lambert, D., Blacklaw, B., Henderson, M., & Manderscheid, R. (2005, January). National estimates for mental health mutual support groups, self-help organizations, and consumer-operated services. *Administration and Policy in Mental Health and Mental Health Services Research, 33,* 92–103.

Gordon, R., Edmunson, E., Bedell, J., & Goldstein, N. (1979). Utilizing peer management and support to reduce rehospitalization of mental patients. *Journal of the Florida Medical Association, 66,* 927–933.

Hodges, J., & Segal, S. (2002). Goal advancement among mental health self-help agency members. *Psychiatric Rehabilitation Journal, 26,* 78–85.

Holter, M. C., Mowbray, C. T., Bellamy, C. D., MacFarlane, P., & Dukarski, J. (2004). Critical ingredients of consumer run services: Results of a national survey. *Community Mental Health Journal, 40,* 47–63.

Hornstein, G. A. (2002, January 25). Narratives of madness, as told from within. *Chronicle Review of Higher Education*, B7–B10.

Johnsen, M., Teague, G., & McDonel-Herr, E. (2005). Common ingredients as a measure for peer-run programs. In S. Clay (Ed.), *On our own together: Peer programs for people with mental illness* (pp. 213–238). Nashville, TN: Vanderbilt University Press.

Kaufmann, C., Ward-Colesante, M., & Farmer, M. (1993). Development and evaluation of drop-in centers operated by mental health consumers. *Hospital and Community Psychiatry, 44,* 675–678.

Kennedy, M. (1990). *Psychiatric hospitalization of GROWers.* Paper presented at the Second Biennial Conference on Community Research and Action, East Lansing, MI.

Kurtz, L. (1988). Mutual aid for affective disorders: The Manic Depressive and Depressive Association. *American Journal of Orthopsychiatry, 58,* 152–155.

Leete, E. (1989). How I perceive and manage my illness. *Schizophrenia Bulletin, 15,* 197–200.

Leff, S., Conley, J., & Elmore, S. (2005). *Making the grade: A review and comparison of selected evidence grading systems.* Cambridge, MA: Human Services Research Institute.

Lewis, L. (2001). Role of mental health patient organizations in disease management. *Practical Disease Management, 9*, 604–617.

Luke, D. A., Roberts, L., & Rappaport, J. (1994). Individual, group context, and individual-group fit predictors of self-help group attendance. In T. J. Powell (Ed.), *Understanding the self-help organization: Frameworks and findings* (pp. 88–114). Thousand Oaks, CA: Sage Publications.

Magura, S., Laudet, A., Mahmood, D., Rosenblum, A., & Knight, E. (2002). Adherence to medication regimens and participation in dual-focus self-help groups. *Psychiatric Services, 53*, 310–316.

Mowbray, C., & Tan, C. (1993). Consumer-operated drop-in centers: Evaluation of operations and impact. *Journal of Mental Health Administration, 20*, 8–19.

National Institute of Mental Health. (1991). *Caring for people with severe mental disorders: A national plan of research to improve services* (DHHS Publication No. ADM 91-1762). Washington, DC: U.S. Government Printing Office.

Nelson, G., Ochocka, J., Janzen, R., Trainor, J., Goering, P., & Lomotey, J. (2007). A longitudinal study of mental health consumer/survivor initiatives: Part V—Outcomes at three-year follow-up. *Journal of Community Psychology, 35,* 655–665.

New Freedom Commission on Mental Health. (2003). *Achieving the promise: Transforming mental health care in America* (DHHS Publication No. SMA-03-3832). Rockville, MD: U.S. Department of Health and Human Services.

Onken, S., Craig, C., Ridgway, P., Ralph, R., & Cook, J. (2007). An analysis of the definitions and elements of recovery: A review of the literature. *Psychiatric Rehabilitation Journal, 31*, 9–22.

Penney, D., & Stastny, P. (2008). *The lives they left behind: Suitcases from a state hospital attic.* New York: Bellevue Literary Press.

Raiff, N. (1984). Some health related outcomes of self-help participation. In A. Gartner & F. Riessman (Eds.), *The self-help revolution* (pp. 183–193). New York: Human Sciences Press.

Roberts, L., Salem, D., Rappaport, J., Toro, P., Luke, D., & Seidman, E. (1999). Giving and receiving help: Interpersonal transactions in mutual-help meetings and psychosocial adjustment of members. *American Journal of Community Psychology, 27*, 841–868.

Rogers, E. S., Teague, G., Lichtenstein, C., Campbell, J., Lyass, A., Chen, R., & Banks, S. (2007). Effects of participation in consumer operated service programs on both personal and organizationally mediated empowerment: Results of multisite study. *Journal of Rehabilitation Research and Development, 44,* 785–800.

Substance Abuse and Mental Health Services Administration. (2005). *National consensus statement on mental health recovery*. Retrieved from http://mental-health.samhsa.gov/publications/allpubs/sma05-4129/

Scott, A. (1993). Consumers/survivors reform the system, bringing a "human face" to research. *Resources, 5*, 3–6.

Segal, S. P., Hardiman, E. R., & Hodges, J. Q. (2002). Characteristics of new clients at self-help and community mental health agencies in geographic proximity. *Psychiatric Services, 53*, 1145–1152.

Stroul, B. (1986). *Models of community support services approaches to helping persons with long-term mental illness*. Boston: Boston University Press.

Trainor, J., Shepherd, M., Boydell, K., Leff, A., & Crawford, E. (1997). Beyond the services paradigm: The impact of consumer/survivor initiatives. *Psychiatric Rehabilitation Journal, 21*, 132–140.

U.S. Department of Health and Human Services. (1999). *Mental health: A report of the surgeon general*. Rockville, MD: Author.

Van Tosh, L., & del Vecchio, P. (2001). *Consumer-operated self-help programs: A technical report*. Rockville, MD: Center for Mental Health Services.

West, S., King, V., Carey, T., Lohr, K., McKoy, N., Sutton, S., & Lux, L. (2002). *Systems to rate the strength of scientific evidence*. Research Triangle Park: Research Triangle Institute, University of North Carolina Evidence-Based Practice Center.

Yanos, P., Primavera, L., & Knight, E. (2001). Consumer-run service participation, recovery of social functioning, and the mediating role of psychological factors. *Psychiatric Services, 52*, 493–500.

Zinman, S. (1986). Taking issue: Self-help: The wave of the future. *Hospital and Community Psychiatry, 37*, 213.

Zinman, S., Harp, H., & Budd, S. (Eds.). (1987). *Reaching across: Mental health clients helping each other*. Riverside: California Network of Mental Health Clients.

CHAPTER 17

Research-to-Practice Example:

Not by Outcomes Alone—Using Peer Evaluation to Ensure Fidelity to Evidence-based Assertive Community Treatment Practice

Gregory B. Teague and Maria Monroe-DeVita

This chapter is one of three research-to-practice examples in the second edition of Outcomes Measurement in the Human Services. *Following in the spirit of the first edition, the three examples illustrate particular issues that are pertinent to integrating or translating research into practice in each of the human service domains featured in the book—physical health, behavioral health, and child and family services. This chapter describes a live project that builds on the development of a new measure of fidelity for an evidence-based mental health practice, assertive community treatment for people with serious mental illness, and uses it to foster outcomes such as improvement in service quality and consumers' lives.*

Fidelity of Evidence-based Practices and Human Service Outcomes: Structural and Process Links

Improving the delivery of human services and its outcomes requires confidence and guidance in the form of valid, specific information about the most effective ways to provide care. One framework often used in specifying program quality is Donabedian's (1988) three-component model (structure, processes, outcomes) for assessing quality of medical care. Here, the structures (for example, staffing, organization) of a program provide a platform for the processes (for example, interactions, procedures) operating within a program or intervention, which in turn yield the desired outcomes. Processes are more immediate to outcomes and therefore more critical, but they cannot be reliably reproduced if program structures to support them are not also in place. In this formulation, the necessary complement to outcome information is information about the structures and processes of care. This may take the form of practice guidelines for individual practitioners to follow in treating specific disorders, areas of assessment, indications for particular treatments, steps to follow at various phases in treatment, termination procedures, and so on.

For more complex programs, this guidance can be built into fidelity measures, typically a combination of qualitative and quantitative indicators that assess the key features of an intervention as implemented relative to the ideal or evidence-based model (Mowbray, Holder, Teague, & Bybee, 2003). A fidelity measure could specify and assess the population to be served, staffing and their training, overall treatment model, details about specific interventions, and so on.

Studies have indicated that fidelity and outcomes are positively correlated: Programs with greater fidelity to an evidence-based model—that is, programs with greater presence of both necessary program structures and critical program processes—achieve better outcomes for those they serve (Becker, Smith, Tanzer, Drake, & Tremblay, 2001; McHugo, Drake, Teague, & Xie, 1999). In this conceptualization, the path to improved outcomes for a specific program leads through improvement in these other two components of quality. A fidelity measure is thus fundamentally a measure of quality, providing the kind of guidance needed to complement outcome information. Viewed at another level, fidelity can itself be viewed as an outcome, where regulatory and structures and training and incentive processes are in place to support fidelity to intended service models.

There are two noteworthy issues here. High scores on a fidelity measure would indicate that programs are of high quality, but their outcomes could still be constrained by possible shortcomings of the fidelity measure itself. Mowbray et al. (2003) stressed the importance of including process in fidelity measurement, not just structure. In the Donabedian (1988) quality framework, processes are closer to outcomes. Yet, much fidelity measurement has favored structure, largely because processes are less well understood and more difficult to observe and measure. For example, it is easier to tally the presence of staff members with specified credentials in a program than to measure their appropriate provision of interventions they appear qualified to perform. But evidence of staff availability is not sufficient; to serve an effective role in improving outcomes, fidelity measures need to include examination of the critical processes that mediate outcome.

A second issue concerns the extent to which fidelity measures capture enough of the necessary dimensions of intervention. Such measures can inevitably tap only selected aspects of an intervention, serving at best as a coarse model of critical ingredients. Selective measurement of particular program elements will inevitably focus greater attention on them relative to those that are not measured. To the extent that important features of programs, for example, clinical processes that are critical to outcomes, are omitted from a fidelity measure, those features may be less frequently or less faithfully carried out, and incentives or sanctions, such as accreditation or funding tied to specific levels of fidelity, could further exacerbate the imbalance of program elements. The resulting distortion to a given service model could undermine its effectiveness, resulting in lost opportunity for consumers, wasted resources for the system, and less valid research conclusions about effectiveness.

In short, to optimize program effectiveness, more information about program quality than just consumer outcomes is needed. For many programs, this can be found by using measures of fidelity to models with demonstrated effectiveness. In the sections below we describe a particularly intensive service model and how fidelity to its most critical components is measured.

Background on the Assertive Community Treatment Fidelity Measurement Project

The Model

Assertive Community Treatment (ACT) is a highly resource-intensive program designed to help a subgroup of people with serious mental illness (that is, people with psychotic or severe bipolar disorders who are frequent users of high-intensity services and whose lives are sufficiently disrupted by their illnesses that they need intensive treatment, rehabilitation, and support) live successfully in the community. Identified as one of five psychosocial evidence-based practices (EBPs) for people with serious mental illness (Substance Abuse and Mental Health Services Administration, 2008), and an essential program within the service continuum for this particular population (Dixon et al., 2010), ACT typically includes an interdisciplinary team (a psychiatrist; nurses; specialists in substance abuse, vocational services, and peer services; clinicians and case managers) serving as the single point of responsibility for all services across a shared caseload, and providing frequent contacts in community settings with availability in some form at any time (Morse & McKasson, 2005). The team directly provides a comprehensive range of individualized treatment, rehabilitation, and support services (for example, medication, psychotherapy, co-occurring disorder treatment, supported employment, wellness management, psychoeducation and support for families and natural supports, and case management assistance). Rather than being an intervention per se, ACT ideally serves as a platform for the individualized delivery of interventions as needed, including other EBPs, such as integrated treatment for people with co-occurring addictive and mental disorders, supported employment, and cognitive–behavioral therapy.

A review of 25 randomized controlled trials concluded that ACT facilitated significantly better outcomes in the following areas: reducing psychiatric hospitalizations, improving stable community housing, retaining consumers in treatment, and facilitating positive consumer and family satisfaction with services; albeit with weaker evidence, it also reduced psychiatric symptoms and improved quality of life (Mueser, Bond, Drake, & Resnick, 1998). For individuals with high rates of service use, ACT is also cost-effective (Latimer, 1999). With acceptance of recovery as a guiding principle in mental health services (New Freedom Commission on Mental Health, 2003), there is increasing attention not only to strengthening incorporation of recovery-oriented practices within ACT but also to emphasizing "graduation" as an important goal for as many participants as possible (Salyers & Tsemberis, 2007). Although ACT services should be time-unlimited, the implicit possibility of lifelong support should not be allowed to limit consumers' ambition to progress toward more independent lives. Commitment to recovery underscores the real possibility of leading a more fulfilling life with less dependence on the treatment system.

ACT Fidelity Measurement: Early Progress and Gaps

In the years after the reported successes of the initial ACT program in Madison, Wisconsin (Stein & Test, 1980), other researchers tested replications and adaptations of the approach. One such study was a statewide multisite trial of an adaptation for people with co-occurring mental and addictive disorders in New Hampshire carried out by a research group based at Dartmouth Medical School (Drake et al., 1998). It became apparent early in the study that not all of the sites fully embraced and implemented the intended model and that it would be important to quantify this variation to properly evaluate the multisite findings.

The Dartmouth researchers therefore developed another fidelity measure (Teague, Drake, & Ackerson, 1995) that used anchored rating scales for a diverse set of items based on expert consensus about critical features of the model, including those that had been validated in an earlier study of fidelity (McGrew, Bond, Dietzen, & Salyers, 1994). The approach entailed combining measurement of diverse types of data—on-site observations and interviews, review of administrative and clinical records—into a set of anchored scales, each representing a feature of the program deemed important to faithful implementation of the intended model. The researchers found a positive relationship between fidelity and both retention in treatment and reduction in hospital admissions (McHugo et al., 1999). The measure was subsequently modified for application and pilot testing in other ACT studies and ultimately became known as the Dartmouth Assertive Community Treatment Scale (DACTS; Teague, Bond, & Drake, 1998).

The DACTS was quickly adopted not only as a useful, standardized way of assessing overall fidelity, but also as a shorthand guide to what proper implementation of the program should look like, despite acknowledgment by the authors that some important features had not been included. The DACTS nonetheless became the standard fidelity measure for ACT (Phillips et al., 2001), in part because it became available in advance of the ACT program manual (Allness & Knoedler, 1998), and in part because of its very convenient format for quick measurement of the model. Salyers et al. (2003) used the DACTS to identify preliminary criteria for adequate performance, and some states used it in funding and certification. The development approach and structure of the measure were incorporated into general practice for developing fidelity measures in psychiatric rehabilitation research (Bond, Evans, Salyers, Williams, & Won-Kim, 2000) and served as the model for corresponding measures for other types of interventions in the national EBP project (McHugo et al., 2007) and their respective SAMHSA ACT toolkit (SAMHSA/CMHS, 2010).

Despite general acceptance and widespread use, however, there were areas of concern:

- Several hypothetically critical ingredients, such as team functioning, assessment, and treatment planning, were either weakly assessed or knowingly omitted altogether.

- Over time, the DACTS became outdated in certain respects: Treatment practices in the field had come to embrace both the broader framework of recovery and provision of EBPs. Because ACT serves as a platform to provide essentially whatever services consumers need, the model itself has evolved along with the field, and model fidelity specifications needed to evolve accordingly (Salyers & Tsemberis, 2007).

- To improve validity and reliability, anchors for some items needed adjustment, and more guidance was needed both for this purpose and to support use in consultation and quality improvement activities.

Addressing Gaps in ACT Fidelity Measurement: The Tool for Measurement of ACT

The establishment of 10 new ACT teams in Washington State in 2007 provided an opportunity to update ACT fidelity measurement. The Washington State Mental Health Division contracted with the Washington Institute for Mental Health Research and Training at the University of Washington to train ACT staff and evaluate teams' fidelity to the ACT model (Bjorklund, Monroe-DeVita, Reed, Toulon, & Morse, 2009). The lead person for ACT implementation from the University of Washington teamed with the lead author of the DACTS (both authors of this chapter) and a seasoned DACTS fidelity reviewer, Lorna Moser. They built on previous discussions, experience with the DACTS, and input from many national colleagues, including those from the ACT Center of Indiana. The new measure, the Tool for Measurement of Assertive Community Treatment (TMACT; Monroe-DeVita, Teague, & Moser, 2010), retained many general features of the DACTS but included substantial additions and modifications.

Designed to support both research and practice, the TMACT provides a standardized set of procedures for detailed review of a program's most critical features, along with a framework for organizing the results, relating them to consensus standards, and providing feedback that teams can use to improve service delivery and ultimately consumer outcomes. Key features as well as principal changes from the DACTS include the following:

- Six subscales contain a total of 47 items rated on five-point anchored rating scales: Operations and Structure (organization of the team, team-based approach, daily team meeting); Core Team (FTE and roles of team leader and medical staff); Specialist Team (FTE and roles of substance abuse, vocational, and peer specialists); Core Practices (for example, direct provision, quality, frequency, intensity, and penetration, of psychiatric and rehabilitative services); Evidence-Based Practices (direct provision, quality, and penetration of specialized services and concordance with the philosophy and delivery of corresponding EBPs); and Person-Centered Planning and Practices (team's facilitation of consumers' recovery by enhancing self-determination and using strengths-based, person-centered planning to guide service delivery.

- Ratings are primarily based on current behavior and activities of enrolled consumers. Some items are directly quantifiable across the team, a selected group of staff, or a sample of consumers; others require synthesis of observations or reports of practice across a number of related dimensions.

- Several items cover individualized or person-centered treatment planning that is oriented to consumers' strengths, promotes consumers' independence and self-determination, and targets a broad range of life goals defined by consumers' own choices.

- Team functioning is assessed through frequency, participation, and content of team meetings; coordination of activities and communication among staff; sharing of caseloads; and roles of specialist staff in support and cross-training other staff.

- Recovery orientation is assessed primarily through items for the person-centered planning process; staffing, penetration, and method of delivery of explicitly recovery-oriented EBPs (supported employment, integrated treatment for co-occurring substance abuse, psychiatric rehabilitation, wellness management, family psychoeducation and support, psychotherapy); and graduation and role of peer specialists.

- Refinements were made to the methods or anchors for most retained DACTS items.

The TMACT is administered in a site visit over a day and a half by two evaluators knowledgeable about ACT. A protocol provides detailed information on all procedures. The introduction describes intent; appropriate use; conduct of an assessment visit; types of data to be provided in advance and on site; and processes for rating, reporting, and follow-up. The main section serves as both detailed guide and data collection document, providing for each item's definitions, specifications, and rationale; data sources and methods (program- and community-based observations to be made, documentation to be reviewed, staff to be interviewed, and probe questions); and data inclusion/ exclusion criteria, tables and checklists, decision rules, and rating guidelines. An appendix includes checklists, forms, and sample letters.

The ACT model is highly complex, so a TMACT fidelity review entails examination of a wide range of program features. To realize its potential and derive valid and reliable scores for research and QI, reviewers must be well trained and practiced in the use of the measure. The next section illustrates how training is being conducted and embedded in one statewide project.

The Florida ACT Fidelity and Outcome Project

Florida's ACT Program

Like mental health authorities (MHAs) in the majority of states, the Florida MHA (the Mental Health and Substance Abuse Program Office of the Department of Children and Families [DCF]) collaborated with family and consumer advocacy groups and providers in seeking and obtaining legislative support to create a statewide ACT program: the Florida Assertive Community Treatment (FACT) program. Beginning in 2000, 31 FACT teams were established across the state using many of the implementation strategies later applied in the national EBP project, such as start-up training and on-site and telephone consultation (Magnabosco, 2006). Ongoing funding through Medicaid and general revenue provided basic support for team personnel and assistance with medication and housing. DCF initially provided training and conducted quality monitoring based on explicit state standards.

After three start-up years, funding for the 31 teams continued but remained flat over the rest of the decade; provider organizations experienced decline in real funding, and continuing pressure to reduce hospital use statewide was not relieved by the creation of new teams. Central resources dwindled over time; training and consultation ended shortly after all programs were in place, and DCF lacked resources to move beyond its initial focus on maintaining contracted teams and monitoring enrollment. Adding to the challenge, outside evidence for the relative advantage ACT has become more equivocal. Thus, in settings where policies significantly limit access to psychiatric hospitals, ACT may lose economic advantage (Latimer, 1999); where alternative services are available to consumers, other types of programs may sometimes compete successfully with ACT in attaining specific outcomes, such as reductions in substance abuse (Essock et al., 2006) and increases in community tenure (Dixon et al., 2010).

The possibility of establishing a more diversified array of service options and perhaps lessening system reliance on FACT teams is constrained by economic conditions, so the concern is with validating or improving the effectiveness of the FACT program as currently constituted. DCF has continued the devolution of its role from providing services, to purchasing services, to contracting with "managing entities" that do the purchasing and oversight, and requirements for a centralized, systematic review and QI effort for even this component of the service system would continue to exceed available resources. How could a severely constrained MHA like this one address this situation? The current project, described next, is the response.

Implementing TMACT in the FACT Evaluation Project

The FACT project has two main components. The first uses a train-the-trainer approach to establish expertise among providers in using the TMACT on a peer-review and peer-consultation basis to measure, track, and enhance fidelity over time. The second entails linking fidelity data to statewide administrative databases containing consumer outcomes information to identify both overall effectiveness and impacts of critical program components.

To begin the fidelity component, four FACT team clinicians were selected from those interested in learning to use the TMACT. In addition to learning to use the tool, they were trained to train others in using it and have trained an additional eight FACT staff members, mostly team leaders. The central DCF FACT coordinator has also participated to ensure that expertise was also developed at the MHA and to serve as a substitute. Training of the first four clinicians began with direct instruction by an outside consultant (the third co-developer of the TMACT, along with the two authors of this chapter). The consultant provided a day-long overview of the measure and all materials, then conducted a fidelity evaluation of a centrally located FACT team, modeling the assessment and feedback process. Trainees were participant–observers, gradually joining in and helping to develop consensus on item-specific ratings and identify the FACT team's underlying strengths and limitations. The consultant shared drafts of the fidelity report with the trainers by e-mail, and all participated in a telephone feedback session with the team. In pairs, the trainers next conducted their own evaluations of two more teams, with the consultant observing and coaching; each trainer pair then evaluated two additional FACT teams and prepared their own feedback reports with telephone consultation as needed.

At the next stage, the previous steps were repeated: Each of the two trainer pairs trained two other pairs of FACT staff, providing initial training, demonstrating evaluation of a team, and observing and coaching the next-generation evaluators in their own initial evaluations. The consultant observed and coached each pair early on in this process and has remained available for distance coaching with these newly trained Florida-based fidelity experts as questions arise. The process is still underway as of the time of this writing; ultimately, all 31 FACT teams will have peer-generated scores and detailed reports of their fidelity to the ACT model.

The fidelity component of the project is designed to establish the capability within the overall FACT program to examine its performance rigorously and to identify and address key areas for improvement on an ongoing basis. Teams with relative strength in a given dimension of the model can provide peer consultation to those less advanced. Building on and sharing its strengths as a system, the FACT program can save scarce resources for additional outside training and consultation on issues for which internal expertise is insufficient. Even if only fidelity data were generated, the FACT project would have value. First, the TMACT provides a link to current information about relatively recent advances in treatment practices—for example, recovery-oriented practices and EBPs—that clinicians in the field can come to own as part of their work. Second, because feedback comes from peer providers using a consistent, objective metric, staff can feel more receptive, and local expertise can be recognized, accepted, and shared among the teams.

Assessing the Value of TMACT Fidelity Data: Implementation and Links to Outcomes

The second main part of the FACT evaluation project will link the TMACT fidelity data to two other types of data. First, consumers are invited to use an anonymous Web-based survey to evaluate the recovery orientation of their teams using the Recovery Oriented Systems Indicator consumer survey. Second, there are several statewide administrative databases covering services and consumer outcomes information, including Medicaid enrollment and claims, services and periodic status assessments from publicly funded behavioral healthcare services, emergency involuntary evaluation, hospitalization in state and other institutions, employment, education, and arrests. Use of these data will allow both examination of changes in key outcome areas over time and comparison with individuals not served through the FACT program but otherwise having similar prior status and service histories.

Using this combination of program- and consumer-level data, the project addresses three main sets of questions:

1. What is the overall fidelity of the FACT program? How does fidelity vary across teams for example, can we identify complementary strengths in some teams to match weaknesses in others? Are there areas where outside consultation will be needed to supplement internal expertise?

2. How effective has the FACT program been, both in fostering gains for FACT consumers over time and relative to comparable people not served in the FACT program? Do these outcomes vary across teams and types of outcome?

3. How does fidelity relate to outcomes? Are there aspects of the ACT model for which greater fidelity is more highly correlated with consumer outcomes and for which efforts to improve these aspects of program quality are needed and should be invested? In many ways, this is the crux of the project.

Assuming that the TMACT yields the anticipated benefits as both research instrument and QI tool (the project is underway at the time of this writing), viability of this approach to QI further depends upon commitments of at least two types. First, provider organizations will need to find this mutual help process valuable enough for continued investment. Second, ongoing central statewide leadership, encouragement, and some level of support will be crucial to ensure that fidelity and outcome findings are used and that system learning needs can be addressed.

Conclusion

Early in this chapter, we argued for more complete data on program quality as a complement to consumer outcome data in ensuring that systems of mental health and other human services are effective. Without having valid data on consumer outcomes, we don't know well enough how the system is doing; without having valid data on the other components of quality, we don't know how the system can do better. The FACT evaluation project, then, is offered to illustrate a desirable integration of data tapping the three components of quality (Donabedian, 1988): structure, process, and outcome.

The FACT evaluation project also illustrates approaches to three of Kelly's (2009) recommendations for creating an effective system of care. First, he highlights the importance of using results-oriented outcome measures and EBPs. The project explicitly evaluates outcomes; ACT is itself an EBP that, in addition, needs to emulate fidelity to the other EBPs it has incorporated, and the TMACT provides a guide for doing so. Importantly, the project also reflects recognition that EBPs are not fixed and immutable; practices evolve. The TMACT has been designed to represent the now-higher standard of performance in this EBP.

Another of Kelly's (2009) recommendations is to empower consumers and families. Like many states, Florida requires that teams have advisory boards, and families are typically well represented on them; the availability of team-level outcome and fidelity information could provide a new impetus for their involvement and advocacy. Consumers have voice in the project.

Kelly (2009) also emphasized the importance of engaging relevant parties in system transformation to preempt possible resistance to change. The national move to infuse recovery and EBPs into the ACT model clearly raises the performance bar; an external mandate to take the work to a much higher level with limited resources could easily inspire resistance. In contrast, the FACT project attempts to apply a practitioners' self-help approach to empowerment that work with consumers already indicates is effective. Through collective ownership of the fidelity self-assessment process, practitioners are more readily inclined to draw on their own creativity and resources for self-improvement to make the changes they come to see as possible and desirable.

The assumptions underlying the TMACT and its use in this project also resonate with recent advances in thinking about health care in general, in which strengths-based approaches, an orientation to prevention, and standardization of outcomes are given increased emphasis. The conception of ACT embodied in the TMACT reflects a strengths-based, recovery orientation. Prevention, too, has a place; although ACT is an approach to treatment for people with illnesses already well manifested, careful monitoring of consumers' well-being includes proactive attention to reducing risks of exacerbation and minimizing the need for more acute care. However, standardization of measurement is only partial. The TMACT is already seeing wide use and may become a standard measure for ACT, but this and similar projects would be both more effective and more generalizable if it were possible to include standard outcome measures.

The approach we have described in this chapter is necessarily shaped around the particulars of one EBP, one new fidelity measure, and one state's situation and constraints, but the approach is generalizable to other EBPs in other settings. Implementation of EBPs without sustained attention to fidelity will ultimately be only skin-deep, if they are implemented or maintained at all (Massatti, Sweeney, Panzano, & Roth, 2008). But resources will always be too limited for centralized, comprehensive monitoring of a wide range of treatments and services; QI—and the motivation that sustains it—must be built in on the ground. Strengths and weaknesses vary; mutual self-help is a way of building on natural affiliations to raise overall performance of people or organizations. Peer evaluation of all components of quality using well-specified fidelity measures, along with consumer outcome measurement, is key to improving the effectiveness of care, especially as the nation embarks on the implementation of health care reform.

References

Allness, D. J., & Knoedler, W. H. (1998). *The PACT model of community-based treatment for persons with severe and persistent mental illnesses: A manual for PACT start-up.* Madison, WI: Programs of Assertive Community Treatment, Inc.

Becker, D. R., Smith, J., Tanzman, B., Drake, R. E., & Tremblay, T. (2001). Fidelity of supported employment programs and employment outcomes. *Psychiatric Services, 52,* 834–836.

Bjorklund, R. W., Monroe-DeVita, M., Reed, D., Toulon, A., & Morse, G. (2009). Washington state's initiative to disseminate and implement high-fidelity ACT teams. *Psychiatric Services, 60,* 24–27.

Bond, G. R., Evans, L., Salyers, M. P., Williams, J., & Won-Kim, H. (2000). Measurement of fidelity in psychiatric rehabilitation research. *Mental Health Services Research, 2,* 75–87.

Dixon, L. B., Dickerson, F., Bellack, A. S., Bennett, M., Dickinson, D., Goldberg, R. W., et al. (2010). The 2009 schizophrenia PORT psychosocial treatment recommendations and summary statements. *Schizophrenia Bulletin, 36,* 48–70.

Donabedian, A. (1988). The quality of care. How can it be assessed? *JAMA, 260,* 1743–1748.

Drake, R. E., McHugo, G. J., Clark, R. E., Teague, G. B., Xie, H., Miles, K., & Ackerson, T. H. (1998). Assertive community treatment for patients with co-occurring severe mental illness and substance use disorder: A clinical trial. *American Journal of Orthopsychiatry, 68,* 201–215.

Essock, S. M., Mueser, K. T., Drake, R. E., Covell, N. H., McHugo, G. J., Frisman, L. K., et al. (2006). Comparison of ACT and standard case management for delivering integrated treatment for co-occurring disorders. *Psychiatric Services, 57,* 185–196.

Kelly, T. (2009). *Healing the broken mind.* New York: NYU Press.

Latimer, E. A. (1999). Economic impacts of assertive community treatment: A review of the literature. *Canadian Journal of Psychiatry, 44,* 443–454.

Magnabosco, J. L. (2006). Innovations in mental health services implementation: A report on state-level data from the U.S. Evidence-Based Practices Project. *Implementation Science, 30,* 1–13.

Massatti, R. R., Sweeney, H. A., Panzano, P. C., & Roth, D. (2008). The de-adoption of innovative mental health practices (IMHP): Why organizations choose not to sustain an IMHP. *Administration and Policy in Mental Health, 35,* 50–65.

McGrew, J. H., Bond, G. R., Dietzen, L., & Salyers, M. (1994). Measuring the fidelity of implementation of a mental health program model. *Journal of Consulting and Clinical Psychology, 62*, 670–678.

McHugo, G. J., Drake, R. E., Teague, G. B., & Xie, H. (1999). Fidelity to assertive community treatment and client outcomes in the New Hampshire Dual Disorders Study. *Psychiatric Services, 50*, 818–824.

Monroe-DeVita, M., Teague, G. B., & Moser, L. (2010). *Tool for measurement of Assertive Community Treatment.* Unpublished manuscript.

Morse, G. A., & McKasson, M. (2005). Assertive community treatment. In R. E. Drake, M. R. Merrens, & D. W. Lynde (Eds.), *Evidence-based mental health practice—A textbook.* New York: W. W. Norton.

Mowbray, C. T., Holder, M., Teague, G. B., & Bybee, D. (2003). Fidelity criteria: Development, measurement, and validation. *American Journal of Evaluation, 24*, 315–340.

Mueser, K. T., Bond, G. R., Drake, R. E., & Resnick, S. G. (1998). Models of community care for severe mental illness: A review of research on case management. *Schizophrenia Bulletin, 24*, 37–74.

New Freedom Commission on Mental Health. (2003). *Achieving the promise: Transforming mental health care in America. Final report* (DHHS Publication No. SMA-03-3832). Rockville, MD: U.S. Department of Health and Human Services.

Phillips, S. D., Burns, B. J., Edgar, E. R., Mueser, K. T., Linkins, K. W., Rosenheck, A. R., et al. (2001). Moving assertive community treatment into standard practice. *Psychiatric Services, 52*, 771–779.

Salyers, M. P., Bond, G. R., Teague, G. B., Cox, J. F., Smith, M. E., Hicks, M. L., & Koop, J. I. (2003). Is it ACT yet? Real-world examples of evaluating the degree of implementation for assertive community treatment. *Journal of Behavioral Health Services and Research, 30*, 304–320.

Salyers, M. P., & Tsemberis, S. (2007). ACT and recovery: Integrating evidence-based practice and recovery orientation on assertive community treatment teams. *Community Mental Health Journal, 43*, 619–641.

Stein, L. I., & Test, M. A. (1980). Alternative to mental hospital treatment: I. Conceptual model, treatment program, and clinical evaluation. *Archives of General Psychiatry, 37*, 392–397.

Substance Abuse and Mental Health Administration (2008). Assertive Community Treatment: The evidence (DHHS Publication No. SMA-08-4344). Rockville, MD: Center for Mental Health Services, Substance Abuse and Mental Health Administration, U.S..Department of Health and Human Services.

Teague, G. B., Bond, G. R., & Drake, R. E. (1998). Program fidelity in assertive community treatment: Development and use of a measure. *American Journal of Orthopsychiatry, 68,* 216–232.

Teague, G. B., Drake, R. E., & Ackerson, T. (1995). Evaluating use of continuous treatment teams for persons with mental illness and substance abuse. *Psychiatric Services, 46,* 689–695.

PART IV

Outcomes Measurement in Child and Family Services

CHAPTER 18

Outcomes Measurement for Child and Family Services:

Successful Approaches for Practice, Management, and Policy

Rose M. Etheridge, Cynthia Klein, Jacqui LaCoste, and Julie T. Marks

Services to children and families with special needs are provided in a diverse range of health and human services agencies and organizations at the federal, state, and local levels. Services such as family assistance with financial and basic needs, child welfare (child protective services, family preservation, and foster care), child care, early childhood health and development, domestic violence, health, mental health and substance abuse services, developmental disabilities, and prevention are supported by separate funding streams and are often spread organizationally across several separate agencies of government, each with different service delivery models and eligibility criteria.

During the 1990s, a number of policy changes and major systemwide reforms occurred at the national level that continue to have far-reaching impacts across the organizational entities that serve children and families. Most notable for children and families, these included managed care, with its emphasis on cost containment; welfare reform that aimed to drastically reduce the number of welfare recipients and return people to work; and changes in leadership at the national level that embraced smaller, decentralized government and devolution of responsibility for vulnerable populations to states and ultimately, a second-tier devolution to localities. These changes gained traction, achieved enduring momentum, and collided with a historic nationwide financial collapse in 2008, a steep rise in housing and business failures and unemployment, and health care reform.

Although these changes are top-down in nature, they have inspired important changes and innovations at the local level. Later in this chapter, for meaningful illustration, we focus on the efforts of Kent County, Michigan, where our team of evaluators has worked in collaboration with county health and human services agencies for the past five years. Michigan's automotive manufacturing industry failure has driven the state's unemployment rate to the highest in the nation. Although Kent County's economy has suffered greatly as a result, the innovations for child and family services the county's agencies and system stakeholders began in the late 1990s have endured, evolved, and become more focused. We detail some of these outcomes-driven system, service, and management innovations in the last half of this chapter, after first briefly examining the larger context and emerging trends in outcomes measurement nationwide.

Context of Outcomes Measurement in Child and Family Services

The current context of outcomes measurement has evolved from, and in many ways is the product of, several large-scale system reforms and smaller, related reforms that began in the 1990s. Two of these reforms, government-sponsored Temporary Assistance to Needy Families (TANF), designed to return unemployed, able-bodied single mothers to work, and managed care, a reform that evolved from the health care sector's adoption of a business model of managing costs, have arisen in part because of a public demand for accountability in how public and private dollars are spent. Both of these systems reforms are unusual in their scope (most reforms proceed incrementally in small steps) and their reach, each having powerful, lasting, and complex impacts on the health and well-being of children and families. TANF is due for reauthorization in 2010.

Findings from a 10-year congressionally mandated evaluation of TANF showed that the initial declines in welfare rolls and unemployment did not persist through the deep recession that began in 2008 (cf. Ziliak, 2009). Unlike TANF, the rapid proliferation of managed care has occurred in the absence of data infrastructures to support consistent and systematic outcomes monitoring and assessment. As a result, efforts to assess its impacts have been difficult to determine. This is both discouraging and concerning because managed care has been incorporated into public programs that serve low-income populations through Medicaid funding, with Medicaid providing the largest share of funding for behavioral health services for children and youth. Overall, Medicaid managed care appears to have improved access to physical and behavioral health care, but its impacts vary considerably by service sector.

A third, smaller and targeted systems reform effort, the Substance Abuse and Mental Health Services Administration's Center for Mental Health Services initiative, the Children's Mental Health System of Care (SOC), began in 1993 with the intent of coordinating access to and provision of cross-sector services for children with severe emotional and behavior disorders and their families. Over time, it has become a driving force in service system reforms. The aims are to avoid unnecessary and expensive institutional care, expand community-based treatment services and supports, and promote respectful integration of consumer youth and families of diverse cultures in decisions affecting their care (Stroul & Friedman, 1986). An ongoing national cross-site evaluation and a local evaluation tailored to individual SOC sites assess the outcomes of the initiative. Empowerment theory, the framework guiding the SOC evaluation, emphasizes full participation of all system partners and stakeholders at all levels of evaluation activities (Fetterman & Wandersman, 2004). The evaluator role is that of collaborative partner rather than outside expert who renders evaluative judgments. This collaborative, participatory approach has come to guide much of the cross-systems work concerning children and families over the past decade, as consumers have become more organized and are asking for inclusion and systems have become more adept at integrating them in decision making.

As of 2010, the SOC initiative has extended its reach to encompass a public health model with an emphasis on prevention and an expansion of services to infants and young children (Blau, Huang, & Mallory, 2010). This expanded definition of a system of care is aligned with the provisions of the newly enacted 2010 health care reform initiative's emphasis on prevention and behavioral health parity (Hyde, 2010; Kaiser Commission on Medicaid and the Uninsured, 2010).

The SOC has been subjected to a number of evaluations with mixed results. Although many individual and cross-site evaluations showed that children receiving treatment and services within an SOC improved over time, findings from a randomized experiment demonstrating no difference between SOC and uncoordinated care have reduced some of the uncritical embrace of systems interventions (Bickman, 1997). As a result, the SOC has begun to shift its emphasis to evidence-based practices and cost effectiveness (Bickman & Athay, 2009).

Common and Emerging Approaches to Measuring Outcomes and Performance in Child and Family Services

The trend toward accountability-driven outcomes measurement has become more prevalent in public sector agencies that serve children and families. This trend is being pursued through quality improvement initiatives and through the adoption of evidence-based practices. These are separate and parallel streams of activity that have yet to be integrated. In response to the Government Performance Results Act of 1993 (GRPA; Office of Management and Budget, 2010), related service sector-specific initiatives followed. With regard to child and family services, the federal Administration for Children and Families launched the Child and Family Services Review (CFSR), which assesses indicators of seven outcomes in the domains of child safety, permanence, and well-being system in each state (D'Andrade, Osterling, & Austin, 2008). Similar quality improvement efforts have been initiated in education, early childhood, juvenile justice, and other agencies that serve children and families, as well as by independent accrediting agencies and professional organizations.

These various efforts in quality improvement over past decade have led to a greater consensus-based understanding of the elements that make up quality care in child and family services. A number of states and localities have initiated outcome monitoring systems and are investing considerable resources in the technological infrastructure to support them. Although some states have fully implemented outcomes systems that link to counties and municipalities, others are in the development phase, many facing impediments caused by budget cuts.

Before these quality improvement efforts can progress to a greater level of utility, some data quality issues require resolution. In child welfare, for example, researchers and administrators have a number of criticisms of the CFSR as a quality-monitoring mechanism. Among these are the following: low reliability of administrative data, lack of concordance between some indicators and the outcome of interest, measurement gaps in capturing caseload dynamics and key client subgroups of interest, absence of contextual measures necessary to explain differences across states, and lack of a longitudinal change capacity inherent in the measurement. To date, few states have achieved substantial conformity with any of the seven CFSR outcomes assessed (D'Andrade et al., 2008).

In this climate of fiscal austerity, both adoption and expanded use of EBPs have become increasingly challenging. Promising alternatives that some sites are pursuing include drawing on core elements from EBPs to inform and improve existing practice, expanding the definition of "evidence" to include findings from research syntheses to create best practices guidelines, and using real-time postsession feedback to clinicians to inform and improve existing practice (Bickman, 2008; Chorpita & Daleiden, 2009; Manderscheid, 2006).

Measurement Domains for Child and Family Services

Although core outcomes for which each child and family services sector is accountable vary by sectors (for example, increased school achievement for education, reduced child abuse and neglect in child welfare), cross-sector collaborative partnerships have helped to establish reasonable agreement about measurement domains (Friesen & Winters, 2003). At the system level, these include increased access to services, improved quality and cost effectiveness of care, and improved child and family well-being and psychosocial functioning. System-level indicators that some communities have adopted included reduced psychiatric hospitalization, reduced restrictiveness of placements, increased housing stability, improved school attendance and reductions in justice system contacts. Over the past few years, SOC initiatives have expanded system-level domains to incorporate system values such as family inclusiveness; broadened agency partnerships; comprehensive, coordinated, efficient, and accountable services; cost-effective, efficient, and sustainable allocation of resources; and consumer-based outcomes such as child and family empowerment and satisfaction with services.

At the practice level, measurement domains include the incorporation of SOC principles and values into practice, and coordination of useful services and supports for families in the community. Recently, researchers have suggested expanding practice-level measures to include the therapeutic alliance to reflect increasing knowledge of how the clinician–client relationship is related to client change and using that information to help clinicians improve treatment decision making (Kelley, Bickman, & Norwood, 2010). At the individual child and family level, domains include reduction in child's distressing symptoms, improved functioning in the home, school, and community; improved family functioning; and reduced caregiver strain. As the SOC has come to incorporate prevention within a public health model, there is a call to incorporate risk and protective factors as important assessment domains (Blau et al., 2010).

At the same time that there is recognition of the practical need for communities to focus on a few key outcomes to assess system and program performance and client improvement, there is a demand for more detailed process measures to help identify the factors that contribute to the outcomes of interest, such as services and supports (Etheridge & Hubbard, 2000). Finally, as illustrated earlier in this overview, external environmental factors such as economic conditions, political climate, laws and regulations, advocacy, and other secular trends can have large impacts on children and families and need to be understood in order to make sound, data-driven decisions.

Challenges in Methodologies, Measurement, and Use of Research Data and Measures in Management, Practice, Policy, and Advocacy

As illustrated above, it is often difficult to link complex human behaviors to policy initiatives and system reforms through research and evaluation efforts. Without continuous and meaningful data of credible quality, the danger exists that ideology, rather than empirically valid information, will drive policy decisions. As information technology has become more sophisticated over the past decade and a culture of accountability and data-driven decision making has become more widespread, public and private managed care and other payor entities are demanding more of outcomes monitoring than a per capita utilization-focused reimbursement and accountability system can provide. Service providers who can demonstrate results, as well as identify factors that contributed to desired outcomes, are most likely to survive in an increasingly competitive market (Mee-Lee, McLellan, & Miller, 2010).

Meeting policymakers' and payers' demand for results will require an investment in the technology to support the continuous availability of cross-sector data over time. In these times of budget contraction, public agencies in particular will need assistance in finding resources to support these infrastructure improvements, moving from systems design to data use at the policy and practice levels as well as the continued adoption and adaptation of EBPs. Continued cross-systems collaboration will be needed to overcome regulatory barriers to sharing both data and responsibility for client outcomes. In addition, researchers must continue to assist in streamlining standardized measures to reduce data-collection burdens.

Finally, consumers and advocacy groups must be encouraged to demand more of treatment and service systems than greater access and quality care. Although necessary, these conditions are not sufficient to insure desirable outcomes (Blau et al., 2010). As awareness of the cost saving to be realized in prevention spreads, existing incentive systems will need to change to support early identification and early intervention while continuing to provide the necessary services and supports for those with more intensive needs.

Kent County: An Example of Outcomes Measurement Across Child and Family Services

The Kent County Prevention Initiative (PI) was established in 2000 with the goal of investing in prevention and early intervention programs as a means to reduce the economic and social burden of youths and families engaged in costly education, justice, mental, and physical health services. The PI provides expanded county funding to four strategic programs:

- Healthy Start (HS) and Bright Beginnings (BB): primary prevention family support programs

- Early Impact (EI): a child abuse and neglect early intervention program;

- Family Engagement Program (FEP): a family-focused substance abuse early intervention program.

Before determining possible prospective benefits from the PI, including the County's long-term return on investment for these programs, it was necessary to examine the county and these programs retrospectively to provide the foundation for future evaluation efforts. To this end, three retrospective studies were completed by February 2007, including:

1. Child safety assessment: a 15-year retrospective analysis of child abuse and neglect in Kent County

2. Evidence-based best practices: a review of program interventions and outcomes analogous to the PI in focus and scope

3. Individual program assessments: program activity and outcome evaluation from 2000 to 2005 on all four of the PI programs

Child Safety Assessment. A child safety assessment was conducted to determine the extent of the child physical abuse and neglect problem within Kent County and as compared with state and national averages since 1990. The assessment revealed that child maltreatment rates for Michigan and Kent County were generally below the national average for the past 15 years. Nationally, child maltreatment data suggested that improvements in conditions for children and families have been occurring over the past decade, as indicated by a downward trend in the physical abuse and neglect rates over this period. However, child maltreatment rates for Michigan and the county, although below the national average, have shown a reverse trend from the national declining one (see Table 18-1). Looking more closely at the data, the county did demonstrate a downward trend in prevalence rates that began in 1993 and ended in 1996, after which the rates climbed steadily through 2005.

Table 18-1: Child Maltreatment Rates: Kent County, State of Michigan, and United States, 1987–2005 (Rate per 1,000 Children)

Year	Kent County	State of Michigan	United States
1987	6.0	—	—
1988	6.4	—	—
1989	6.5	—	—
1990	5.8	10.9	13.4
1991	6.4	11.1	14.0
1992	6.0	10.8	15.1
1993	5.6	8.1	15.3★
1994	5.2	9.2	15.2
1995	4.3	8.4	14.7
1996	4.3	8.3	14.7
1997	4.5	8.8	13.7
1998	6.2	8.9	12.9
1999	8.3	9.6	11.8
2000	8.7	10.3	12.2
2001	9.4	11.0	12.5
2002	10.5	11.2	12.3
2003	11.2	11.3★	12.2
2004	12.0★	11.1	11.9
2005	10.5	—	—

Note: Dashes indicate data not available.
★Rate peaked.

This pattern was generally mirrored by Michigan's maltreatment rates over this period and indicated an increasing problem of child safety for both the county and the state. The increase in child maltreatment at the state and county levels during the period when national rates were declining appeared to be driven primarily by increases in child neglect in Kent County (and at the state level) as opposed to increases in physical and sexual abuse. This income-sensitive form of child maltreatment may be reflective of the economic circumstances in Kent County over the past 10 years.

Evidence-based Practices. A comprehensive review of best practices and outcomes from similar programs was conducted and shared with the PI programs for consideration in their service provision. Similar programs found to be efficacious demonstrated such characteristics as

- Assessment with a valid and reliable instrument
- Mutual service recipient–provider involvement in goal setting
- Goal-based intervention planning with regular progress assessment and updates
- Home visitation rather than office-based service delivery
- Family empowerment
- Family strengths focus
- Respect for and competence in cultural diversity
- Readiness to change model of intervention
- Cross-service sector involvement (for example, health, welfare, education, mental health, juvenile justice)
- Individualized service provision
- High-quality program implementation
- Adequate knowledge and skills of service providers
- Positive relationships between service recipients and providers.

Individual Program Assessments. Retrospective program evaluations were completed in February 2007, looking at services provided from 2000 to 2005. These evaluations were conducted to assess program activities and implementation, determine which populations were being reached, and examine each program's ability to collect and provide useable data for the long-term evaluation.

Through the review and analysis of initial program data, the county was able to identify gaps in data measures and recommend data collection improvements to each program. This initial assessment led to increased collection of similar demographic data points (that is, race, income, and education were collected uniformly across programs) and improved outcomes measures for short-term program goals.

There were also several issues identified during this initial assessment, including lack of a mechanism to track participants on exit from PI services or any ability to determine other community services received by PI participants, strength of the relationship between the current intensity and frequency of service reported in the short-term evaluation and the likelihood of producing the long-term outcomes desired by the PI, and sufficient sample sizes and outcome measure sensitivity to detect program effects given the program population (that is, the findings of very low prevalence of Child Protective Services [CPS] dispositions at baseline among some of the programs suggested this metric may not be appropriate to reflect changes).

Table 18-2: Long-Term Child Evaluation Outcomes

Program	Outcome	Component Outcomes
Bright Beginnings and Healthy Start	Child education	Child health Child welfare Juvenile substance abuse Juvenile justice
Early Impact	Child welfare	Juvenile justice Child health Child education Child/adult substance abuse Adult welfare
Family Engagement	Youth/adult substance abuse	Education Juvenile justice Child health Child/adult welfare

With the retrospective analysis in place, the county underwent a prospective, long-term evaluation study of the impact of the PI programs on key indicators of family health and well-being in Kent County. The scope of this evaluation included linking participation in one or more of the PI programs with external outcomes, such as improved educational achievement, decreased juvenile justice contacts, improved health, and the sustained protection of children from abuse and neglect. The anticipated primary and secondary outcomes associated with each program are shown in Table 18-2.

For the long-term impact analysis, the Kent County Health Department coordinated the collection, deidentification, and linking of data on children from the following external sources:

- Kent Intermediate School District (education)
- Department of Human Services data warehouse (child welfare)
- Juvenile Justice database (youth substance abuse, juvenile justice)
- Michigan Care Improvement Registry, hospital records (child health).

An annual cycle of data collection and analysis has been established for the process, short-term, and long-term outcome measures. To date, two cycles of this annual evaluation have been conducted.

Although it is too early to evaluate long-term academic achievement outcomes, such as high school graduation rates and special educational placements, immunization evaluations showed children in the Healthy Start program appear to have higher immunization rates than children typically found in Kent County. Significantly lower percentages of children who participated in the Bright Beginnings program used the emergency department relative to children in the comparison group, and emergency department visit rates (number of visits) were significantly lower for children in Healthy Start and Bright Beginnings. A lower percentage of children in Early Impact, Healthy Start, and Bright Beginnings were associated with CPS referrals relative to the comparison group across all CPS categories.

For the economic evaluation (as conducted through 2009), when program costs are compared with benefits, the net savings per program are positive. Thus, the initial program cost is more than offset by subsequent savings. For every dollar invested in Bright Beginnings, there is $4.28 in later savings; for Healthy Start, the return is $2.93, and for Early Impact, the return is $6.96.

In the face of a declining economy, Kent County chose to invest in primary prevention and to create sustained improvements in the health and well being of individuals that will ultimately lead to a productive and healthier population, thereby reducing both financial and social burden on institutions such as schools, courts, and health care systems. Furthermore, rather than cutting program evaluation funds, Kent County chose to invest in evaluation as an approach to data-driven decision making about its programs, including an economic component to yield a measure of return on public funds invested. Looking forward, Kent County is moving to invest in a systemwide data infrastructure to support the capacity for continuous cross-system monitoring to better coordinate and evaluate its primary prevention efforts.

Conclusion

The experiences of the past decade, along with legislative reforms, have important implications for continued improvements in human services policy and clinical practice for child and family services. First, the Personal Responsibility and Work Opportunity Reconciliation Act of 1996 (welfare reform) clarified the reduced role of government as the responsible entity for the financial well-being of families. Going forward, it will be important to ensure that welfare reform's push to reduce welfare rolls and increase employment does not come at the expense of the health and well-being of children. Because the human services field does not have a strong, well-organized advocacy component, the need for continued cultivation of champions and citizen coalitions to monitor the status of children and families in our communities remains a priority. Successful advocacy efforts will rest heavily on the availability of relevant status and outcomes indicators to inform its activities.

Because child and family services are spread across many systems, it is critical to have system-level data infrastructures that yield continuous, high-quality data to monitor child and family outcomes across service sectors. This will require continued cross-systems collaboration at the policy and practice levels and ongoing efforts to reduce barriers to information sharing across agencies. The potential benefits and cost savings from system-level monitoring are many and strongly support communities' move to a population-based public health model based on prevention, early cross-sector risk identification, and anticipation of needs that new reforms—such as the 2010 health care reform—set in motion.

Finally, as research continues to yield more evidence-based interventions in child and family services, researchers will likely continue to find slow progress in implementing these practices, particularly in an era of extreme constraints in public agency budgets. Researchers will be challenged to redefine their roles as collaborators, joining with practitioners and administrators in finding ways to promote improved dissemination and use of research findings to improve practice.

References

Bickman, L. (1997). Resolving issues raised by the Ft. Bragg findings: New directions for mental health services research. *American Psychologist, 52*, 562–565.

Bickman, L. (2008). A measurement feedback system (MFS) is necessary to improve mental health outcomes. *Journal of the American Academy of Child and Adolescent Psychiatry, 47*, 1114–1119. doi: 10.1097/CHI. obo13e3181825af8.

Bickman, L., & Athay, M. (2009). The worst of all possible program evaluation outcomes. In A. R. Stiffman (Ed.), *The field research survival guide* (pp. 174–204). New York: Oxford University Press.

Blau, G. M., Huang, L. N., & Mallory, C. J. (2010). Advancing efforts to improve children's mental health in America: A commentary. *Administration and Policy in Mental Health Services Research, 37*, 140–144. doi: 10.1007/s10488-010-0290-3.

Chorpita. B. F., & Daleiden, E. L. (2009). Mapping evidence-based treatments for children and adolescents: Application for the distillation and matching model to 615 treatments from 322 randomized trials. *Journal of Consulting and Clinical Psychology, 77*, 566–579.

D'Andrade, A., Osterling, K. L., & Austin, M. J. (2008). Understanding and measuring child welfare outcomes. *Journal of Evidence-Based Social Work, 5*, 135–156.

Etheridge, R. M., & Hubbard, R. L. (2000). Conceptualizing and assessing treatment structure and process in community-based drug dependency programs. *Substance Use & Misuse, 35*, 1757–1796.

Fetterman, D. A., & Wandersman, A. (2004). *Empowerment evaluation: Principles in practice.* New York: Guilford Press.

Friesen, B. J., & Winters, N. C. (2003). The role of outcomes in systems of care. In A. J. Pumariega & N. C. Winters (Eds.), *The handbook of child and adolescent systems of care* (pp. 459–486). San Francisco: Jossey-Bass.

Hyde, P. (2010). *The Affordable Care Act & mental health: An update.* Retrieved from http://www.healthcare.gov/news/blog/mentalhealthupdate.html

Kaiser Commission on Medicaid and the Uninsured. (2010). *Medicaid beneficiaries and access to care.* Retrieved from http://www.kff.org/medicaid/upload/8000-02.pdf

Kelley, S. D., Bickman, L., & Norwood, E. (2010). Evidence-based treatments and common factors in youth psychotherapy. In B. L. Duncan, S. D. Miller, B. E. Wampold, & M. A. Hubble (Eds.), *The heart and soul of change* (2nd ed., pp. 325–356). Washington, DC: American Psychological Association.

Manderscheid, R. W. (2006). Some thoughts on the relationships between evidence based practices, practice based evidence, outcomes, and performance measures. *Administration and Policy in Mental Health Services Research, 33*, 646–647. doi: 10.1007/s10488-006-0056-0.

Mee-Lee, D., McLellan, A. T., & Miller, S. D. (2010). What works in substance abuse and dependence treatment. In B. L. Duncan, S. D. Miller, B. E. Wampold, & M. A. Hubble (Eds.), *The heart and soul of change* (2nd ed., pp. 393–318). Washington, DC: American Psychological Association.

Office of Management and Budget. (2010). *Government Performance and Results Act of 1993.* Retrieved from http://www.whitehouse.gov/omb/mgmt-gpra/gplaw2m

Stroul, B., & Friedman, R. (1986). *A system of care for children and youth with severe emotional disturbance.* Washington, DC: Georgetown University Child Development Center, National Technical Assistance Center for Children's Mental Health.

Ziliak, J. P. (Ed.). (2009). *Welfare reform and its long-term consequences for America's poor.* Cambridge, England: Cambridge University Press.

CHAPTER 19

Cost and Outcomes Analysis of Child Well-Being

M. Rebecca Kilburn

Cost and outcome analysis has become an increasingly popular complement to traditional evaluation findings in informing human services policy decisions. This is particularly apparent in the area of early childhood services, where cost–benefit arguments have played a central role in the growing acceptance of early childhood intervention programs (or programs with targeted services delivered to young children and their families with the purpose of promoting developmental, health, or other outcomes) as a more effective and efficient way of improving a range of social ills. Nobel-prize winning economists (Heckman, 2006) and Federal Reserve Bank finance experts (Rolnick & Groenwald, 2003) offer calculations showing that early childhood programs might be a good financial investment in terms of their long-term benefits relative to their costs. Furthermore, several decades of research have accumulated a body of evidence documenting that targeted intensive services for young children and their families have the potential to improve outcomes for both children and their parents across a range of outcomes (Center on the Developing Child at Harvard University, 2007; Karoly, Kilburn, & Cannon, 2005; Kilburn & Karoly, 2008), including emotional and cognitive development, child welfare, educational attainment, health, criminal activity, public assistance receipt, and earnings (Karoly, Kilburn, Bigelow, Caulkins, & Cannon, 2001).

Comparisons of the upfront costs of early childhood programs to the monetary value of long-term benefits of these children's services show that the value of the benefits exceeds the costs in many cases (Karoly et al., 2005). Cost–benefit arguments not only account for part of the growth in public and private support for early childhood programs in the last decade, but this line of reasoning also changed the nature of social policy discussions in other areas as well (Aos, 2009; Wang & Holton, 2007).

In addition to providing a compelling argument that resonates with policy-makers, there are additional reasons to incorporate cost and outcome analysis into human services research and decision making. Such analyses provide the following:

- *Useful metrics for choosing among policy alternatives.* Cost and outcome analysis offers an approach for summarizing very different alternatives using a common metric: total dollar values. Hence, there is standardization when comparing prevention approaches to treatment approaches, and approaches that may diverge in terms of the timing of public costs and benefits, as well as whether health providers, early childhood agencies, criminal justice departments are the service providers.

- *Extremely valuable information when trying to replicate services.* In addition to helping policymakers choose among alternatives, knowing the costs of services helps them plan budgets and assess the degree to which services are being implemented with fidelity.

- *Information that can promote program improvement.* For instance, if faced with options to make tradeoffs among staff with different salaries, it may be tempting to substitute lower cost staff for more expensive staff. However, cost and outcome analysis might lead to a better informed choice. If more expensive personnel produced client outcomes that were greater by a factor larger than their salary premium, the organization might be able to produce better outcomes by employing more of the better paid staff rather than less.

The rest of this chapter describes the major types of cost and outcome analysis and the data required to conduct the different types of analysis; provide some examples of their use for children's programs; and conclude with some implications for policy, research, and practice.

Types of Cost and Outcome Analysis

This section describes four major types of cost and outcome analysis approaches, along with types of data required to conduct each type of analysis and examples of each from the children's services field. (Any analysis that calculates the monetary costs of a policy option and the monetary benefits is often referred to as "cost–benefit" analysis, when in fact cost–benefit analysis is one type of cost and outcome analysis.)

Cost Analysis

This type of analysis focuses on the costs of policy options rather than on monetizing the benefits of policy options. This is useful for benchmarking against cost standards in the field, informing decision makers about resource requirements for replicating services, and contributing to other types of resource allocation decisions.

An example of this type of analysis is found in *Examining the Cost of Military Child Care* (Zellman & Gates, 2002). The authors of this study provided the military child care system, the nation's largest system of employer-sponsored child care, with information about the costs of providing child care in alternative settings. The Department of Defense (DoD) provides child care in Child Development Centers, Family Child Care homes, and centers operated by outside providers under contract to the DoD. The DoD requires outsourcing for services that are 10 percent less expensive when operated by contractors, and these estimates indicated that the contractor-run centers were more expensive to operate than DoD-run centers. Furthermore, the analysis showed that DoD might be able to realize savings or increase child care services by shifting some care to Family Child Care homes, which had lower costs than either type of center. Finally, the analysis allowed DoD to compare their cost structure to that of employer-sponsored care provided by other employers.

Cost-Effectiveness Analysis

This class of cost and outcome analysis can provide two types of information: the amount of spending required to realize a given outcome level, or what level of outcome results from a particular expenditure. Cost-effectiveness analysis focuses on one particular outcome rather than providing a full accounting of all benefits from a program or service.

A study of two curricula for teaching math to fifth-graders (Levin & McEwan, 2001; Quinn, Ban Mondfrans, & Worthen, 1984) demonstrates the use of cost-effectiveness analysis. The authors compared mathematics scores on the Iowa Test of Basic Skills for children assigned to one of two curricula: Goal-Based Educational Management System Proficiency Mathematics (or GEMS Math), which was a highly individualized approach using special instructional methods for teaching math, or Text Math, which was a more traditional, text-based approach. The GEMS Math program cost $288 per student per year, compared with $194 per student per year for the Text Math program. However, the authors found that the scores of students in the GEMS Math classes were higher than those of students in the Text Math program. Cost-effectiveness analysis provides a way to assess whether the gains achieved in the GEMS Math class were large enough to justify the greater costs. The authors divided the average raw score points on the Iowa Test of Basic Skills by the cost per student to create a cost-effectiveness ratio. Despite its higher average total cost per student, the GEMS Math program had lower costs per raw score point on the math test: GEMS cost $11.48 per raw score point compared with $13.45 per raw score point for Text Math. This cost-effectiveness analysis shows that the GEMS approach exhibits the lowest cost per unit of outcome—test score points in this case.

Cost–Benefit Analysis

This analysis compares services' costs to society with their benefits to society in dollar terms. Cost–benefit analysis indicates whether a service is of value to society at large in terms of generating benefits that outweigh the costs. A type of cost–benefit analysis that is often of particular interest for human service decision makers is *cost-savings analysis*. This type of analysis focuses exclusively on the costs and benefits that accrue to government or other specific stakeholder rather than to society as a whole. This kind of analysis is often used to determine whether a publicly provided program "pays for itself" and is thus justified not only by whatever human services benefits it may render, but also on financial terms.

The costs and savings that result from an intervention are typically compared by taking their difference, and if the savings to are greater than the costs, then the program is said to pay for itself. The difference between the savings and the costs might be termed "net benefits" in reports. Another approach used to compare costs and savings is to create a ratio of the two, a benefit:cost ratio. If the ratio of benefits to costs is greater than one, then the program benefits are greater than the costs. A final way to compare costs and savings to government is by creating an internal rate of return, which is the interest rate that would be required for the activities up-front costs to produce a stream of returns equal to the realized sequence of benefits.

In their study of universal preschool for California, Karoly and Bigelow (2005) express the costs and outcomes using many variants of cost–benefit analysis and from the perspective of multiple actors in society. In their model, in which families pay for preschool on a fee schedule that subsidizes lower-income families, they present net benefits, the benefit:cost ratio, and the internal rate of return for government and total society. Their government calculations include state and local as well as a federal government costs and benefits, and the estimates for total society add costs and benefits for preschool families and the rest of society.

The results differ substantially depending on the perspective from which the analysis is conducted. The net benefits per child for the State of California and local government of this policy scenario are negative (–$342 per child), the benefit–cost ratio is less than one (0.87), and the internal rate of return is 2.2 percent, implying that the program would not provide a return to state and local government for the expenditures required to deliver the services. However, if one considers the costs and outcomes for government as a whole—combining state, local and federal—the net benefits per child are positive ($1,952 per child), the benefit:cost ratio is 1.75, and the internal rate of return is 5.4 percent. From this perspective, the service does more than pay for itself. When Karoly and Bigelow (2005) aggregate all of the costs to society and all of the benefits, they obtain estimated costs and benefits for total society across the United States. This calculus produces net benefits of $9,329 per child, a benefit:cost ratio of 3.15, and an internal rate of return of 11.2 percent.

Data Elements for Different Types of Cost and Outcome Analysis

Before embarking on cost and outcome analysis, it is necessary to determine whether the data exist to be able to conduct the analysis, and whether those data meet minimal standards, such as the completeness of the cost information. Below is an overview of the cost and outcome data that would be needed to undertake the types of analyses described in the last section.

Cost Data

All of the types of cost and outcome analyses described above require similar cost data. Despite the fact that the analytical and design challenges inherent in collecting cost data are often less formidable than those present when collecting outcomes data—such as needing to have a rigorous research design, requiring many years of follow-up, or involving advanced statistical methods—policy choices under consideration often are more likely to have outcomes rather than cost data available. For instance, a review of the programs and policies catalogued in "best practices" projects, such as Department of Education's What Works Clearinghouse (http://ies.ed.gov/ncee/wwc), the Cochrane Collaboration (http://www.cochrane.org), and the Promising Practices Network (http://www.promisingpractices.net), reveals that cost data are rarely reported for the hundreds of programs for which these projects report evaluation findings.

The paucity of cost data available on many policy options under consideration is partly because this information is typically not generated by the research process in the same way that outcome data often are: through program evaluations or other research studies. Furthermore, there is less incentive for researchers to collect cost data for its own sake: Although research reporting on program effectiveness is likely to result in journal publication, research that reports the cost of a program or service is generally not given the same value in scientific journals, and it would be unusual if this accounting resulted in journal publication.

It can also be time consuming and challenging to obtain the information needed to estimate costs from administrative sources. One reason is that many organizations do not organize their budgets in a way that assigns portions of broad categories of expenses—rent, utilities, insurance, management and human resources functions, and computer networks, for example—to particular projects or agencies. It is likely to be particularly challenging if one is trying to estimate costs for a program that was delivered a decade or more ago. The best option for obtaining reliable cost data is to collect the cost information at the time a program is in operation when possible.

Whenever the cost data are collected and whatever the context, it is important to consider the full resources required to implement the program or policy, not just the direct monetary costs to the implementing organization. This implies that a full accounting of costs would need to consider the costs to clients or participants in the activity, not the only the costs to the organization providing the services. For example, one parenting program may be delivered in the client's home whereas a second is delivered at a family support center that is a half-hour bus ride away. The first program incurs no time or money costs of transportation for the client, but the second may. The total costs of the second program would need to account for the time and money clients spend getting to the facility.

Resources that are donated are important to capture as well as those that require a direct cash outlay. In interviews with seven sites implementing the First Born Program home visiting model, there was wide variance in the amount of personnel time, facilities, and materials that were donated (Kilburn & Cannon, in press). Donated time ranged from the time of the site director to that of a part-time administrative assistant. Other resources that did not show up in program budgets at different sites but that represent real resources required to deliver the program included donated space; office maintenance and cleaning; and equipment for participating families such as children's books, clothing, toys, or car seats.

Another example of costs that may be easy to miss is indirect or overhead costs. Some of these may be difficult to assign to a particular program or agency within an organization, such as building security or human resources functions. These indirect costs may also include costs associated with delivering a service that are not directly related to that service per se. An example of this is the Baby College operated by Harlem Children's Zone (HCZ). Of the $1.2 million that HCZ spent to deliver Baby College as of 2008 (Tough, 2009) more than $100,000 included expenses that were not related to the classroom experience itself, such as outreach workers that helped recruit families for the courses, lunch and breakfast for the parents who attended the courses, $10 and $25 gift certificates that are raffled off after each class, a $100 check for each parent who completed the course, and gift baskets containing baby essentials and safety equipment for graduating parents (Tough, 2009). It is clear that if HCZ had not accounted for these expenditures that were not incurred as part of teaching the course itself, they would not have captured the full cost of implementing Baby College.

In general, the categories of costs that would need to be captured for a full accounting of human services include personnel; client time; facility, including rent, capital depreciation, utilities, security, maintenance, and cleaning; equipment, such as computers and other electronics, furniture, and office supplies; and client consumables, like worksheets, food and drinks, fliers about services, information sheets, and calendars

Details about the methods for collecting costs for human services cannot be provided here, but some references that readers may want to consult for more information about this topic include Levin and McEwan (2001), Karoly et al. (2001), and Yates (1996).

Outcome Data

As mentioned above, all four types of cost and outcome analysis described in the first section require similar types of cost data, which account for the full resources required to deliver a service. However, the four types of cost and outcome analysis have different requirements in terms of outcome data.

Cost Analysis. Cost analysis requires no outcome data.

Cost-Effectiveness Analysis. Cost-effectiveness analysis compares the dollar amount required to produce one unit of a particular outcome. The outcome changed is divided by the cost of producing that change to generate an estimate of the cost of each unit changed. The example above that compared the two math curricula shows that the outcome data required for cost-effectiveness analysis is the measurement of the impact of an activity for only one outcome measure, but it only makes sense in the context of collecting the outcome for more than one program alternative. This is because cost-effectiveness analysis compares the cost of producing a unit change in a particular outcome for different intervention options.

Cost–Benefit Analysis. Cost–benefit analysis places a monetary value on the resources required to deliver services and compares them with the monetary value of benefits to all of society. A related type of analysis, *cost-savings analysis*, compares the costs of an intervention to government to the savings to government. Another variant of cost–benefit analysis calculates an *internal rate of return*. This is the implicit interest rate that produces the observed sequence of monetized program costs and benefits. For instance, if a program costs $100 today, and then provides $103 in real benefits next year, the rate of return is 3 percent.

Note that for cost–benefit analysis, data on only one policy option or multiple policy options might be incorporated into the analysis. This depends on what types of questions the analysis is designed to address. If the question is "Does this intervention save the government more money that it costs?", only cost and outcome data for the intervention in question are needed. However, if the purpose of the analysis is to compare two alternative options, and the question is "Which of these interventions saves the government more money?", then cost and outcome data would be needed for all the alternatives being compared.

Estimating a monetary value for the benefits requires a full accounting of the benefits resulting from a service for all of the potential beneficiaries in society. Beneficiaries of human services would include not only program participants, but also potentially other members of society. In order to calculate the monetary value of the benefits, an analyst would need a measure of the size of the change in outcome cause by receipt of the service. For example, this might take the form of 0.23 fewer children placed in special education in one year for each child served, or 0.11 fewer teens incarcerated for each youth served. The second piece of information required would be the monetary value of each of these changes. This allows a value to be placed on the change in the outcome. Using special education placement as an example, if it is known that each special education placement costs $3,000 more than a regular education per year, then placing 0.23 fewer children in special education in a year would be valued at 0.23 times $3,000, or $690 a year. The changes that result from a service might benefit different actors in society and would generally include one or more of these groups: government, program participants, other members of society besides program participants (such as potential victims of crimes or people who no longer breathe polluted air).

Limitations to Cost and Outcome Analysis

Whichever approach one takes to cost and outcomes analysis, it is important to recognize that there are inherent limitations. Here are a few of the most important ones to consider:

Adjustments for Variations in Context. One issue in applying the results of cost and outcome analysis is that the analysis is generally based on findings of evaluations done on small model programs. It is unclear whether similar results would be obtained if such programs were "scaled up" to the broader settings that are usually the subject of policy decisions. Although the results of larger, scaled-up programs could in theory be larger or smaller than those from smaller scale model programs, it is often assumed that the results from scaled-up programs would be smaller. This would be because it may be more difficult to duplicate a program with fidelity as it becomes larger, and because it is often assumed that the program developer is more able to deliver the program effectively than others. In addition, local adaptations to model programs—perhaps necessitated because of differences in public transportation, weather, labor laws or other uncontrollable factors—may also lead to deviations from the original model program site.

Estimating Future Benefits. Some outcomes may have an immediate and short-term benefit, such as the monetary value of an avoided emergency room visit. This happens at a very discrete point in time and has a relatively clear monetary value. However, many of the outcomes improved by human services do not have that quality and in fact may result in a stream of changed outcomes over a person's entire life. Such outcomes may include obtaining a high school degree, avoiding a teen pregnancy, improving achievement scores, and preventing trauma from experiences such as child maltreatment or family violence. Not only is it difficult to place a monetary value on these outcomes at the time they are measured in an evaluation, but it is also not straightforward to generate an estimate of the entire path of better outcomes that this would be associated with for the remainder of the person's life. This is not an impossible task, however.

Uncertainty. One way to characterize the majority of limitations of cost and outcome analysis is with one word: uncertainty. The two considerations just discussed fall into this category.

Another concerns the fact that most analysts do not report standard errors for cost and benefit calculations. That is, the analysts report point estimates or average values based on their calculations but do not include an estimate of the degree of uncertainty surrounding the estimates. This is potentially important, because as is the case for evaluation results, if the estimated net benefit of a program is $1,200, but a 95 percent confidence interval includes zero, it may be the case that the net benefit should be considered positive.

Another type of uncertainty that influences the utility of cost and outcome findings is the fact that many outcomes are not measured by the evaluations on which the benefit findings are based. For example, Heckman, Moon, Pinto, Savelyev, and Yavitz's (2010) analysis of the Perry Preschool Program—a 2.5 hours-a-day free preschool program—showed program evaluations included outcome data only for participating children. However, it is likely that their mothers also realized improved outcomes from the program, which could result in large monetary benefits such as higher family earnings or lower public assistance use. The implication of this type of uncertainty is that the monetary benefits from many human services are likely to be undercounted.

A final type of uncertainty that vexes the interpretation of cost and outcome findings is related to the assumption that the state of the world will remain largely constant in the future. This is related to such issues as assuming that high school will continue to go up to grade 12 for the current crop of entering preschool students, that Social Security will exist when we retire, and other policy assumptions that underlie cost and outcome analysis.

Implications for Policy, Research, and Practice in Children's Services

Although cost and outcome analysis has attractive features, such as expressing diverse programs with very different types of outcomes in a common metric (dollars), there are some weaknesses in the analysis in general. The primary one is that there can be many sources of uncertainty that make it difficult to compare outcomes across policy options. As a result, given the current state of the field of human services, the primary value of cost and outcome analysis for policy decisions is to assess whether the benefits of a service are likely to exceed its costs.

The results of cost and outcome analysis can be a valuable tool in helping to inform policy choices, but it is also the case that cost and outcome analysis is but one option among many tools that contribute to decisions. Indeed, there is no shortage of detractors from cost–benefit analysis, with criticisms including the lack of attention to morality, distributional implications of policies, and others (for example, Frank, 2000; Richardson, 2000; Vining & Weimar, 2010). Rather than debating whether cost and outcome analysis is the penultimate tool for informing decisions, it is likely to be more productive to recognize the strengths and weaknesses of this approach, be informed about the pitfalls to watch out for in individual studies, and use well-designed analyses in their most appropriate setting. For instance, supplementing widely available impact evaluations with information about alternative programs' costs would likely help decision makers select an option that not only improves clients' well-being, but also does so at the least cost to taxpayers. In recognition of the potential value of expanding the availability of cost and outcomes analysis for human services, and children's services in particular, many recent federal government requests for proposals to evaluate child and family services have required a cost–benefit component.

This chapter has also pointed out several implications for research in child and family services and human services more generally. One of the most important is a call to collect more cost data. A very small fraction of the policy options that have been evaluated for effectiveness have collected cost data, which profoundly limits the application of these methods and the advancement of methodologies in the field of human services. In addition, the discussion highlighted several areas where investments in methodologies would substantially improve the field's utility. These are primarily in the areas of developing methods for valuing the long-term benefits from improved outcomes and methods for accounting for uncertainty in estimates. These are both currently active areas of research, with some of the advances being documented by the National Research Council and Institute of Medicine (2009). These areas are particularly pressing in evaluations of services for children, as children's services are more likely than many types of interventions to produce gains in the long run. Furthermore, children's services are increasingly described as social "investments" with an increasing emphasis on prevention rather than treatment, both of which emphasize a temporal sequence in which costs occur upfront and benefits accrue in the future (Kilburn & Karoly, 2008).

Some arguments in favor of the recent health care reform legislation also focus on the potential monetary benefits of spending more on up-front prevention costs in order to realize greater health care savings in the future. However, whether the long-term cost savings that result from better prevention truly pay for themselves may vary by condition, age of the patient, and other factors, and the net balance of whether prevention can help pay for health care reform will require much more additional research (Thorpe & Ogden, 2010).

Last, individuals who manage and deliver children's services may have had the impression that the cost–benefit analysis had value in the policy and research arenas but had little utility for practice. This chapter has discussed several other types of cost and outcome analysis that are in fact highly useful for improving children's services or other human services. These include cost analysis, which can help providers understand the costs of replicating specific program models and to identify sites within a multisite environment that can be targets of reengineering or other operational improvement measures. Monitoring costs and outcomes for specific services and activities can also help organizations engage in continuous quality improvement programs, identifying best practices in delivering services at lower costs or achieving better outcomes despite limited budgets.

References

Aos, S. (2009). *Return on (taxpayer) investment: Evidence-based prevention and intervention*, Olympia: Washington State Institute for Public Policy. Retrieved from http://www.wsipp.wa.gov/rptfiles/09-12-1202.pdf.

Center on the Developing Child at Harvard University. (2007). *A science-based framework for early childhood policy: Using evidence to improve outcomes in learning, behavior, and health for vulnerable children.* Retrieved from http://www.developingchild.harvard.edu.

Frank, R. H. (2000). Why is cost–benefit analysis so controversial? *Journal of Legal Studies, 29*, 913–930.

Heckman, J. J. (2006, June 30). Skill formation and the economics of investing in disadvantaged children. *Science, 312*, 1900–1902.

Heckman, J. J., Moon, S. H., Pinto, R., Savelyev, P. A., & Yavitz, A. (2010). The rate of return to the HighScope Perry Preschool Program. *Journal of Public Economics, 94*, 114–128.

Karoly, L. A., & Bigelow, J. A. (2005). *The economics of investing in universal preschool education in California* (Report No. MG-349). Santa Monica, CA: RAND Corporation.

Karoly, L. A., Kilburn, M. R., Bigelow, J. H., Caulkins, J. P., & Cannon, J. (2001). *Assessing costs and benefits of early childhood intervention programs: Overview and application to the Starting Early Starting Smart program* (Report No. MR-1335-CRP). Santa Monica, CA: RAND Corporation.

Karoly, L., Kilburn, M. R., & Cannon, J. (2005). *Early childhood interventions: Proven results, future promise* (Report No. MG-341). Santa Monica, CA: RAND Corporation.

Kilburn, M. R., & Cannon, J. S. (in press). *Factors that influence successful start-up of home visiting sites: Lessons learned from replicating the First Born® program.* Santa Monica, CA: RAND Corporation.

Kilburn, M. R., & Karoly, L. A. (2008). *The economics of early childhood policy: What the dismal science has to say about investing in children* (Report No. OP-227). Santa Monica, CA: RAND Corporation.

Levin, H. M. & McEwan, P. J. (2001). *Cost-effectiveness analysis: Methods and applications* (2nd ed.). Thousand Oaks, CA: Sage Publications.

National Research Council & Institute of Medicine, Committee on Strengthening Benefit–Cost Analysis Methodology for the Evaluation of Early Childhood Interventions. (2009). *Strengthening benefit–cost analysis for early childhood interventions: Workshop summary.* Washington, DC: National Academies Press.

Quinn, B., Ban Mondfrans, A., & Worthen, B. D. (1984). Cost-effectiveness of two math programs as moderated by pupil SES. *Educational Evaluation and Policy Analysis, 6,* 39–52.

Richardson, H. S. (2000) The stupidity of the cost–benefit standard. *Journal of Legal Studies, 29,* 971–1003.

Rolnick, A., & Grunewald, R. (2003, December). Early childhood development: Economic development with a high public return. *Region,* 6–12. Retrieved from http://minneapolisfed.org/research/studies/earlychild/abc-part2.pdf

Thorpe, K. E., & Ogden, L. L. (2010). The foundation that health reform lays for improved payment, care coordination, and prevention. *Health Affairs, 29,* 1183–1187.

Tough, P. (2009). *Whatever it takes: Geoffrey Canada's quest to change Harlem and America.* New York: Houghton Mifflin Harcourt.

Vining, A. R., & Weimer, D. L. (2010). An assessment of important issues concerning the application of benefit–cost analysis to social policy. *Journal of Benefit–Cost Analysis, 1,* 1–38.

Wang, C.-T., & Holton, J. (2007). *Total estimated cost of child abuse and neglect in the United States.* Retrieved from http://www.preventchildabuse.org/about_us/media_releases/pcaa_pew_economic_impact_study_final.pdf.

Yates, B. T. (1996). *Analyzing costs, procedures, processes, and outcomes in human services: An introduction.* Thousand Oaks, CA: Sage Publications.

Zellman, G. L., & Gates, S. M. (2002). *Examining the cost of military child care* (Report No. Mr-1415-OSD). Santa Monica, CA: RAND Corporation.

CHAPTER 20

Practice-to-Research Example:

Implementation of Child and Family Services Reviews: Progress and Challenges

Brenda G. McGowan and Elaine M. Walsh

This chapter is one of three research-to-practice examples in the second edition of Outcomes Measurement in the Human Services. *Following in the spirit of the first edition, the three examples illustrate particular issues that are pertinent to integrating or translating research into practice in each of the human service domains featured in the book—physical health, behavioral health, and child and family services. This chapter describes policies and outcome measurements that are integral to practice and evaluation of child welfare programs at individual, program and system levels of analysis.*

This chapter discusses the implementation of the Child and Family Service Reviews (CFSRs) that were introduced in 2000 by the U.S. Department of Health and Human Services (DHHS). These reviews were the first effort to focus on the outcomes rather than the processes of the various child welfare programs supported by Title IV-B and Title IV-E of the Social Security Act. These programs include child protective services, foster care, adoption, and family preservation and support services. DHHS had been authorized by the 1994 amendment to the Social Security Act to ensure accountability by reviewing state compliance with the procedural requirements of these programs, but the accountability focused on service processes, not outcomes. Reflecting the lack of attention to program outcomes in federal laws and funding requirements, neither public nor contracted child welfare agencies gave systematic attention to outcomes measurement before the current decade. This chapter illustrates how the shift to a focus on outcomes measurement in program funding and evaluation has created new emphases in child welfare practice.

The lack of attention to outcomes in child welfare was highlighted in the first edition of this book (Mullen & Magnabosco, 1997). Commenting on the discussions during the symposium, McGowan and Cohen (1997) wrote, "There was widespread agreement that the field of outcome measurement in child and family services as a whole is in sorry shape and that little is known about what should be measured, how it should be measured, or by whom it should be measured" (p. 297).

The Child and Family Service Reviews (CFSRs) demonstrate a major effort to address this criticism. In 2000, when announcing the new results-oriented approach to federal monitoring of state child welfare programs, DHHS Secretary Donna Shalala commented, "This regulation demonstrates a critical and significant shift in holding states accountable for children's safety and permanency while promoting their well-being" (DHHS, 2000). Implementation of these reviews has been accompanied by numerous efforts to develop results-oriented accountability at the state and local levels.

The CFSR Process

CFSRs are administered by the U.S. Children's Bureau of the Administration for Children and Families (ACF) within DHHS in collaboration with the states. In addition to ensuring systems accountability, they are designed to help states improve child welfare services by achieving specific outcomes related to safety, permanency, and child and family well-being. These outcomes are defined as follows (DHHS, ACF, 2009a, 2009b, 2009c):

- Safety: Children are first and foremost protected from abuse and neglect; children are safely maintained in their homes whenever possible and appropriate.

- Permanency: Children have permanency and stability in their living situations; the continuity of family relationships and connections is preserved for families.

- Family and Child Well-Being: Families have enhanced capacity to provide for their children's needs; children receive appropriate services to meet their educational needs; children receive adequate services to meet their physical and mental health needs.

Child safety has long been an objective of the child welfare system. The early child protective services started in the 19th century were based on the legal principle of *parens patriae* derived from its use in England to justify state intervention in family life on behalf of children. The permanency objective was first enunciated in the Adoption and Child Welfare Act of 1980, passed in response to a number of studies documenting the large numbers of children remaining in foster care for many years in what has been termed a "foster care limbo." Although child welfare practitioners have long hoped they were contributing to child well-being, family and child well-being was not formally introduced as a child welfare objective until the passage of the Adoption and Safe Families Act of 1997. The importance of these objectives is illustrated by the fact that in 2008, the most recent year for which such data are available, an estimated 772,000 children in the United States were determined to be victims of child abuse or neglect (DHHS, ACF, Administration for Children, Youth and Families Children's Bureau, 2010). Moreover, some 748,000 were in foster care that year, down from 800,000 in 2002, with some in care for brief periods, and others waiting years for permanent homes through reunification with their biological parents or adoption.

In addition to examining attainment of these objectives for children and families, the CFSRs also examine seven systemic factors in each state that reflect management objectives: (1) statewide information system; (2) case review system; (3) quality assurance system; (4) staff and provider training; (5) service array and resource development; (6) agency responsiveness to the community; and (7) foster and adoptive parent licensing, recruitment, and retention. Each of these system components is assumed to contribute to the desired outcomes of safety, permanency, and well-being.

The CFSR is a two-stage process that consists of a statewide assessment and an on-site review. The first round of reviews was conducted from 2001 to 2004. The second round was initiated in 2007 and was completed in 2010. The third round is expected to start in 2012. As this range suggests, each review is a very lengthy process, described below, that involves the statewide assessment and on-site review, publication of the final report, and development and implementation of the Program Improvement Plan. A wide range of stakeholders is expected to be involved in each of these stages.

Statewide Assessment

The statewide assessment conducted by the state government is based in part on aggregate data prepared by the U.S. Children's Bureau. The data profiles, which focus on safety and permanency outcomes, are derived from data submitted by the state for the Adoption and Foster Care Analysis Reporting System (AFCARS) and the National Child Abuse and Neglect Data System (NCANDS). AFCARS is a federal data collection program that provides child-specific information on all children covered by the protections of Title IV-B and Title IV-E of the Social Security Act. All states are required to submit to the Children's Bureau on an annual basis data concerning each child in foster care and each child who has been adopted under the authority of the state's child welfare agency. These databases are designed to address policy and program management issues at the state and federal levels. NCANDS is a voluntary national data collection and analysis system created in response to the requirements of the National Child Abuse and Treatment Act, as amended (P.L.93-247). It consists of two components. One, the Summary Data Component, is a compilation of key aggregate child abuse and neglect statistics from all states. The other, the Detailed Case Data Component, is a compilation of case-level data from those child protective agencies across the country able to provide electronic child abuse and neglect records. Both of these data collection systems provide valuable information for research and planning, but they do not provide the information required to hold states accountable for achieving specific outcomes

An additional section of the statewide assessment requires a narrative analysis of the outcome areas profiled in the data provided by the Children's Bureau and information about any improvements in these areas since the previous statewide assessment. The next major section of the statewide assessment describes the state's child welfare system's characteristics and presents a narrative discussion of the seven systemic factors. It must also evaluate changes in policy, practice, and performance initiated since the last assessment. The final section must assess the strengths and challenges in the state's child welfare system and identify issues and geographic locations that should be examined in the on-site review.

The statewide assessment is completed by a team consisting not only of staff in the state child welfare system, but also of stakeholders from a range of voluntary and state agencies, court and tribal representatives, youth, and foster and adoptive parent representatives. In addition to reviewing all relevant data sources, the state agency is encouraged to hold focus groups with various stakeholders and to conduct surveys to ensure wide input into the report. This same process is followed in every state.

On-Site Review

The on-site review in every state is a week-long process conducted by a joint federal and state team. The federal representatives are staff members from the Children's Bureau; the state representatives include staff from the state agency responsible for children's services and external experts in child welfare and children's services. The on-site review consists of a random sample of 65 cases in three different areas of each state. The largest metropolitan area in each state must be included as one of the study sites. The team members review case records, interview children and parents receiving services, and hold intensive interviews with the relevant stakeholders in each case. In New York, for example, the last on-site view was in May 2008 and had 15 teams of two members each, one each from the state and from the Children's Bureau. They reviewed cases from Onondaga and Rockland counties and New York City.

Report on the CFSR

A report is prepared for each state presenting the findings of the Statewide Assessment, the State Data Profile prepared by the Children's Bureau, the cases reviewed in the onsite review, and the interviews and focus groups conducted during the review. The CFSR assesses state performance on 23 items related to the seven outcomes presented above, and 22 items related to the seven systemic factors also identified above. A rating of "strength" or "area needing improvement" is assigned to each of the 23 outcome items reviewed, and the ratings are aggregated to determine the state's performance on each of the seven key outcomes. The outcome can be rated substantially achieved, partially achieved, or not achieved. It is expected that these reports to the states, which are made available to interested stakeholders and the public at large, will be used as the basis for the states' plans for improvement in child and family service delivery. To be in substantial conformity on an outcome in round 1, 95 percent of the cases reviewed had to be rated as substantially achieved. The minimum amount of improvement required in round 2 is based on the national sampling error adjusted for the level of the state's baseline year performance.

Safety and permanency outcomes are also evaluated on the basis of state performance in relation to six national data standards. Both the national standards for each indicator and the case review requirements must be met for the state to be in substantial conformity on these outcome measures. Each item included in each of the systemic factors section of the report is rated either as a strength or an area needing improvement on the basis of whether the state performance meets the federal standards specified in the Child and Family Services Plan (DHHS, ACF, 2009a).

Program Improvement Plan

Every state not in conformity with particular outcomes or systemic factors must develop a Program Improvement Plan (PIP) to address those deficits. The PIP, which will be used to make improvements in the state's child welfare system, is developed by the responsible state agency in consultation with relevant stakeholders and must be submitted to the Children's Bureau promptly after the final report is received. The PIP is expected to explain the state's primary strategy and goal; the outcomes on the specific factors being addressed, based on specific items identified in the final report as requiring improvement; the action steps to be taken; benchmarks; and responsible personnel. It is usually structured around the key outcome areas of safety, permanency, and well-being. There is often an ongoing dialogue over many months between the federal agency and the state, and various revisions must be made before the PIP is approved. To illustrate, New York's PIP was submitted in May 2008, was revised several times, and was not approved until January 2010. Ultimately, if the PIP is not accepted, and specific improvements specified in the PIP are not achieved within two years after approval of the PIP, serious financial penalties can be imposed on the state. The ACF determines the amount of Title IV-A and Title IV-E funds to be withheld by means of a very complex formula (see Federal Register, 65:16 [January 25, 2000], Rules and Regulations, 4081–4082).

States' Performance and Experience with CFSRs

As the above description suggests, the ACF has established high performance and outcome standards for the states. All 50 states, the District of Columbia, and Puerto Rico completed their first round by 2004, and none complied fully with the federal standards; all were found to violate one or more. All were required to submit PIPs to avoid substantial penalties ranging from 2.3 to 18.2 million dollars (Pear, 2004).

Although some improvement has been noted in the second round of reviews, many states have failed to achieve substantial conformity on the different outcomes and systemic factor measures (for example, statewide information system, case review system, quality assurance system, staff and provider training, service array and resource development, agency responsiveness, parent licensing, recruitment and retention). To date, none of the states has achieved "substantial compliance" at the initial stage in all of the measures or systemic factors studied, and all have had to submit PIPs (Schuerman & Needell, 2009a, 2009b). The two outcome areas in which the states demonstrate the lowest level of compliance are permanency outcome 1 (children have permanency and stability in their living situations), and well-being outcome 1 (families have enhanced capacity to provide for their children's needs).

Despite the disappointing statistical results reported, in 2008 a majority of the Federal CFSR Teams reported several improved trends in round 2 reviews. These included the following (Adams, 2008):

- Increased efforts to improve family involvement in case decision making and planning

- Increased efforts to protect the safety of children through use of standardized tools in initial and ongoing assessment of risk, community involvement in safety, planning and supervisory oversight in decision making

- Increased community and local partnerships

- Enhanced quarterly assessment systems to measure practices promoted by the CFSRs.

The CFSR team also made a number of observations indicating that there had been improvement since round 1 in the timeliness of adoptions and an increase in permanency for children who had been in care more than two years. At the same time, little improvement was noted in the proportion of children experiencing three or more moves while in placement.

The introduction of specific outcome measures in the CFRS process enabled the review teams to note specific areas of progress. However, it is impossible to say whether the emphasis on outcome measures actually contributed to these changes. The whole CFRS process is likely to focus administrative and staff attention on these issues, but larger environmental factors are likely to have a greater influence. For example, it is widely expected by experts in the field that the current economic recession will contribute to increased child abuse and neglect complaints, and increasing lay offs in child welfare agencies will result in delays in family reunification and adoption planning. Hence, there may be some decline in the round 3 measures.

States' Experience with CFSRs

The National Association of Public Child Welfare Administrators conducted mail and telephone surveys in 2008 with state child welfare administrators about their experiences to gather information with issues the states identified as problems ($N = 44$ states, the District of Columbia, and Puerto Rico). Analysis revealed little difference by federal region, so the results were reported as a whole. Some of these findings are as follows:

- The planning phase for the outside review is generally very collaborative between the state and the federal regional offices and contractors, as is the onsite collaboration between the onsite federal and state teams.

- These teams "cannot truly be called a partnership since the Federal Government is clearly in charge" (p. 2).

- There are inconsistencies across study sites and states in the way cases are rated.

- Planning for the on-site reviews and the actual reviews require an enormous amount of time and expense on the part of states. (The National Association of Public Child Welfare Administrators later estimated that the state cost for the on-site review is at least $500,000.)

- Although states are provided a high level of technical assistance from the federal regional offices and the National Child Welfare Resource Centers in the development of their PIPs, they are frustrated by the delays in receipt of final reports and variations in the PIP requirements.

- Potential fiscal penalties are a concern for all states (although few have actually been assessed).

- Most states have developed their own Quality Service Reviews that align with the on-site review of the CFSR and believe they could provide information that would be more useful to the states and to different areas of each state than is the information gathered through the federal process. (National Association of Public Child Welfare Administrators, 2008a)

Despite all these concerns, a letter summarizing the results of this survey to the Associate Commissioner of the Children's Bureau concluded,

> *We all acknowledge the need for monitoring and the benefits of a federal review to ensure that the momentum of the child welfare reform through out the nation continues. Our members are committed to strengthening families and improving outcomes for all children. Their ability to do so has evolved significantly since the first round of CFSRs and PIPs. (National Association of Public Child Welfare Administrators, 2008b, p. 9)*

Critiques of the CFSR System and Implications for Outcomes Measurement

There is widespread agreement in the child welfare system about the value of monitoring service outcomes. In that sense, the goals of the CFSRs have been widely applauded. Concern has been raised, however, about specific aspects of the implementation of this program. In its major report of foster care, the Pew Commission on Children in Foster Care (2004) not only noted the need for more flexibility and an increase in funding, but also outlined several recommended improvements in the CFSRs. These include such items as improved measures of child-well being, use of longitudinal data, continuation of federal matching funds for the State Automated Child Welfare Information Systems, and reinvestment of a portion of the penalties that may be assessed in the state's PIP.

Courtney, Needell, and Wultzyn (2003) were among the first to identify problems with the national standards being used to assess state performances on safety and permanency. As they point out, these standards are derived from information reported by states for AFCARS and NCANDS. These are both very useful data sets, but they do not contain any longitudinal data. Cross-sectional samples such as these create a selection bias in favor of children who have been in care longer. Moreover, exit cohorts tend to be biased toward children with relatively brief stays in care. Selection bias in outcome measures such as those presented by use of these standards presents two problems. First, bias makes it impossible for states to measure their progress over time. Second, "bias creates an unfair basis for the federal government to determine which States must embark upon performance improvement plans and upon which States to assess financial penalties" (Courtney et al., 2003, p. 1146). Individual case tracking over time from the point of entry would be the only way to correct for the selection bias inherent in these cross-sectional samples.

Another serious concern identified by these critics is that the standards are not "risk adjusted" because they do not take into account the demographic differences in the characteristics of children and families receiving services. They recommend that standards be based on entry cohort, use longitudinal data, and shift the focus from compliance measurements to study of which states are achieving particular constellations of outcomes. They conclude that increased data management and analysis capacity will be required at both the state and federal level to make full use of the CFSR data for program planning and evaluation and policy analysis.

Zeller and Gamble (2007) raised serious concern about using retrospective versus prospective data and did a fascinating analysis of the difference in results that could be obtained by examining prospective and retrospective data on the reunification and reentry patterns in the 23 largest counties of a northeastern state. The results raise serious question about the validity of the retrospective measures used in the CFSRs. These measures may determine the relative standing of states, but they do not provide the information necessary to improve outcomes. Because these measures cannot be used to determine the factors that contribute to success or failure in achieving specific outcomes, they do not lead to valid judgment about what should be changed in order to improve state performance. There are clear trade-offs inherent in the use of retrospective versus prospective data. Retrospective data present obvious savings in time and cost and provide immediate information about outcomes. However, only prospective data can provide the information the states need about which types of inputs lead to which types of outcomes over what time frames.

In response to the experiences in the field and criticisms raised about the first round of CFSR completed in 2004, ACF contracted with a consultant to study the process and recommend potential revisions. The consultant convened a workgroup that included state administrators and child welfare researchers. One of the primary suggestions, which was implemented in round 2, was to replace the single-outcome data measures from which national standards were established in round 1 with data composites that incorporate more performance items related to a particular domain. It was assumed that expanding the scope of data would provide a more holistic and more accurate assessment of state performance. This recommendation was followed. To illustrate, the national standard used in round 1, Length of Time to Achieve Reunification, was changed in round 2 to Timeliness of Reunification, measured by a composite of three measures: exits to reunification in less than 12 months; exits to reunification, median stay; and entry cohort reunification in less than 12 months.

Interestingly, although composite measures are being used, ACF decided not to respond to other recommendations that they eliminate national standards and instead assess performance on the basis of continuous improvements over time on the data measures within each state. Their stated rationale for the decision not to accept these recommendations was that setting national goals is important for ensuring that all agencies remain focused on achieving the highest level of results for all children. Similarly, ACF refused to respond to the repeated request that separate performance standards be established for children of different ages or races, or with different reasons for entering care. The rationale for their decisions was that children have the same need for safety and permanency as specified in the tenets of the Adoption and Safe Families Act of 1997 (DHHS, AFC, 2007).

It is too early to determine the full response of state administrators to the shift to composite measures and the refusal to consider other proposed changes. However, Schuerman and Needell (2009b) have recently written a full critique of the CFSR process. They point out that although ACF addressed some of the limitations identified in round 1, some of the early flaws were repeated in round 2, and new problems were introduced. Their analysis focuses on the four national standards derived from 15 measures of permanency and their associated composite measures. Like some of the earlier critics, they point out the problems inherent in overlooking demographic differences among children and families across states and the lack of longitudinal data. They also identify issues related to differences in state criteria for accepting children with different types of problems on their caseloads and the problem inherent in weighting all states equally despite enormous differences in population size.

In a prior report based on a careful reanalysis of the data set used to develop the national standards, Schuerman and Needell (2009a) state that the current national standards "employ a complicated statistical method, principal components analysis, when it is not evident that such a method is in any way required or superior to simpler and more transparent approaches to measurement [and] make many arbitrary and statistically inappropriate decisions in the use of the PCA procedures" (p. 19).

Writing from a somewhat different perspective, the authors of the American Public Human Service Association's (APHSA) *Focal Point*, a document designed as a blueprint for the Obama Administration, identify many of the same issues in the CFSRs. They state, "Child and Family Service Reviews do not measure what they are designed to do and therefore do not accurately reflect State performance.... States are concerned for a variety of reasons that the measures are flawed" (APHSA, 2009, p. 24). More specifically, they point out the lack of longitudinal data, the lack of attention to demographic differences of children, and to the small sample size ($N = 65$) in each state, which cannot give an accurate picture of how the larger states are performing. In addition, APHSA highlights the fact that the CFSRs are very labor intensive before and during the on-site reviews, the states and counties receive different guidance from regional offices about what is expected, and states are forced to start developing the PIPs before the final CFSR is received. Ultimately, APHSA argues that states need additional funds to make improvements approved under the PIPs and that the states should be provided with financial incentives, not penalties under the CFSRs (APHSA, 2009).

Conclusion and Implications for Child Welfare Policy and Practice

It is important to note that there are significant differences between the child welfare system and the health and behavioral health systems discussed in other chapters in this book. These differences have important implications for outcomes measurement. Child welfare services are legislatively mandated at the federal and state levels, and approximately half the costs of child welfare services are paid by the federal government through grants to the states under Titles IV-A and IV-E of the Social Security Act. Consequently, the demand for outcome measurement and accountability is focused on the states, and the focus is on aggregate data, not individual case outcomes.

Despite these differences, there are a number of initiatives parallel to developments in health and behavioral health. To illustrate, a number of public and voluntary agencies have organized different types of consumer advisory boards to ensure a consumer role in local program and policy decisions. Many state and voluntary agencies are experimenting with ways to encourage their staff members to use evidence-based interventions to reach different objectives. And some of the leading child welfare researchers have started to focus on ways to introduce outcome measurement into programming and practice at different levels. See, for example, Testa and Poertner's (2010) recent book, *Fostering Accountability*, which argued for results-oriented accountability to guide child welfare policy and practice. And Wulczyn, Barth, Yuan, Harden, and Landsverk's (2005) recent book, *Beyond Common Sense*, which presented a framework for assessing child well-being outcomes through a developmental and ecological perspective.

There is no doubt that the introduction of the CFSRs has served an important function in focusing attention on outcomes measurement in child welfare. Voluntary agency executives, as well as public administrators at the county and state levels, now raise multiple questions about the outcomes of the services they are funding. Front line practitioners are being trained to evaluate the results as well as the process of their interventions. Moreover, there is now a common language and a strong consensus across the states that the primary objectives of child welfare services should be safety, permanency, and well-being.

This conceptual agreement is clearly a step forward. However, it ignores the conflicts frequently experienced in practice between the goals of safety and permanency. If there is any risk of child abuse, child protective workers often find it safest to remove children from their homes, and they are often reluctant to return them. Yet foster care workers eager to ensure permanency for children in care will argue for as speedy a return as possible. In other words, concern about children's well-being can lead to different practice decisions, geared at times to the safety objective and at other times to the permanency objective.

Complicating this inherent tension among the objectives at the practice level is the fact that the performance measures—or what McDonald and Testa (2010) termed the "operational definitions" of these objectives—focus on processes, not objectives. This is particularly obvious in the CFSR definition of child and family well-being that specifies, for example, receipt of appropriate services to meet children's educational and health needs.

In addition to the conceptual difficulties, many problems have been identified with the actual process of the CFSRs. One issue is the very high performance expectations. Another is the standards imposed and how they were established. Child welfare researchers and administrators alike have raised questions about the reliance on cross-sectional data and the failure of ACF, when establishing standards, to consider differences in the size of the state population and differences in the age, race, ethnicity, gender, and reasons for placement among the children and families involved in the child welfare system. Concerns have also been raised about the method of selection and small size of the sample in the on-site reviews. These research issues all lead to questions about the validity of the data on which the CFSRs are based.

Other concerns have been raised about the implementation process. Although the Children's Bureau and regional office staff members provide extensive consultation and technical assistance, there are differences in expectations across states and localities. The lengthy and repeated exchanges around the PIPs can be very frustrating because of the time delays. Moreover, the whole process is very time, cost, and resource consuming for the states, and there is no real federal cost-sharing. (National Association of Public Child Welfare Administrators, 2008). The CFSR is essentially an unfunded mandate to the states, which creates tensions related to the costs associated with the review process itself and the costs of implementing the PIP.

The multiple implementation issues—at national, state, and local levels—that have arisen with the CFSRs are somewhat puzzling because the program was not initiated without careful prior planning. The day the final regulation was issued governing the CFSRs, the ACF reported, "Because the shift to outcome-focused monitoring represents such an important change in the way child welfare programs are held accountable, DHHS initially conducted numerous pilot tests with the States to refine its approach. In addition, a number of focus groups were conducted" (DHSS, 2000). This suggests that outcome measurements in child welfare were so new that those who participated in the pilot studies and other planning ventures could not anticipate the implementation issues that would arise.

Now that the system has been institutionalized and is likely to remain in place, we would argue for some important revisions before the introduction of round 3 in 2012. The multiple procedures spelled out by the Children's Bureau emphasize heavy involvement of multiple stakeholders from the states, voluntary agencies, the courts, and other service systems in different aspects of the CFSR. Given the federal expectations for stakeholder involvement in the CFSR process, why is ACF not listening to the stakeholder critiques of the process at the implementation stage? The Children's Bureau should be working to put in place a review process that will produce data that are more useful for each of the states and the child welfare system as a whole.

The experience with the CFSRs suggests that any federal system for monitoring human service outcomes at the state level should be carefully pretested to account for the enormous population differences among states. Moreover, it is essential that all stakeholders be engaged in the design process to avoid the multiple frustrations and complaints that can arise during the implementation process. Although one can applaud the commitment to developing outcomes for the national child welfare system, it is not enough to put the concept in place. The real value would be having CFSRs that are valid, reliable, and meaningful for all.

References

Adams, D. (2008, September). Spotlight on the CFSRs: What are we learning from round two? *Children's Bureau Express, 9,* 1–2. Retrieved from http://cbexpress.acf.hhs.gov/index.cfm

American Public Human Services Association. (2009). *Focal point.* Retrieved from http://www.unity of purpose.org/

Courtney, M., Needell, B., & Wultzyn, F. (2003). *National standards in the Child and Family Services Reviews: Time to improve on a good idea.* Retrieved from http://Eric.ed.gov/EricWebPortal

McDonald, T., & Testa, M. F. (2010). Outcomes monitoring in child welfare. In M. F. Testa & J. Poertner (Eds.), *Fostering accountability: Using evidence to guide and improve child welfare policy* (pp. 101–135). New York: Oxford University Press.

McGowan, B. G., & Cohen, S. D. (1997). Comments on outcomes measurements in child and family services. In E. J. Mullen & J. L. Magnabosco (Eds.), *Outcomes measurement in the human services* (pp. 297–301). Washington, DC: NASW Press.

Mullen, E. J., & Magnabosco, J. L. (Eds.). (1997). *Outcomes measurement in the human services*. Washington DC: NASW Press.

National Association of Public Child Welfare Administrators. (2008a). *CFSR/ PIP all state telephone discussion summary conducted March 3, 2008–April 3, 2008*. Retrieved from http://www.napcwa.org/youth/docs/CFSR-PIP summary.pdf

National Association of Public Child Welfare Administrators. (2008b). *Letter to Christine Calpin, U.S. Department of Health and Human Services, Administration of Children and Families, Children's Bureau*. Retrieved from http:www. mapcwa.org

Pear, R. (2004, April 24). U.S. finds fault in all 50 states' child welfare programs, and penalties may follow. *New York Times*, p. 16.

PEW Commission of Children in Foster Care. (2004, May 18). *Fostering the future: Safety, permanence and well-being for children in foster care*. Retrieved from http://pewfostercare.org/research/docs/Final Report.pdf

Schuerman, J. R., & Needell, B. (2004). *The Child and Family Services Review composite scores: Accountability off the track*. Chicago: Chapin Hall.

Schuerman, J. R., & Needell, B. (2009a). *The Child and Family Services Review composite scores: Accountability off the track*. Chicago: Chapin Hall.

Schuerman, J. R., & Needell. B. (2009b). *The Child and Family Services Review composite scores: A critique of method* [Issue brief]. Chicago: Chapin Hall.

Testa, M. F., & Poertner, J. (Eds.). (2010). *Fostering accountability: Using evidence to guide and improve child welfare policy*. New York: Oxford University Press.

U.S. Department of Health and Human Services. (2000). *HHS issues final child welfare regulations to improve services and outcomes for children*. Retrieved from http://archive.hhs.gov/news/press/2000pres/20000125.html

U.S. Department of Health and Human Services, Administration for Children and Families. (2000). *Title IV-E foster care eligibility reviews and Child and Family Services state plan reviews; final rule*. Retrieved from http://www.acf. hhs.gov/programs/cb/laws_policies/cblaws/fed_reg/fr012500.htm

U.S. Department of Health and Human Services, Administration for Children and Families. (2007). *Corrected Federal Register announcement*. Retrieved from http://www.acf.hhs.gov/programs/cb/cwmonitoring/legislation/ fed_reg.htm

U.S. Department of Health and Human Services. (2009a). *Administration of Children and Families, Children's Bureau. New York Child and Family Services review executive summary, final report*. Retrieved from http://www.acf.hhs. gov/programs/cb/cwmonitoring

U. S. Department of Health and Human Services, Administration for Children and Families. (2009b). *Children's Bureau, Child and Family Service reviews fact sheet.* Retrieved from http://www.acf.hhs.gov/programs/cb/cwmonitoring/recruit/cfsrfactsheet.htm

U.S. Department of Health and Human Services, Administration of Children and Families. (2009c). *Final report: New York Child and Family Services review.* Retrieved from http://www.acf.hhs.gov/programs/cb/cwmonitoring

U.S. Department of Health and Human Services, Administration for Children and Families, Administration for Children, Youth and Families Children's Bureau. (2010). *Child maltreatment 2008.* Washington, DC: Author.

Wulczyn, F., Barth, R. P., Yuan, Y.-Y.T., Harden, B. J., & Landsverk, J. (2005). *Beyond common sense: Child welfare, child well-being, and the evidence for policy reform.* Piscataway, NJ: Aldine Transaction.

Zeller, D. E., & Gamble, T. J. (2007). Child welfare performance: Retrospective and prospective approaches. *Child Welfare, 86,* 97–122.

PART V

Special Topics in Outcomes Measurement in the Human Services

CHAPTER 21

The Veterans Health Administration:

Lessons Learned from Implementing Performance Measurement, Electronic Health Records, and Evidence-based Practice[1]

Joseph Francis

Public support of veterans with medical conditions and disabilities related to their military service dates back to colonial times and as such is a deeply held American value. The United States provides the most comprehensive benefits to veterans of any nation and is unique in its managing a national health care system specifically focused on their needs. With a medical care budget of $42 billion in Fiscal Year 2010, the Veterans Health Administration (VHA) is the largest integrated health care system in the United States, serving nearly 6

---

[1]The views presented in this chapter are those of the author and do not necessarily represent the views of the U.S. Department of Veterans Affairs.

million of the nation's 23 million military veterans. (Comprehensive medical benefits are available to all *enrolled* veterans, but not all veterans are eligible to enroll. High-priority groups for the VHA include veterans with service-connected disabilities, former prisoners of war, veterans determined to be housebound or catastrophically disabled, and low-income veterans. Recently, the VHA extended enrollment eligibility to all returning service members, including reservists and National Guard members, for five years following discharge from active duty and relaxed income restrictions for other nonservice connected veterans with service needs [see http://www.va.gov/healtheligibility].) The VHA provides a full range of primary care, mental health, medical specialty, surgical, and rehabilitative services to enrolled veterans. It employs more than 240,000 staff (including 65,000 health professionals) and manages more than 1,400 sites of care, including 153 medical centers, 951 outpatient clinics, 134 nursing homes, and 232 counseling centers. In addition to its comprehensive medical care mission, the VHA performs medical, prosthetics, and health services research relevant to veterans' health needs ($580 million in Fiscal Year 2010) and, through affiliations with 107 medical schools and 1,200 other schools, trains more than 100,000 health professionals and researchers annually. Given the broad scope and complexity of its mission, the VHA provides a rich laboratory for health policymakers and researchers as well as an informative case study of the potential for performance measurement, electronic health records (EHRs), and evidence-based practices to transform U.S. health care.

Historical Context: Challenge and Transformation in the 20th-Century VA

Health care in the VHA is the product of many decades of innovation in response to evolving challenges. After the Revolutionary War, Congress provided pensions for veterans and other benefits. The growing scale of combat, along with improvements in battlefield and rehabilitative medicine, made the Civil War a turning point for the medical care of veterans. Recognizing the need for coordinated national efforts to assist disabled veterans, President Lincoln, in his second inaugural address, called on Congress "to care for him who shall have borne the battle and for his widow, and his orphan." This statement subsequently defined the mission of the Department of Veterans Affairs. After the Civil War, federally supported homes for disabled soldiers provided institutional care along with medical services. An organized system of hospitals developed after the large influx of World War I veterans prompted Congress to transfer management of 57 existing hospitals from the Public Health Service to a newly formed Veterans Bureau, as well as authorize construction of new hospitals to serve veterans. In 1930, the Veterans Bureau was renamed the Veterans Administration (VA; Department of Veterans Affairs, 2005).

VA's next challenge came after 1945, when it faced a surge of more than 15 million veterans returning from World War II. Traditional Civil Service rules presented barriers to hiring highly qualified medical personnel, but policy decisions that established formal affiliations with the nation's medical schools for the purpose of recruiting medical faculty and postgraduate trainees gave VA the ability to quickly gain capacity to provide state-of-the-art medical and rehabilitative care. The new missions of education and research and the alliance with academic medicine also laid the foundation for an organization that encouraged critical thinking, learning, innovation, and discovery among its staff. For instance, VA-supported cooperative clinical studies since 1946 have challenged prevailing clinical practice and helped to define the scientific underpinnings for the treatment of tuberculosis, hypertension, diabetes, coronary artery disease, prostate cancer, schizophrenia, post-traumatic stress disorder, and other chronic disorders (Henderson et al., 2001).

In 1988, President Reagan signed legislation that elevated VA to Cabinet status. The Department of Veterans Affairs, led by the Secretary of Veterans Affairs, became the second largest of the 14 Cabinet departments. (Only the Department of Defense employs more individuals. It should be noted that the Military Health System—which comprises Army, Air Force, and Navy medical facilities as well as networks of civilian providers managed as part of TRICARE, the military's health plan—serves active duty military, their families, and military retirees. The general public and news reporters often do not distinguish VHA from military treatment facilities.) The reorganized VA now comprised three agencies: the VHA, responsible for health care; the Veterans Benefits Administration, responsible for compensation, pensions, as well as education and housing benefits; and the National Cemetery Administration, responsible for death and burial benefits and the administration of veterans' cemeteries. VHA missions were defined under statute to include medical care, medical and prosthetics research, medical education, backup to the Department of Defense health system, and national support during major disasters.

With elevation to Cabinet status, the VA experienced a corresponding increase in oversight and scrutiny by Congress, Veterans Service Organizations, the media, and other stakeholder groups. It soon became apparent that the hospital-centered system established in 1930 was not designed to enhance population health; for example, acutely ill veterans could be hospitalized, but only a limited number of veterans were eligible for the primary care that might have avoided the hospital admission. Administrative, financial, and legal factors created additional inefficiencies; for example, hospitals were funded on the basis of a census of occupied beds, creating incentives for excessive lengths of stay. These factors combined to form a poor public image and widespread consensus about the need for major overhaul, if not elimination, of an aging and costly bureaucracy. In 1995, amid ongoing national debate on health care reform, the VHA began a multifaceted reengineering effort led by Dr. Kenneth Kizer, an emergency physician and former Director of the California Department of Health who was appointed Undersecretary for Health in the VHA. Kizer's leadership resulted in the VHA reorganizing its loose confederation of hospitals into 22 (later 21) Veterans Integrated Service Networks (VISNs) accountable for clinical and financial outcomes; decentralizing operational decision making to the VISN administrative level; establishing an enrollment system and universal access to primary care; and developing a system for allocating the VHA's medical budget to reflect the health needs and geographic distribution of the veteran population. Between 1995 and 1999, those changes resulted in a reduction of 40,000 inpatient beds, an increase of 650 community-based care sites, and a growth in the number of veterans served from 2.5 million in 1995 to 3.6 million in 1999 (Kizer & Dudley, 2009).

Such sweeping organizational transformation as experienced by the VHA offers many lessons and perspectives (Young, 2000). A principal driver of change was the establishment of a disciplined approach to measuring organizational performance and holding senior managers accountable for attaining specific performance targets. This emphasis on performance and outcomes fueled an investment in robust information systems, including systemwide implementation of a fully integrated EHR. Underlying all these efforts was a commitment to implementing evidence-based clinical and management practices in order to ensure the best possible quality of care.

Performance Measurement to Drive Value in the VHA

Health care quality became a serious topic of public discussion in the 1990s. The traditional framework for assessing the performance of health care organizations has been that of Donabedian (1996): *structure*, defined as those features that determine capability to deliver care, such as staffing and facilities; *process*, the actual care provided; and *outcome*, the health state of the patient that results from the care received. Although outcome measures represent the desired end results of health care, evidence-based process measures (those health care activities shown scientifically to result in improved patient outcomes) have dominated most of the measurement systems that are reported to consumers, payers, and regulators, because they represent actions under the immediate control of health care providers, require less observation time, and can be assessed with reasonable precision by using samples of patients (Rubin, Pronovost, & Diette, 2001). In contrast, outcome measures were seen as more dependent on factors outside the control of the health system, such as patient case mix or socioeconomic status, for which risk adjustment is often not yet adequate (Lilford, Brown, & Nicholl, 2007).

VHA stakeholders demanded to know that the public's investment in the care of veterans was achieving consistently high levels of technical quality and, in addition, addressing patient-centered needs for timely access, coordination, and involvement in their care. Accordingly, VHA leadership committed to objectively demonstrate equal or better value than what was offered by the private sector. Value was conceptualized as a function of five domains: access to care, quality of care, patient functional status, and customer satisfaction, divided by the cost or price of the care (Kizer & Dudley, 2010):

Value = (Access + Quality + Functional Status + Satisfaction) ÷ Cost.

Although the quotient was never actually calculated, in practice, this conceptual model strongly informed the shape of performance measurement. Each of the five domains of value became a dimension within the VHA's organizational scorecard, with no single dimension optimized at the expense of others. This thinking was further embedded in a new performance management system launched in 1995 that used standardized metrics and an annual contract with senior health system leaders to clarify expectations, communicate priorities, and quantify progress toward strategic goals. VISNs became the VHA's fundamental unit of operations and accountability, although performance contracts were expected to be translated down to smaller operating units such as medical centers and the larger community-based clinics. Feedback on performance (for example, adherence to evidence-based clinical guidelines) was shared with clinicians on a regular basis and provided a strong stimulus to improvement, consistent with the literature on audit and feedback (Jamtvedt, Young, Kristofferson, O'Brien, & Oxman, 2006). Although senior executive compensation was partly dependent on achieving performance goals, individual clinicians were not subject to pay-for-performance until Congress passed the Health Care Personnel Enhancement Act of 2004 (P.L. 108-445), which made provisions for market and performance-based pay adjustments for physicians.

Performance measurement began modestly, and the initial performance plan included only 10 metrics, many of which were structural (for example, establishing primary care teams) or process oriented (for example, checking annually the level of glycosylated hemoglobin in diabetics in order to assess glucose control). Once the power of setting performance expectations became evident, and additional organizational priorities were identified and agreed on by senior leadership, the number of performance measures quickly grew. This included evidence-based measures endorsed by external groups such as the National Committee on Quality Assurance (NCQA). The VHA performance plan incorporated measures from NCQA's Healthcare Effectiveness Data and Information Set (HEDIS), such as rates of immunization for influenza and pneumococcal pneumonia (both examples of process measures), and inter-mediate outcome measures, such as levels of blood pressure and cholesterol in patients with ischemic heart disease (see http://www.ncqa.org/tabid/187/default.aspx). Choosing to adopt externally endorsed measure systems such as HEDIS had two effects: It validated the measures the VHA chose for assessing value, and it allowed direct comparison (benchmarking) between the VHA and private sector performance.

The impact of monitoring, feedback, and reward of senior executives for reaching quality targets was substantial; within a few years, VHA clinical per-formance had overtaken and surpassed private sector comparators, particularly for those indicators that were directly measured (Asch et al., 2004; Jha, Perlin, Kizer, & Dudley, 2003). One concern about performance measurement is the potential for "teaching to the test," but in the case of the VHA, more than just the specific measures improved. For instance, Asch et al. (2004) identified a "halo effect," in which all the indicated care processes for a given care process, such as diabetes care, showed improvement, even if only a portion were being actively tracked. Performance measurement in the VHA, it appears, created real change in underlying systems and practices of care, which allowed the gains to be sustained over time (Ross et al., 2008). Today, more than 300 measures are tracked by the VHA and incorporated either directly into performance con-tracts or used as less formal operating monitors. As originally designed, perfor-mance *measures* were used for rating senior executive and agency performance, focused on indicators of health care quality, and had specific targets and goals. *Monitors*, on the other hand, included a growing number of indicators related to compliance with agency policy and other government requirements as well as measures that were tracked to ensure stable or continually improving performance for areas not specified in the performance contract. In practice, however, VHA leaders are held accountable for addressing unfavorable varia-tion among any of these indicator sets. In 2009, senior clinical executives were directly accountable for 120 measures in their performance contracts, includ-ing 81 measures of clinical quality, 29 measures of access, seven measures of functional status, and three measures of patient satisfaction. That current VHA performance continues to compare quite favorably with Medicare, Medicaid, and commercial health plans is shown in Table 21-1.

Table 21-1: Veterans Administration (VA) and Healthcare Effectiveness Data and Information Set (HEDIS) Clinical Quality Comparisons

Clinical Indicator	VA Average 2009 (%)[a]	VA Average 2008 (%)[a]	HEDIS Commercial 2008 (%)[b]	HEDIS Medicare 2008 (%)[b]
Breast cancer screening	87	87	70	68
Cervical cancer screening	92	92	80	N/A
Cholesterol management for patients with cardiovascular conditions				
LDL < 100 mg/dL	67	66	60	57
LDL-C screening	96	94	89	89
Colorectal cancer screening	80	79	59	53
Comprehensive diabetes care				
Blood pressure control (<140/90)	80	78	66	60
Eye exams	88	86	57	61
HbA1c testing	98	97	89	88
LDL-C control (<100 mg/dL)	69	68	46	49
LDL-C screening	96	95	85	86
Medical attention for nephropathy	95	93	82	88
Poor HbA1c control	16	16	28	29
Controlling high blood pressure	77	75	63	59
Flu shots for adults				
Age 50–64	69	69	50	N/A
Age 65 and older[c,d]	83	84	N/A	71
Smoking cessation				
Advising smokers to quit[e]	96	89	77	N/A
Discussing medications[e]	90	84	54	N/A
Discussing strategies	96	92	50	N/A
Immunizations: Pneumococcal[c,d]	95	94	N/A	67

Note: Because of population differences and methodology variations, not all HEDIS measures are comparable to VA measures. Therefore, this is not a comprehensive list of indicators, but this comparison does contain those indicators that are closely aligned in content and methodology. LDL = low-density lipoprotein.
[a]VA comparison data are obtained by abstracting medical record data using similar methodologies to matched HEDIS methodologies. There are noted differences in eligibility and exclusions for end of life care.
[b]HEDIS data were obtained from the 2009 State of Health Care Quality Report, available on the National Committee for Quality Assurance (NCQA) Web site: http://www.ncqa.org.
[c]Behavioral Risk Factor Surveillance System (BRFSS) reports are available on the CDC Web site: http://www.cdc.gov.
[d]BRFSS Survey scores are median scores. VA Scores are averages obtained by medical record abstraction.
[e]HEDIS is obtained by survey. VA is obtained by medical record abstraction.

Many of the VHA's core clinical quality measures, such as Joint Commission ORYX (see http://www.jointcommission.org/PerformanceMeasurement/PerformanceMeasurementSystems) measures for inpatient care and outpatient HEDIS measures, require close review of clinical documentation and are obtained through human abstraction (albeit currently from an electronic rather than a paper-based record). Because of the cost of abstraction, VHA performance for those areas is calculated from a probability sample limited to approximately 350,000 veteran users, which allows for reasonably precise estimates of performance at the level of individual facilities or divisions, but insufficient data to rate individual clinicians. (VHA facilities use a variety of means to assess individual physicians, ranging from peer review to locally developed electronic tracking systems.) With improvements in the EHR (discussed later) and data standardization, performance measures are increasingly being generated directly from electronic data systems and based on full samples of defined populations.

In the 1990s, VHA clinicians and researchers began to develop methods to track certain patient-level outcomes using robust internal clinical risk-adjustment models derived from observing large cohorts of veterans. For example, the National Surgical Quality Improvement Program provided risk-adjusted surgical mortality and complication rates (expressed as a ratio of observed to expected events) to facility, VISN, and national clinical leaders, along with consultative site visits and other opportunities for sharing best practices. Other outcomes, such as a reduction in harm as a result of medical care, were pursued less through measurement than through system interventions, such as the introduction of bar coding for medication administration and the establishment of a National Center for Patient Safety, which emphasized careful root cause analysis of untoward events rather than the blame or punishment of individuals (Weeks & Bagian, 2000).

From the patient's perspective, other outcomes, such as improved function or satisfaction with care, can be critical. The measurement of functional status in clinical settings has been a challenge, as clinician-administered functional status instruments imposed time demands on staff and were not widely adopted outside of research settings, except for specific groups of high-risk veterans. Although more generic health assessments such as the Short Form-36 and Short Form-12 have been administered in the VHA via mailed surveys to assess the larger population of ambulatory care users (Jones et al., 2001), using such surveys on a recurring basis for purposes of performance measurement imposes considerable burden on respondents and comes at a high cost, so their use has been limited to date. Self administered assessment questionnaires using Web-based or computer kiosk technologies at the point of care may overcome these barriers.

With regard to satisfaction, the VHA has had an extensive program of assessing patient perceptions of the inpatient or outpatient services via mailed questionnaires. Beginning in 1995, using the proprietary Picker-Commonwealth patient satisfaction survey, the VHA was able to demonstrate early gains in veteran satisfaction with overall quality, access, coordination of care, and communication with physicians and nurses. However, because this instrument was never widely adopted by the private sector, benchmarking proved difficult. In 2009, the VHA switched to the Consumer Assessment of Health Providers and Systems survey tool, which has the advantage of being a public-domain instrument that is widely used in the health industry, allowing for comparative benchmarking (see http://www.cahps.ahrq.gov).

Progress in the final domain of value, cost, has also been challenging to quantify. Initially, the VHA experienced significant gains in operational efficiency by closing unneeded beds and divesting non-health care–related assets such as golf courses, fire stations, and laundries (Kizer & Dudley, 2009). Improved primary care access was believed to result in a reduction in costs per patient, although critics contend the larger impact may have been the enrollment of healthier veterans who came to the VHA to take advantage of its pharmacy benefits, while continuing to rely on private health plan or Medicare benefits for inpatient care (Oliver, 2007). Nonetheless, when the actual costs of specific episodes of care are examined in depth, it appeared that the VHA had a significant cost advantage compared with Medicare fee-for-service (Nugent, Hendricks, Nugent, & Render, 2004), in part because of lower pharmacy costs. (The VHA leverages its purchasing power and its National Formulary to extract deep discounts from pharmaceutical suppliers, something that Medicare is currently not permitted to do.)

VHA's Integrated EHR

The health information infrastructure in the United States was historically designed to support financial and administrative tasks such as charge capture and billing. Because this infrastructure was not originally designed to encompass the development and implementation of EHRs, relatively few physicians or hospitals have implemented EHRs so far (DesRoches et al., 2008). In contrast, because the VHA was both funder and provider, it has had the latitude to develop health information systems to directly support patient care. In the early 1980s, clinicians and programmers began working together to create the Decentralized Hospital Computer Program, one of the first EHR systems to support multiple health care sites and settings. Over time, continuous innovation and improvement of this system led to the system now known as the

Veterans Health Information Systems and Technology Architecture (VistA), an assemblage of more than 100 software applications that support clinical, financial, and administrative functions. Access to VistA was made possible through a graphical user interface known as the Computerized Patient Record System (CPRS). Nationwide implementation of CPRS/VistA was mandated in 1997 and completed by December 1999. A decade later, the VHA remains one of a handful of benchmark institutions that have successfully implemented the EHR and begun using the data captured in the process of clinical care to measure health system performance (Chaudhry et al., 2006; Congressional Budget Office, 2009).

VHA providers now work within an entirely paperless environment, accessing patient information gathered anywhere in the VHA, updating a patient's medical history as needed, directly placing orders, and reviewing test results wherever they can securely access a computer. Embedded decision support, such as clinical alerts, notifications of test results, and prompts for evidence-based interventions such as disease screening and health prevention, promote both the delivery and measurement of evidence-based practices, including measures that support wellness, such as counseling for at-risk drinking and physical activity. Electronic capture of key clinical information in CPRS/VistA facilitates many aspects of measurement, including collection of clinically relevant variables needed for specific patient registries (for example, automated registries of veterans with HIV or hepatitis C can be generated by using laboratory data extracts), outcomes assessment using risk adjustment, and measurement of health disparities. Recent examples of these approaches include the construction of a longitudinal diabetes registry that tracks improvements in glucose control among a specific cohort (Kupersmith et al., 2007), assessment of risk-adjusted mortality in critically ill veterans (Render et al., 2008), tracking of the relationship of nurse staffing to inpatient mortality (Sales et al., 2008), and the identification of care disparities among veterans with mental illness (Frayne et al., 2005; Kilbourne, Welsh, McCarthy, Post, & Blow, 2008).

As an early adopter of the EHR, the VHA offers many lessons for the U.S. health care system. Although the up-front investment and maintenance costs have been considerable, the benefits of ensuring 100 percent availability of the medical records, avoidance of duplicative testing, and support of evidence-based practice (Hynes et al., 2010) have been estimated, on the basis of computerized cost–benefit modeling, to have yielded a potential cumulative benefit net of costs of more than $3 billion by 2007 (Byrne et al., 2010). Furthermore, EHRs offer an unprecedented ability to engage patients and families more directly. For example, in 2003, the VHA introduced the next phase of the EHR, My Health*e*Vet (see http://www.myhealth.va.gov), a Web-based personal health record designed to give veterans access to their own health care data and empower them to play a more active role in their health. The full functionality of My Health*e*Vet will permit veterans to plan and coordinate their own care on line, refill medications, view laboratory and diagnostic test results, and communicate with their health care team via encrypted e-mail. This move toward "virtual health care" has the potential to transform the delivery of health care in the 21st century as profoundly as the move from hospital care to primary care in the late 20th century.

Evidence-based Practice in the VHA

Thoughtful observers believe that improving health outcomes may rely more on implementing known evidence than in making investments in new discovery (Woolf, 2008). Such knowledge-translation or implementation activities have been strongly supported in the VHA and have made an important contribution to the improvement of health care quality. Many VHA performance measures (for example, those related colorectal and breast cancer screening and diabetes care) are themselves the direct embodiment of the commitment to evidence-based practice guidelines, deriving from a structured approach to synthesizing scientific evidence into specific recommendations for clinical care, a process that the VHA does in collaboration with the Department of Defense in order to ensure clinical relevance to needs of veterans (Francis & Perlin, 2006).

Summarizing and presenting scientific knowledge in the form of clinical practice guidelines and other dissemination vehicles is an important first step, but alone, it is insufficient to change the behavior of health care providers or systems. (As defined by the Institute of Medicine, *clinical practice guidelines* are systematically developed statements to assist practitioner and patient decisions about appropriate health care for specific clinical circumstances. VHA clinical practice guidelines adhere to inclusion criteria specified by the National Guideline Clearinghouse [see http://www.guideline.gov]). Recognizing the difficulties of translating research into practice, in 1998, the VHA made a significant investment in the nascent science of implementation, launching a Quality Enhancement Research Initiative (QUERI) program that facilitates active participation and collaboration among a multidisciplinary group of VA researchers, managers, and other stakeholders to ensure that research activities can be purposely linked to clinical care in as close to real time as possible.

QUERI activities typically are focused on a defined population (for example, specific QUERI centers have been established to improve outcomes of veterans with diabetes, spinal cord injury, ischemic heart disease, serious mental illness, and other high-profile conditions such as HIV) and prioritized to address quality or outcome gaps identified through performance measurement or the EHR (see http://www.queri.research.va.gov). QUERI has provided a structured, disciplined approach to implementation and measurement (see Table 21-2) to ensure that its efforts yield durable insights into the best means to translate evidence into clinical and management practice (Stetler, Mittman, & Francis, 2008). The engagement of researchers interested in accelerating the implementation of evidence-based care with VHA clinicians and leadership has facilitated the introduction of many evidence-based practices, with many activities directly related to patient outcomes or evidence-based process measures. In addition, QUERI projects have provided many important insights into the process of health system improvement that can be generalized to other situations. These include the critical importance of facilitation (Stetler et al., 2006), as well as the resource intensity and organizational cost of quality improvement work (Liu et al., 2009).

Table 21-2: Steps in the Veterans Administration Quality Enhancement Research Initiative Process

Step and Phase	Action
1	Select conditions per patient populations associated with high risk of disease, disability, and/or burden of illness for veterans
2	Identify evidence-based guidelines, recommendations, and best practices
3	Measure and diagnose quality and performance gaps
4	Implement improvement programs
Phase 1	Pilot projects (single site) to develop intervention and evaluate feasibility
Phase 2	Multisite clinical demonstration to refine intervention for large-scale deployment
Phase 3	Regional rollout (3–5 VISNs)
Phase 4	National rollout of tested, refined strategy
5 (Applied to each of above Phases)	Assess improvement program feasibility, implementation, and impacts on patient, family, and health care system processes and outcomes
6 (Applied to each of above Phases)	Assess improvement program impacts on health-related quality of life

Note: VISN = Veterans Integrated Service Network.

New Challenges for a 21st-Century VA

As in the mid-1990s, the debates regarding health care access, quality, costs, and outcomes in the United States are prompting reexamination of the role and value of VHA health care. Although the VHA continues to demonstrate superior performance in providing recommended ambulatory and acute inpatient services, continued homelessness among veterans (see http://www.va.gov/HOMELESS/chaleng.asp), instances of inadequate specialty care (Bogdanich, 2010), high suicide rates among combat veterans (Bowser, 2008), and gaps in provision of women's health services (Government Accountability Office, 2009) have drawn the attention of Congress, the public, and the VHA itself. Although some of these criticisms are based on anecdotal material rather than fair outcome comparisons, others note that the VHA may have become a "victim of its own success" (Oliver, 2007) as a result of rising public expectations and increased demands on the system from the growth of users such as veterans returning from multiple deployments in Iraq and Afghanistan.

In addition, the clientele served by the VHA is changing. The combat injuries are different; body armor now protects soldiers from gunshots, and the majority of serious wounds in Iraq and Afghanistan now are the result of blast injury from improvised explosive devices. Blast injuries are "polytraumatic" in nature, involving various combinations of brain injury, hearing or vision loss, limb amputation, pain, and posttraumatic stress disorder. This has required rethinking the underlying care platform and moving away from a physician-driven, primary-care model toward more comprehensive team-based approaches that engage both patients and their families in a "medical home," as well as new and different measures of patient, organizational, and systems measures of outcomes and performance. Other changes are evident among the veterans themselves: They are more likely to be female (women now constitute 14 percent of the military), computer savvy, accustomed to near-instant service, and empowered to challenge authority. The aggregate impact of all these developments is creating significant pressure to transform a care delivery system originally designed for a largely male, World War II– or Vietnam-era population toward one that is more client centered, oriented toward timeliness and consistency of access, and proactive with communication and outreach (Shinseki, 2009).

Most veterans have access to, and in fact receive, care from sources in addition to those available from the VA (Congressional Budget Office, 2009). While the trajectory of 21st-century health care reform cannot be predicted, it is likely that veterans will continue to have a choice of where to go for care, and that they and their families will make their health care decisions on the basis of what they learn by consulting the Internet, as they now do for other types of decisions. In contrast to the VHA transformation of the 1990s, which relied on the internal feedback of performance to system leaders and clinicians, the transformation of the 21st-century VHA will require a new approach to performance measurement, in which the motivation derives less from performance contracts and internal reporting, and more from transparency and public reporting of comparative performance. Transparency and public reporting, widely believed to be transforming principles for health care (Leape, 2010), began in earnest in the VHA in 2008 with the reporting of site-specific performance data using a patient-friendly Web site (see http://www.qualityofcare.va.gov). This was followed in 2009 by the online publication of detailed facility-level statistics (see http://www.va.gov/health/HospitalReportCard.asp), and subsequently the posting of comparative hospital performance data on the Department of Health and Human Services' Hospital Compare Web site (http://www.hospitalcompare.hhs.gov). By providing credible and understandable comparisons of its performance with that of other health providers, both public and private, it is hoped that the VHA can maintain the trust of veterans, families, and the American taxpayer, and inspire others to learn from its health care delivery experiences.

Lessons for the VHA and Other Organizations

It is a management truism that what gets measured gets managed, and the VHA experience with performance measurement highlights how the commitment to measuring value can transform health care. There is also a downside evident in the VHA's performance measurement journey. The complexity of the current performance measurement system makes it a challenge for managers and clinicians to focus their time and attention on a limited number of priorities. Despite strong quantitative evidence that evidence-based processes have increased in frequency, it is less clear that outcomes have changed. Arguably, the measures themselves are defined primarily by professional rather than patient-centered values (client-centered measures of health care quality are still in their infancy), and recent studies of health consumers (not veterans) have highlighted significant misunderstandings regarding evidence-based care and quality (Carman et al., 2010).

For these reasons, it is important that human services organizations realize that measurement alone cannot guarantee positive client outcomes. Measures are one tool for guiding transformation, but equally important are accountable leaders who set clear priorities and expectations and ensure that financial incentives do not create counterproductive behaviors. Other enabling factors include robust and clinically relevant information systems and the organizational capacity to generate and implement new knowledge. The interaction of these factors in a dynamic environment that balances local innovation with centralized strategy is likely to be an additional critical element. The active and intense dialogue among the policy, clinical, academic, and veteran communities has enhanced the VHA's capacity to adapt to changing circumstances and argues for its ability to continue serving veterans well into the 21st century. To the extent that health care reform in the United States adopts similar strategies, the VHA experience holds valuable lessons for others.

References

Asch, S. M., McGlynn, E. A., Hogan, M., Hayward, R. A., Shekelle, P., Rubenstein, L., et al. (2004). Comparison of quality of care for patients in the Veterans Health Administration and patients in a national sample. *Annals of Internal Medicine, 141,* 938–945.

Bogdanich, W. (2010, January 26). As technology surges, radiation safeguards lag. *New York Times,* p. A1.

Bowser, B. A. (2008, November 10). Military, VA confront rising suicide rates among troops. *The NewsHour with Jim Lehrer* [Television broadcast]. New York and Washington, DC: Public Broadcasting Service.

Byrne, C. M., Mercincavage, L. M., Pan, E. C., Vincent, A. G., Johnston, D. S., & Middleton, B. (2010). The value from investments in health information technology at the U.S. Department of Veterans Affairs. *Health Affairs, 29,* 1–10.

Carman, K. L., Maurer, M., Yegian, J. M., Dardess, P., McGee, J., Evers, M., & Marlo, K. O. (2010). Evidence that consumers are skeptical about evidence based health care. *Health Affairs, 29,* 1–7.

Chaudhry, B., Wang, J., Wu, S., Maglione, M., Mojica, W., Roth, E., Morton, S. C., & Shekelle, P. G. (2006). Systematic review: Impact of health information technology on quality, efficiency, and costs of medical care. *Annals of Internal Medicine, 144,* 742–752.

Congressional Budget Office. (2009). *Quality initiative undertaken by the Veterans Health Administration* (Publication No. 3234). Retrieved from http://www.cbo.gov/doc.cfm?index=10453

Department of Veterans Affairs. (2005). *VA history in brief.* Retrieved from http://www.va.gov/opa/publications/archives/docs/history_in_brief.pdf

DesRoches, C. M., Campbell, E. G., Rao, S. R., Donelan, K., Ferris, T. G., Jha, A., et al. (2008). Electronic health records in ambulatory care: A national survey of physicians. *New England Journal of Medicine, 359,* 50–60.

Donabedian, A. (1996). Evaluating quality of medical care. *Milbank Quarterly, 10*, 477–483.

Francis, J., & Perlin, J. B. (2006). Improving performance through knowledge translation in the Veterans Health Administration. *Journal of Continuing Education in the Health Professions, 26*, 63–71.

Frayne, S. M., Halanych, J. M., Miller, D. R., Wang, F., Lin, H., Pogach, L., et al. (2005). Disparities in diabetes care: Impact of mental illness. *Archives of Internal Medicine, 165*, 2631–2638.

Government Accountability Office. (2009). *Preliminary findings on VA's provision of health care services to women veterans* (Publication No. GAO-09-899T). Washington, DC: Author.

Henderson, W. G., Lavori, P. W., Peduzzi, P., Collins, J. F., Sather, M. R., & Feussner, J. R. (2001). Cooperative Studies Program, U.S. Department of Veterans Affairs. In C. R. Redmond & T. Colton (Eds.), *Biostatistics in clinical trials* (pp. 99–115). New York: John Wiley & Sons.

Hynes, D. M., Weddle, T., Smith, N., Whittier, E., Atkins, D., & Francis, J. (2010). Use of health information technology to advance evidence-based care: Lessons from the VA QUERI program. *Journal of General Internal Medicine, 25*(Suppl. 1), 44–49.

Jamtvedt, G., Young, J. M., Kristofferson, D. T., O'Brien, M. A., & Oxman, A. D. (2006). Audit and feedback: Effects on professional practice and health care outcomes. *Cochrane Database of Systematic Reviews, 19*, CD000259.

Jha, A. K., Perlin, J. B., Kizer, K. W., &. Dudley, R. A. (2003). Effect of the transformation of the Veterans Affairs health care system on the quality of care. *New England Journal of Medicine, 348*, 2218–2227.

Jones, D., Kazis, L., Lee, A., Rogers, W., Skinner, K., Cassar, L., et al. (2001). Health status assessments using the Veterans SF-36 and SF-12: Methods for evaluating outcomes in the Veterans Health Administration. *Journal of Ambulatory Care Management, 24*, 1–19.

Kilbourne, A. M., Welsh, D., McCarthy, J. F., Post, E. P., & Blow, F. C. (2008). Quality of care for cardiovascular disease-related conditions in patients with and without mental disorders. *Journal of General Internal Medicine, 23*, 1628–1633.

Kizer, K. W., & Dudley, R. A. (2009). Extreme makeover: Transformation of the veterans health care system. *Annual Review of Public Health, 30*, 313–339.

Kupersmith, J., Francis, J., Kerr, E., Krein, S., Pogach, L., Kolodner, R. M., & Perlin, J. B. (2007). Advancing evidence-based care for diabetes: Lessons from the Veterans Health Administration. *Health Affairs, 26*, w156–w168.

Leape, L. L. (2010). *Transparency and public reporting are essential for a safe health care system* (Commonwealth Fund Publication No. 1381). Washington, DC: Commonwealth Fund.

Lilford, R. J., Brown, C. A., & Nicholl, J. (2007). Use of process measures to monitor the quality of clinical practice. *British Medical Journal, 335,* 648–650.

Liu, C. F., Rubenstein, L.V., Kirchner, J. E., Fortney, J. C., Perkins, M.W., Ober, S. K., et al. (2009) Organizational cost of quality improvement for depression care. *Health Services Research, 44,* 225–244.

Nugent, G. N., Hendricks, A., Nugent, L., & Render, M. L. (2004). Value for taxpayer's dollars: What VA care would cost at Medicare prices. *Medical Care Research and Review, 61,* 495–508.

Oliver, A. (2007). The Veterans Health Administration: An American success story? *Milbank Quarterly, 55,* 5–35.

Render, M. L., Deddens, J., Freyberg, R., Almenoff, P., Connors, A.F., Wagner, D., & Hofer, T. P. (2008). Veterans Affairs intensive care unit risk adjustment model: Validation, updating, recalibration. *Critical Care Medicine, 36,* 1031–1042.

Ross, J. S., Keyhani, S., Keenan, P. S., Bernheim, S. M., Penrod, J. D., Boockvar, K. S., et al. (2008). Use of recommended ambulatory care services: Is the Veterans Affairs quality gap narrowing? *Archives of Internal Medicine, 168,* 950–958.

Rubin, H. R., Pronovost, P., & Diette, G. B. (2001). The advantages and disadvantages of process-based measures of health care quality. *International Journal for Quality in Health Care, 13,* 469–474.

Sales, A., Sharp, N., Li, Y. F., Lowy, E., Greiner, G., Liu, C. F., et al. (2008). The association between nursing factors and patient mortality: The view from the nursing unit level. *Medical Care, 46,* 938–945.

Shinseki, E. K. (2009, January 14). *Hearing on presumptive nomination of General Eric K. Shinseki, to be Secretary of Veterans Affairs. Opening statement of Eric K. Shinseki , Secretary-designate of Veterans Affairs before the Committee on Veterans Affairs, United States Senate.* Washington, DC: U.S. Senate Committee on Veterans' Affairs.

Stetler, C. B., Legro, M.W., Rycroft-Malone, J., Bowman, C., Curran, G., Guihan, M., et al. (2006). Role of "external facilitation" in implementation of research findings: A qualitative evaluation of facilitation experiences in the Veterans Health Administration. *Implementation Science, 1,* 23. Retrieved from www.implementationscience.com/content/1/1/23

Stetler, C. B., Mittman, B. S., & Francis, J. (2008). Overview of the VA Quality Enhancement Research Initiative (QUERI). *Implementation Science, 3*, 8. Retrieved from www.implementationscience.com/content/3/1/8

Weeks, W. B., & Bagian, J. P. (2000, November/December). Developing a culture of safety in the Veterans Health Administration. *Effective Clinical Practice*. Retrieved from www.acponline.org/clinical_information/journals_publications/ecp/novdec00/weeks.htm

Woolf, S. H. (2008). The meaning of translational research and why it matters. *JAMA, 299*, 211–213.

Young, G. (2000). Managing organizational transformations: Lessons from the Veterans Health Administration. *California Management Review, 43*, 66–82.

CHAPTER 22

Measuring Outcomes in Criminal Justice

Susan Turner

The criminal justice system in the United States casts a wide net over the country's population. According to recent Pew Center on the State reports, one out of every 100 Americans is incarcerated in jail or prison (Pew Center on the States, 2008); one in 33 is under some form of correctional control (Pew Center on the States, 2009). In 2008, of the estimated 1.38 million violent crimes committed, 600,000 resulted in arrests (Federal Bureau of Investigation [FBI], 2010). Correctional budgets consume large portions of states' general funds: In California, the California Department of Corrections and Rehabilitation budget is more than $8 billion, serving more than 300,000 offenders in prison and on parole (California Department of Correction and Rehabilitation [CDCR], 2009).

How do we measure the outcomes of such a large and expensive system? This chapter discusses how outcomes are measured in criminal justice. It begins with a discussion of the criminal justice system, followed by traditional outcome measures of crime and recidivism, recent efforts to move beyond traditional outcomes, dissemination of best practices for good outcomes, and challenges in the measurement of outcomes. It concludes with a short discussion of what other sectors in human services can learn from outcomes measurement in criminal justice.

The U.S. Criminal Justice System

The main agencies involved in the criminal justice system are the police; prosecution, courts, and defense; jails; probation; prison and parole; and other governmental and private agencies that partner with each of these, including education, vocational, health, mental health, substance use, and social services. The criminal justice system is called a system for a very good reason. Each of the decision points is linked with the next, with outcomes in one sector of the system affecting the operations of others down the line. For example, once a person is arrested by the police, they work up the case for the prosecutor, who determines whether to proceed with the case. If police policies change to focus on a particular issue, say drug sweeps, this affects workload and case processing of the prosecutor's office. Whether the prosecutor decides to proceed with the case affects the courts; the more prosecutor dismissals, the less the court workload, and so on.

The entry point for many into the system is arrest by a law enforcement officer. Depending on the seriousness of the crime, individuals may be booked into a jail and either released (on bail or their own recognizance) or remain in jail awaiting the outcome of their case. In the United States, approximately one half of all persons in jails are there awaiting trial; in other words, they have not been convicted of any crimes. Not all persons who are arrested for crimes are convicted. Statistics show approximately 27 adults are sentenced for every 100 crimes (Clear, Cole, & Reisig, 2008), although conviction rates for felonies are higher (Bureau of Justice Statistics [BJS], 2004b). When individuals are not convicted, it is generally because their cases are dismissed for lack of evidence; a small percentage is acquitted at trial. Those who are convicted generally face one of two sanctions: to remain in the community, generally under some form of community supervision with terms and conditions they abide by, or they are incarcerated in either jails (generally reserved for sentences less than year) or state-level incarceration, in other words, prison. Virtually all prisoners are released from prison back into the community at some point, often under some form of postrelease community supervision, often known as parole (Petersilia, 2003; Travis, 2005).

In addition to each state's criminal justice system, the federal system is responsible for processing and supervising defendants charged with federal crimes. The state and federal systems operate independently; the federal system is smaller, with approximately 300,000 in prison or on probation or parole as compared with almost 7 million state offenders (BJS, 2004a). This chapter concentrates on state justice systems, although concepts and outcomes are applicable to the federal system as well.

Traditional/Historical Outcome Measures

Crime rates and offender recidivism, two major outcomes with which the public is familiar, are also two of the most traditional measurement domains in the criminal justice field. The most frequently used indicator of the crime rate is that published by the FBI as part of the Uniform Crime Reporting Program. Approximately 17,000 law enforcement jurisdictions collect information on reported crimes, which is sent electronically to the FBI and compiled annually in statistical publications. Part I crimes—the most serious—are the focus of most media and public concerns and are often used to gauge the state of crime in the nation. These offenses include homicide, forcible rape, robbery, aggravated assault, burglary, larceny theft, motor vehicle theft, and arson (FBI, 2010). For these offenses, data on both crimes reported and arrests are gathered and reported. Rates are generally represented as the number of crimes per 100,000 population, allowing comparisons to be made between states, counties, and cities. Such comparisons are used, for example, by *Forbes Magazine* to determine winners of the America's Safest Cities award.

Crime rates tell us little about an individual offender's successful return to society after having had a case handled in the criminal justice system. The most common outcome for an individual is referred to as *recidivism*. Despite its common use, there exists no agreed-on and consistently used definition of this word. Recidivism can mean a number of different things, in terms of both the behavior and the length of time during which the recidivism is measured. For example, a new arrest may be considered recidivism. For probationers and parolees—who must abide by terms and conditions of their community supervision—a frequently used measure is a technical violation of these terms. Violations of these terms are not necessarily new law violations (for example, failure to report to probation officer or parole agent, failure to obtain a job), but they are sanctioned by the justice system in their efforts to hold offenders accountable in the community.

Oftentimes, the data available drive the choice of a measure to use. For example, in California, prisoner recidivism has historically been measured as return to the CDCR (either for a new crime or a technical violation) because the CDCR has readily available data on who enters and leaves their prison system. The BJS, whose mission is to "collect, analyze, publish, and disseminate information on crime, criminal offenders, victims of crime, and the operation of justice systems at all levels of government" (BJS, 2010), often uses a three-year window for recidivism. The different definitions result in "apples and oranges" comparisons, quite unlike discussions of the crime rate in which states use consistent definitions for crimes.

Focus on Additional Agency-Level Outcomes

Both crime rates and recidivism are coarse measures of agency and offender behavior. Recent efforts by agencies, in particular, have tried to move the conversation beyond these traditional measures into ones more closely aligned with agency goals and practices. These efforts can be seen as part of the movement toward total quality management and "reinventing government" that has been occurring in public agencies over the past two decades (Osborne & Gaebler, 1992).

Such a focus is seen in landmark compilation of discussion papers sponsored by the BJS and Princeton University, which challenged the justice system's focus on crime rates and recidivism. Nationally recognized authors presented new visions of outcomes for components of the justice system (police, prosecutors, courts, community corrections, prisons) that go beyond measures of crime rates and recidivism, such as recognizing four civic duties of doing justice, promoting secure communities, providing restitution to crime victims, and promoting noncriminal options. Of particular note is a common theme among the authors: Components of the justice system should be measured not by distal outcomes—those far in the future— but by the processes in which they are engaged. For example, Logan (1993) argues that prisons should focus on tasks associated with the business of confining offenders, such as security, safety, order, care, and activities (such as educational and vocational training, treatment). These measures are of what happens within the prison walls, not outside them, quite unlike recidivism, which focuses on behavior after an offender has left the prison. Education, training, and work are seen not as tools for rehabilitation, but as opportunities for inmates who will make productive use of them.

Using outcomes that are realistically under the sphere of influence, competence, and accountability of community corrections is also apparent in Petersilia's (1993) measures for success. Rather than using postsupervision recidivism as the major measure, she recommends measures such as assessing individual's suitability for placement, capturing contacts and supervision of offenders, payment of restitution, participation in programming, and other required activities, with indicators of parole violation and arrests only during the time the offender is under supervision.

Outcome measures serve another important need in community corrections, whose budgets are often slighted at the expense of institutional programs: If community corrections agencies have established mission statements and derived performance measures for which they can show success, they are less vulnerable to budget cuts.

One of the more publicized measurement systems has been the Comp-Stat (Computer Statistics) model, which was developed by Commissioner Bill Bratton of the New York Police Department. Key principles of CompStat are accurate and timely intelligence, rapid deployment of resources, effective tactics, and relentless follow-up and assessment (Burrell & Gelb, 2007). Using a heavy reliance on mapping crime in the city, New York City CompStat has been credited for much of the reduction in crime in the city in the 1990s. CompStat provides the basis for a continuous evaluation of an agency's performance in which statistics on key indicators are compiled and reviewed in weekly sessions. Executive and senior managers attend these sessions, and unit commanders are held accountable for outcomes in their jurisdictions.

The CompStat principles have begun to be incorporated in other criminal justice agencies. The Pew Charitable Trusts recently published a report on how to use a CompStat approach for community corrections agencies, which the authors argue has lagged behind in the movement toward performance measurement. Echoing themes of the BJS/Princeton compendium, Burrell and Gelb (2007) suggest that community corrections agencies select a few measureable indicators of success that can be reported on quickly and accurately to help demonstrate they are delivering results and ensure taxpayers are getting a strong return on their investment. Although there are several major components to the CompStat model, the live audits, in which department managers present and review their own and others' performance, are key.

Focus on Additional Individual Offender Outcomes

In keeping with the desire to move beyond crime rates and recidivism as the primary criminal justice agency outcomes, criminal justice has also moved toward assessing offenders in more multidimensional domains, particularly those that are associated with recidivism. Over the past 20 years, a number of instruments have been developed. Many instruments were developed to assess offender's risk of recidivism; however, more recent instruments have been developed to measure risk and needs that are related to criminal behavior. Perhaps the most influential work on this area has been done by Andrews and his colleagues on the psychology of criminal conduct model. This model is a combination of social learning, cognitive–behavioral, and social cognition theories, which posits the importance of the "Big Four" variables—antisocial attitudes, antisocial associates, antisocial behavioral history, and antisocial personality—in the prediction and influences on human behavior. These variables are moderated or influenced by other domains of the family, school and work, leisure and neighborhood, and substance use (Andrews & Bonta, 2003, p. 10). This work has given risen to the widely used Level of Service Inventory–Revised (LSI-R; Andrews & Bonta, 1995), consisting of 54 items that measure offender risks and needs that research has shown to be associated with criminal conduct. The LSI-R is used to identify areas for the provision of services, and research has shown that changes in a person's LSI-R score are related to changes in recidivism. What instruments like the LSI-R have also done is broaden the measurement of an offender's performance from distal measures of recidivism to the more proximate outcomes such as attitudes, criminal associates, substance use, educational and vocational attainment, and so on. Of course, the hope is that improvements in these proximal measures will help ensure reductions in ultimate recidivism.

How to Predict Offender Recidivism

Although definitions of recidivism may different, practitioners have been interested in the ability to determine which offenders under their supervision pose the most risk to reoffend. Risk prediction has been a flourishing field since the early 1920s, when early prediction models sought to determine who would succeed or fail on parole (Harcourt, 2007). Now, risk prediction instruments are used at virtually all points in the criminal justice system—from a determination of whether an individual should be released from jail pending their case decision (pretrial release), to classification in a correctional system for violence, to risk to recidivate on probation or parole. A national survey of adult prisons, jails, and community corrections agencies revealed than slightly more than one third use a standardized risk assessment tool to gauge an offender's risk to public safety (Taxman, Cropsey, Young, & Wexler, 2007). The field is far from utilizing a single instrument, although the LSI-R and some version of the Wisconsin tool (Eisenberg, Bryl, & Fabelo, 2009) dominate. Risk assessment tools contain standardized items, often measuring an individual's prior criminal behavior, performance on supervision, and other areas of a person's life (for example, alcohol and drug use, education, employment). Statistical predictions are then made regarding an individual's probability or likelihood of recidivating within some specified time period on the basis of scores on the scale items.

As the field has been moving toward widespread use of risk assessment tools, several issues remain regarding adoption and use. One continues to be the debate about whether actuarial tools (such as the LSI-R) are superior to clinical judgment. Since as far back as the mid-1900s, research has shown actuarial tools to be superior to clinical judgment (Egisdottir et al. 2006; Meehl, 1954). Despite this, many practitioners resist using actuarial tools for prediction, preferring to use their experience, skills, and judgment to predict whether someone will succeed or fail returning to the community after jail or prison (Latessa & Lovins, 2010). Lack of acceptance by practitioners is a major impediment to incorporating risk assessment into ongoing supervision.

A second issue relates to the types of items that are included in risk assessment tools. Earlier tools often used items that are considered static, including age, prior records, and family criminality, factors that cannot be changed. Instruments like the LSI-R include factors referred to as *dynamic*. These are things that can be changed, such as drug use, criminal attitudes, and association with criminal peer groups, factors referred to as *criminogenic needs*, which are correlated with risk of recidivism. Controversy exists over the predictive utility of needs items in the prediction of risk (Baird, 2009). Some suggest that the inclusion of needs items does not increase the ability to predict recidivism, arguing for shorter instruments that include items that are significantly correlated with recidivism (Baird, 2009). Others advocate for the inclusion of both types of factors for the best prediction (Latessa & Lowenkamp, 2005).

Although actuarial tools have thus far been proven to be more accurate than clinical judgment, they are not without error. Tools are not 100 percent accurate. Because they are developed on the basis of groups of individuals with certain characteristics, they are probabilistic. Risk assessment tools being used often rate slightly below good predictability (Turner, Hess, & Janetta, 2009). Some offenders who are predicted to be low risk do recidivate; some offenders who are predicted to be high risk do not. Each type of error has significant ramifications. Those who are predicted not to recidivate and do are known as *false negatives*. Errors of this kind can cause considerable political backlash when, for example, someone who has been released early or placed on a low level of supervision commits a particularly heinous crime. Conversely, the case of an individual who is erroneously predicted to be high risk and is denied opportunities or sanctioned more severely raises concerns about fairness and justice. In addition, instruments with high false positive rates lead to inefficient allocation of scare resources. There is also the concern that increasing efforts to predict future offending result in increasing criminal behavior (Harcourt, 2007).

Identification and Dissemination of Best Practices for Good Outcomes

The drive to achieve positive outcomes in all governmental agencies has spawned an interest in identifying particular programs (for example, drug treatment) and practices (for example, cognitive–behavioral techniques) that are associated with good outcomes for justice system clients. Programs that are geared toward reductions in recidivism can be delivered in a variety of settings, including institutions and in the community (while offenders are under probation or parole supervision). There are a number of ways in which effective programs are identified, with three prominent ones used in criminal justice: meta-analysis, the Colorado *Blueprints for Violence Prevention* (Mihalic, Fagan, Irwin, Ballard & Elliott, 2002), and cost–benefit studies.

Meta-analysis—the analysis of individual study findings in a quantitative manner—has become popular over the past 20 years as a way to increase the rigor of research summaries. In meta-analysis, effect sizes from individual studies are analyzed to determine whether there is an overall treatment effect and whether certain variables may moderate the effect. Numerous meta-analyses have been conducted of correctional programs (for example, drug courts, boot camps). For example, in a recent review, Lipsey (2009) examined more than 540 studies of juvenile programs. Key findings were that higher risk juveniles evidence the largest program effects—a finding that many might find counterintuitive—and that programs implemented with higher quality also produced better recidivism outcomes (Lipsey, 2009).

The Center for the Study and Prevention of Violence at the University of Colorado established the *Blueprints for Violence Prevention*, a list of proven and promising program models that have been shown to be effective in reducing recidivism for youth. For Blueprints to certify a program as proven (that is, a model program), the program must demonstrate its effects on problem behaviors with a rigorous experimental design, show that its effects persist after youth leave the program, and be successfully replicated at least once. In order for a brand name program to be certified as promising, the program must demonstrate effects using a rigorous experimental design. Despite the numerous juvenile programs in operation today, only 11 have been classified as model programs, and only 19 as promising programs by Blueprints (for example, Big Brothers and Big Sisters of America, Multi-Systemic Therapy, and Nurse–Family Partnership).

As criminal justice budgets continue to decline, despite increasing population pressure, practitioners and policymakers search for programs that promise to deliver good outcomes at acceptable costs. The Washington State Institute for Public Policy (WSIPP) is a widely recognized agency that produces cost-effectiveness meta-analyses on correctional programs and practices for adult and juvenile programs and services. WSIPP cost analyses measure the impact of programs on recidivism on the basis of findings from individual studies conducted in the field. For example, estimates of the effect on crime for 21 studies examining drug treatment in prison (therapeutic community or outpatient) show a reduction of 6.4 percent in crime outcomes, with benefits to crime victims of more than $9,000, and benefits to taxpayers of almost $5,000, relative to program costs of slightly more than $1,600, per individual (Drake, Aos, & Miller, 2009).

Challenges in the Measurement of Criminal Justice Outcomes

Although crime rates and recidivism have historically been the most often used metrics, one of the continuing challenges in the field is the definition of outcomes and agreement on common metrics. Fortunately, many agencies are tackling this issue, partly in response to increased pressure to show accountability in public agencies. CompStat, in which benchmarks are established and reported on regularly, is a model that can be utilized not only by police, but also by other justice agencies. A continuing point of difference is the time period of measurement. Does an agency consider as applicable outcomes that are measured during the time an offender is under their jurisdiction, or do they also assume responsibility after jurisdiction has ended? This may be similar to questions asked about treatment for drugs or alcohol: Do treatment providers measure treatment outcomes by successful completion of program components or by long term sobriety after a client has left a program? The answer may be tied to an agency's explicit mission, but even if an agency narrowly scopes its outcomes, the public may demand better long term outcomes as well.

Closely related to the definition of outcomes is the explosion of data by which to report them. Automation and new technology have increased the availability of data that can be used to report outcomes. For example, in 2005, the National Center of State Courts unveiled CourTools, a list of 10 performance measures for court administrators that included time to disposition and collection of monetary penalties (Corbett, 2007). Global positioning systems can show movements of sex offenders 24 hours a day, seven days a week. By using commercial software products, many jurisdictions are able to systematically report on similar outcomes. However, the increased availability of readily accessible data, particularly records concerning financial data, parties to legal proceedings and treatment, has some critics concerned about individuals' privacy (Corbett, 2007; Pattavina & Taxman, 2006). Privacy provisions of the federal Health Insurance Portability and Accountability Act restrict the use of these data if personal identifiers are included; however, the integration of data across systems often requires identifiers. Available data do not always result in increased sharing; interagency competition also occurs because some agencies are unwilling to share data developed and maintained by their group with other components of the justice system. Next steps for corrections might include efforts to systematize outcomes across and within jurisdictions in order to compare outcomes.

What Can Human Services Sectors Learn from Criminal Justice?

Experiences in the use and development of outcome measures in criminal justice may be useful to other human services sectors. Undoubtedly, criminal justice and human services sectors are all affected by the widespread focus on accountability. For example, the No Child Left Behind Act of 2001 (P.L. 104-110) highlights the intensity of efforts across the states to improve educational outcomes for youth in which receipt of federal funds is tied to achievement of measurable goals. The justice system's focus on two primary outcomes—crime rates and offender recidivism—has perhaps helped focus efforts toward accountability, although it is clear that individual components of the system see the importance of other outcomes that are more process, rather than outcome, focused. Transparent efforts like CompStat help link efforts with outcomes and help align agencies with their missions. They can also provide evidence to the public about what they are getting for their tax investment, which can focus accountability even further.

Experiences in the criminal justice realm also highlight potential pitfalls. Although automation is key to the efficient collection of large amounts of information and the ability to report outcomes, it also raises issues having to do with privacy, accuracy in risk assessment tools that incorporate automation, and areas of data ownership and sharing among agencies. Successful efforts to share information may come from coordinated efforts to address particular issues, for example, when parole and law enforcement must work together in the supervision of high-risk sex offenders.

Although crime and recidivism are primary outcomes, the criminal justice system is also interested in other outcomes for individuals under its umbrella. Large numbers of offenders suffer from drug and alcohol problems, mental and physical health challenges, and family dysfunction (Cullen, 2002; Davis et al., 2009; Farrington, 2002), and many offenders appear as clients not only in the justice system, but also in other public agency caseloads as well. To the extent that criminal justice and other human service sectors find ways to share information, they may be able to provide more comprehensive and integrated information on offender needs, provide appropriate services, and ultimately assist in reducing crime rates and offender recidivism. Key to this, however, will be removing many of the hurdles offenders face when accessing services in their efforts to reintegrate into the community (Petersilia, 2003; Travis, 2005).

References

Andrews, D. A., & Bonta, J. (1995). *LSI-R: The Level of Service Inventory–Revised.* Toronto: Multi-Health Systems.

Andrews, D. A., & Bonta, J. (2003). *The psychology of criminal justice conduct* (3rd ed.). Cincinnati, OH: Anderson Publishing.

Baird, C. (2009). *A question of evidence: A critique of risk assessment models used in the justice system.* San Francisco: National Council on Crime and Delinquency.

Bureau of Justice Statistics. (2004a). *Probation and parole in the United States, 2003* (Bulletin No. NCJ 205336). Washington, DC: U.S. Department of Justice.

Bureau of Justice Statistics. (2004b). *State court sentencing of convicted felons, 2004 statistical tables, NCJ217995, Table 1.8.* Retrieved from http://bjs.ojp.usdoj. gov/index.cfm?ty=pbdetail&iid=1533.

Bureau of Justice Statistics. (2010). *About the Bureau of Justice Statistics.* Retrieved from: http://bjs.ojp.usdoj.gov/index.cfm?ty=abu

Burrell, W., & Gelb, A. (2007). *You get what you measure: CompStat for community corrections.* Washington, DC: Pew Center on the States, Pew Charitable Trusts.

California Department of Corrections and Rehabilitation. (2009). *California prisoners and parolees, 2008.* Sacramento, CA: Author.

Clear, T. R., Cole, G. F., & Reisig, M. D. (2008). *American corrections.* Belmont, CA: Wadsworth Publishing.

Corbett, R. P. (2007). The courts and soft technology. In J. Byrne & D. Rebovich (Eds.), *The new technology of crime, law and social control* (pp. 211–226). Monsey, NY: Criminal Justice Press.

Cullen, F. T. (2002). Rehabilitation and treatment programs. In J. Q. Wilson & J. Petersilia (Eds.), *Crime: Public policies for crime control* (2nd ed., pp. 253–289). Oakland, CA: Institute for Contemporary Studies.

Davis, L. M., Nicosia, N. Overton, A., Miyashiro, L., Derose, K. P, Fain, T., & Williams, E., III (2009). *Understanding the public health implications of prisoner reentry in California: Phase I report* (RAND/TR-687-TCE, RAND Research Brief, RB-9458-TCE). Santa Monica: CA: RAND Corporation.

Drake, E., Aos, S., & Miller, M. G. (2009). Evidence-based public policy options to reduce crime and criminal justice costs: Implications in Washington state. *Victims and Offenders, 4,* 170–196.

Egisdottir, S., Hite, M., Spengler, P. M., Maugherman, A. S., Anderson, L. A., Cook, R. S., et al. (2006). The Meta-Analysis of Clinical Judgment Project: Fifty-six years of accumulated research on clinical versus statistical prediction. *Counseling Psychologist, 34*, 341–382.

Eisenberg, M., Bryl, J., & Fabelo, T. (2009). *Validation of the Wisconsin Department of Corrections risk assessment instrument.* New York: Council of State Governments.

Farrington, D. P. (2002). Families and crime. In J. Q. Wilson & J. Petersilia (Eds.), *Crime: Public policies for crime control* (pp. 129–148). Oakland, CA: Institute for Contemporary Studies.

Federal Bureau of Investigation. (2010). *2008 crime in the United States.* Retrieved from http://www.fbi.gov/ucr/cius2008/index.html

Harcourt, B. (2007). *Against prediction: Profiling, policing and punishing in an actuarial age.* Chicago: University of Chicago Press.

Latessa, E. J., & Lovins, B. (2010). The role of offender risk assessment: A policy maker guide. *Victims and Offenders, 5,* 203–219.

Latessa, E. J., & Lowenkamp, C. T. (2005, 4th quarter). What are criminogenic needs and why are they important? *For the Record*, 15–16.

Lipsey, M. (2009). The primary factors that characterize effective interventions with juvenile offenders: A meta-analytic overview. *Victims and Offenders, 4*, 124–147.

Logan, C. (1993). Criminal justice performance measures for prisons. In *Performance measures for the criminal justice system* (pp. 19–59). Washington, DC: Bureau of Justice Statistics.

Meehl, P. (1954). *Clinical vs statistical prediction.* Minneapolis: University of Minnesota Press.

Mihalic, S., Fagan, A., Irwin, K., Ballard, D. S., & Elliott, D. (2002). *Blueprints for violence prevention replications: Factors for implementation success.* Boulder, CO: Institute of Behavioral Sciences.

No Child Left Behind Act of 2001, P.L. 104-110, 115 Stat. 1425 (2001).

Osborne, D., & Gaebler, T. (1992). *Reinventing government.* Reading, MA.: Addison-Wesley.

Pattavina, A., & Taxman, F. (2006). Community corrections and soft technology. In J. Byrne & D. Rebovich (Eds.), *The new technology of crime, law and social control* (pp. 327–346). Monsey, NY: Criminal Justice Press.

Petersilia, J. (1993). Measuring the performance of community corrections. In *Performance measures for the criminal justice system* (pp. 61–86). Washington, DC: Bureau of Justice Statistics.

Petersilia, J. (2003). *When prisoners come home: Parole and prisoner reentry.* Oxford, England: Oxford University Press.

Pew Center on the States. (2008). *One in 100: Behind bars in America.* Washington, DC: Pew Center on the States, PEW Charitable Trusts.

Pew Center on the States. (2009). *One in 31: The long reach of American corrections.* Washington, DC: Pew Center on the States, Pew Charitable Trusts.

Taxman, F. S., Cropsey, K. L., Young, D. W., & Wexler, H. (2007*)*. Screening, assessment, and referral practices in adult correctional settings: A national perspective. *Criminal Justice and Behavior, 34,* 1216–1234.

Travis, J. (2005). *But they all come back: Facing the challenges of prisoner reentry.* Washington, DC: Urban Institute Press.

Turner, S., Hess, J., & Jannetta, J. (2009, November). *Development of the California Static Risk Assessment Instrument (CSRA).* Irvine: University of California at Irvine Center for Evidence-Based Corrections.

CHAPTER 23

U.S. Faith-based Human Services:
The Current State of Outcomes Assessment

Richard Flory, Hebah Farrag, Brie Loskota, and Tobin Belzer

Increasingly, various public entities in the United States, including governmental agencies and political leaders, are turning to faith-based organizations (FBOs) and other religious institutions to provide the types of services and resources that government is finding increasingly difficult to provide. The slow dismantling of the social safety net has left FBOs and other religious institutions and organizations as some of the last remaining entities that can provide needed services for large segments of the underserved population. In some respects, this is nothing new. Organizations like the Salvation Army, as well as many rescue missions found in the core of large urban areas like Los Angeles, Chicago, and New York, have been a part of the landscape of American society for well over 100 years, providing food and shelter for the homeless, as well as other services for vulnerable populations. These organizations have traditionally provided services as a part of their larger Christian mission, and they have generally operated outside of any associations with public service providers. Recently, however, FBOs are being encouraged and depended on by different governmental entities, from the state to the county and even city levels, to provide a broad range of social services. In turn, they have many more opportunities for seek public funding to support for their efforts.

Beginning with former President Clinton's Welfare-to-Work program in the 1990s, and continuing through the faith-based initiatives of former President George W. Bush and current President Obama, public institutions have increasingly sought to utilize faith-based services, outreach, and leadership. This has occurred largely because of FBOs' unique access to different populations, their perceived effectiveness in a wide range of arenas, and their status as the only organizations remaining that can provide the types of services needed in many communities (Daly & Dionne 2009; Sager, 2010).

The increasing attention being paid to FBOs by the federal government is a measure of their unique place and value in the American landscape, and has resulted in creating a clearer path to their inclusion in public life, as well as to public funding. President Obama has expanded the office established by former President George W. Bush from "faith-based initiatives" to the Office of Faith-Based and Neighborhood Partnerships, indicating not just a name change, but an expanded set of responsibilities. By expanding the previous efforts at including FBOs in the public life of the United States, the current administration has made clear its intention to give FBOs an opportunity to voice their opinions, experiences, and concerns along with other community stakeholders, rather than simply giving them an opportunity to increase their requests for public funding. Yet, with this increased opportunity, much depends on the ability of FBOs to demonstrate their ability to move beyond this newfound acceptance in the public sphere and show the effectiveness of their programs in improving the lives of those they serve.

FBOs, including but certainly not limited to religious congregations—the "armies of compassion" as former President George W. Bush called them, are often seen as embodying many characteristics that make them effective service providers and desirable partners. Congregations and other religious organizations are a ubiquitous force in many communities, with religious leaders generally seen as legitimate authorities with social capital, moral vision, and spiritual motivation to act because of their convictions, beliefs, and organizations. Congregations and FBOs are among the few voices that can reach and speak authentically to, and for, underrepresented communities. They have physical space that can be used for service provision and outreach, and in times of crisis and emergency, they are most often among the first responders on the scene. As well, they are adept at conflict resolution and uniquely qualified to provide hope and guidance (Miller & Orr, 1994). The social roles of religious organizations and institutions include, but are not limited to, direct service (food, clothing, shelter), economic development (housing, jobs), personal reformation (drugs, gangs, prison reentry), community development (social capital, education, training), political advocacy (policy creation), community organizing, emergency preparedness, and health (screenings, information).

As many scholars have noted, FBOs are receiving increased visibility as a result of their expanded role in the provision of diverse health, mental health, and social services, not only in the United States, but also globally, through such organizations as the World Bank's development partnerships with local religious organizations (Chaves, 1999; DiIulio, 2002; Pipes & Ebaugh, 2002). Yet, many potential pitfalls are associated with FBOs receiving public support to provide social and human services, both for these organizations and for the separation of church and state. Many criticisms have been leveled against public funding of FBOs, ranging from their potential for proselytizing those they seek to serve to whether they should be allowed to hire only fellow believers rather than being required to hire those of other, or no, religious convictions. At the same time, many FBOs are concerned about the potential effects of public money on their religiously motivated organizational mission.

These concerns notwithstanding, FBOs currently, and into the future, will continue to provide a wide range of human services, particularly to underserved communities. Yet, FBOs are both understudied and, to the extent that their efforts have been studied, are still not understood in all the complexity that they represent. That is, simply by defining a field as being composed of FBOs suggests a similarity of organizations and mission that does not exist in reality. An accurate understanding of the many different types of organizations that can be considered faith based, and the wide range of understandings that they have of religious faith, its role in their organizations and service provision programs, and its role in the lives of individuals, is a key element to assessing both the claims to success and the level of accountability of these organizations. As such, the ability to adequately and accurately understand and evaluate the field of FBOs and their programs lags behind the rapid growth of this sector of human service provision.

In this chapter, we present an overview of the current state of research on FBO human services outcomes, focusing on the various claims to success and effectiveness made by FBOs and their supporters, FBO accountability to both funders and constituencies, and the different roles that faith may play in FBO organizations and programming. In conclusion, we suggest several areas that need to be developed further to improve research and understanding of FBOs in general, and their outcomes in particular.

Claims Making and Effectiveness in Faith-based Services

The past decade has seen a dramatic increase in the number of federally funded FBOs that deliver social services, yet the evaluation of the often high rates of success claimed by these programs has not developed at the same pace (Fischer, 2003). Scholars who study FBOs fairly unanimously acknowledge the need for more frequent, rigorous, and comprehensive evaluation of human services delivered by these organizations. According to sociologist Jodi Lane, "research on faith-based programming is in its infancy, and policymakers and practitioners should withhold judgment regarding its effectiveness" (Lane, 2009, p. 330). Many scholars contend that the research designs and methods used to study faith-based programs are often questionable, which makes it difficult to evaluate their claims of success (Ferguson, Wu, Spruijt-Metz, & Dyrness, 2007). Most FBO personnel have not received training that would enable them to implement outcome measures, analyze data, or utilize study findings (Morley, Vinson, & Hatry, 2001).

Beyond the limitations of existing studies of FBO effectiveness, there is also a gap in the literature that compares research on faith-based with that on secular programs (Leake et al., 2007). Amirkhanyan and colleagues assert that the "literature on the comparative performance of FBOs and secular nonprofit organizations has a variety of methodological limitations" (Amirkhanyan, Kim, & Lambright, 2009). For example, many studies are based on cross-sectional data and focus on specific states or communities, giving them limited generalizability (Amirkhanyan et al., 2009). Campbell and colleagues found that a number of studies failed to specify any theoretical framework (Campbell et al., 2007). Ferguson and colleagues found that effectiveness has been most often measured solely by focusing on client outcomes (Ferguson et al., 2007). The most prevalent method of data analysis has also been descriptive statistics, rather than more advanced statistical models that would help to better "explain how faith-based programs operate [and] what specifically contributes to their effectiveness" (Ferguson et al., 2007, p. 272).

In general, there is little empirical evidence relating to claims about the effectiveness of faith-based social services. Among studies that conclude that faith-based services are effective, relatively few identify the specific faith components related to successful outcomes. The different emphases on faith have generally been inadequately operationalized, and thus inadequately measured, for any effects they may have on outcomes (Ferguson et al., 2007). Research has typically relied on a single measure of religiosity: frequency of church attendance (Mears, Roman, Wolff, & Buck, 2006). As a result, it remains difficult to determine what specific characteristics of faith-based programs lead to positive outcomes (Ferguson et al., 2007). Without an existing instrument that assesses the role of faith in achieving successful outcomes in faith-based programs (Ferguson et al., 2007), FBOs and other stakeholders will continue to face the challenge of how to accurately communicate the role of faith in FBO programs (Fischer, 2003).

However, a variety of qualitative and quantitative methods have been utilized to measure outcomes claims made by FBOs, presenting some promising directions for outcomes measurement, including self-reporting (DeHaven, Hunter, Wilder, Walton, & Berry, 2004); surveys; semistructured telephone interviews (Kegler, Kiser, & Hall, 2007); and biological measures, or outcome measures of health conditions (DeHaven et al., 2004). Likewise, some nutritional intervention programs have been evaluated by using an "effectiveness trial," in which churches collected self-administered baseline and follow-up surveys that assessed fruit and vegetable consumption; participant demographics; and health and potential psychosocial mediators, such as social support and self-efficacy (Campbell et al., 2007).

Another methodology that has been used to evaluate FBOs is a community-based participatory approach, in which community members and service providers collaborate in the research process (Kaplan, Calman, Golub, Ruddock, & Billings, 2006). Other methodologies such as process evaluation (which assess the extent to which program implementation corresponds with the program plan), efficiency evaluations (or cost–benefit analyses), and evaluations of relevance (which assess the extent to which the program addresses concerns relevant to the target population) have also been used (Wilson, 2000). Although FBOs often claim that their programs are effective, there is a lack of research that supports these claims (Ferguson et al., 2007). For example, Johnson (2002) examined more than 800 studies of faith-based social service interventions to discover that only 25 attempted to evaluate their programs, and that among those that did, evaluation designs lacked rigorous methodologies. Given the higher visibility of FBOs in the new millennium, their acceptance of public funding, and their increasing role in public life, many questions and controversies have arisen over the issue of FBO program effectiveness and accountability. According to the White House Office of Faith-Based and Community Initiatives (2001), "Federal funds should be awarded to the most effective organizations, whether public or private, large or small, faith-based or secular, and all must be allowed to compete on a level playing field." Thus, the ability of FBOs to continue to gain funding for their programs will be largely dependent on their ability to demonstrate their effectiveness in comparison with other programs, by using measures that are widely agreed on by professionals in the field.

Significant questions remain regarding the impact of FBO programming, particularly whether FBOs are more or less effective than secular organizations, and further, whether religious faith empowers organizations to more effective action (Ferguson et al., 2007). This however, may be a function of where the field currently is in its development of standardized measurements. Developing such methodological capacity and standardization is important to future FBO service programs and will go a long way toward overcoming any suspicions and misunderstandings of the motives of FBOs.

Accountability of FBOs

For many scholars, the process of evaluating faith-based programs raises a number of issues related to accountability, as religious organizations are not subject to the standards of accountability that are commonplace for state health and welfare agencies (Walton, 2007, p. 172). Among legal scholars, there has been much constitutional debate about the role of accountability in charitable choice, a legislative provision designed to remove barriers to the receipt of certain federal funds by FBOs (Gilman, 2002, p. 887). Hall notes that formal legal protections that had shielded FBOs from accountability have been eroding (Hall, 2002, p. 7).

Within organizations, many FBO service providers prioritize their accountability to God, rather than to the population they serve (Garland, Netting, Katherine, & Yancey, 2004, p. 2). In their qualitative study of 15 faith-based human service programs, O'Connor and Netting (2008) found that most service providers "assumed that accountability was an expectation from those both inside the organization such as professionals and clients themselves, as well as from a myriad of outside forces" (p. 350). Such tensions are one major factor that underlies the trend that research about FBOs has not generally focused on the faith component of outcomes measurement, and illustrate why pursuing measures that systematically include faith as a component is one of the more important developments that needs to take place in this field.

The "Faith Factor" in FBO

Although faith motives have been used by different groups to draw suspicion to FBO service provision, the "faith factor" is an often overlooked element in the construction of outcomes measurement tools for use with FBOs (Ferguson et al., 2007, p. 271). Although secular organizations and FBOs often operate in parallel areas, providing similar if not exactly the same services, often the only component that is different in their work is the added layer of religion or religious practice. At their core, FBO social services programs contain many of the same elements as their secular counterparts (Fischer, 2003), but are in different ways infused with the faith component. For example, one might expect that an organization that receives federal funding to deliver counseling services to homeless single men should be held accountable to the same indicators of success, regardless of whether the service provider is a FBO or a secular nonprofit agency (Fischer, 2003). The key outcome indicators could include specific accomplishments by participants, such as the completion of a training program, finding employment, and/or remaining clean and sober for a specified period (Fischer, 2003). The degree to which the services are infused with a faith or spiritual component simply could be seen as a reflection of a difference in the underlying service model, which is often the case (Fischer, 2003). Rather than ignore the faith factor, these differences need to be understood and clearly specified in evaluating FBO outcomes (Fischer, 2003).

Part of the tension and confusion over what role faith may play in different outcomes is a result of a lack of clarity on what exactly faith means in any given organizational context. In some programs, faith is not necessarily a component of programming, even though the program may be operated by a church (Mears et al., 2006, p. 353). Other programs incorporate religious and spiritual components that are outside of the purview of conventional evaluation methods (Harden, 2006, p. 482). Ferguson and colleagues note that the role of faith is more commonly assessed as a contextual factor (for example, being located in a faith-based environment) than as a component of a program (Ferguson et al., 2007, p. 273).

According to DeHaven and colleagues, "faith-placed" programs (that is, those brought into a congregation by professionals from the outside) are more likely to report outcome data than faith-based programs (that is, those that originate inside a congregation; DeHaven et al., 2004, p. 17). The distinction between faith-placed and faith-based is important to note here in that whereas faith-placed programs may have a better record of outcomes reporting than faith-based programs, any reporting that fails to define and analyze the role of faith in the program does not clearly add to the body of knowledge about what difference—if any—faith makes in outcomes.

Much of the impetus behind the increased interest among policymakers in using faith-based programs to intervene with at-risk populations is the substantial empirical evidence showing that individuals who score high on measures of religiosity are more inclined to exhibit prosocial behaviors (Benda & Corwyn 1997; Johnson, Jang, Larson, & De Li, 2001; Richard, Bell, & Carlson 2000; Roman, Wolff, & Correa, & Buck, 2007). In their study of a faith-based substance abuse treatment program, Duke and Wolf-Branigin (2007) showed that the availability of a spiritual activity component provided a valuable attractor for persons who successfully completed treatment. Youth participation in faith-based programs has also been linked to strong positive developmental traits such as identity formation, educational aspiration and achievement, and mental and physical health (Donahue & Benson, 1995; Donelson, 1999; Regnerus, 2000).

A central challenge for FBOs, then, and a missing link in the development of tools for empirical outcome measurement, has been the inability to accurately communicate the specific role of faith as a dimension of the program model (Ferguson et al., 2007). Faith-based elements in programming and service delivery could include a broad range of elements such as the routine use of prayer in meetings, outreach, and programming, or the incorporation of religious concepts into program activities (Fischer, 2003). These faith-based elements should be clearly understood, quantified, and assessed as a key aspect of the program itself (Fischer, 2003). Regardless of the characteristics of the faith elements, their assessment and measurement is vitally important to the understanding of program outcomes.

With this in mind, it is striking that most studies fail to systematically account for the role of faith in the social and human services programs of FBOs. Johnson, Tompkins, and Webb (2002) noted the lack of measures of "religious commitment, religiosity or a quantifiable measure of the key independent variables that defines the nature of the FBO." Ferguson et al. (2007) study of FBO effectiveness found that despite considerable empirical attention to diverse effectiveness indicators within faith-based programs, only five of the 29 studies they examined explored how faith and religion specifically contributed to particular program outcomes. The narrow focus of most evaluation studies has led to an approach that fails to consider not only the impact of faith on the client, but also the impact of faith-based services on other aspects of the organization and the surrounding milieu, which can also reflect program success (Ferguson, et al., 2007).

The "faith" in faith-based may not only lend itself to producing different outcomes, but may also influence how organizations perceive effectiveness and success. For example, O'Connor and Netting (2008) analyzed the process of evaluation by a sample of exemplar (that is, FBOs whose programs operated as a model of excellence and effectiveness and were, therefore, recognized as top tier FBOs) FBOs and found that faith-based groups often look at outcomes measurement in unique ways. Their study revealed that these exemplar FBOs were adept at program evaluation and outcomes measurement, with responses revealing multiple types of evaluation mechanisms, including assessing staff performance reviews, conducting consumer satisfaction surveys, communicating with consumers and collaborators, generating service statistics (outputs), and collecting outcome measurements. It also revealed that these exemplar FBOs prioritized values such as communication, relationship building, stewardship, responsiveness and flexibility, and accountability in ways that made them unique in relation to their secular counterparts (O'Connor & Netting, 2008). On the basis of this research, understanding concepts such as faithful stewardship and its accompanying service orientation is key to developing effective evaluative tools for FBOs.

These findings suggest several implications for program evaluators—whether internal or external to the organization—to consider when involved in faith-based human service evaluation. The faith factor in these programs becomes a critical dimension in determining what constitutes quality in mission-driven FBOs. O'Connor and Netting (2008) believe that given FBOs added layer of faith, their approach to accountability and evaluation, their attention to stewardship and presence of committed stakeholders, faith-based programs might be potential grounds for innovation in which new program evaluation designs can be developed. They suggest that, "in an era when effectiveness in the form of outcome-based measurement is advantaged... [FBOs] may help to shed light on the interaction between quality, responsive human service programming and traditional program evaluation methods" (O'Connor & Netting, 2008, p. 354).

Conclusion

At a time of economic crisis and major changes in the human services sector (such as what is taking place with health care reform), outcome measurement and effectiveness become key factors in ensuring that taxpayer dollars go only to organizations that can prove their impact. A results orientation is crucial to FBOs gaining legitimacy and understanding. It is also vital that federal agencies, foundations, and the public at large pay closer attention to the added value of faith in organizational life and client receptivity, as well as to the role faith may play in evaluation and effectiveness. Although FBOs continue to generate suspicion in some quarters, whether on the basis of perceived faith motives, the fear of proselytization in a secular society, or exclusionary hiring practices, what faith can offer is of value for a variety of stakeholders and clients and critical to the identity development and sustainability of FBOs. (Recently, a long-raging debate over whether religious organizations that accept funds from the government should be allowed to discriminate when hiring was reignited [Mooney, 2009]. Some religious groups contend that it is their right to exclude homosexuals from their organizations on the basis of their religious practice and beliefs.) More studies are needed on the impact of faith and religious orientation on effectiveness and organizational capacity in order to relieve many of the misunderstandings that remain.

It is clear that furthering research on FBOs and their associated outcomes is an important step in demonstrating their program effectiveness, rationale for public funding, and place in the spectrum of human services. Several studies have made sound suggestions to improve measurement. Wolf-Branigin and Duke (2007) suggest that future research should seek to better understand what attracts different participants to different programs in order to more effectively use spirituality as an attractor. Campbell and colleagues note a lack of studies about groups other than African Americans and suggest that the field would greatly benefit from studies offering greater diversity of groups (Campbell et al., 2007). DeHaven and colleagues note that data collection methods should not be beyond the expertise of service providers, and suggest developing "user-friendly workshops and tools" that could be used by service providers who are accustomed to program/service delivery, but not evaluation (DeHaven et al., 2004, p. 1034). These suggestions may go a long way toward easing data collection and providing a better understanding of client motivation and diversity, but improved methodology is only one aspect of developing approaches to measure and demonstrate outcomes that are meaningful, useful, and comparable.

In addition to the above suggestions, we argue that scholars and practitioners need to go further and address the following three areas in order to provide better analytical tools for categorizing FBOs and understanding their successes and failures in service delivery: (1) develop a typology, or classification system, of FBOs that accurately describes and classifies their organizational structures and service delivery in all their complexity; (2) create language that describes religion, faith, and spirituality within organizations that moves beyond Judeo-Christian frameworks; and (3) work to create sources of funding for real evaluation and for forums for sharing lessons learned, both failures and successes, that contribute to an understanding this field that goes beyond organizational competition for dollars.

The first area—developing a typology—would help to classify faith-based programs in a way that more accurately reflects the role that faith plays in FBOs, both in how they are organized and conceive of themselves, and in their programs (cf. Mears et al., 2006). A typology of this sort would allow a deeper look into the ways in which organizations might incorporate religious and spiritual elements in their different organizational levels and ultimately in their programs, thereby establishing the different ways that FBOs are organized around religious/faith issues. Such a typology would need to minimally include three primary categories that would describe (1) the role of faith in the organization—that is, the degree to which faith is actually a part of the organization and its programs—what we might call a "faith saturation index"; (2) the different strategies FBOs pursue in their programs, and (3) the different forms of authority, or leadership style, that characterize particular FBOs (our thanks to Donald Miller, Executive Director of the USC Center for Religion and Civic Culture, for suggesting these categories).

Within the category of the role of faith in the organization, we also suggest identifying different levels of faith saturation, ranging from "faith placed" groups—that is, those groups that are otherwise secular but form a relationship with a congregation or other organization for operating their programs—to denominational organizations (that is, sponsored by a particular religious denomination), ecumenical FBOs (those that include several different faith perspectives or that work with many different faith groups), and conversionist FBOs (organizations who use their human service programs to make contact with different populations and ultimately convert them to their particular religious perspective). In each of these different classifications, the level of faith saturation would vary and could be easily measured through interviews and documentary evidence from the organization. This basic understanding of the primary faith saturation of the FBO would then be combined with knowledge about the strategies they pursue in their programs, whether direct service provision, community and/or economic development, personal reformation, or other related strategies. And, finally, how authority or leadership style is infused within the FBO: whether they have a bureaucratic structure, a charismatic leader/authority, or a traditional organizational structure in which programs have always been operated in a particular way out of a commitment to tradition and/or faith requirements.

All of this, then, would allow for comparisons of outcomes within categories of similar FBOs, across different types of FBOs, and between FBOs and secular service organizations and programs. Taking such an approach would allow for differentiating the role of faith in diverse settings and allow a more precise determination of what, if any, difference faith makes in social and human service provision outcomes. Key to accomplishing this is the need to address the fact that most studies of FBO effectiveness have focused on organizations with Jewish or Christian affiliations, yet there are both increasing numbers of FBOs being established, and increasing numbers of potential clientele, that do not share that Judeo-Christian heritage. Thus, categories of analysis need to be broad enough to describe various religious traditions and commitments so that they can be properly operationalized, analyzed, and compared with each other, both within and across traditions and with secular programs. Such description could include, for example, how monotheistic and overtly religious programs might compare with other traditions and those that are implicitly spiritual (Roman et al., 2007).

The obstacles to proper outcomes assessment and evaluation, however, are not simply limited to having the correct categories of religion or creating a better vocabulary that reflects religious pluralism. As with many things in the independent sector, the process of evaluation is one that requires significant financial investment (Francis & Liverpool 2009). Funders, working with FBOs, need to set aside resources to collaboratively undertake evaluation that engages and addresses any training needs of FBO staff and creates relationships with outside evaluators and field experts.

As funders play more of a role in determining priorities for funding, they also indirectly and directly play a role in developing vocabularies, outcomes measures and measurement tools, and standardization for, and with, the recipients of funds. Top-down efforts from funding sources will not fill all the gaps, and funders need to be wary of leaving service providers out of the conversation: There is great power in foundations convening groups of other funders and stakeholders, even more so when they are also willing to support outcomes evaluations that benefit grantee goals.

Evaluations themselves, of course, are not the end but only a means to greater understanding of what works and what doesn't work in programming. Too often, evaluations—especially those that might reveal programmatic shortcomings—are not shared with others outside the organization or foundation. A culture shift that makes publicly sharing the products of evaluation in a way that advances the knowledge of field is perhaps the final frontier. Accordingly, DeHaven and colleagues recommend increasing collaboration between FBOs and professionals in targeted areas of interest to improve outcomes assessment, evaluation and dissemination of findings, and innovation (DeHaven et al., 2004). After all, what good are the proper tools, analytical frameworks and resources if the lessons learned, and the failures endured, stay within the pages of reports on the bookshelves?

References

Amirkhanyan, A. A., Kim, H. J., & Lambright, K. T. (2009). Faith-based assumptions about performance: Does church affiliation matter for service quality and access? *Nonprofit and Voluntary Sector Quarterly, 38,* 490–521.

Benda, B. B., & Corwyn, R. F. (1997). Religion and delinquency: The relationship after considering family and peer influences. *Journal for the Scientific Study of Religion, 36,* 81–92.

Campbell, M. K., Hudson, M. A., Resnicow, K., Blakeney, N., Paxton, A., & Baskin, M. (2007). Church-based health promotion interventions: Evidence and lessons learned. *Annual Review of Public Health, 28,* 213–234.

Chaves, M. (1999). Religious congregations and welfare reform: Who will take advantage of "charitable choice"? *American Sociological Review, 64,* 836–846.

Daly, L., & Dionne, E. J., Jr. (2009). *God's economy: Faith-based initiatives and the caring state.* Chicago: University of Chicago Press.

DeHaven, M. J., Hunter, I. B., Wilder, L., Walton, J. W., & Berry, J. (2004). Health programs in faith-based organizations: Are they effective? *American Journal of Public Health, 94,* 1030–1036.

DiIulio, J. J. (2002). The three faith factors. *Public Interest, 149,* 50–64.

Donahue, M. J., & Benson, P. L. (1995). Religion and the well-being of adolescents. *Journal of Social Issues, 51,* 145–160.

Donelson, E. (1999). Psychology of religion and adolescents in the United States: Past to present. *Journal of Adolescence, 22,* 187–204.

Duke, J., & Wolf-Branigin, M. (2007). Spiritual involvement as a predictor to completing a Salvation Army substance abuse treatment program. *Research on Social Work Practices, 17,* 239–245.

Ferguson, K. M., Wu, Q., Spruijt-Metz, D., & Dyrness, G. (2007). Outcomes evaluation in faith-based social services: Are we evaluating faith accurately? *Research on Social Work Practice, 17,* 264.

Fischer, R. L. (2003, March 6). *The devil is in the details: Implementing outcome measurement in faith-based organizations.* Paper presentation at the Independent Sector 2003 Spring Research Forum: The Role of Faith-Based Organizations in the Social Welfare System, Bethesda, MD.

Francis, S. A., & Liverpool, J. (2009). A review of faith-based HIV prevention programs. *Journal of Religion and Health, 48,* 6–15.

Garland, D., Netting, E., Katherine, M., & Yancey, G. (2004). *Belief systems in faith-based human service programs: Orientation to faith-based social services resource.* Waco, TX: Baylor University School of Social Work.

Gilman, M. E. (2002). "Charitable choice" and the accountability challenge: Reconciling the need for regulation with the First Amendment religion clauses. *Vanderbilt Law Review, 54,* 799–888.

Hall, P. D. (2002, November). *Accountability in faith-based organizations and the future of charitable choice.* Paper presentation at the Panel on Understanding Accountability in Faith-Based Organizations, Accountability in Faith-Based Organizations, Association for Research on Non-profit Organizations and Voluntary Action (ARNOVA), Montreal, Canada.

Harden, M. (2006). Towards a faith-based program theory: A reconceptualization of program theory. *Evaluation Review, 30,* 481–504.

Johnson, B. R. (2002). Assessing the impact of religious programs and prison on recidivism: An exploratory study. *Texas Journal of Corrections, 28,* 7–11.

Johnson, B. R., Jang, S. J., Larson, D. B., & De Li, S. (2001). Does adolescent religious commitment matter? A reexamination of the effects of religiosity on delinquency. *Journal of Research in Crime and Delinquency, 38,* 22–44.

Johnson, B. R., Tompkins, R. B., & Webb, D. (2002). *Objective hope—Assessing the effectiveness of faith-based organizations: A review of the literature.* Philadelphia: University of Pennsylvania, Center for Religion and Urban Civil Society.

Kaplan, S., Calman, N., Golub, M., Ruddock, C., & Billings, J. (2006). The role of faith-based institutions in addressing health disparities: A case study of an initiative in the southwest Bronx. *Journal of Health Care for the Poor and Underserved, 17,* 9–19.

Kegler, M. C., Kiser, M., & Hall, S. (2007). Evaluation findings from the Institute for Public Health and Faith Collaborations. *Public Health Reports, 122,* 793–802.

Lane, J. (2009). Faith-based programming for offenders. *Victims and Offenders, 4,* 327–333.

Leake, R., Green, S., Marquez, C., Vanderburg, J., Guillaume, S., & Gardner, V. (2007). Evaluating the capacity of faith-based programs in Colorado. *Research on Social Work Practice, 17,* 216–228.

Mears, D., Roman, C., Wolff, A., & Buck, J. (2006). Faith-based efforts to improve prisoner reentry: Assessing the logic and evidence. *Journal of Criminal Justice, 34,* 351–367.

Miller, D., & Orr, J. (1994). *Politics of the spirit: Religion and multiethnicity in Los Angeles.* Los Angeles: University of Southern California.

Mooney, A. (2009, February 5). *Controversy surrounds Obama's faith office.* Retrieved from http://edition.cnn.com/2009/POLITICS/02/05/obama.faith.based/index.html

Morley, E., Vinson, E., & Hatry, H. (2001). *Outcome measurement in nonprofit organizations: Current practices and recommendations.* Washington DC: Independent Sector.

O'Conner, M. K., & Netting, F. E. (2008). Faith-based evaluation: Accountable to whom, for what? *Evaluation and Program Planning, 31,* 347–355.

Pipes, P. F., & Ebaugh, H. R. (2002). Faith-based coalitions, social services, and government funding. *Sociology of Religion, 63,* 49–68.

Regnerus, M. D. (2000). Shaping schooling success: Religious socialization and educational outcomes in metropolitan public schools. *Journal for the Scientific Study of Religion, 39,* 363–370.

Richard, A. J., Bell, D. C., & Carlson, J. (2000). Individual religiosity, moral community, and drug user treatment. *Journal for the Scientific Study of Religion, 39,* 240–246.

Roman, C. G., Wolff, A., Correa, V., & Buck, J. (2007). Assessing intermediate outcomes of a faith-based residential prisoner reentry program. *Research on Social Work Practice, 17,* 199–215.

Sager, R. (2010). *Faith, politics, and power: The politics of faith-based initiatives.* New York: Oxford University Press.

Walton, E. (2007). Evaluation of faith-based programs: An introduction from the guest editor. *Research on Social Work Practice, 17,* 171–173.

White House Office of Faith-Based and Community Initiatives. (2001). *Unlevel playing field: Barriers to participation by faith-based and community organizations in federal social service programs.* Washington, DC: Author.

Wilson, L. (2000). Implementation and evaluation of church-based health fairs. *Journal of Community Health Nursing, 17,* 39–48.

Wolf-Branigin, M., & Duke, J. (2007). Spiritual involvement as a predictor to completing a Salvation Army substance abuse treatment program. *Research on Social Work Practice, 17,* 239–245.

CHAPTER 24

Social, Health, and Mental Health Outcomes:
Global Linkages

Vijay Ganju

Ultimately, the goal of most societies is to improve the lives of its members through reduction in poverty, betterment of health and education, and enhancement of the quality of life. Whether in high-income countries such as the United States or the United Kingdom, or in middle- or low-income countries such as in South America, there is a naturalistic imperative to link mental health and substance use interventions to broader societal goals and outcomes such as increased employment, reduction in poverty, maternal and child health, higher rates of literacy, and improved school performance. Internationally, there has been remarkable consensus on the overarching goal of eliminating dire poverty. In 2000, more than 200 countries jointly adopted the United Nation's Millennium Development Goals (MDGs; see http://www.un.org/millenniumgoals) to eliminate poverty and hunger through concrete goals and time-bound targets related to universal education, maternal health, child mortality, public health, environmental sustainability and biodiversity. There is broad-based recognition that these goals cannot be achieved without addressing broader health issues such as noncommunicable diseases and mental health.

On the 10-year anniversary of the adoption of the MDGs, a high-level plenary was convened at the United Nations (UN) headquarters to review successes, best practices, and lessons learned. Overall, the world is on track to halve the number of people in extreme poverty, primary school enrollment rose from 83 percent to 89 percent, and the Global Fund (established in 2002 to focus resources in fighting three of the world's most devastating diseases: AIDS, tuberculosis, and malaria; see http://www.theglobalfund.org/en/fighting/?langen) saves 4,000 lives a day. Although targets are unlikely to be achieved, there has been a 34 percent decline in maternal and child mortality. HIV/AIDS targets are also not on track. A critical point is the emergent understanding that these targets cannot be achieved without addressing broader health and mental health issues. As efforts are made to streamline and accelerate the MDG process, the next generation of activity is expected to explicitly include these aspects.

In these intersectoral linkages, the relationship between health and mental health is primary. People with mental health conditions experience substantial disability and premature death (World Health Organization [WHO], 2010a, 2010b). Globally, mental health conditions account for 13 percent of the total burden of disease, and 31 percent of all years lived with disability (WHO, 2009). By 2030, depression alone is likely to be the single highest contributor to burden of disease in the world, more so than heart disease, stroke, road traffic accidents, and HIV/AIDS.

These burden-of-disease calculations do not reflect the full impact of the problem. People with mental health conditions are more likely than others to develop significant physical health conditions including diabetes, heart disease, stroke, and respiratory diseases (World Health Organization, 2010a). People with mental health conditions also are more likely than the general population to die prematurely. Systematic reviews of studies conducted in many countries have shown that people with schizophrenia and depression have an overall increased risk of premature death that is 1.6 and 1.4 times greater, respectively, than that expected in the general population.

As the WHO has noted, four chronic illnesses—cardiovascular, diabetes, cancer and respiratory illnesses—are responsible for 60 percent of the world's deaths. Understanding of the relationship between these chronic illnesses and mental illness has increased dramatically in the past two decades. It is now known that persons with these chronic illnesses have much higher rates of depression and anxiety than the general population (see chapters 8 and 12 in this volume). Major depression among persons experiencing chronic medical conditions increases the burden of their physical illness and somatic symptoms, causes an increase in functional impairment, and increases medical costs. The presence of mental illness with long-term illnesses impairs self-care and adherence to treatment regimens and causes increased mortality.

The bottom line is that mental illnesses occur as chronic mental conditions in many persons, causing significant role impairment, work loss, and work cutback. They also worsen prognosis for heart disease, stroke, diabetes, HIV/AIDS, cancer, and other chronic illnesses. Many factors point to reasons that mental illnesses are not adequately addressed in this context. Consumer, provider, and system factors all contribute to poor quality of care. Consumers and family members may not recognize or correctly identify symptoms or may be reluctant to seek care. The providers may not have the right training, equipment, or support to provide appropriate interventions. Systems may have constraints and limitations related to financing and the availability of and access to mental health treatment.

To complicate the picture even further, people with mental health conditions are denied employment and other income-generating opportunities, lack educational opportunities, have poorer educational outcomes, and often experience restrictions in the exercise of their civil and political rights. According to the National Human Rights Commission (see http://www.hhrc. nic.in) mental illness has been strongly associated with social exclusion and stigma, human rights violations, and institutionalization, both formal and in other guises. Many studies also indicate how policies and programs outside the health sector have an impact on health outcomes (Organization for Economic Co-Operation and Development, 2003). For example, a study in India showed that, contrary to the aims of health policy, when safety nets such as food subsidies were weakened, detrimental effects on the overall state of health throughout the nation resulted.

In 2008, the UN Secretary-General Ban Ki-moon called for "more [integration] of mental health awareness into all aspects of health and social policy, health-system planning, and primary and secondary general health care" (World Health Organization, 2010a, p. 7). The UN, therefore, in an international context, has begun to address the importance of recognizing mental health disorders as an important cause of long-term disability and dependency. Similarly, WHO has attributed 32 percent of all years lived with disability to neuropsychiatric conditions, namely, unipolar depression, alcohol use disorder, schizophrenia, bipolar depression, and dementia (WHO, 2005) and links mental health issues (especially depression) to poor prognosis of diabetes, chronic heart disease, respiratory diseases, and cancer. Reports in the United States echo these statistics as recent studies have shown that there is gap in mortality of 25 years between persons with serious mental illnesses and the general population (Druss & Bornemann, 2010). The Convention of the Rights of

Persons with Disabilities (2006) provides momentum to highlight the importance of the nexus between disabilities and mental health, not only in the context of human rights and humanitarian response, but also in the context of development. For example, the UN's Department of Economic and Social Affairs is promoting and mainstreaming the rights of persons with disabilities, including mental and psychosocial disabilities, into community development responses. In the United States, the National Outcomes Measures proposed by the Substance Abuse and Mental Health Services Administration have outcomes related to reduced involvement with the criminal justice system, increased employment, and improved school performance.

Despite this newfound momentum, a recent series of articles in *Lancet* (see http://www.thelancet.com) on the Global Mental Health Movement illustrate that mental health and substance use are missing from policy frameworks for health improvement and poverty reduction, and from the targets and outcomes that are indicators for these broader health, social, and economic goals. For example, the MDGs sets out a vision for international health (for example, reducing extreme poverty and hunger, reducing child mortality rates, and fighting disease epidemics such as malaria and HIV/AIDS) and education (for example, elimination of gender disparity in primary and secondary education) goals for low- to middle-income countries that all 192 United Nations member states—and at least 23 international organizations—have agreed to achieve by the year 2015 (Patel, 2007).

Regardless of the close links between mental health outcomes and many of the individual MDGs, and the fact that improving health of poor people is central to the MDG, mental health is not included as an MDG in and of itself. This is extremely concerning at multiple levels in society: Serious mental illnesses impoverish people through cost of health care, lost employment, and social ostracism. A major reason children are not enrolled in schools or do not complete primary education is poor physical and mental health status. Depression is a common health problem during pregnancy and after childbirth (Patel, 2007; Prince et al., 2007). Mental disorders increase the risk for communicable and noncommunicable diseases. Mental disorders affect the rate of and recovery from other health conditions and, as stated earlier, are associated with risk factors such as obesity, hypertension, poor diet, onset of Type 2 diabetes, and increased risk of contracting HIV/AIDS.

The bottom line is that the relationships among outcomes related to health, mental health, and human services, especially as they pertain to societal goals, are complex, nonlinear, interactive, and often bidirectional. The tendency is to minimize this complexity. From a measurement perspective, reducing this complexity is a sine qua non. However, from a policy perspective, understanding and incorporating this complexity is critical: Without an appreciation of these relationships, especially among the different levels and types of outcomes, models become simplistic, distorting reality and making it more difficult for outcomes to contribute to desired and meaningful change.

Achieving Multiple Human Services Outcomes: Tensions in Planning and Implementation

A major challenge then is how to make the enterprise of mental health and substance use outcomes more relevant within the larger context of international health. Clearly, as health reform initiatives occur, attention to mental health is becoming more prominent. Health care reform in the United States has clearly identified mental health and substance use as key components, and has introduced parity legislation to normalize delivery of care and payment for physical health, mental health, and substance use disorders. In the United Kingdom, with reform including the abolition of the National Trust and more direct funding to provider systems, a major component is based on an outcomes paradigm, including those for behavioral health.

One major component to meeting the aforementioned challenge is that mental health and substance use outcomes have been used variably around the world, being driven by different contexts and purposes, different applications of outcomes, and different ways of including consumers and family members. Thus, several tensions are inherently present within the quest to make mental health and substance more internationally codified into planning for common or comparable outcomes, and to related them to the larger societal and health contexts of which they are a part. Such tensions are described below.

Science versus Traditional Culture

As health providers and other stakeholders glibly talk about mental health and mental disorders as the problems to be addressed, there needs to be recognition at the outset that these are concepts that, in many languages, have no direct equivalent. For example, in the Zimbabwean Shona language, there are no terms for depression or anxiety. Also, in Zimbabwe, multiple somatic complaints such as headaches and fatigue are the most common presentations of depression (Patel, Abas, Broadhead, Todd, & Reeler, 2001). As a result, case records that require health workers to state a diagnosis show far lower numbers for depression than is expected. An alternative could be to identify local, traditional concepts related to depression for inclusion. In Shona, the concept of *kufungisisa* ("thinking too much"); in India, *ghabrahat* ("related to anxiety"); or, in Botswana *pelo y tata* ("heart too much") are described as local illness categories that overlap with depression. That is, the underlying tension is the identification of the mental health problem to be addressed and how culturally based symptom manifestations and issues of language are critical in identifying persons to whom services will be targeted and for whom outcomes will be obtained and monitored. For example, Asian cultures tend to exhibit or express depression more somatically than Western cultures (Parker, Gladstone, & Chee, 2001).

Accountability versus Quality Improvement

This is perhaps the most fundamental tension in the implementation of mental health outcome systems internationally. At one level, mental health and substance use outcome systems are implemented to prove the value and utility of mental health and substance use programs to funders and policymakers. Typically, data are reported one way: upward, from the local program to the state level or from the state level to the national level. Issues that arise in such systems are often differences in eligible populations, the initial status of persons served, the range of interventions a particular jurisdiction may have under its purview, data quality, and the like, resulting in comparisons across jurisdictions being somewhat suspect. A major issue is that the focus of many of these accountability systems is reporting. Although feedback is provided, such feedback is often not integrated into a quality improvement framework. Another approach to outcomes is monitoring at the individual level so that clinicians have feedback to inform care and treatment. Some of these systems are implemented in real time. This is an extreme version of a quality improvement framework. (Data on outcomes aggregated at the clinician or program or provider agency level can also be used for quality improvement purposes.)

In many systems, the initial driving concept is to simultaneously address both accountability and quality improvement perspectives (for example, please see chapter 21, on the Veteran's Health Administration, in this volume). This is indeed possible but requires a coordinated strategic approach and strong leadership that obtains a commitment from clinicians and managers and provides resources for implementation and training. Clearly, as noted in reports and studies in various countries—the United Kingdom and Australia, for example—the pressure to use outcomes measures in routine clinical practice is increasing (Pirkis et al., 2005). A Mental Health Outcomes Compendium (National Institute of Mental Health in England, 2008) recognizes the diversity of applications of outcomes and is designed to support clinicians engaged in service delivery and development who wish to gauge clinical effectiveness and recovery. The increased use of electronic health records may facilitate the use of mental health outcomes in clinical settings.

Clinician versus Consumer Perspectives

What constitutes a good outcome depends on one's perspective. Clinicians emphasize outcomes related to symptoms and functioning; consumers tend to have a more holistic approach, with a focus on recovery with quality of life and use of perception of care as integral components. In fact, the New Zealand approach to mental health outcomes includes five perspectives: consumer, clinical, cultural, family caregiving, and public (Krieble, 2003). The underlying idea of multiple perspectives is that they contribute to a richer understanding of whether or not mental health services are making a difference, taking into account differences in expectations across stakeholders. In New Zealand, the consumer measure has strong recovery and quality-of-life dimension and is supported through the developmental of regional and consumer networks that participate in service planning. The clinical perspective is supported by a number of evidence-based practice initiatives and by the promotion of an outcome-focused culture. The cultural perspective is based on Hua Oranga, a Maori mental health measure, and by the establishment of Kaupapa Maori mental health services. The family care perspective focuses on the measurement of caregiving burden among families. From a public perspective, a cost–benefit framework is being developed to guide future mental health allocations. This New Zealand outcomes initiative illustrates the tension related to perspective. This is especially a consideration as the cost of implementing an outcome system has become an important deciding factor when technical precision and data quality need to be taken into account.

Standardized Use versus Idiosyncratic Application of Measures

There are an enormous number and variety of clinical outcomes measures in current use in clinical practice and research, particularly in relation to adult mental health. In the United Kingdom, it has been noted that four recently published trials assessing counseling and primary care did not share a single measure in common (Ward et al., 2000). The Mental Health Outcomes Compendium (NIMHE, 2008) for Wales and England identified 69 instruments that scored highly on quality, instruments recommended by the practice group, and instruments proposed by the Royal Colleges of Psychiatry and Nursing and the British Psychological Society.

This plethora of outcomes instruments allows for the choice of instruments for appropriate application. At the same time, this diversity results in a lack of standardization that does not establish a universal metric that can be used as an outcome measure. Also, in many situations, locally created instruments are used.

What proves to be even more of a problem is that many instruments widely used at the national level often do not have adequate research to support instrument reliability and validity. For example, there are few outcomes studies related to consumers receiving treatment for mental illnesses in humanitarian emergencies (Souza, Yasuda, & Cristofani, 2009). In a small study conducted in Darfur, researchers acknowledged that standardized instruments for adults could not be used because of their length and need for specialized personnel (Souza, Yasuda, & Critofani, 2009). Outcomes for children were not monitored because of the lack of simple and short instruments and because clear case definitions of children's mental health in conflict situations (for example, enuresis, posttraumatic stress disorder) did not exist. At the same time, humanitarian agencies are often in a bind because donors have provided funding for interventions, and evaluation or outcomes studies may go against the grain of donor intent.

Generic Programs versus Specific Interventions

Mental health and substance use outcomes can be associated with generic programs that are often an ill-defined collection of interventions or with interventions that are well specified and defined. For example, outcomes may be associated with hospitalization during which pre and post measures are obtained, but the set of interventions that were provided in the hospital setting is not clear. Outcomes in this situation are associated with programs within which individualized care may occur but individual interventions are not specified. On the other hand, outcomes may be associated with specific interventions that may even have their own fidelity measures. In a quality-improvement framework, these distinctions are important. In the United States, there is renewed emphasis on comparative effectiveness research as a way to identify what works with which patients under what circumstances (Institute of Medicine, 2009). In terms of research priorities, psychiatry ranked 6th and substance use ranked 12th.

Technical Precision versus Implementation Costs of Outcome Systems

An ongoing debate arises from the tension between resources required for the implementation of outcomes into practice and/or policy, such as the management and resources needed for the implementation of programs and interventions that produce the outcomes. The argument is that outcomes are important but the need for technical precision is the penchant of academicians and researchers and is therefore excessive.

For the most part, there is agreement that the concepts addressed in an outcomes system must be related directly to the needs and priorities being addressed by the programs, and to the purposes for which the outcomes data will be used. The issue of technical precision can be considered as analogous to the precision in a financial statement or audit. The rationale for precision in a financial statement or audit is to be able to make a definitive statement. That is also true for outcomes: Technical precision allows for statements related to programs and interventions to be more definitive.

The challenge of technical precision is both significant and multifaceted. Often, the same outcomes instrument is used for a large range of diagnoses or disorders and for persons who enter programs at varying levels of dysfunction. The applicability of one or two instruments to cover these different types of spectrums is nontrivial. Another aspect of technical precision is the monitoring of meaningful change using an outcomes instrument. The technical arsenal to address these issues exists. However, the application of these techniques is often arcane and, therefore, easily dismissed.

Conclusion

Regardless of these tensions, more international attention is being paid to the role that mental health and substance use disorders play in reaching societal goals that are both health and non–health related. In order to help keep such attention and international initiatives evolving, this chapter concludes with recommendations that may help move forward an international outcomes agenda for health, mental health, and substance use:

Conduct Research Related to Relationships between Mental Health and Substance Use Outcomes and Larger Societal Outcomes

This chapter provides a thumbnail overview of these relationships that need to be explicated and elaborated. The WHO (2010a) report titled *Mental Health and Development—Integrating Mental Health Into All Development Efforts Including Millennium Development Goals* delineates current research in this area. The report demonstrates how persons with mental and psychosocial disabilities are a marginalized group facing stigma, discrimination, and human rights violations and identifies how governments can prioritize mental health care to address these issues. From a policymaker's or a funder's vantage point, mental health is not "sexy": It cannot be dressed up, eradicated, or eliminated. Mental health issues will always be present. Recognition is needed that addressing mental health helps achieve health and development outcomes much the same way as does addressing nutrition and water safety. Essentially, both research and marketing are needed for the recognition of mental health as a public health good, essential for the well-being and prosperity of a population.

Include Financial and Economic Outcomes

Related to the first recommendation is the need to relate mental health outcomes to economic and financial benefits, whether in terms of reduced health care costs or increases in human capital and productivity. As described above, this is an objective of some outcomes systems (such as the one in New Zealand). Explicit inclusion of such outcomes would help make the case for both mental health interventions and outcomes.

Conduct Research Related to Mental Health Outcomes

Many of the initiatives related to outcomes have resulted in outcome system based on instruments and measures that do not have an adequate psychometric footing. There are issues of validity applicability to diverse population, the meaning and use of the change scores derived, benchmarking, and reporting to various audiences. These are all issues addressed by various implementers and mental health outcome systems: A first step would be the compilation of best practices in these areas, which could then be the basis of a more rigorous research program.

Use of Outcomes by Different Stakeholder Groups

To a large extent, the focus of outcome systems has been to support management or to justify programs to funders or policymakers. The use of outcomes by clinicians and providers is beginning to occur, mostly in higher income countries. This is the trend that will continue and will be accelerated through the implementation of electronic health records. Another critical area that needs emphasis is use of outcomes by consumers and family members to both inform and advocate for their own care.

Develop Outcomes-based Cultures

There is consensus both within the behavioral health world and more generally that outcomes measurement is a necessary and beneficial process, but often this recognition is more in the realm of rhetoric than in the realm of application and use. Outcomes are used in a superficial way to justify programs and expenditures and often there is a tacit conspiracy that the outcomes being reported suffice to justify continuation of programs that have not been reviewed or analyzed vigorously. That is, even as outcomes are used, the decisions made as a result are oriented more toward policy than toward improvement in patient care. As other chapters in this volume also attest, an important consideration for the future is how mental health outcomes are integrated into every perspective—management, clinical, consumer—so that outcomes can truly inform health and mental health transformation and improve the lives of people with mental illness everywhere.

In closing, over the past decade there has been a growing recognition that considering mental health, substance use, physical health, and social outcomes as separate domains is retrogressive, and more a reflection of funding streams and organizational arrangements than the realities experienced by people in their attempt to lead better lives. New models are under development for integrating health and mental health, and for recognizing the role of health and mental health in producing desired social outcomes such as reduction in poverty, increased employment, and improved school performance. These are as important in high-income countries such as the United States (where health care reform is underway) and the United Kingdom (where the National Health Trust system is being revamped) as they are in middle- and low-income countries.

The world of outcomes has not kept pace with the changes that are occurring at the systems level and with the emergent knowledge of the linkages and complexities of the inter-relationships among social, health, and mental health components. Clearly, the tensions identified in this chapter will not evaporate; however, recognition of these interrelationships and tensions will better inform the next generation of outcomes in a substantive and meaningful way.

References

Druss, B.G.& Bornemann, T. (2010). Improving health and health care for persons with serious mental illness. *JAMA, 303,* 1972–1973.

Institute of Medicine. (2009). *Initial national priorities for comparative effectiveness research.* Washington, DC: National Academies Press.

Krieble, T. (2003). Towards an outcome-based mental health policy for New Zealand. *Australasian Psychiatry, 11,* S78–S82.

National Institute of Mental Health in England. (2008). *Outcomes compendium: Helping you select the right tools for the best mental health care practice in your field* (Gateway reference 10934). London: Barts and the London School of Medicine and Dentistry.

Organization for Economic Co-Operation and Development. (2003). *Annual report No. 81911 2003.* Paris: Author.

Parker, G., Gladstone G., & Chee, K.T. (2001). Depression in the planet's largest ethnic group: The Chinese. *American Journal of Psychiatry, 158,* 857–864.

Patel, V. (2007). Alcohol use and mental health in developing countries. *Annals of Epidemiology, 17,* S87–S92.

Patel, V., Abas, M., Broadhead, J., Todd, C., & Reeler, A. (2001). Depression in developing countries: Lessons from Zimbabwe. *British Medical Journal, 322,* 482–484. doi: 10.1136/bmj.322.7284.482

Pirkis, J., Burgess, P., Coombs, T., Clarke, A., Jones-Ellis, D., & Dickson, R. (2005). Routine measurement of outcomes in Australia's public sector mental health services. *Australia and New Zealand Health Policy, 2,* 8. doi: 10.1186/1743-8462-2-8

Prince, M., Patel, V., Saxena, S., Maj, M., Maselko, J., Phillips, M., & Rahman, A. (2007). No health without mental health. *Lancet, 370,* 859–877.

Souza, R., Yasuda, S., & Cristofani, S. (2009). Mental health treatment outcomes in a humanitarian emergency: A pilot model for integration of mental health into primary care in Habila, Darfur. *International Journal of Mental Health Systems, 3.* doi: 10.1186/1752-4458-3-17

Victorian Government Department of Health and Community Services, Psychiatric Services Division. (1996). *Victoria's Mental Health Service: The framework for service delivery—Better outcomes for area mental health services.* Victoria, Australia: Author.

Ward, M., King, M., Lloyd, M., Bower, P., Sibbald, B., & Farrelly, M. (2000) Randomised controlled trial of non-directive counselling, cognitive–behaviour therapy, and usual general practitioner care for patients with depression. I: Clinical effectiveness. *British Medical Journal, 321,* 1383–1388. doi: 10.1136/bmj.321.7273

WHO World Mental Health Survey Consortium. (2004). Prevalence, severity and unmet need for treatment of mental disorders. *JAMA, 291,* 2581–2590.

World Health Organization. (2005). *Report from the WHO European Ministerial Conference: Mental health—Facing the challenges, building solutions.* Copenhagen, Denmark: WHO Press.

World Health Organization. (2009). *Disease and regional injury estimates for 2004.* Retrieved from http://www.who.int/healthinfo/global_burden_disease/estimates_country/en/index.html

World Health Organization. (2010a). *Mental health and development—Integrating mental health into all development including millennium development goals.* Geneva: WHO Press.

World Health Organization. (2010b). *Mental health and development: Targeting people with mental health conditions as a vulnerable group.* Geneva: WHO Press.

CHAPTER 25

Concluding Comments

Jennifer L. Magnabosco and Ronald W. Manderscheid

The timing of this second edition of *Outcomes Measurement in the Human Services* could not be better: It will be released just as the U.S. Department of Health and Human Services, the health care field, and its partners begin to implement national health reform. This juxtaposition is very symbolic: National health reform cannot succeed without using outcomes and performance measures—particularly consumer outcomes measures—as one essential yardstick of its progress.

Thus, this update to the understanding of the state of outcomes measurement has much to offer those involved in health care reform, as well as to major efforts that are underway in other human service fields. Although we have made important conceptual and operational strides in outcomes measurement, we close this volume with a pressing call to action.

To date, no strong, overarching, integrated approach to outcomes has been established within the human services. There has yet to be thorough discussion and development of a common outcomes language. Conceptual models and measures vary across human service fields, and standardization of outcomes and performance measurement continues to plod slowly. Human service professionals vary tremendously in how much they embrace the use of outcomes and/or performance measures, outcomes processes (such as continuous quality improvement), outcomes management, and evidence-based practices. Private sector organizations have increasingly limited the types of populations they serve. And the once-distinct lines between private and public sector responsibilities to serve those in need have become increasingly blurred.

With this level of variability, it will be exceedingly difficult to reach many of the goals that are part of reforms underway in health, behavioral health, and child and family services, especially with regard to defining (and, in turn, measuring) the range of outcomes that reflect the whole person (and whole community), developing and utilizing a strengths-based (versus problems-first) and quality-improvement approach to service delivery and recovery, and assuredly "bending the cost curves." Like the pushes for increased accountability in the late 1990s, reaching out across disciplines and professional lines is becoming a requirement to design and execute the implementation of current reforms, to revise approaches that enhance infrastructures that promote individual and community well-being, and to fairly calculate effectiveness of human services programs and policies.

As such, efforts to implement reform are laden with opportunities for participation from stakeholders, including consumers, who previously may not have been involved. In health, and behavioral health especially, stakeholders are taking hold of opportunities to work together to shape the quality of the initiatives undertaken, and the outcome measures used to assess them. Despite this, no multidisciplinary effort or consortium of organizations has been formed to work on the development of a common human services outcomes measurement culture.

If we are to successfully usher in the new era of personalized health care (that is, customized care to the particular needs of consumers and families), achieve human services reforms, and meet impending human service challenges in the United States and abroad, we advocate that such a consortium be formed. Such a consortium has the potential to significantly extinguish further fracturing (Mullen & Magnabosco, 1997) of conceptual and operational foundations of outcomes measurement in the human services, and forge a common culture of outcomes measurement across human services fields. We suggest that such a consortium include organizations and individuals that represent the array of human service professionals (such as the National Council for Community Behavioral Health, the American Medical Association, the American Psychological Association, the American Psychiatric Association, the National Association of Social Workers, the American Psychiatric Nurses Association, the Child Welfare League of America, and other organizations involved in the Whole Health Coalition [http://www.lac.org]); educational programs that prepare human service workers and researchers; government, nonprofit, for-profit, funding, and research entities; and consumer advocacy groups.

Accordingly, we suggest that readers and other stakeholders (consumers/families, providers, managers, policymakers, advocates, researchers, educators and students) involved in the human services "scale up" (Fixsen, 2009) the ability to build consensus, as well as the ability to conduct new types of holistic (integrated) critical assessments that synthesize approaches, definitions, metrics and workforce issues related to outcomes measurement across fields of practice and disciplines. Moving the collective consciousness (Skocpol, 1985) toward an integrated outcomes measurement culture can only ensure that consumer-centered health and well-being priorities are met during this era of reform, and that quality of care and outcomes are prioritized over cost. Nothing else is more challenging or more gratifying!

References

Fixsen, A.A.M. (2009, December). *Defining scaling up across disciplines: An annotated bibliography.* Chapel Hill: University of North Carolina.

Mullen, E. J., & Magnabosco, J. L. (Eds.). (1997). *Outcomes measurement in the human services: Cross-cutting issues and methods.* Washington, DC: NASW Press.

Skocpol, T. (1985). Bringing the state back in: Strategies of analysis in current research. In B. Evan, D. Rueschemeyer, & T. Skocpol (Eds.), *Bringing the state back in* (pp. 3–42). New York: Cambridge University Press.

The Editors

Jennifer L. Magnabosco, PhD, currently is co-principal investigator and projects director at the Center for Implementation Research and Practice Support and health science research specialist at the Center of Excellence, Center for the Study of Health Care Provider Behavior, Veterans Health Administration, Department of Veterans Affairs, North Hills, CA. Concurrently she is management consultant and principal investigator for the Los Angeles County Department of Mental Health; adjunct professor in the Department of Social Work, California State University, Los Angeles; and part-time research faculty member at Yo San University of Traditional Chinese Medicine, Los Angeles. Previously she was associate director and senior research associate at the Thomas and Dorothy Leavey Center for the Study of Los Angeles at Loyola Marymount University, Los Angeles; associate policy researcher at the RAND Corporation, Santa Monica, CA; director of administration and operations at the Center for the Study of Social Work Practice at Columbia University, New York; and staff psychotherapist at the Postgraduate Center for Mental Health, New York. Dr. Magnabosco is co-chair of the Research Interest and Emerging Leader groups of ACMHA—The College for Behavioral Health Leadership-and a governing council member and member of the action board for the Mental Health Section of the American Public Health Association. She has also held several alumni association volunteer positions, including vice president of the University of Chicago National Alumni Board of Governors and board member of the Columbia University School of Social Work National Alumni Board of Directors.

Ronald W. Manderscheid, PhD, currently serves as executive director of the National Association of County Behavioral Health and Developmental Disability Directors, Washington, DC. The Association represents county and local authorities and provides a national program of technical assistance and support. Concurrently, he is adjunct professor in the Department of Mental Health, Bloomberg School of Public Health, Johns Hopkins University, Baltimore; a member of the Secretary of Health and Human Services' Advisory Committee on Healthy People 2020; and president of ACMHA—The College for Behavioral Health Leadership. Dr. Manderscheid serves on the boards of the Employee Assistance Research Foundation, the Danya Institute, the FrameWorks Institute, and the Council on Quality and Leadership. Previously, he served as the director of mental health and substance use programs at the Global Health Sector of SRA International, Rockville, MD. Throughout his career, he has emphasized and promoted consumer and family concerns.

The Contributors

Joie D. Acosta, PhD, is associate behavioral scientist, the RAND Corporation, Santa Monica, CA.

John Bartlett, MD, MPH, is senior advisor, Primary Care Initiative Mental Health Program, The Carter Center, Atlanta.

Barbara Berkman, PhD, DSW, is Helen Rehr/Ruth Fizdale Professor of Health and Mental Health, School of Social Work, Columbia University, New York.

Richard H. Beinecke, DPA, ACSW, is chair, Public Management Department, and associate professor, Public Management Department and Member Healthcare Department, Sawyer Business School, Suffolk University, Boston.

Tobin Belzer, PhD, is sociologist, Center for Religion and Civic Culture, University of Southern California, Los Angeles.

Jean Campbell, PhD, is research associate professor, Missouri Institute of Mental Health, University of Missouri–Columbia.

Dasha Cherepanov, PhD, AHRQ, is a fellow, University of California at Los Angeles/the RAND Corporation in Santa Monica, CA.

Matthew Chinman, PhD, is behavioral scientist, the RAND Corporation, Pittsburgh, and health science specialist, VISN-4 Mental Illness, Research and Clinical Center, Department of Veterans Affairs, Pittsburgh.

Kevin Corcoran, PhD, JD, is professor, School of Social Work, Portland State University, Portland, OR, and School of Social of Public Policy and Practice, University of Pennsylvania, Philadelphia.

Ian D. Coulter, PhD, is Samueli Chair for Integrative Medicine, the RAND Corporation, Santa Monica, CA; senior health policy analyst and professor, School of Dentistry, University of California, Los Angeles; and research professor, at the Southern California University of Health Sciences, Whittier, CA.

Rose M. Etheridge, PhD, is a research and evaluation consultant, Durham, NC.

Hebah Farrag, MA, is project manager, Center for Religion and Civic Culture, University of Southern California, Los Angeles.

Richard Flory, PhD, is associate research professor, Sociology, and senior research associate, Center for Religion and Civic Culture, University of Southern California, Los Angeles.

Joseph Francis MD, MPH, is chief quality and performance officer, Department of Veterans Affairs, Washington, DC.

Vijay Ganju, PhD, is secretary general and chief executive officer, World Federation for Mental Health, Woodbridge, VA.

Jean K. Gornick, is an independent evaluation consultant and former executive director, Damiano (Community-Based Poverty Agency) of Duluth, MN.

Harry P. Hatry, MS, is distinguished fellow and director of the Public Management Program at the Urban Institute, Washington, DC.

Ron D. Hays, PhD, is professor, School of Medicine, University of California, Los Angeles.

Nikki Hozack, MSW, is doctoral candidate, Social Welfare, School of Public Policy, University of California at Los Angeles.

Daniel B. Kaplan, LICSW, LMSW, CSW–G, QDCS, is a doctoral fellow, Hartford Geriatric Social Work Initiative; a doctoral candidate, School of Social Work, Columbia University, New York; and a program evaluator, Hartford Geriatric Social Work Faculty Scholars Program, New York.

Timothy A. Kelly, PhD, is coordinator of behavioral health services and clinical psychologist, Parkway Health Medical Centers, Shanghai Centre Medical Center, Shanghai, China.

Peter M. Kettner, PhD, MSW, is professor emeritus, School of Social Work, Arizona State University, Phoenix.

Raheleh Khorsan, MA, is research associate, Integrative Medicine and Military Medical Research Programs, Samueli Institute, Alexandria, VA.

M. Rebecca Kilburn, PhD, is senior economist and director, RAND Child Policy, the RAND Corporation, Santa Monica, CA.

Thomas A. Kirk Jr., PhD, is an independent consultant in Connecticut and former commissioner, Department of Mental Health and Addiction Services, State of Connecticut.

Cynthia Klein, PhD, is research and evaluation project director, SRA International, Atlanta.

Jacqui LaCoste, BA, is evaluation project manager, SRA International, Durham, NC.

Brie Loskota, PhD, is manager director, Center for Religion and Civic Culture, University of Southern California, Los Angeles.

Julie T. Marks, PhD, is research and evaluation consultant, SRA International, Durham, NC.

Lawrence L. Martin, PhD, MSW, is professor and director, Center for Community Partnerships, College of Health and Public Affairs, University of Central Florida, Orlando.

Brenda G. McGowan, DSW, MSW, is professor and James R. Dumpson Chair of Child Welfare Studies, Graduate School of Social Service, Fordham University, New York.

Maria Monroe-DeVita, PhD, is director, the Washington Institute for Mental Health Research and Training, Seattle, and acting assistant professor, Department of Psychiatry and Behavioral Science, School of Medicine, Division of Public Behavioral Health and Justice Policy, University of Washington, Seattle.

Thomas Packard, DSW, CSWM, is associate professor, School of Social Work, San Diego State University, San Diego.

Michael Quinn Patton, PhD, is an independent consultant, former president of the American Evaluation Association, and author of *Utilization-Focused Evaluation*.

James Siemianowski, MSW, is director of Evaluation, Quality Management and Information, Department of Mental Health and Addiction Services, State of Connecticut.

Gregory B. Teague, PhD, is associate professor, Department of Mental Health Law and Policy, University of Southern Florida, Tampa.

Bruce A. Thyer, PhD, LCSW, is professor, College of Social Work, Florida State University, Tallahassee, and editor, *Research on Social Work Practice*.

Susan Turner, PhD, is professor and director, Center for Evidence-Based Corrections, Department of Criminology, Law and Society, University of California, Irvine.

Elaine W. Walsh, PhD, LCSW, MSW, is associate professor, Urban Affairs and Planning, and director of the Graduate Program in Urban Affairs and the Public Service Scholars Program, Hunter College, City University of New York.

Brian T. Yates, PhD, is professor, Department of Psychology, American University, Washington, DC.

James R. Zabora, ScD, MSW, is dean and professor, National Catholic School of Social Service, Catholic University of America, Washington, DC.

Index